LEGITIMACY AND INTERNATIONAL COURTS

One of the most noted developments in international law over the past twenty years is the proliferation of international courts and tribunals. They decide who has the right to exploit natural resources, define the scope of human rights, delimit international boundaries, and determine when the use of force is prohibited. As the number and influence of international courts grow, so too do challenges to their legitimacy. This volume provides new interdisciplinary insights into international courts' legitimacy: what drives and undermines the legitimacy of these bodies? How do drivers change depending on the court concerned? What is the link between legitimacy, democracy, effectiveness, and justice? Top international experts analyze legitimacy for specific international courts, as well as the links between legitimacy and cross-cutting themes. Failure to understand and respond to legitimacy concerns can endanger both the courts and the law they interpret and apply.

NIENKE GROSSMAN is an associate professor of Law and Deputy Director of the Center for International and Comparative Law at the University of Baltimore School of Law.

HARLAN GRANT COHEN holds the Gabriel M. Wilner/UGA Foundation Professorship in International Law at the University of Georgia School of Law.

ANDREAS FOLLESDAL is Professor of Political Philosophy in the Faculty of Law and Codirector of PluriCourts, a Centre for the Study of the Legitimate Roles of the Judiciary in the Global Order, at the University of Oslo.

GEIR ULFSTEIN is Professor of International Law in the Department of Public and International Law and Codirector of PluriCourts, a Centre for the Study of the Legitimate Roles of the Judiciary in the Global Order, at the University of Oslo.

STUDIES ON INTERNATIONAL COURTS AND TRIBUNALS

General Editors
Andreas Follesdal, University of Oslo
Geir Ulfstein, University of Oslo

Studies on International Courts and Tribunals contains theoretical and interdisciplinary scholarship on legal aspects as well as the legitimacy and effectiveness of international courts and tribunals.

Other Books in the Series

Mads Andenas and Eirik Bjorge (eds.) *A Farewell to Fragmentation: Reassertion and Convergence in International Law*

Cecilia M. Bailliet and Nobuo Hayashi (eds.) *The Legitimacy of International Criminal Tribunals*

Amrei Müller with Hege Elisabeth Kjos (eds.) *Judicial Dialogue and Human Rights*

Nienke Grossman, Harlan Grant Cohen, Andreas Follesdal and Geir Ulfstein (eds.) *Legitimacy and International Courts*

LEGITIMACY AND INTERNATIONAL COURTS

Edited by

NIENKE GROSSMAN
University of Baltimore School of Law

HARLAN GRANT COHEN
University of Georgia School of Law

ANDREAS FOLLESDAL
University of Oslo

GEIR ULFSTEIN
University of Oslo

CAMBRIDGE
UNIVERSITY PRESS

University Printing House, Cambridge CB2 8BS, United Kingdom

One Liberty Plaza, 20th Floor, New York, NY 10006, USA

477 Williamstown Road, Port Melbourne, VIC 3207, Australia

314-321, 3rd Floor, Plot 3, Splendor Forum, Jasola District Centre, New Delhi - 110025, India

79 Anson Road, #06-04/06, Singapore 079906

Cambridge University Press is part of the University of Cambridge.

It furthers the University's mission by disseminating knowledge in the pursuit of
education, learning and research at the highest international levels of excellence.

www.cambridge.org
Information on this title: www.cambridge.org/9781108423854
DOI: 10.1017/9781108529570

© Cambridge University Press 2018

This publication is in copyright. Subject to statutory exception
and to the provisions of relevant collective licensing agreements,
no reproduction of any part may take place without the written
permission of Cambridge University Press.

First published 2018

A catalogue record for this publication is available from the British Library

Library of Congress Cataloging-in-Publication Data
Names: Symposium on Legitimacy and International Courts (2014 : Baltimore, Md.) |
Cohen, Harlan Grant, editor. | Follesdal, Andreas, editor. | Grossman, Nienke, editor. |
Ulfstein, Geir, 1951- , editor.
Title: Legitimacy and international courts / edited by Harlan Grant Cohen,
Andreas Follesdal, Nienke Grossman, and Geir Ulfstein
Description: Cambridge, United Kingdom ; New York, NY, USA:
Cambridge University Press, 2018. | Series: Studies on international courts and tribunals |
Includes papers presented at the Symposium on Legitimacy and International Courts,
September 18-19, 2014, at the University of Baltimore, sponsored by the
University of Baltimore School of Law, the American Society of International Law,
and PluriCourts of the University of Oslo. | Includes bibliographical references and index.
Identifiers: LCCN 2017037930 | ISBN 9781108423854 (Hardback) |
ISBN 9781108438520 (paperback)
Subjects: LCSH: International courts–Congresses.
Classification: LCC KZ6250 .S97 2014 | DDC 341.5/5–dc23
LC record available at https://lccn.loc.gov/2017037930

ISBN 978-1-108-42385-4 Hardback
ISBN 978-1-108-43852-0 Paperback

Cambridge University Press has no responsibility for the persistence or
accuracy of URLs for external or third-party internet websites referred to in
this publication, and does not guarantee that any content on such websites is,
or will remain, accurate or appropriate.

CONTENTS

List of Contributors   vii

1   Legitimacy and International Courts – A Framework   1
HARLAN GRANT COHEN, ANDREAS FOLLESDAL,
NIENKE GROSSMAN, AND GEIR ULFSTEIN

PART I   The Legitimacy of Particular Dispute
Settlement Mechanisms   41

2   Solomonic Judgments and the Legitimacy of the
International Court of Justice   43
NIENKE GROSSMAN

3   The Global–Local Dilemma and the ICC's Legitimacy   62
MARGARET M. DEGUZMAN

4   Justice as Legitimacy in the European Court of
Human Rights   83
MOLLY K. LAND

5   Legitimacy and Jurisdictional Overlap: The ICC and the
Inter-American Court in Colombia   114
ALEXANDRA HUNEEUS

6   The Legitimacy of the European Court of Justice:
Normative Debates and Empirical Evidence   143
MARK A. POLLACK

7   The International Tribunal for the Law of the Sea:
Seeking the Legitimacy of State Consent   174
ANASTASIA TELESETSKY

8   Who Decides Matters: The Legitimacy Capital of
WTO Adjudicators versus ICSID Arbitrators   216
JOOST PAUWELYN

CONTENTS

9 The Legitimacy of the International Centre for Settlement of Investment Disputes 234

ANDREA K. BJORKLUND

10 The Human Rights Treaty Bodies and Legitimacy Challenges 284

GEIR ULFSTEIN

PART II Legitimacy – Cross-Cutting Issues 305

11 Constitutionalization, Not Democratization: How to Assess the Legitimacy of International Courts 307

ANDREAS FOLLESDAL

12 Democracy, Justice, and the Legitimacy of International Courts 338

MORTIMER N. S. SELLERS

13 Stronger Together? Legitimacy and Effectiveness of International Courts as Mutually Reinforcing or Undermining Notions 354

YUVAL SHANY

Index 372

CONTRIBUTORS

ANDREA K. BJORKLUND is Full Professor and L. Yves Forties Chair in International Arbitration and International Commercial Law at McGill University Faculty of Law in Quebec, Canada.

HARLAN GRANT COHEN is Gabriel M. Wilner/UGA Foundation Professor in International Law at the University of Georgia School of Law, Georgia, USA.

ANDREAS FOLLESDAL is Professor and Co-Director of PluriCourts at the Centre for the Study of the Legitimacy of the International Judiciary at the University of Oslo, Norway.

NIENKE GROSSMAN is Associate Professor of Law and Deputy Director of the Center for International and Comparative Law at the University of Baltimore School of Law, Maryland, USA.

MARGARET M. DEGUZMAN is Associate Professor of Law at Temple University Beasley School of Law, Pennsylvania, USA.

ALEXANDRA HUNEEUS is Associate Professor of Law and Director of the Global Legal Studies Center at the University of Wisconsin Law School, Madison, Wisconsin, USA.

MOLLY K. LAND is Professor of Law and Human Rights at the University of Connecticut School of Law and Associate Director of the University of Connecticut's Human Rights Institute, Connecticut, USA.

JOOST PAUWELYN is Professor of International Law and Co-Director of the Centre for Trade and Economic Integration at The Graduate Institute Geneva, Switzerland.

viii CONTRIBUTORS

MARK A. POLLACK is Professor of Political Science and Law, Jean Monnet Chair in European Integration Studies, as well as Director of the Global Studies Program at Temple University, Pennsylvania, USA.

MORTIMER N. S. SELLERS is Regents Professor of the University System of Maryland and Director of Center for International and Comparative Law at the University of Baltimore School of Law, Maryland, USA.

YUVAL SHANY is Professor of Law, Hersch Lauterpacht Chair in Public International Law, and Dean at The Hebrew University of Jerusalem, Israel. Shany is also Vice-Chair of the UN Human Rights Committee.

ANASTASIA TELESETSKY is Professor of Law at the University of Idaho College of Law, Idaho, USA.

GEIR ULFSTEIN is Professor of Law and Co-Director of PluriCourts at the Centre for the Study of the Legitimacy of the International Judiciary at the University of Oslo, Norway.

1

Legitimacy and International
Courts – A Framework

HARLAN GRANT COHEN, ANDREAS FOLLESDAL,
NIENKE GROSSMAN, AND GEIR ULFSTEIN[*]

I Why Relevant? Why Important? Why Interdisciplinary?

One of the most noted developments in international law in the past twenty years is the multiplication of international courts, tribunals, and other adjudicatory and quasi-adjudicatory bodies (ICs, or international courts).[1] They include the International Court of Justice (ICJ); the World Trade Organization's panels, Appellate Body, and the Dispute Settlement Body (the WTO-DSB); ad hoc tribunals under the auspices of the International Centre for the Settlement of Investment Disputes (ICSID); and the European Court of Human Rights (ECtHR), among many others.

These bodies are deciding disputes with implications for our planet and its people, such as when the use of force is legal, what natural resources belong to whom, and the content of sovereign rights and obligations with respect to human rights, the environment, and trade. Their decisions frequently transcend the parties immediately before them. They shape and promote specific normative regimes like international investment, human rights, humanitarian law, and trade law. Even when decisions are not formally binding, advocates before them, scholars, politicians, and judicial opinions frequently cite them as if they set precedent – yet stare decisis is not the prevailing rule.[2] Decisions are

---

[*] First drafts of the chapters in this volume were presented and discussed at a conference in September 2014, sponsored by the University of Baltimore School of Law and the University of Oslo's PluriCourts centre, in honor of the University of Baltimore School of Law's Center for International and Comparative Law's twentieth anniversary. Drafts were then edited and revised in preparation for publication.

[1] Karen J. Alter, *The New Terrain of International Law: Courts, Politics, Rights* (Princeton, NJ: Princeton University Press, 2014), pp. 3–4.

[2] *See* N. Grossman, "The Normative Legitimacy of International Courts," *Temple Law Review*, 86 (2013), 68–72.

frequently used as focal points in driving domestic and international political debates.[3] States not involved in a particular dispute look to international court decisions that may affect the standards by which their conduct may be judged in the future.

As international courts' numbers and influence grow, so too do questions about their legitimacy. Political actors query why a state should abide by the decisions of a court located thousands of miles away and composed of foreign nationals, and why a state should subject itself to the jurisdiction of a court that may decide a dispute against a state's perceived self-interest. Scholars seek a theoretical framework for understanding the sources of international courts' authority. What qualities must international courts possess for their authority to be justified? In what circumstances should states subject themselves to the jurisdiction of international courts? What drives the audiences of international courts – states, international organizations, individuals, and nongovernmental organizations – to support or disparage international courts?

Legitimacy provides one theoretical lens through which to assess and critique the work of international courts. Although many have written about the legitimacy of specific international courts, there has been little effort to link these discussions and to determine to what extent they are theoretically consistent with each other. What is common across criticisms and analyses of the legitimacy of international courts? How do differences depend on particular characteristics of individual institutions – their role or impact within a complex of actors including states, international organizations, and civil society actors? This book seeks to fill these gaps in two ways. First, it highlights and evaluates some cross-cutting themes that may affect legitimacy no matter what court may be involved, such as democracy, justice, and effectiveness. Second, it brings together experts on specific international courts to consider what legitimacy means and how it applies to their court. This book lets readers consider the legitimacy of international courts from a comparative perspective. The stakes are high. Failing to understand and respond to legitimacy concerns endangers both the international courts and the

---

[3] H. Cohen, "Theorizing Precedent in International Law," in A. Bianchi et al. (eds.), *Interpretation in International Law* (Oxford, UK: Oxford University Press, 2015), pp. 268–89; H. Cohen, "International Precedent and the Practice of International Law," in M. Helfand (ed.), *Negotiating State and Non-State Law: The Challenge of Global and Local Legal Pluralism* (Cambridge, UK: Cambridge University Press, 2015), pp. 172–94.

law they interpret and apply. If international courts lack justified authority, so too will their interpretations of international law.

The set of contributions in this book examines what underpins and undermines legitimacy, or the justification of authority, of international courts and tribunals. The authors explore what strengthens and weakens the legitimacy of various different international courts, while also considering broader theories of international court legitimacy. Some chapters highlight the sociological or normative legitimacy of specific courts or tribunals, while others address cross-cutting issues such as representation, democracy, independence, and effectiveness. A solid understanding of the complexities of legitimacy require a set of scholars who bring a range of different methodologies to the table – drawing from law, philosophy, and political science – and bring a range of perspectives – having studied courts and tribunals as academics, practitioners, government officials, and judges. The authors hail from several countries and institutions around the world.

The result is a broader understanding of the underpinnings of legitimacy for international courts. This volume helps readers understand how legitimacy challenges differ from one court with one subject matter to the next, and how older, more traditional tribunals may learn from newer ones, and vice versa.

This initial chapter surveys some of the key contributions of this book and distills some of the lessons of its varied chapters for the legitimacy of international courts. Sections II and III are largely conceptual in approach, exploring what legitimacy means for each and all of the courts. Section II explores the concept of legitimacy as it pertains to international courts, examining the relationship between source, process, and results-oriented aspects of IC legitimacy and the relationship between legitimacy, justice, democracy, and effectiveness. Section III looks more closely at the chapters in this book and explores their contributions to the preceding discussions, as well as their lessons regarding the relationship between sociological and normative legitimacy.

Section IV takes a more functional approach, exploring how various factors internal or external to particular courts have contributed to those courts' normative or sociological legitimacy. It considers international courts in their context, examining the relationship between the specific goals, design choices, audiences, institutional contexts, and IC legitimacy. It explores three models of how these factors interact in this book's chapters to either support or undermine an international court's sociological or normative legitimacy. Section V provides thumbnail summaries of each the chapters that follow.

II Legitimacy Approaches

A Sociological and Normative Legitimacy: Source, Process, and Result-Oriented Factors

Legitimacy is often criticized as a notoriously slippery concept. It is defined in myriad ways by many different authors, frequently to justify a set of reforms for a particular institution. Yet it is a meaningful concept because it seeks to explain why those addressed by an authority should comply with its mandates in the absence of perceived self-interest or brute coercion. A legitimate power is broadly understood to mean one that has "the right to rule."[4] A legitimate court, therefore, possesses a justifiable right to issue judgments, decisions, or opinions, which those normatively addressed must obey, or at least consider with due care.

While normative legitimacy is concerned with the right to rule according to predefined standards, sociological legitimacy derives from *perceptions or beliefs* that an institution has such a right to rule.[5] Assessments of normative legitimacy may apply legal, political, philosophical, or other standards. Sociological legitimacy is subject to empirical analysis, such as by measuring the degree or type of support that an institution enjoys. Sociological legitimacy may fluctuate over time and vary by the constituency or audience whose support is being measured.[6]

---

[4] D. Bodansky, "Legitimacy in International Law and International Relations," in J. L. Dunoff and M. A. Pollack (eds.), *Interdisciplinary Perspectives on International Law and International Relations: The State of the Art* (Cambridge, UK: Cambridge University Press, 2013), p. 324; D. Bodansky, "The Concept of Legitimacy in International Law," in R. Wolfrum and V. Röben (eds.), *Legitimacy in International Law* (Berlin: Springer-Verlag, 2008), p. 313; D. Bodansky, "The Legitimacy of International Governance: A Coming Challenge for International Environmental Law?" *American Journal of International Law*, 93 (1999), 603–4; A. Buchanan and R. O. Keohane, "The Legitimacy of Global Governance Institutions," *Ethics and International Affairs*, 20 (2006), 405; A. Buchanan, "The Legitimacy of International Law," in S. Besson and J. Tasioulas (eds.), *The Philosophy of International Law* (Oxford, UK: Oxford University Press, 2010), p. 79; J. Tasioulas, "The Legitimacy of International Law," in *The Philosophy of International Law*, p. 97; A. Follesdal, "Legitimacy Deficits Beyond the State: Diagnoses and Cures," in A. Hurrelmann et al. (eds.), *Legitimacy in an Age of Global Politics* (Basingstoke, UK: Palgrave Macmillan, 2007), pp. 211–28.

[5] *See, e.g.*, Buchanan and Keohane, "The Legitimacy of Global Governance Institutions," 405.

[6] Mark A. Pollack (Chapter 6 in this volume), citing I. Hurd, "Legitimacy and Authority in International Politics," *International Organization*, 53 (1999), 379, 381; *see also* N. Grossman, "Legitimacy and International Adjudicative Bodies," *George Washington International Law Review*, 41 (2009), 117.

"Legitimacy capital" may increase or decline over time.[7] While "internal legitimacy" looks at the perceptions of regime insiders, or constituencies working within the institutional regime concerned, "external legitimacy" refers to the beliefs of outsiders, or constituencies beyond the institution itself.[8] Previous empirical analyses have evaluated "specific support," which relates to the extent to which an institution's specific decisions coincide with individuals' policy preferences, and "diffuse support," which looks to individuals' favorable dispositions toward a court generally and willingness to tolerate unpalatable decisions.[9]

Considerations and concerns about legitimacy can be usefully split into source-, process-, and results-oriented factors.[10] For example, consent to be bound is a powerful source-based justification for the exercise of authority over the bound subject, also called "legal legitimacy."[11] Because states are sovereign and independent, they enjoy a presumption that they cannot be coerced without their consent. Thus, a court that acts beyond the scope of authority granted to it, or *ultra vires*, exceeds the bounds of state consent and lacks justified authority.[12] Moreover, it is expected that courts, as legal organs, apply generally accepted methods of interpretation. Source-based legitimacy may arguably require the consent of affected nonstate stakeholders, such as civil society in nondemocratic states, or transnational groups, as well as that of states.

---

[7] *See* Yuval Shany, *Assessing the Effectiveness of International Courts* (Oxford, UK: Oxford University Press, 2014), pp. 145–7.

[8] *See, e.g.,* Joost Pauwelyn, in Chapter 8 of this volume, citing J. Weiler, "The Rule of Lawyers and the Ethos of Diplomats: Reflections on the Internal and External Legitimacy of WTO Dispute Settlement," *Journal of World Trade*, 35 (2001), 193.

[9] Mark A. Pollack, in Chapter 6 of this volume, citing Y. Lupu, "International Judicial Legitimacy: Lessons from National Courts," *Theoretical Inquiries in Law*, 14 (2013), 440–2. The canonical origin of the terms is David Easton, *A Systems Analysis of Political Life* (New York: Wiley, 1965).

[10] R. Wolfrum, "Legitimacy of International Law from a Legal Perspective: Some Introductory Considerations," in R. Wolfrum and V. Röben, *Legitimacy in International Law*, p. 6.

[11] J. Klabbers, "Setting the Scene," in J. Klabbers et al. (eds.), *The Constitutionalization of International Law* (Oxford, UK: Oxford University Press, 2009), p. 39; L. H. Meyer and P. Sanklecha, "Introduction," in L. H. Meyer (ed.), *Legitimacy, Justice and Public International Law* (Cambridge, UK: Cambridge University Press, 2009), pp. 3–4; Bodansky, "The Legitimacy of International Governance," 596, 597, 605; Buchanan and Keohane, "The Legitimacy of Global Governance Institutions," 412–13.

[12] Bodansky, "The Legitimacy of International Governance: A Coming Challenge for International Environmental Law?" 605.

Regarding process-oriented factors, fair and even-handed procedures and the open-mindedness of judges are also considered essential to legitimacy. If an international court does not provide equal opportunities to be heard to all the relevant parties, then its authority may suffer.[13] In recent years, and as discussed later, questions have been raised about who those relevant parties may be and what kinds of procedural rights they should be afforded.[14]

Finally, results-oriented factors that concern how well the international court performs its "functions" are variously defined. A first set of performance factors concern how well ICs perform the functions that states intended them to serve. For example, do courts issue judgments in the cases brought before them in a reasonably quick and efficient fashion?[15] A second form of performance factors pertains to how well ICs contribute to solving the problems that states established specific ICs to address, be it protecting and promoting human rights, increasing foreign direct investment, or bringing justice to peoples suffering from violations of international criminal law. It can also be asked how well a court performs functions beyond dispute settlement between the disputing parties, such as setting precedents or giving general guidance on interpretation; participating in judicial law-making; and serving as an integral part of an international regime, including compliance functions. A final kind of performance factors concerns the extent to which ICs may transform international relations, for example, to what extent the European Court of Justice has promoted European integration.[16]

---

[13] *See* Thomas M. Franck, *Fairness in International Law and Institutions* (Oxford, UK: Oxford University Press, 1995), p. 7 (discussing both procedural and substantive fairness); Bodansky, "The Legitimacy of International Governance," 612 (stating that "authority can be legitimate because it involves procedures considered to be fair"); J. H. H. Weiler, "The Rule of Lawyers and the Ethos of Diplomats: Reflections on the Internal and External Legitimacy of WTO Dispute Settlement," *Journal of World Trade*, 35 (2001), 204 (explaining that the legitimacy of courts is largely based on their ability "to listen to the parties, to deliberate impartially favouring neither the powerful nor the meek, to have the courage to decide and then, crucially, to motivate and explain the decisions").

[14] *See, e.g.,* Grossman, "The Normative Legitimacy of International Courts," 82.

[15] Martin Shapiro, *Courts: A Comparative and Political Analysis* (Chicago: University of Chicago Press, 1981); L. Helfer, "The Effectiveness of International Adjudication," in K. Alter et al. (eds.), *Oxford Handbook of International Adjudication* (Oxford, UK: Oxford University Press, 2014), pp. 464–82; Armin von Bogdandy and Ingo Venzke, *In Whose Name? On the Functions, Authority, and Legitimacy of International Courts* (Oxford, UK: Oxford University Press, 2014); Karen J. Alter, *The New Terrain of International Law: Courts Politics, Rights* (Princeton, NJ: Princeton University Press 2014), pp. 10–13.

[16] A. M. Burley and W. Mattli, "Europe before the Court: A Political Theory of Legal Integration," *International Organization*, 47 (1993), 41–76.

B Standards for Assessing Normative Legitimacy

1 Justice

According to Raz's service conception of authority, the legitimacy of an institution concerns whether it helps a state to better act in accordance with rules that bind it independently.[17] Thus Allan Buchanan and Robert Keohane have argued that the legitimacy of global governance institutions depends on respecting standards of "minimal moral acceptability."[18] Nienke Grossman has proposed a legal standard: if states are better at complying with international law acting on their own – in courts' absence – then it is difficult to justify international courts' authority.[19] In other words, if courts fail to help states comply with normatively acceptable law, including universally accepted human rights obligations, they are illegitimate.[20]

These understandings of legitimacy have several implications. For example, some treaties and their ICs may violate standards of global justice. Their legitimacy is thus threatened from the outset; some critics of the WTO regime appear to hold such views.[21] To the extent that standards of global justice apply to all international actors, they may affect how judges on international courts should reason when interpreting vague terms and specifying the treaty obligations and may create a tension between legal legitimacy based on an interpretation of the obligations as set out in the treaty and justice-based legitimacy.

2 Democracy

Some have sought to connect democratic theory or values with both normative and sociological legitimacy. Several debates about the legitimacy deficits of international governance institutions concern their lack of democratic accountability – thus many critics have complained that the European Union bodies are undemocratic.[22] Likewise, authors who address the legitimacy deficits of ICs propose their "democratization," by which the authors often mean to increase their transparency,

---

[17] Joseph Raz, *The Morality of Freedom* (Oxford, UK: Oxford University Press, 1986), pp. 47, 53.

[18] Buchanan and Keohane, "The Legitimacy of Global Governance Institutions," 405–37.

[19] Grossman, "The Normative Legitimacy of International Courts," 100.   [20] Ibid., 101.

[21] T. Pogge, "The Role of International Law in Reproducing Massive Poverty," in S. Besson and J. Tasioulas (eds.), *The Philosophy of International Law* (Oxford, UK: Oxford University Press, 2010), pp. 417–35.

[22] A. Follesdal and S. Hix, "Why There Is a Democratic Deficit in the EU: A Response to Majone and Moravcsik," *Journal of Common Market Studies*, 44 (3) (2006), 533–62.

accountability or participation by various parties.[23] At the same time, such calls for democratization should give pause because national courts are seldom subject to similar norms of democratic election and accountability as are national parliaments or the executive.

As regards ICs, such calls for increased democratic accountability may best be understood along one of three strands. First, they may be proposals to improve the selection of judges to secure more equitable representation of the population, such as calls for more women and minorities as judges of ICs.[24] Second, there may be proposals to make the treaties or the jurisprudence of the IC less skewed toward the interests of some states rather than others.[25] A more "democratic" IC should be less biased. Such calls must, of course, be specified carefully. For instance, some authors assume that states represent and protect the interests of their people, so that inclusion of all states also ensures that the citizens of these states will have their interests better secured. However, this assumption cannot easily be maintained in the face of highly undemocratic states.[26] A third set of recommendations calls for more transparency, accountability, and participation concerning ICs.[27] However, such changes may be of value for reasons other than as building blocks of democracy. More transparency, accountability, or participation is often, but not always, beneficial in this regard: partial increases in accountability or participation, for example, may render the ICs less normatively acceptable for some but not all stakeholders. Transparency may also deter some actors from using ICs. Moreover, such changes toward more transparency can be valuable even when they do not advance democracy.

3 Legitimacy and Performance, or Effectiveness

Unless ICs *in fact* promote their stated objectives or otherwise promote recognized values, they may have no moral claim on actors to defer. In other words, if an IC is not effective in this sense, its normative

---

[23] von Bogdandy and Venzke, *In Whose Name? On the Functions, Authority, and Legitimacy of International Courts*.

[24] N. Grossman, "Achieving Sex Representative International Court Benches," *American Journal of International Law*, 110 (2016), 82.

[25] *E.g.* S. D. Franck, "International Arbitrators: Civil Servants? Sub Rosa Advocates? Men of Affairs?" *ILSA Journal of International and Comparative Law*, 12 (2006), 499, 501.

[26] Y. Shany, "Assessing the Effectiveness of International Courts: A Goal-Based Approach," *American Journal of International Law*, 106 (2012), 241.

[27] Grossman, "The Normative Legitimacy of International Courts," 61–105; Buchanan and Keohane, "The Legitimacy of Global Governance Institutions," 405–37.

legitimacy is at stake. In this vein, Yuval Shany has proposed a "goal-based" approach to the study of the effectiveness of ICs in which a court's aims or goals, as described by its mandate providers, are measured against whether it has achieved them.[28] Goals might also, however, be articulated by nonmandate providers, and it is essential that goals be explicitly stated for effectiveness to be properly measured.

What about the relationship between compliance with an IC's decisions and legitimacy? Persistent and widespread noncompliance, which amounts to free riding among state signatories, especially if it shifts excessive burdens onto compliers, may thus challenge the normative legitimacy of the IC. For other ICs, noncompliance by some states may be less worrisome. For instance, there may be several benefits of a regional human rights court even if its rulings are only complied with by some of the state signatories.

Challenges to the legitimacy of an IC that relate to its effectiveness may arise if institutions other than courts would secure the objectives more efficiently or with greater certainty. Further legitimacy dilemmas may arise if an IC is "too effective." For example, popular resentment against an IC may develop if its judgments are seen to intrude on state sovereignty once they take effect. Also, a large backlog of cases, as in the case of the European Court of Human Rights, may affect that institution's effectiveness and, thereby, its legitimacy.

III Contributions to the Legitimacy Literature – Sociological and Normative Legitimacy

As the next sections of this chapter show, this book significantly deepens our understanding of (1) the factors driving sociological legitimacy, as well as interactions between normative and sociological legitimacy and (2) the relationship between normative legitimacy and various substantive outcomes, such as justice, democracy, and effectiveness.

A Normative Legitimacy and Its Relationship to Sociological Legitimacy

One might assume that if a court possesses normative legitimacy, perceptions of the court as legitimate will follow. Nonetheless, factors that

---

[28] Shany, "Assessing the Effectiveness of International Courts: A Goal-Based Approach," 241.

contribute to sociological legitimacy may differ from those necessary for normative legitimacy, or may interact in interesting ways. The focus of many chapters in this book on specific international courts provides new and more concrete insights into what drives sociological legitimacy and the relationship between normative and sociological legitimacy in the context of a specific international court.

For example, as **Mark A. Pollack** demonstrates in Chapter 6, although the European Court of Justice is one of the most trusted institutions in Europe, its legitimacy rests on a "thin base of knowledge about the Court" and appears to be more rooted in general attitudes toward Europe and the rule of law than particular characteristics of the court itself. In other words, he suggests that familiarity with and normative legitimacy of a specific international court may not be the ultimate determinant of sociological legitimacy. Instead, how it is embedded within and among other institutions and regimes, and its relationship to a broader political institution and regime, may be more relevant.

Andrea K. Bjorklund argues in Chapter 9 that while defenders of the International Centre for the Settlement of Investment Disputes tend to rely on normative legitimacy arguments, critics employ a more sociological lens. Defenders of ICSID highlight state consent to investment treaties and the ICSID Convention, as well as procedural safeguards in investment treaty arbitrations. Detractors, on the other hand, focus on the public interest implications of arbitration, impact on regulation for desirable social purposes, decision makers' identity, and the "correctness" of tribunal decisions. The distinction between normative and sociological legitimacy thus helps to explain why these two groups are "talking past each other," and why defenses of an institution's normative legitimacy may not satisfy constituencies' concerns stemming from sociological legitimacy.

Alexandra Huneeus draws related insights in Chapter 5 from her case study of the involvement of the International Criminal Court (ICC) and the Inter-American Court of Human Rights (IACHR) in the Colombian peace process. She suggests that the sociological legitimacy of one international court, or of all international courts, may impact the legitimacy of another court. For example, the ICC and the IACHR, through a dynamic of "constructive interference," boosted each other's legitimacy by both working toward the same end of accountability for the crimes of the paramilitary in the Colombian conflict. To the extent that their goals coincide, their authority is reinforced and considered more justified. She argues that the ICC prosecutor's use of the jurisprudence of the IACHR heightens the sociological legitimacy of both courts, although it may also represent an expansion of its mandate, which would be inconsistent with its normative legitimacy.

Nienke Grossman suggests in Chapter 2 that when the International Court of Justice appears to "split the baby" with little deference to the governing law, it may threaten its legitimacy by exceeding the scope of authority granted by states in its governing statute. She also proposes that such judgments are inherently unfair, and therefore a threat to legitimacy, because they grant the more legally meritorious party less than the law provides. She invokes Joseph Raz's service conception of authority to argue that a subset of Solomonic judgments may result in a failure to assist states in better complying with the governing law than they would in the Court's absence. This constitutes another threat to its legitimacy.[29] She considers the impact of perceptions of Solomonism on the Court's sociological legitimacy as well.

Geir Ulfstein in Chapter 10 considers challenges to the normative legitimacy of the United Nations human rights treaty bodies with respect to their court-like function of ruling on the merits of individual petitions. He proposes that legitimacy for these bodies requires (1) independent, impartial, and highly competent treaty body members; (2) application of procedures that allow both parties to be heard and ensure that relevant facts are taken into account; (3) respect for the legal mandate established in their constitutive instruments; (4) effectiveness; and (5) accountability to international and national organs. Treaty bodies possess unique features, which complicate the legitimacy analysis, such as their emphasis on the protection of human rights, their ever-growing caseload, the nonbinding nature of their decisions, and their ability to produce state reports and General Comments, in addition to responding to individual complaints.

B Legitimacy and Substantive Outcomes

As discussed in Section II, normative legitimacy has been linked to justice, democracy, and effectiveness. Perceptions of justice, democracy, and effectiveness may also affect sociological legitimacy. Although relationships between these concepts and legitimacy are found in existing literature, this book adds new insights by considering

---

[29] J. Raz, "The Problem of Authority: Revisiting the Service Conception," *Minnesota Law Review*, 90 (2006), 1003–44.

these topics in relation to international courts as a whole and with reference to specific international courts.

1 Legitimacy and Justice

In Chapter 4, **Molly K. Land** examines the relationship and tensions between doing justice and legitimacy on the European Court of Human Rights, through the lens of prisoner voting rights cases. She proposes that justice is an aspect of normative legitimacy, like legality, and considers the extent to which just decision making affects perceptions of legitimacy. Land defines "just outcomes" as those that "expand human rights protection," especially for society's most vulnerable people. She argues that the prisoner voting cases show two ways in which the pursuit of justice can enhance the legitimacy of a court: (1) legitimacy can increase when compliance constituencies consider its decisions just and (2) even when decisions may conflict with national policy preferences, a robust domestic human rights culture raises the costs of non-compliance. So long as the Court appears to be a moral actor, dissonance between domestic policy and the Court's decisions may ultimately promote compliance and bolster legitimacy. Also, pursuing just outcomes may be less risky and more legitimacy-enhancing for mature courts, like the European Court of Human Rights, because they already possess general legitimacy. Yet, courts that issue decisions with domestic political consequences must be conscious that they may meet with resistance if they are perceived to be overreaching by doing justice. Although a court must be sensitive to domestic political concerns, the prisoner voting rights cases suggest that too much deference may undermine the compliance pull of a court's decisions.

For **Mortimer N. S. Sellers,** justice is the linchpin of legitimacy. In Chapter 12, he defines legitimacy as "the status of being correct according to some external standard" or in light of "the most *appropriate* standard for evaluating the practice in question." Although a court that is "actually legitimate" fulfills such standards, for "sociologically legitimate" courts, subjects are persuaded to act as if a rule or institution is legitimate. The extent to which a law or legal institutions secure or advance justice provides the standard for measuring actual legitimacy. Thus, actually legitimate courts advance justice, while sociologically legitimate courts are believed to do so.

Margaret M. deGuzman, as discussed further later, examines the ICC's failure to prioritize explicitly between global and local justice concerns as potentially affecting the Court's legitimacy in Chapter 3.

2 Legitimacy and Democracy

Andreas Follesdal raises doubts in Chapter 11 about the link that many scholars have made between democratic theory and the legitimacy of international courts. Follesdal suggests that scholars misuse the term *democracy* because their proposals are seldom about standards or institutions unique to democratic governance. While reform proposals emanating from these critiques may enhance the legitimacy of international courts, they rarely recommend standards or institutions unique to democratic governance. While transparency, accountability, and participation are often, but not always, beneficial, they can be valuable even when they do not advance democracy. To deepen our understanding about legitimacy and these ideals, legitimacy scholars should distinguish between democratic institutions of decision making, the normative principles that justify those institutions, and important features of those institutions that contribute to their justification. Follesdal suggests that calls for democratization are better understood as suggestions for constitutionalization of the combination of international and domestic law constituting a "Global Basic Structure." A global constitutionalist perspective helps address contested issues concerning the functions of constitutions: to create, curb, and channel the use of institutions and to specify rules for changing de facto constitutions. Further, it provides a normative justification that also provides reasons for valuing democracy: institutions deferred to must treat all people with the respect owed political equals.

Mortimer N. S. Sellers, too, questions the utility and theoretical consistency of linking democracy and legitimacy in Chapter 12. Democracy, in his view, has little to do with legitimacy because it has little to do with justice. Instead, democracy has the potential to threaten judicial independence and impartiality and, thereby, legitimacy. On the other hand, the "illusion" of democracy may indirectly buoy legitimacy by securing broader public support for judicial decisions legitimate on other grounds. It is purely instrumental in its relationship to legitimacy. Democratic practices and procedures legitimate international courts only to the extent that they advance the purposes that justify international courts in the first instance.

3 Legitimacy and Effectiveness

Yuval Shany proposes in Chapter 13 that legitimacy and effectiveness tend to operate in a mutually reinforcing manner but can be mutually undermining. Legitimacy can help a court to be more effective, and effective courts may be considered more legitimate. In addition, he argues that judicial illegitimacy can produce ineffectiveness and vice versa. Sociological legitimacy – or perceptions of justified authority – may be particularly important in sustaining judicial effectiveness by inviting support and cooperation by relevant constituencies. Put otherwise, when states believe courts are legitimate, they are more likely to implement their decisions and to provide them with resources. At the same time, legitimacy and effectiveness are not always unidirectional. For example, sometimes protecting the legitimacy of an international court may require the adoption of ineffective judicial decisions, and occasionally, effective judicial bodies are not legitimate. Shany concludes by pointing out that gaps between judicial outcomes and the preferences of courts' constituencies can result in sociological legitimacy.

Margaret M. deGuzman in Chapter 3 identifies and analyzes the importance of clear missions for international courts, questions the ICC's failure to prioritize between local and global justice, and suggests this lacuna affects both the effectiveness and legitimacy of the ICC. She proposes that existing theories of ICC legitimacy do not properly take into account ambiguities in the Court's goals and priorities. Without clearly defined objectives, the Court cannot be effective, and a limited capacity for effectiveness translates into dubious capacity for legitimacy. Consequently, clarifying and prioritizing the Court's goals with respect to global justice – the building of global norms to prescribe and prevent international crimes – and local justice – providing justice to victims of international crimes – can translate into strengthened legitimacy.

Andrea K. Bjorklund adds to the conversation in Chapter 9 by pointing out that a tribunal that actually resolves issues effectively may thereby reduce its normative legitimacy in the eyes of some critics. This may appear to be the case for the investment regime, which is criticized for impermissible infringements of state sovereignty.

IV   The Legitimacy of International Courts in Context

This book not only makes contributions to the literature on sociological and normative legitimacy and their interaction, but also it raises new insights about the context in which these courts operate and its link to legitimacy. Many discussions of the legitimacy of international courts take place in the abstract, focusing on general principles of normative or sociological legitimacy that might apply to international adjudication generally. The accounts of specific international courts in this volume, informed by their authors' expertise in those courts' histories and affairs, highlight a range of contextual factors that influence courts' respective legitimacy. The different courts have different normative goals, reflect different design choices, speak to different audiences, and inhabit different environments. These chapters describe the complex ways that these contextual elements interact with one another to either sustain or diminish the legitimacy of these various courts.

The full range of contextual elements that might be taken into account is too long to list here, but a general survey is useful. Some of these elements are beyond a particular court's or its designers' control; others reflect choices each must make in both designing and managing a particular court.

A Types of Contextual Elements

1 Normative Goals

Different international courts will operate with a focus on different normative goals such as dispute resolution, rule development, and substantive justice. A court might be charged with or see itself as primarily concerned with *dispute settlement* – resolving discrete disputes between the parties, as opposed to development of a consistent and coherent normative regime. This might be an ad hoc exercise, an appeal to a neutral arbiter to divide some set of fought-over spoils in a manner acceptable to both parties, based on law or ex acqueo et bono. For example, Nienke Grossman suggests that the ICJ may, at times, be engaged in this model of dispute settlement when it issues Solomonic judgments seemingly detached from concrete norms.[30]

Sometimes, though, courts or those appearing before them have broader aspirations than resolving a single case. They may be engaged instead in *rule development*, using discrete disputes to help clarify ambiguities in a legal regime, providing guidance and predictability to regime actors. For example, the International Tribunal for the Law of the Sea (ITLOS) is involved in more than just the settlement of a particular dispute; it is also involved in developing law of the sea rules more broadly. The creation of a permanent WTO Appellate Body and the development of compulsory jurisdiction were arguably efforts at achieving similar goals for trade law.

A third possible goal for an international court might be substantive *justice*. This can take a variety of forms even for a particular tribunal.

---

[30] Grossman (Chapter 2 in this volume).

16   COHEN, FOLLESDAL, GROSSMAN, AND ULFSTEIN

It might be justice as defined by the values of a particular regime. For Molly Land, a desire to achieve justice explains and underpins the ECtHR's adoption of expansive, rather than minimalist, readings of the rights it is tasked with protecting.[31] This form of justice is largely prospective, aimed at making each state under its supervision a little more just in the future. For the ICC, justice is retrospective or restorative, designed to remedy past wrongs. Still, as Margaret deGuzman describes, the ICC faces choices between local and global justice.[32]

Of course, the lines between these different goals are fuzzy; specific courts may embrace multiple or all of these goals simultaneously or over time, depending on the specifics of the case before them. Resolving disputes by applying the law may provide justice to the party in the right. It may also help develop the rules, providing certainty, predictability, and guidance. Various actors – members of a court, litigants, stakeholders – may also disagree on the normative goals for particular courts. But as will be discussed later, matching expectations about those goals with other features of a particular court may be important in determining whether it will possess normative or sociological legitimacy.

2   Design Choices

Myriad choices face those designing or seeking to reform a particular international court or tribunal. These choices include structure, personnel, case initiation, procedures, and effect, among others. For example, will the court be embedded within a particular international regime[33] as the WTO-DSB is within the trade regime, ITLOS is within the law of the sea convention, or human rights courts and bodies are within particular human rights treaties, or will it be independent of any particular regime as in the case of the ICJ? Embeddedness itself can take a range of forms – a court's jurisdiction could be limited to a specific treaty or treaties or limited in the sources or rules it can apply. Additionally or alternatively, a court could be embedded within particular institutional structures, establishing relationships between the court and other bodies that may

---

[31] Land (Chapter 4 in this volume).   [32] deGuzman (Chapter 3 in this volume).
[33] A regime is defined here as a set of "principles, norms, rules, and decision-making procedures around which actor expectations converge in a given issue-area." S. D. Krasner, "Structural Causes and Regime Consequences: Regimes as Intervening Variables," in S. Krasner (ed.), *International Regimes* (Ithaca, NY: Cornell University Press, 1983), pp. 1, 185.

support it, monitor it, or hold it accountable.[34] As Joost Pauwelyn suggests, it may be the panel's deep embeddedness within a broader set of institutional structures at the WTO that allows it to use largely nonlawyer panelists.[35] Will an adjudicative body be a permanent body with a set group of judges like the ICJ or WTO AB or a system for setting up ad hoc tribunals like ICSID or WTO panels? Who will make the decisions – will the court have professional judges or other types of experts? What credentials will be required?

How will cases come to the court? Will jurisdiction be compulsory, optional, or something in between? As Anastasia Telesetsky explains, ITLOS has compulsory jurisdiction over prompt release cases, but only optional jurisdiction over maritime delimitation cases.[36] Prompt release cases may function like free samples designed to convince states to opt for ITLOS in other cases.[37] ITLOS may on the flipside have some discretion on whether to issue advisory opinions.[38] Who can initiate cases – state parties as in the WTO, ITLOS, or ICJ; national courts as with the ECJ; private parties as in ICSID; or human rights courts and bodies, or a prosecutor, as in the case of the ICC?

When it comes to procedural choices, will there be oral arguments, or will the case be solely on the written record, as with most human rights treaty bodies? What role will nonparties play in the proceedings, whether victims of crimes, amicus curiae state or amicus curiae NGOs? These are questions that the various bodies – the ICC, the WTO dispute settlement system, and ICSID arbitrations – continue to struggle with.

Court designers must consider the effects of a body's decisions. For example, will the decisions of a particular court or tribunal be binding or nonbinding? How much precedential effect will decisions in one case have for future similar ones? The ICJ Statute gives prior decisions little more than persuasive authority; in practice, the court itself may give its

---

[34] For example, the ECtHR and WTO-DSB are both limited in their jurisdiction and embedded within an institutional structure that supports and oversees it. The ICJ is open to disputes arising under a range of treaties and regimes, limited only by the agreements of the parties, and except where otherwise agreed, applies the general sources of international law. The ICJ is nonetheless embedded within the institutional structure of the United Nations, issuing advisory opinions at the request of UN bodies and looking to the Security Council for enforcement of its decisions.

[35] Pauwelyn (Chapter 8 in this volume).   [36] Telesetsky (Chapter 7 in this volume).

[37] Ibid.   [38] Ibid.

18　　COHEN, FOLLESDAL, GROSSMAN, AND ULFSTEIN

own decision greater weight.[39] The WTO AB has interpreted the Dispute Settlement Understanding to create at least vertical stare decisis – in the AB's view, WTO panels must follow AB decisions.[40] ICSID arbitrators and advocates have appealed to a loose *jurisprudence constante*.[41] And the Rome Statute specifies that "[t]he Court may apply principles and rules of law as interpreted in its previous decisions."[42] What methods of enforcement will be available to a particular court or tribunal – the power to order particular interim or final measures; questions that have arisen for the ICJ, ITLOS, and the Human Rights Committee; enforcement by a Council of Ministers like the ECJ and the Committee of Ministers for the EtCHR; or appeal to the UN Security Council like the ICJ?

These are, of course, only a small sampling of the design choices that international courts might exhibit. As will be discussed later, the legitimacy of specific international courts and tribunals will often depend on how well these choices are aligned with other aspects of a court's context.

3　Audiences

The courts in this study also highlight the various audiences to which any particular court or tribunal will speak. These audiences might be the litigants in a particular case or the other participants in a particular legal regime more generally. The ICJ, argues Nienke Grossman, by both its title and statute, speaks to the broader community subject to international law.[43] Its legitimacy, she argues, is at least partly derived from its ability to help other actors beyond the litigants in a specific case discern lawful from unlawful actions.[44] Solomonic judgments trade legitimacy with that audience for what the court perceives (wrongly in Grossman's view) will be viewed as legitimate by the specific litigants before it.[45] Concerns about ICSID's legitimacy, Andrea K. Bjorklund suggests, have tracked shifts in the practical audiences for ICSID decisions.[46] ICSID's designers made choices designed to legitimate decisions with discrete litigants who had directly agreed to arbitration in contracts or

---

[39] Mohamed Shahabuddeen, *Precedent in the World Court* (Cambridge, UK: Cambridge University Press, 1996).

[40] *See* H. Cohen, "Theorizing Precedent in International Law"; M. Crowley and R. Howse, "US–Stainless Steel (Mexico)," *World Trade Review*, 9 (2010), 122–4.

[41] Bjorklund (Chapter 9 in this volume).

[42] Rome Statute of the International Criminal Court (adopted 17 July 1998), 2187 UNTS 90, Art. 21.2.

[43] Grossman (Chapter 2 in this volume).　　[44] Ibid.　　[45] Ibid.

[46] Bjorklund (Chapter 9 in this volume)

concession agreements.[47] The rapid multiplication of Bilateral Investment Treaties, the consequent widening of access to arbitration, and the range of public policies now challengeable before ICSID panels, however, has broadened interest in ICSID panel decisions and required ICSID and ICSID arbitrators to legitimate their decisions to a much broader audience.[48] The design features chosen to guarantee equality of arms and fair proceeding may be insufficient to do so.

This hints at another distinction between audiences. The audiences may be technical, professional audiences or they may be much broader, including the public at large. Audiences may include trade diplomats, the elite investment law bar, foreign ministries, national court judges, transnational advocacy networks, or domestic publics at large. The court may be speaking primarily to regime insiders – Joost Pauwelyn suggests that this had long been the case within the trade law.[49] To the extent the issues they decide remain of low salience to those outside the regime, legitimacy with those insiders may be sufficient. If, on the other hand, those issues become salient to broader populations, as in the case of felon disenfranchisement laws described in Molly Land's chapter on the ECtHR,[50] a court may need to legitimate its decisions in different ways. Sometimes a court may choose to legitimate its decisions with a broader audience at the expense of a narrower one. This might be the strategy employed by human rights courts and bodies when they choose broader evolutive interpretations fought by state parties. Or as Margaret deGuzman explains, an international criminal court like the ICC may choose global justice goals over local ones.[51] As a result, it may choose cases and procedures that legitimate its actions in global eyes, rather than local ones. It might, for example, choose to emphasize independence from local politics rather than sensitivity to it.[52] As deGuzman suggests, achieving maximum legitimacy with both global and local audiences may be impossible.[53]

4 Institutional Environment

Finally, international courts and tribunals do not operate in a vacuum. Instead, they exist within an ecosystem of courts, tribunals, and other international and domestic institutions, and their normative and sociological legitimacy may depend on finding the proper role to play within

---

[47] Ibid. [48] Ibid. [49] Pauwelyn (Chapter 8 in this volume).
[50] Land (Chapter 4 in this volume). [51] deGuzman (Chapter 3 in this volume).
[52] Ibid. [53] Ibid.

it. Some courts will be first movers, like the ICJ, providing the first real fora for particular disputes. Such courts may have a lot of room (and time) to establish their legitimacy. They will face a range of decisions about the scope of their jurisdiction, their procedures, and their methods of interpretation. As Yuval Shany explains, the right decisions can produce virtuous cycles where initial investments of "legitimacy capital" translate into effectiveness, initial effectiveness bolsters legitimacy, and so on.[54] An older, successful court will, in turn, have legitimacy capital to expend. It may be able to take riskier decisions, perhaps ones that bolster legitimacy with some audience members at the expense of some others, without threatening its overall legitimacy.[55] The European Court of Rights, with its increasingly aggressive scrutiny of the states under its jurisdiction, may demonstrate that point.[56]

Other courts or tribunals may be latecomers, like ITLOS. As Anastasia Telesetsky explains, ITLOS has had to compete with the ICJ for jurisdiction in maritime boundary delimitation cases.[57] As the latecomer, ITLOS must give states reasons to choose it over the predictability that comes from the ICJ's longer track record. As Telesetsky explains, ITLOS thus uses prompt release cases, over which it has exclusive jurisdiction, to make the argument to states that its decisions are particularly attentive to state consent.[58] Those cases thus become proving grounds for the tribunal's legitimacy relative to other courts.

Overlapping jurisdiction may also create substantive regulatory competition between courts and tribunals. The divergent logics of international criminal law and the traditional rules of state responsibility may pit the International Criminal Tribunal for the former Yugoslavia (ICTY) against the ICJ.[59] The competing logics of liberalized trade and human rights may pit the WTO against UN human rights bodies. In these cases, overlapping jurisdiction risks disorder, highlights the limits of specific tribunals' logics and mandates, and demonstrates the limits of their effectiveness, all of which in turn may threaten their perceived

---

[54] Shany (Chapter 13 in this volume).   [55] Ibid.
[56] *See* Land (Chapter 4 in this volume).   [57] Telesetsky (Chapter 7 in this volume).
[58] Ibid.
[59] Compare *Prosecutor v. Tadić*, Case No. IT-94-1-A, Judgment in the Appeals Chamber, ¶¶ 115–45 (July 15, 1999) (rejecting the ICJ's "effective control" test) *with* Application of the Convention on the Prevention and Punishment of the Crime of Genocide ¶ 223 (Bosn. & Herz. v. Serb. & Mont.) (Judgment of February 26, 2007), *available at* http://www.icj-cij.org/files/case-related/91/091-20070226-JUD-01-00-EN.pdf ¶ 406 (reasserting the "effective control" test after *Tadic*).

legitimacy with both outsiders and insiders. Disagreement over the content of international law may undermine any and all tribunals' claims to legitimate authority to interpret it.

In other situations, overlapping jurisdiction may be mutually reinforcing. Alexandra Huneeus tells the story of the ICC and Inter-American Court of Human Rights' interaction in Colombia.[60] In that case, overlapping jurisdiction has allowed each to borrow, reference, and appeal to the complementary work of the other, strengthening the authority and sociological legitimacy of each, so much so that their normative legitimacy may now be in question.[61]

B Models of Interaction

These numerous and varied contextual elements, summarized in Table 1.1 interact in complex ways to affect the legitimacy of international courts. For example, specific audiences at specific times are more or less likely to be interested in achieving particular normative goals or to view attempts at achieving those goals as desirable and legitimate. Achieving particular normative goals in a legitimate manner may require specific design choices – methods of initiating disputes, types of adjudicators, processes of adjudication, or even substantive rules. A court's specific environment – whether it is a new or old court, whether it faces competition or not – may affect the relative legitimacy of its options, priorities, and opportunities. The chapters in this book help to illuminate a few of these different interactions and suggest avenues for further research.

The importance of these interactions becomes most obvious when these factors – normative goals, design features, audiences, and environments – end up misaligned, whether at the outset or as a result of changes to each over time. When that happens, the legitimacy of a particular international court may be brought into doubt. ICSID, as Andrea K. Bjorklund explains, was designed to provide dispute settlement services for discrete investment disputes between consenting parties, yet various treaties have thrust it into a different role, in which arbitrators are seemingly asked to sit in judgment over state public policy.[62] Whereas arbitrators once spoke only to states and investors, they now find themselves speaking to national publics as well. Procedures designed primarily to protect investors and to guarantee procedural fairness in discrete

---

[60] Huneeus (Chapter 5 in this volume).   [61] Ibid.
[62] Bjorklund (Chapter 9 in this volume).

Table 1.1 *Factors Relevant to IC Legitimacy*

Normative Goals	Design Choices	Audience	Environment

• Dispute Settlement
  • Ad Hoc
  • Rule-based
• Rule/Regime Development
• Justice
  • Global
  • Local
	• Structure
	  • Regime Dependent or Independent?
	• Personnel
	  • Permanent or Ad Hoc?
	• Adjudicators
	  • Method of Appointment
	  • Credentials
	• Case Initiation
	  • Compulsory or Ad Hoc Jurisdiction?
	  • States
	  • Supervisory Body (Commission, Security Council, etc.)
	  • Prosecutor
	  • Investors
	  • Individuals
	• Procedures
	  • Public or Closed?
	  • Written Submissions
	  • Oral Arguments
	  • Participation by:
	    • Interested Third Parties
	    • Amici
	    • Victims
	• Effect
	  • Binding?
	  • Precedential?
		• State Parties
		• Bureaucrats
		  • Trade Diplomats
		  • Foreign Ministries
		  • National Judges
		• Professional Bar
		• Investors
		• Transnational Advocacy Networks
		• General Public
		  • Global
		  • Local
			• Age of Tribunal
			• Availability of Other Fora

disputes, may no longer seem legitimate for what may been seen by this new audience as a public law dispute.[63]

As Joost Pauwelyn recounts, the appointment of nonlawyer, insider, trade diplomats to the former General Agreement on Tariffs and Trade (GATT) and now WTO dispute settlement panels may have been adequate when disputes were technical, and the audience was trade ministries. But when disputes pit trade against other concerns, for example, the environment or animal welfare, other stakeholders, suddenly interested in WTO dispute settlement, may deem the same arbitrators inadequate and illegitimate.[64] Nienke Grossman describes a different type of misalignment, one between a court's perceived and actual role.[65] Solomonic judgments divorced from relevant law may reflect the ICJ's judgment that its role is to divide entitlements such that both parties are equally pleased and displeased.[66] But as Grossman explains, Solomonic judgments conflict with ICJ's role as a court of justice, expected to apply and develop law.[67] The ICJ might be buying itself some limited sociological legitimacy (states continue to choose it over ITLOS, as Anastasia Telesetsky explains,[68] no doubt because states prefer the expected outcome), but in so doing, the ICJ undercuts its broader normative legitimacy.[69] In a sense, it may be argued, the ICJ's chosen audience conflicts with its broader structure, design, and mandate.

To protect both normative and sociological legitimacy, courts and their supporters must be cognizant of these relationships between contextual factors and work to keep these various elements aligned. Courts may have to make choices. They may not be able to be or do all things for all audiences. As Margaret deGuzman explains, legitimately providing global justice or local justice may require the ICC to choose different procedures and strategies.[70]

1   Regime-Embedded versus Regime-Independent Tribunals

One set of interactions with importance for questions of legitimacy revolves around the choice of whether to embed a court or tribunal within a particular regime or whether set it up as independent of any

---

[63] Ibid.   [64] Pauwelyn (Chapter 8 in this volume).
[65] Grossman (Chapter 2 in this volume).
[66] *Cf.* E. A. Posner and J. C. Yoo, "Judicial Independence in International Tribunals," *California Law Review*, 93 (2005), 1, 17–18.
[67] Ibid.   [68] Telesetsky (Chapter 7 in this volume).
[69] Grossman (Chapter 2 in this volume).   [70] deGuzman (Chapter 3 in this volume).

particular regime.[71] Examples of the former (regime-specific courts) in this book include the WTO Dispute Settlement Understanding (DSU), ITLOS, European Court of Justice, European and Inter-American Courts of Human Rights, and UN Human Rights Committee, established pursuant to and as part of the WTO, United Nations Convention on the Law of the Sea (UNCLOS), the European Union, ECHR and American Convention on Human Rights, and International Covenant on Civil and Political Rights, respectively. Examples of the latter (regime-neutral courts) include the ICJ and ICSID, neither of which is tied to a specific set of substantive laws. Instead, each is available to help decide disputes arising under a range of treaties or laws when relevant parties so choose. The chapters suggest that the choice between these two models has significant implications for these courts' respective legitimacy. The choice acts as a key organizing principle dictating how other contextual elements are or will need to be aligned.

At the most basic level, the chapters in this book help illuminate why IC designers might tie an IC more or less closely to a particular regime. Regime-specific courts cater most effectively to repeat players who operate regularly under the shadow of the regime and court and who seek, above all, predictable rules. The WTO-DSB might be an archetype of such a regime-specific court. GATT members explicitly moved to a model of compulsory jurisdiction and a permanent Appellate Body in the hopes that WTO-DSB would help develop clearer, more predictable rules for international trade. The ECtHR's move toward compulsory jurisdiction can be described in much the same way, as an attempt to develop clear, generally applicable rules of European human rights that can provide state parties, their legislatures, and their courts, all of whom are repeat players with regard to human rights, with forward-looking guidance. Regime-specific courts help achieve these goals through relative insulation from other areas of international law. Designed to develop the laws of a particular regime, their mandates often limit them to considering its rules, their meaning, and their objectives. The DSU limits on the jurisdiction of the WTO dispute settlement are a perfect example.[72]

Regime-neutral courts, on the other hand, make most sense when their primary consumers are not repeat players and the issues are ones that do

---

[71] For the definition of regime, see note 34.

[72] WTO Dispute Settlement Understanding, Article 3.2, provides that "Recommendations and rulings of the DSB cannot add to or diminish the rights and obligations provided in the covered agreements."

not come up as often, particularly for that state. Fair dispute resolution, rather than rule development, is the primary goal sought by its consumers. Maritime boundary delimitation might be a typical example. Most states will have few of those disputes and may be less interested in the development of clear rules on the subject. Future cases may not be that relevant to them. Where states or other consumers are interested in prospective rule development, regime-neutral courts are more likely to put those rules in a broader context by embedding them within the larger corpus of international law. Neither of these points should be overstated. When states delegate disputes under a particular treaty to the ICJ, for example, the Vienna Convention on Consular Relations, they undoubtedly hope that over time, the treaty's provisions may be clarified by a corpus of cases. That goal, though, seems secondary.

The choice between regime-specific and regime-neutral courts may also turn, to some extent, on the traditional rules-standards divide.[73] Regime-specific courts are useful where states or other actors can only agree on vague standards and hope to delegate rule development to other institutions. Human rights and trade, again, fit the bill. Where states or other actors choose more determinate rules designed to govern discrete interactions, ad hoc dispute resolution may be the more apt choice.

These insights have a number of implications for legitimacy. For one thing, these choices suggest specific chains of contextual factors that need to be aligned to support these courts' legitimacy. It suggests the connection of normative goals, for example, rule development, with specific structures like an embedded court and compulsory jurisdiction (to avoid fragmentation and conflicting interpretations), and a specific audience, usually regime insiders (though regime insiders may be a broad and numerous group in the case of a regime like human rights). It also suggests certain types of processes and decision making. To legitimately develop rules from specific cases for the broader regime, the courts' processes must allow for sufficient involvement or intervention by other regime participants, whether other states or amici. It may also suggest the need for proper accountability mechanisms, like democratic control or legislative overrides.

These legitimacy chains can also help explain conflicts over certain courts' legitimacy. As Andrea K. Bjorklund explains, ICSID was designed to legitimate resolutions of discrete disputes between parties in privity

---

[73] P. J. Schlag, "Rules and Standards," *UCLA Law Review*, 33 (1985), 379.

who had agreed on both the specific substantive rules governing their relationship – the contract – and the jurisdiction of a tribunal to resolve it.[74] Ad hoc, secretive, but procedurally fair, dispute resolution may have been normatively and sociologically legitimate. But as the type and scope of disputes before ICSID tribunals has expanded through bilateral investment treaties (BITs) and other agreements, this chain has broken.[75] To many, investment law looks like a de facto regime, and secretive, ad hoc dispute resolution no longer looks appropriate. Both arbitrators and advocates have sought greater consistency, predictability, transparency, and participation. But these moves only break the chain further. Based not on a single set of substantives rules, but on a vast array of similar treaties and agreement, consistency, through forms of stare decisis, for example, may be illegitimate from the standpoint of legality or consent. They also may be illegitimate in the absence of effective review and accountability mechanisms. Annulment proceedings, sufficient accountability for ad hoc arbitration, may be too weak and too narrow to guarantee that rules develop in directions acceptable to investment law's swelling stakeholder ranks. It is those sorts of concerns that undergird the powers of NAFTA's Foreign Trade Commission and calls for a permanent investment law appellate body.

A different sort of challenge to this chain can be seen in the history and development of the WTO-DSB. A regime-specific tribunal may be a legitimate means of developing trade law within the WTO and among trade insiders. But as the WTO has moved from regulating tariffs and quotas to other regulatory trade barriers, trade law has come into potential conflict with other concerns like health or the environment and become salient to a much broader audience that cares about those issues. A closed regime that considered only trade law may have been legitimate to and for an audience of trade insiders. But as reaction to the Tuna–Dolphin dispute[76] and the 1999 protests in Seattle demonstrated, a regime that failed to consider other external concerns was illegitimate in the eyes of many regime outsiders. The WTO AB's response, visible in its resolution of the Shrimp–Turtle dispute,[77] was to open the regime up, at least partly, to other concerns. Opening WTO dispute settlement

---

[74] Bjorklund (Chapter 9 in this volume).   [75] Ibid.

[76] Report of the Panel, United States-Restrictions on Imports of Tuna, DS2I/R (Sept. 3, 1991), GAIE B.I.S.D. (39th Supp.), 155 (1993).

[77] Appellate Body Report, *United States – Import Prohibition of Certain Shrimp and Shrimp Products*, WT/DS58/AB/R (October 8, 1998).

proceedings to the public, allowing amici, and considering outside areas of international law have all been on the table as well. The alternative to changing these design features, as the conflict over affordable medicines demonstrated, would have been for regime outsiders to seek out other more friendly fora for their disputes, threatening the DSB's control over the development of trade law.[78]

Regime-specific courts' legitimacy may also be inextricably intertwined with the legitimacy of the broader regime. As Yuval Shany[79] and Mark A. Pollack[80] suggest in their respective chapters, a regime-specific court may both gain and lose legitimacy along with the regime in which it is embedded. And Andrea K. Bjorklund describes the legitimacy debates around ICSID in similar terms.[81] As the number of BITs and BIT arbitrations has multiplied, investment law has become a de facto regime. ICSID, she argues, is no longer judged on the basis of its own legitimacy alone, but also on the legitimacy of the investment regime it supports.[82] ICSID's procedures could be nothing but fair, but as long as they are used to support normative ends viewed by many as unjust, like putting the interests of investors ahead of democratically enacted state public policy, ICSID's legitimacy will suffer.

2 Bindingness, Stakes, Exit, and Voice

Another key relationship illuminated by the chapters is between legitimacy, exit, and voice. Geir Ulfstein's chapter on the UN treaty bodies adds a factor that goes undiscussed in most of the others – bindingness.[83] As Ulfstein explains, the UN treaty bodies diverge from the other courts and tribunals described here in a number of ways. Communications are considered by experts rather than judges, who serve on the treaty bodies on a near-volunteer basis. In some cases, legal expertise among the group may be limited. The experts consider the communications before them on an extraordinarily truncated timeline, there are no oral arguments, and decisions are made solely on the written record. Separation-of-powers concerns abound; the same experts issue general comments expounding the treaties they supervise and decide discrete disputes over

---

[78] *See, e.g.*, L. R. Helfer, "Regime Shifting: The Trips Agreement and New Dynamics of International Intellectual Property Lawmaking," *Yale Journal of International Law*, 29, (2004), 49–51, 65–9 (describing how developing states brought their demands for access to affordable medicine to human rights bodies rather than to WTO dispute settlement).
[79] Shany (Chapter 13 in this volume).   [80] Pollack (Chapter 6 in this volume).
[81] Bjorklund (Chapter 9 in this volume).   [82] Ibid.
[83] Ulfstein (Chapter 10 in this volume).

the treaties' application. The UN General Assembly, to which the bodies technically report, does little to hold the bodies accountable for their interpretations and decisions.[84] And yet, the treaty body claims broad powers to declare state parties in violation of their human rights obligations and to require them to take remedial actions. The lack of process, the low levels of participation and the absence of accountability for its decisions seem incongruous with the vast powers of review the treaty bodies claim. Although many have questioned the legitimacy of the treaty bodies' work, those bodies have not crumbled in the face of a perceived legitimacy deficit. If anything, the opposite has happened: state parties to the treaties have sought to strengthen the bodies and provide them more tools to do their work. How can this seeming paradox be explained?

Part of the answer, as Ulfstein suggests, is the fact that the decisions of the treaty bodies are generally accepted to be nonbinding.[85] As Ulfstein suggests, if the bodies' decisions were to be binding, major reforms would be needed to their structure and processes.[86] The Human Rights Committee and the other human rights treaty bodies would have to look more like traditional courts – the ECtHR, for example.

The broader insight is that the legitimacy of a particular court or tribunal may not be dependent solely on structural factors like who decides cases, under what processes, or even in service of which goals. The legitimacy of any particular tribunal may depend as much on what, or how much, it asks of its audiences. A body issuing nonbinding decisions asks less of participants. Compliance may not be "voluntary," but it is also not obligatory. Such a body may need to do less to legitimate its decisions. We have described legitimacy as "justified authority." Most of the chapters in this book focus on the "justification" prong of that equation. Bindingness focuses us on the other variable, "authority." The less authority a body claims or asserts, the less justification it needs to do so legitimately.

Although bindingess in a legal sense is binary, this focus on the authority exercised by a tribunal or court highlights how authority might be increased or decreased in a variety of ways. It might be calibrated through control of jurisdiction: The court or tribunal will claim much more authority when jurisdiction is compulsory than where states or other actors can opt in or out of jurisdiction. So too where a court or tribunal's jurisdiction is exclusive – leaving open the possibility to forum

---

[84] Ibid.   [85] Ibid.   [86] Ibid.

LEGITIMACY AND INTERNATIONAL COURTS – A FRAMEWORK   29

shop may soften a court or tribunal's claims to authority. Relative authority might be calibrated through precedent: the more precedential the decisions of the tribunal the broader its claim of authority. Or it might be calibrated through substantive scope: the narrower the court or tribunal's substantive mandate, the less authority it needs to justify. In fact, the level of authority might be thought of as a function of stakes. The more that is asked of participants, both in terms of substance and obligation, the more justification participants will expect and require. As Molly Land describes, the ECtHR's progressive narrowing of the margin of appreciation and more aggressive review of national legislation has been met with increasing demands from member states for justification.[87]

The effect of varying the stakes or authority can be conceptualized as a form of the well-known relationship between exit and voice.[88] Decreasing the level of authority claimed by a court or tribunal – making decisions nonbinding, making jurisdiction optional, narrowing the scope of its mandate – essentially increases the opportunity for participants to exit the regime. They can refuse to follow the decision (at least technically). They can refuse jurisdiction or shop for more favorable fora. They can choose to comply in narrower or easier ways. Less work will need to be done to justify their acceptance of the court or tribunal's authority. Arguably, the possibility of exit acts as an ongoing form of specific consent that can always be rescinded or limited.

As opportunities to exit decrease, however, demands for voice, participation or control grow. This can be seen in the stories of the courts and tribunals described in this book. As the authority of each increases, so too do demands for greater participation in decision making. Thus compulsory, exclusive jurisdiction in the WTO DSU has been met by calls for (depending on who is calling) greater openness and transparency, more opportunities to be heard, and more room for legislative correction by WTO members. Some, like Joost Pauwelyn, have argued that exit too might need to be recalibrated to establish the DSU's legitimacy, perhaps through broader readings of exceptions or safe harbors within trade agreements or something like a margin of appreciation.[89] BITs have

---

[87] Land (Chapter 4 in this volume).

[88] Albert O. Hirschman, *Exit, Voice and Loyalty – Responses to Decline in Firms, Organizations, and States* (Cambridge, MA: Harvard University Press, 1970); *see also* E. Benvenisti, "Exit and Voice in the Age of Globalization," *Michigan Law Review*, 98 (1999), 167; J. H. H. Weiler, "The Transformation of Europe," *Yale Law Journal*, 100 (1991), 2403.

[89] J. H. B. Pauwelyn, "The Transformation of World Trade," *Michigan Law Review*, 104 (2005), 1–66.

made exit from ICSID more difficult, and the rapidly increasing number of cases has increased the power of de facto precedent. While some have used the exit options they have left – explicit carve outs from ISDS have been included in newer agreements, and Venezuela, Ecuador, Bolivia, and Argentina have all withdrawn from ICSID jurisdiction – others have called for greater transparency, more participation through amici, or more opportunities for meaningful review.[90]

In this sense, higher stakes may require more legitimacy and lower stakes less. But as Yuval Shany suggests, the relationship may run in the opposite direction as well.[91] Although weak, narrow, or timid courts or tribunals may need less legitimacy capital to support their work and their authority, that same weakness, narrowness, or timidity will make them less effective and, in turn, less legitimate. As Shany suggests, the timidity of the ICJ's *Southwest Africa* decision damaged the ICJ's perceived legitimacy for decades. By contrast, the boldness of the ICJ's later approach to Nicaragua's case against the United States suggested that the ICJ could handle high-stakes cases effectively, kicking off a virtuous legitimacy cycle for the court.[92] A court may choose a lower legitimacy burden by asking less of stakeholders. When it does so, however, it risks limiting its legitimacy more broadly. If and when that court wants to take bolder action in the future, it may have insufficient legitimacy capital to support it.

The following figure illustrates this relationship between the level and depth of obligation and legitimacy.

---

[90] *See also* S. Williams, "Aggression, Affected States, and a Right to Participate: A Response to Koh and Buchwald," *AJIL Unbound*, 109 (2016), 246 (arguing for third-party intervention in future ICC aggression cases).
[91] Shany (Chapter 13 in this volume). [92] Ibid.

As the level and depth of obligations increase, more legitimacy capital is required to support them. At the same time, stronger and deeper obligations will also increase the court's legitimacy capital for the future. Choosing where to be on one of the two vectors dictates where a court will be on the other.

For the UN treaty bodies, this suggests an uncomfortable trade-off. Justifying binding decisions might require changes to the treaty bodies' structure, personnel, and processes that seem politically and logistically implausible. Among other things, such reforms would require massive infusions of additional resources. Binding decisions might require full-time judges, longer and/or more frequent meetings, oral arguments, and opportunities to respond, among other things. So long as their pronouncements remain nonbinding, however, their existing arrangements – part-time experts, short meetings, written submissions alone – may largely suffice. The treaty bodies may not need to work as hard to legitimate their work. The treaty bodies' inability to bind states, however, cripples their effectiveness, guaranteeing that many of their boldest pronouncements will be ignored. Its legitimacy capital will essentially be capped. Given its resources, is limited effectiveness and limited legitimacy enough? Maybe.

3   Raising Legitimacy Capital

A final way to imagine the interaction between the contextual elements described in these chapters is in relation to each court's or tribunal's quest for "legitimacy capital."[93] Yuval Shany develops the idea of "legitimacy capital" as a way to capture the functional role a court's normative or sociological legitimacy might play. It treats a court's normative or sociological legitimacy as an asset that the court needs to accomplish its goals. One might imagine international courts or tribunals as startups seeking infusions of capital from interested investors. In this case though, the key investment is not ordinary capital (though they need that too), but legitimacy capital. The court or tribunal will only be able to operate if someone will fund it, someone will send it cases, and someone will be influenced by its decisions. None of those things will happen, however, if no one is interested or willing to see that court, its cases, or its overall project as legitimate.

This startup model suggests that a court or tribunal interested in legitimacy capital must consider three sets of contextual factors:

---

[93] *See* Shany (Chapter 13 in this volume).

(1) audience, (2) product, and (3) packaging. Proponents of the startup court must decide from whom to seek legitimacy capital. Are their potential investors – those who the court will rely on to support its jurisdiction and decisions[94] – states, bureaucrats, national court judges, investors, transnational or local advocacy groups, or the general public either in specific countries or globally? They will need to decide what they are selling to those potential investors – dispute settlement, monitoring, predictability, rule development, or some form of justice, whether remedial or restorative, local or global. Proponents of the court will also need to consider packaging. Will the court be permanent or ad hoc? Will it have professional judges, experts, or other types of arbitrators? How will they be appointed and for how long? Will the court be embedded within a regime or independent of any? What processes will it follow for case initiation, case management, deliberation, and decision making?

A court, its designers, or its proponents can look at these factors in whatever order they choose. Once they make decisions, though, about one of these categories, those decisions will affect the options available to it in the others. If one starts with a group of investors, say states, the next question has to be what states want. For Margaret deGuzman, the ICC's initial choice is whether to seek legitimacy capital from local or global constituencies.[95] Each will want different types of justice and will expect different types of procedures. And choosing the wrong procedures may alienate the chosen audience. An ICC that ignores local concerns and local norms in an effort to project independence, neutrality, and universality may cost itself the support of the communities affected by the crimes it prosecutes. Alternatively, one could start with a product, for example, substantive human rights justice. The challenge for a court or its proponents then becomes finding audiences interested in supporting that goal and willing to invest legitimacy capital in a court willing to provide it. It may be that states' interest in that product is limited. A human rights court or body might thus seek to augment its legitimacy capital by shopping its product to others, whether transnational advocates or national judges and lawyers. This strategy appears to have been embraced by the ECtHR[96] and the Inter-American Court of Human

---

[94] This group overlaps with but is distinct from the court's audience.

[95] deGuzman (Chapter 3 in this volume).

[96] E. Voeten, "Does a Professional Judiciary Induce More Compliance?: Evidence from the European Court of Human Rights" (2012), Georgetown University, 4–6 <http://papers.ssrn.com/sol3/papers.cfm?abstract_id=2029786> accessed 22 March 2014.

Rights,[97] among others. Courts may even start with the packaging. The WTO DSU and ITLOS are limited in what they can offer and to whom by their origin within the trade and law of the sea regimes, respectively. The key is that building a court's legitimacy capital requires that the choices in the three categories be properly aligned.

Courts face these choices throughout their lifetimes. Maintaining legitimacy capital requires constantly reassessing whether choices are aligned to guarantee sufficient investment. Initial assumptions about the market in legitimacy capital can turn out to be wrong. The ICJ's decision to reject Ethiopia's and Liberia's standing in the *Southwest Africa* decision[98] may have reflected a belief among ICJ judges that states, the court's primary audience, wanted it to be cautious before stepping into politically sensitive disputes. Although some state parties may have wanted or preferred that, the court's track record after that case suggests that the interest in such a conservative court was limited. The ICJ's decision cost the court considerable credibility and led many developing states to turn away from it.[99] The ICJ took a different approach in its *Nicaragua* decision, however. A court willing to decide politically difficult cases and confront politically powerful states turned out to be much more popular with states than the opposite. The Nicaragua decision arguably reopened the flow of legitimacy capital.[100]

Anastasia Telesetsky describes ITLOS as a court focused on states and offering dispute settlement.[101] Perhaps judging that such an audience would be attuned to issues of state consent, it has sought to emphasize legality in its decisions.[102] And yet, its docket of cases remains small. As Telesetsky lays out in her chapter, ITLOS has decided only one maritime boundary delimitation case since its founding. One other case is pending. During that same period, the ICJ has decided ten cases on maritime delimitation or maritime rights.[103] Perhaps states are less willing to invest much legitimacy capital for such cases in ITLOS in the face of the ICJ's more established jurisprudence. The challenge for ITLOS thus becomes finding a new audience, product, or both. Telesetsky mentions the Sub-Regional Fisheries Commission request for an advisory opinion.[104]

---

[97] *See* A. Huneeus, "Constitutional Lawyers and the Inter-American Court's Varied Authority," *Law and Contemporary Problems*, 79 (2016), 179.

[98] *South West Africa* (Liberia v SA; Ethiopia v SA), 1966 ICJ 6.

[99] Shany, "Assessing the Effectiveness of International Courts," pp. 104–5.

[100] *See* Shany (Chapter 13 in this volume). [101] Telesetsky (Chapter 7 in this volume).

[102] Ibid. [103] Ibid. [104] Ibid.

In defiance of state parties who argued that the tribunal could not exercise advisory jurisdiction, ITLOS accepted the request. Could advisory opinions on issues like environmental protection provide ITLOS with a new audience interested in investing legitimacy capital in the tribunal? The interactions described here suggest it might be worth exploring.

V Chapter Summaries

This book deepens and broadens prevailing understandings of international courts and legitimacy by comparing legitimacy across courts and seeking to probe the relationship between cross-cutting concepts such as democracy, effectiveness, and justice to legitimacy. This Introduction has already referred to the book's authors in discussing their individual and collective contributions to the legitimacy and international courts literature. Following is a brief summary of each chapter for easy reference.

Nienke Grossman examines the impact of Solomonic judgments on the legitimacy of the International Court of Justice. Solomonic judgments may represent a point within a set of reasonable legal outcomes whereby the Court has awarded each of the litigating parties some, but not all, of what they seek. Alternatively, Solomonic judgments may prioritize pleasing and displeasing the litigating parties in relatively equal amounts over deciding disputes in strict accordance with the law. Grossman suggests that Solomonic decision making is a potential danger to the normative legitimacy of the ICJ when it exceeds the scope of States' delegated authority and because it is biased against parties with significantly stronger legal cases. Also, Solomonic judgments that "split the baby" may result in unsound legal reasoning, and they do not assist those normatively addressed to better comply with the law. The perception that the Court is acting in a Solomonic fashion, even when it may not be, may harm its sociological legitimacy, when detracting from the Court's adjudicatory function. On the other hand, perceptions that the Court is making decisions that are rooted in law and also Solomonic may enhance the Court's effectiveness and thereby its sociological legitimacy.

Margaret M. deGuzman identifies and analyzes the importance of clear missions for international courts, questions the ICC's failure to prioritize between local and global justice, and suggests this lacuna affects both the effectiveness and legitimacy for the ICC. She proposes that existing theories of ICC legitimacy do not properly take into account ambiguities in the Court's goals and priorities. Without clearly defined objectives, the Court cannot be effective, and a limited capacity for effectiveness translates into dubious capacity for legitimacy. Consequently, clarifying and prioritizing the Court's goals can translate into strengthened legitimacy. The Court's objectives can be grouped into two categories, which may at times overlap: a pursuit of "global justice," or the building of global norms to prescribe and prevent international crimes, or "local justice," to provide justice to the victims of international crimes. These two different objectives may shape the way one understands and analyzes the Court's legitimacy of origin, decision maker legitimacy, legitimacy of exercise, and output legitimacy. While legitimacy of origin refers to whether the ICC is legitimate based on the manner in which it was created, "personal legitimacy" is concerned with the major actors at the ICC: judges and prosecutors. "Legitimacy of exercise" deals with the operational practices and procedures of the court, while "output legitimacy" looks to the results or outputs created by the Court. For example, democratic representativeness among the creators of the ICC may be less important for "legitimacy of origin" if the Court's goal is global justice because human rights are universal norms not grounded in state consent. If the goal is to engender local justice, perhaps decision makers should take into account to a greater degree the desires of the state where atrocities took place. In the same vein, the selection of cases and situations may sometimes be legitimate when a global – but not local – justice approach is utilized.

Molly K. Land examines the relationship and tensions between doing justice and legitimacy on the European Court of Human Rights, through the lens of prisoner voting rights cases. She proposes that justice is an aspect of normative legitimacy, like legality, and considers the extent to which just decision making affects perceptions of legitimacy. Land defines "just outcomes" as those that "expand human rights protection," especially for society's most vulnerable people. She argues that the prisoner voting cases show two ways in which the pursuit of justice can enhance the legitimacy of a court: (1) legitimacy can increase when compliance constituencies consider its decisions just and (2) even when decisions may conflict with national policy preferences, a robust domestic human rights culture raises the costs of noncompliance. So long as the Court appears to be a moral actor, dissonance between domestic policy and the court's decisions may ultimately promote compliance and bolster legitimacy. Also, pursuing just outcomes may be less risky and more legitimacy-enhancing for mature courts, like the European Court of Human Rights, because they already possess general legitimacy.

Yet, courts that issue decisions with domestic political consequences must be conscious that they may meet with resistance if they are perceived to be overreaching by doing justice. Although a court must be sensitive to domestic political concerns, the prisoner voting rights cases suggest that too much deference may undermine the compliance pull of a court's decisions.

Alexandra Huneeus's chapter examines the International Criminal Court and the Inter-American Court of Human Rights' engagement with the Colombian peace process and its impact on the legitimacy of both courts. Professor Huneeus proposes that complementary work, such as influencing the state's response to atrocity crimes through different bodies of law and different national actors, yielding different kinds of changes in state behavior, does not appear to heighten or lessen legitimacy. When both courts are working toward the same goal, however, such as accountability for crimes of the paramilitary, the legitimacy of one appears boosted by the work of the other, through a dynamic of constructive interference. Both courts support the same underlying goal, making it and the institutions advocating for it appear more legitimate. Normative legitimacy questions may arise when one court relies on or incorporates the work of the other to justify its own actions, such as when ICC Prosecutor Fatou Bensouda threatened to open a case in Colombia if it did not comply with the Inter-American Court's jurisprudence. Although perceptions of both courts' legitimacy might be enhanced by promotion of consistent legal rules, the ICC may be acting beyond the scope of authority delegated to it by invoking another Court's case law. Also, it may undermine its legitimacy if it is perceived as derailing a fragile peace process by taking away options from the Colombian government. Understanding the relationship between multiple international courts operating in the same factual context and its impact on legitimacy promises to be an increasingly fertile field of inquiry.

Mark A. Pollack examines both normative debates and empirical evidence about the legitimacy of the European Court of Justice (ECJ). The first part provides a basic theoretical framework, defining legitimacy as "the right to rule," consistent with Dan Bodansky's understanding of the term, and distinguishing between normative and sociological conceptions of the term. Next, it examines the normative legitimacy of the ECJ, considering three possible criteria. The third part of the chapter surveys empirical evidence about the sociological legitimacy of the ECJ. Finally, the fourth part proposes that the Court is subject to greater normative criticism and lower levels of public support than previously. Pollack finds that both the normative and sociological legitimacy of the court are "more fragile and contested than they first appear." Although the Court is one of the most trusted legal or political institutions in Europe, "the apparent public legitimacy of the court rests on a very thin base of public knowledge about the court," which seems to borrow legitimacy from attitudes toward Europe and the rule of law. Consequently, impacts on the legitimacy of the EU may ultimately impact perceptions of the legitimacy of the ECJ.

Anastasia Telesetsky's contribution considers the challenges of generating legitimacy for one of the youngest courts discussed in this book: the International Tribunal for the Law of the Sea (ITLOS). She suggests that the legitimacy, or justified or justifiable authority, of ITLOS, will depend largely on whether States actively support it by referring cases and providing financial assistance and whether the court is trusted to protect both core sovereign interests and the international rule of law. Through an analysis of their decisions thus far, Telesetsky argues that ITLOS judges have already taken steps to attempt to institutionalize legitimacy, for example, by providing detailed jurisdictional analysis, detailing the legal questions to be addressed, citing directly to specific provisions of the United Nations Convention on the Law of the Sea, employing a cautious incrementalist approach by carefully building on preexisting case law, and citing and relying on decisions of other international courts. To bolster legitimacy within the tribunal, as opposed to for external stakeholders alone, Telesetsky points to the importance of a rule of law culture, the introduction and justification of new legal standards for itself, respect for sovereigns, abstaining from deciding issues unnecessary to resolve the dispute, and creating an ethical environment. Finally, she suggests that the court revise some of its current practices to address possible perceptions of partiality and overreaching, and the lack of enforcement options.

Joost Pauwelyn examines differences between the pools of individuals deciding World Trade Organization disputes, as opposed to investor-state disputes within the framework of the International Centre for the Settlement of Investment Disputes, and suggests the differences in the pools may affect the sources and limits of legitimacy for the tribunals and the broader legal system within which the tribunals operate. He finds striking differences among adjudicators, including nationality, professional background, diversity, status, and ideology. For example, WTO panel and Appellate Body members tend to be technocrats from developing countries, while ICSID arbitrators are likely to be high-powered, elite private lawyers or academics from Western Europe or the United States. While the ICSID pool is relatively closed, with a small number of ideologically polarized individuals serving multiple times as arbitrators, WTO panelists have relatively low reappointment rates and are more ideologically homogeneous. These differences suggest that "legitimacy capital" comes from different sources for ICSID, as compared to the WTO. For Pauwelyn, sociological legitimacy for the WTO comes from inside its diplomatic, governmental surroundings. The WTO Appellate Body and panels are embedded in a thick bureaucratic regime, where the quality of the broader WTO system and internal communication between adjudicators and WTO member countries is essential to maintaining its legitimacy. ICSID's legitimacy, on the other hand, relies more heavily on the individual quality and impartiality of its arbitrators, as it is situated within a thin institutional platform, no diplomatic community surrounds or interacts with it, and no appellate body exists. On the other hand, concerns arise about ICSID arbitrators' representativeness and impartiality.

Andrea K. Bjorklund explores the legitimacy of the International Centre for the Settlement of Investment Disputes. She proposes that many of ICSID's legitimacy problems arise from a mismatch between its design and current expectations from relevant publics. While ICSID was designed to resolve specific and discrete disputes, it is now a symbol of investment law and policy and is the recipient of critiques that should be leveled against states rather than ICSID. Bjorklund notes that defenses of ICSID rely on formalistic criteria linked to normative legitimacy, while criticisms focus on criteria linked to both normative and sociological legitimacy. Bjorklund relies on Yuval Shany's insights about the relationship between effectiveness and normative legitimacy and on factors related to normative sociological legitimacy drawn from Thomas Franck for international law generally, and then modified and expanded on by Nienke Grossman in the framework of international courts and tribunals. She then reviews the legitimacy criticism of investment treaty arbitration generally and of ICSID arbitrations in particular to probe the dissonance between sociological and normative legitimacy. Her analysis concludes by showing a shift in expectations and standards over time.

Geir Ulfstein considers challenges to the normative legitimacy of the United Nations Human Rights Treaty Bodies with respect to their court-like function of ruling on the merits of individual petitions. Drawing, in part, on prior scholarship on legitimacy and international courts, he proposes that legitimacy for these bodies requires (1) independent, impartial, and highly competent treaty body members; (2) application of procedures that allow both parties to be heard and ensure that relevant facts are taken into account; (3) respect for the legal mandate established in their constitutive instruments; (4) effectiveness; and (5) accountability to international and national organs. Ulfstein considers the treaty bodies' legitimacy through the lens of each of these legitimacy prerequisites, explaining in detail how they may apply differently in the treaty body context, as compared to traditional international adjudication. Treaty bodies possess unique features that complicate the legitimacy analysis, such as their emphasis on the protection of human rights, their ever-growing caseload, the nonbinding nature of their decisions, and their ability to produce state reports and General Comments, in addition to responding to individual complaints. He makes specific recommendations for enhancing the legitimacy of these institutions.

Andreas Follesdal questions the utility of linking "democratization" or "democratic values" with the legitimacy of international courts. He suggests that scholars misuse the term because their proposals are seldom about standards or institutions unique to democratic governance. Although reform proposals coming out of these critiques may enhance the legitimacy of international courts, they rarely recommend standards or institutions unique to democratic governance. Although transparency, accountability and participation are often, but not always, beneficial, they can be valuable even when they do not advance democracy. To deepen our understanding about legitimacy and these ideals, legitimacy scholars should distinguish between democratic institutions of decision making, the normative principles that justify those institutions, and important features of those institutions that contribute to their justification. Follesdal suggests that calls for democratization are better understand as suggestions for constitutionalization of the combination of international and domestic law constituting a "Global Basic Structure." A global constitutionalist perspective helps address contested issues concerning the functions of constitutions: to create, curb, and channel the use of institutions and specify rules for changing de facto constitutions. Further, it provides a normative justification that also provides reasons for valuing democracy: institutions deferred to must treat all people with the respect owed political equals.

Mortimer Sellers probes the relationship between democracy, justice, and legitimacy. He defines legitimacy as "the status of being correct according to some external standard" or in light of "the most *appropriate* standard for evaluating the practice in question." While a court that is "actually legitimate" fulfills such standards, for "sociologically legitimate" courts, subjects are persuaded to act as if a rule or institution is legitimate. The extent to which a law or legal institutions secure or advance justice provides the standard for measuring actual legitimacy. Thus, actually legitimate courts advance justice, while sociologically legitimate courts are believed to do so. Democracy, however, has little to do with legitimacy because it has little to do with justice. Instead, democracy has the potential to threaten judicial independence and impartiality, and thereby legitimacy. On the other hand, the "illusion" of democracy may indirectly buoy legitimacy by securing broader public support for judicial decisions legitimate on other grounds. It is purely instrumental in its relationship to legitimacy. Democratic practices and procedures legitimate international courts only to the extent that they advance the purposes that justify international courts in the first instance.

Yuval Shany's chapter explores the relationship between effectiveness and legitimacy. In his view, the two can either mutually reinforce or undermine each other. Effective courts may be viewed as more legitimate, and legitimacy can assist a court in improving its effectiveness. Judicial illegitimacy may undermine effectiveness, and ineffectiveness can undermine judicial legitimacy. Perceptions of justified authority from relevant constituencies may assist in sustaining judicial effectiveness by resulting in increased support and cooperation. In other words, when states believe courts are legitimate, they are more likely to implement their decisions and to provide them with resources. At the same time, legitimacy and effectiveness are not always unidirectional. For example, sometimes protecting the legitimacy of an international court may require the adoption of ineffective judicial decisions, and occasionally, effective judicial bodies are not legitimate. Shany concludes by pointing out that gaps between judicial outcomes and the preferences of courts' constituencies can result in sociological legitimacy.

PART I

The Legitimacy of Particular Dispute Settlement Mechanisms

2

Solomonic Judgments and the Legitimacy of the International Court of Justice

NIENKE GROSSMAN

On January 27, 2014, the International Court of Justice (ICJ) issued its ruling in *Maritime Dispute (Peru v. Chile)*.[1] Peru requested that the Court delimit the maritime boundary between the two states in the form of an equidistance line, arguing that no maritime boundary agreement was in force between the two states. Chile, on the other hand, asserted that the maritime boundary was fully delimited by a 1952 treaty between the parties, and it consisted of a parallel of latitude extending westward from a point on the coast out to a distance of at least 200 nautical miles. The Court determined that a tacit maritime boundary existed, which neither party argued, and that it consisted of a line of latitude extending 80 nautical miles from the coast, followed by an equidistance line up to 200 nautical miles.[2] The Court's judgment was widely described as "Solomonic."[3]

The term *Solomonic* dates to the Biblical story of King Solomon. Two women each claimed to be the mother of the same infant, and the king

---

[1] *Maritime Dispute (Peru v. Chile)*, Judgment, ICJ (2014), *at* http://www.icj-cij.org/files/case-related/137/137-20140127-JUD-01-00-EN.pdf. The author, who is an Associate Professor at the University of Baltimore School of Law, served as a Legal Advisor to the Government of Chile in this dispute. She wrote this article in her personal capacity, and the views expressed are her own and do not necessarily represent the views of the Chilean government. She is grateful for excellent suggestions and feedback from the editors and participants in the University of Baltimore School of Law/PluriCourts joint symposium on International Courts and Legitimacy.

[2] Ibid., 67, para. 196

[3] *See, e.g.,* Peru-Chile Deal Will Strengthen Economies, *World Affairs* (4 February 2014), at www.worldaffairsjournal.org/blog/juan-de-onis/chile-peru-deal-will-strengthen-econ omies; Maritime Dispute between Peru and Chile Ends in a Tie More or Less, *The World Daily Blog* (28 January 2014), at www.thestar.com/news/the_world_daily/2014/02/mari time_dispute_between_peru_and_chile_ends_in_a_tie__more_or_less.html; Pragmatism wins the day in ICJ's Maritime Dispute Ruling Involving Peru and Chile, *Arent Fox* (27 January 2014), at www.arentfox.com/newsroom/alerts/pragmatism-wins-day-icjs-mari time-dispute-ruling-involving-peru-and-chile#.VaQbrLtRGM8.

declared it should be cut in half.[4] Although King Solomon used this provisional judgment to determine the identity of and grant custody to the biological mother, Solomonic judgments are generally understood as the "split-the-baby" provisional approach. Solomonic or compromise judgments reject the winner-take-all approach that characterizes most modern common law adjudication.[5] Rather than recognizing legal rights or duties as belonging to one party alone, a Solomonic court finds ways to split the issues or allocate remedies somewhat evenly. A Solomonic judgment may represent a point within a set of reasonable legal outcomes whereby the Court has awarded each of the litigating parties some, but not all, of what they seek. On the other hand, sometimes Solomonic courts may prioritize pleasing and displeasing the litigating parties in relatively equal amounts over deciding disputes in strict accordance with the relevant law. They may prize Solomonism over law.

Peru v. Chile is not the Court's first judgment deemed "Solomonic." Rather, the term is frequently used to describe ICJ judgments.[6] The implications of Solomonic decision making for the Court's legitimacy, however, are underexplored. A legitimate court possesses justified authority, and its rulings are worthy of respect and ought to be followed, even when against the perceived interests of a particular party. Normatively legitimate courts possess the "right to rule," while sociologically legitimate courts are perceived to have it.[7] While normative

---

[4] The New Annotated Bible with the Apocrypha (Oxford, UK: Oxford University Press, 1994), pp. 16–28.

[5] J. Jaconelli, "Solomonic Justice and the Common Law," *Oxford Journal of Legal Studies*, 12 (1992), 480.

[6] *See, e.g.,* V. Dimitrijevic and M. Milanovic, "The Strange Story of the Bosnian Genocide Case," *Leiden Journal of International Law*, 21 (2008), 85 (discussing the Bosnian Genocide case); L. F. Damrosch, "The Impact of the Nicaragua Case on the Court and Its Role: Harmful, Helpful or in Between?" *Leiden Journal of International Law*, 25 (2012), 145 (referring to Bosnian Genocide and Oil Platforms case); J. B. Rhinelander et al., "Testing the Effectiveness of the International Court of Justice: The Nuclear Weapons Case," *American Society of International Law Proceedings*, 91 (1997), 8 (analyzing the Nuclear Weapons case); T. Ginsburg and R. McAdams, "Adjudicating in Anarchy: An Expressive Theory of International Dispute Resolution," *William & Mary Law Review*, 45 (2004), n. 247 (discussing the Haya de la Torre case).

[7] D. Bodansky, "The Concept of Legitimacy in International Law," in R. Wolfrum and V. Roben (eds.), *Legitimacy in International Law* (Berlin: Springer-Verlag, 2008), p. 313; A. Buchanan and R. Keohane, "The Legitimacy of Global Governance Institutions," in L. H. Meyer (ed.), *Legitimacy, Justice and Public International Law* (Cambridge, UK: Cambridge University Press, 2009), p. 29; D. Bodansky, "The Legitimacy of International Governance: A Coming Challenge for International Environmental Law?" *American Journal of International Law*, 93 (1999), 604.

legitimacy is prescriptive and derived from philosophical and theoretical approaches, sociological legitimacy is agent-relative, dynamic, and subjective.[8] Source-, procedure, and result-oriented factors may affect the legitimacy of an institution.[9] This chapter explores the relationship between legitimacy and Solomonic judgments. It suggests that Solomonic decision making is a potential danger to the normative legitimacy of the ICJ when it exceeds the scope of states' delegated authority and because it is inherently biased against parties with significantly stronger legal cases. Judgments aimed at splitting the baby may result in unsound legal reasoning, and they do not assist those normatively addressed to better comply with the law.[10] The perception that the Court is acting in a Solomonic fashion, even when it may not be, may harm its sociological legitimacy or states' perceptions of its justified authority when it detracts from the Court's adjudicatory function. On the other hand, perceptions that the Court is making decisions that are rooted in law and also Solomonic may enhance the Court's effectiveness and, thereby, sociological legitimacy.

I   Delegated Authority

The legitimacy of the ICJ rests, in significant part, on the consent of states to its jurisdiction and the Court's acting within the confines of state consent.[11] The ICJ lacks the authority to bind sovereign and independent states without their consent, or to make decisions that are ultra vires, or exceed the limits of delegated authority. Both the ICJ and its predecessor, the Permanent Court of International Justice, have emphasized the importance of consent. For example, in *Application of the International Convention on the Elimination of All Forms of Racial Discrimination (Georgia v. Russian Federation)*, the Court wrote: "The Court's jurisdiction is based on the consent of the parties and is confined to the extent

---

[8] Bodansky, "The Concept of Legitimacy in International Law," p. 313; N. Grossman, "Legitimacy and International Adjudicative Bodies," *George Washington International Law Review*, 41 (2009), 116.

[9] R. Wolfrum, "Legitimacy of International Law from a Legal Perspective: Some Introductory Considerations," in R. Wolfrum and V. Roben (eds.), *Legitimacy in International Law* (Berlin, Heidelberg: Springer-Verlag, 2008), p. 6.

[10] The latter idea is drawn from Joseph Raz's service conception of authority. *See* below, Section IV.

[11] Bodansky, "The Legitimacy of International Governance: A Coming Challenge for International Environmental Law?" p. 605.

accepted by them."[12] To the extent that Solomonic judgments exceed the scope of delegated authority, they threaten the Court's legitimacy.

The United Nations Charter and the Court's Statute establish the function of the Court and prescribe the limits of its authority. According to the Charter, the ICJ is the United Nations' "principal judicial organ."[13] In the first paragraph of the ICJ Statute's Article 38, states specified that the Court's "function is to decide in accordance with international law" disputes submitted to it.[14] The Court must apply conventions, customary international law, general principles of law, and as a subsidiary means for the determination of rules of law, judicial decisions and the teachings of highly qualified publicists. The second paragraph of Article 38 states that the Court may decide a case *ex aequo et bono* "if the parties agree thereto."[15]

These instruments demonstrate that states distinguished between adjudicative and other functions when establishing the ICJ, and they provide insights into what states authorized the Court to do. States charged the Court with adjudication, as distinguished from political or other roles. Filing a case at the ICJ is supposed to bring a dispute among states into the adjudicative realm, which is characterized by the application of law to a set of facts. The ICJ is a place for judicial settlement, and not for other kinds of dispute resolution, such as conciliation or mediation. The Court is to decide cases "in accordance with international law."

Just as the Court's foundational instruments distinguish between adjudicative and other functions, so too have scholars and ICJ judges. For example, Cesare P. R. Romano, Karen Alter, and Yuval Shany recently wrote that international adjudication is a "law-based way of reaching a

---

[12] *Application of the International Convention on the Elimination of All Forms of Racial Discrimination (Georgia v. Russian Federation), Preliminary Objections*, ICJ Reports (2011) 124–5, para. 131 (*citing Armed Activities on the Territory of the Congo*); *see also Status of the Eastern Carelia, Advisory Opinion*, P.C.I.J. 1923 (ser. B) No. 5, para. 33 ("It is well established in international law that no State can, without its consent, be compelled to submit its disputes with other States either to mediation or to arbitration, or to any other kind of pacific settlement."); *Armed Activities on the Territory of the Congo (New Application: 2002) (Democratic Republic of the Congo v. Rwanda), Provisional Measures*, ICJ Reports (2002) 219, para. 57 ("... one of the fundamental principles of its Statute is that it cannot decide a dispute between states without the consent of those States to its jurisdiction.").

[13] Charter of the United Nations, San Francisco, 26 June 1945, in force 24 October 1945, 3 Bevans 1153; 59 Stat 1031; TS 993, art. 92.

[14] Statute of the International Court of Justice, 26 June 1945, in force 24 October 1945, 3 Bevans 1179; 59 Stat 1031; TS 993; 39 AJIL Supp. 215, art. 38.

[15] Article 38(2) of the UN Charter.

final decision" and that the "law-based nature of adjudicative decision-making distinguishes adjudication from other processes, such as political decision-making and mediation."[16] In the same vein, ICJ Judge Weeramantry opined in the *Lockerbie* case that the ICJ, "by virtue of its nature and constitution applies to the matter before it the concepts, the criteria and the methodology of the judicial process which other organs of the United Nations are naturally not obliged to do. The concepts it uses are juridical concepts, its criteria are standards of legality, its method is that of legal proof."[17] The point is that a judicial process is characterized by unique "concepts," "criteria," and "methodology." Consequently, the Court may issue a compromise or Solomonic judgment and still act consistent with the authority delegated to it by states in two situations: (1) if the parties express consent to such an approach concerning a particular case or (2) if the law requires or allows the Court to incorporate a Solomonic approach into its reasoning.

The second paragraph of Article 38 of the ICJ Statute provides for one circumstance where the Court may issue judgments that prize Solomonic results over law. The Court may decide a case ex aequo et bono "if the parties agree." The literal translation of ex aequo et bono is "from equity and goodness."[18] The Oxford *Guide to Latin in International Law* adds that it is a "manner of deciding a case pending before a tribunal with reference to the principles of fairness and justice in preference to any principle of positive law."[19] Ian Brownlie wrote that it "involves elements of compromise and conciliation."[20] Resolution ex aequo et bono is generally considered distinct from equity, despite that *aequo* literally means "equity."[21] Equity is concerned with fairness, fair dealing, and

---

[16] C. P. R. Romano, K. J. Alter, and Y. Shany, "Mapping International Adjudicative Bodies, the Issues, and Players," in C. P. R. Romano, K. J. Alter, and Y. Shany (eds.), *The Oxford Handbook of International Adjudication* (Oxford, UK: Oxford University Press, 2014), pp. 4–5.

[17] *Case Concerning Questions of Interpretation and Application of the 1971 Montreal Convention Arising From the Aerial Incident at Lockerbie (Libyan Arab Jamahiriya v. United Kingdom)*, Provisional Measures, ICJ Reports (1992) 56 (Dissenting Opinion of Judge Weeramantry).

[18] Aaron Fellmeth and Maurice Horwitz, *Guide to Latin in International Law* (Oxford, UK: Oxford University Press, 2009), p. 91.

[19] Ibid.

[20] Ian Brownlie, *Principles of Public International Law*, 7th ed. (Oxford, UK: Oxford University Press, 2008), pp. 26, 720. *See also Cayuga Indians (Gr. Brit. v. U.S.)*, 6 R.I.A.A. 171, 183 (Perm. Ct. Arb. 1925) (referring to ex aequo et bono as calling for "a degree of compromise").

[21] *See, e.g., Cayuga Indians (Gr. Brit. v. U.S.)*, 6 R.I.A.A. 171, 183 (Perm. Ct. Arb. 1925).

principles of justice, but it is considered "a part of the normal judicial function,"[22] while ex aequo et bono "may not be easy to reconcile with the judicial character" of the ICJ.[23] The ICJ drew the distinction between equity and ex aequo et bono in the *North Sea Continental Shelf Cases*:

> Whatever the legal reasoning of a court of justice, its decisions must by definition be just, and therefore in that sense equitable. Nevertheless, when mention is made of a court dispensing justice or declaring the law, what is meant is that the decision finds its objective justification in considerations lying not outside but within the rules, and in this field it is precisely a rule of law that calls for the application of equitable principles. There is consequently no question in this case of any decision *ex aequo et bono*, such as would only be possible under the conditions prescribed by Article 38, paragraph 2, of the Court's Statute.[24]

The adjudicative function must consider the justice of the result, but it is constrained by the substantive legal context. Ex aequo et bono, on the other hand, operates beyond the normal scope of the judicial function.

Equity, which the Court may resort to as a general principle of law pursuant to Article 38(1)(c) of the Court's Statute, is intended to "correct the law's generality by filling gaps in the law, by adjusting conflicts and tensions among legal provisions, and by making exceptions in cases in which the rule leads to unanticipated results."[25] If relevant law on a disputed point exists and was intended to apply to the facts at hand, equity's role is limited to situations where application of the law works an unacceptable injustice. *Ex aequo et bono*, on the other hand, disfavors positive law and is driven by judges' notions of what is good or fair. Just as the members of the Court in the *North Sea Continental Shelf Cases* understood the two concepts to differ, so too did the drafters of the ICJ Statute; that is why they required explicit consent by litigants to its application.

What about when the law is unclear or when a gap exists in the law? Is the use of Solomonic judgments authorized by states in such circumstances? Prosper Weil argues that once states consent to the jurisdiction of a tribunal, they confer on it "the normative and quasi-legislative power

---

[22] Ibid.; B. A. Garner (ed.), Definition of "Equity," *Black's Law Dictionary* (St. Paul, MN: West Group, 2001), p. 241; Brownlie, *Principles of Public International Law*, pp. 25–6.

[23] Brownlie, *Principles of Public International Law*, p. 720.

[24] *North Sea Continental Shelf (Federal Republic of Germany v. Denmark)* ICJ Reports (1969) 3, para. 88.

[25] L. B. Solum, "Equity and the Rule of Law," in I. Shapiro (ed.), *Nomos XXXVI* (New York: New York University Press, 1994), p. 124.

necessary" to settle the dispute.[26] The tribunal must rule because the states are asking for judicial resolution, even if the law is unclear or riddled with gaps. A lack of law or clarity on a particular issue may be remedied, suggests Weil, either by recourse to general principles of law, found in national legal systems, equity, or through application of the *Lotus* principle – states may engage in conduct that is neither prohibited nor required by international law.[27] Yet nowhere does Weil argue that equity and ex aequo et bono are equivalent or coextensive, nor does he suggest that equity requires compromise judgments. Rather, equity, understood as fairness, fair dealing, and principles of justice, may require the Court to recognize that one litigant has the significantly stronger or weaker case, not to split the entitlements or the remedies equally. Finally, because they required states to authorize decisions ex aequo et bono pursuant to Article 38(2), the drafters of the Statute could not have intended the Court to fill gaps in the law through judgments that prioritize compromise over law.

Does the law permit or mandate compromise or Solomonic decision making in any other contexts? In other words, in what circumstances might treaties or customary international law require or allow a Solomonic approach? Maritime boundary delimitation is probably a good candidate. The delimitation of the continental shelf is to be done "in order to achieve an equitable solution," pursuant to the United Nations Convention on the Law of the Sea.[28] When the Court uses equidistance lines in the process of delimiting the continental shelf in the absence of a binding treaty, it frequently splits maritime spaces equally. Nonetheless, the Court's analysis does not stop once it generates an equidistance line. It is also required to consider relevant circumstances that may require adjustment or shifting of the line, including existing agreements, and finally, whether the shares of the relevant area are markedly

---

[26] P. Weil, "'The Court Cannot Conclude Definitively...' Non Liquet Revisited," *Columbia Journal of Transnational Law*, 36 (1998), 115.

[27] Weil, "The Court Cannot Conclude Definitively," 11–12; *see also* D. Bodansky, "*Non liquet* and the incompleteness of international law," in L. Boisson de Chazournes and P. Sands (eds.), *International Law, The International Court of Justice and Nuclear Weapons* (Cambridge, UK: Cambridge University Press, 1999), pp. 159–66.

[28] *See, e.g.,* United Nations Convention on the Law of the Sea, Montego Bay, 10 December 1982, in force 16 November 1994, 1833 U.N.T.S. 3, art. 83. "1. The delimitation of the continental shelf between States with opposite or adjacent coasts shall be effected by agreement on the basis of international law, as referred to in Article 38 of the Statute of the International Court of Justice, in order to achieve an equitable solution."

disproportionate to the relevant coasts.[29] And UNCLOS states that the Court is to achieve an equitable solution "on the basis of international law" as found in Article 38 of the ICJ Statute. In other words, even in the area of maritime boundary delimitation, the Court's articulated methodology requires it to consider nongeographical circumstances with legal weight. At least in theory, preexisting positive law may strongly influence how the baby is split, distinguishing it from a pure ex aequo et bono approach.

What about Solomonic judgments for the sake of peace? If they are rooted in generally accepted legal discourse, Solomonic judgments to promote reconciliation among the parties may not exceed the scope of states' consent to the Court's authority. Solomonic judgments can help to maintain and nurture social relationships or aid in reconciliation of litigating parties.[30] States created the United Nations, of which the ICJ is a part, to "save succeeding generations from the scourge of war."[31] The Court cannot ignore the implications of its rulings on the ground or engage in formalistic, decontextualized reasoning. Issuing decisions that depart from strong political consensus, such as took place in the *South-West Africa Cases*, can result in searing critiques and calls for reform and can harm perceptions of legitimacy of the Court.[32]

Yet, as Joseph Jaconelli explained in regard to domestic common law courts, Solomonic judgments for the purpose of reconciliation alone "would be a denial of the judicial role conceived as an adjudicatory role. It would be entirely improper for a court to form the view that *p* is the legally required result, and for it then to decree *q* in the interests of conciliation."[33] The ICJ was created as a "judicial organ," and its function is to "decide in accordance with international law."[34] The Court serves the cause of peace by the exercise of its jurisdiction, through application of law. In this vein, the Court noted in the *United States Consular and*

---

[29] *Territorial and Maritime Dispute (Nicaragua v. Colombia)*, Judgment, ICJ Reports (2012) 624, paras. 190–93, 219.

[30] N. E. Simmonds, "Book Review of Random Justice: On Lotteries and Legal Decision-Making" (N. Duxbury), *Cambridge Law Journal*, 60 (2001), 216; Jaconelli, "Solomonic Justice and the Common Law," 484–5.

[31] Preamble of the UN Charter.

[32] *See, e.g.,* Richard Falk, *Reviving the World Court* (Charlottesville: University Press of Virginia, 1986), pp. xiii, xv.

[33] Jaconelli, "Solomonic Justice and the Common Law," 484.

[34] Article 92 of the United Nations Charter; Article 28 of the Statute of the International Court of Justice.

SOLOMONIC JUDGMENTS AND THE LEGITIMACY OF THE ICJ 51

Diplomatic Staff in Tehran case, that "the resolution of ... legal questions by the Court may be an important, and sometimes decisive, factor in promoting the peaceful settlement of the dispute."[35] Other forums exist for other kinds of dispute settlement. If the Court takes on a purely conciliatory role, it eliminates the option of judicial dispute resolution, an important mechanism for protecting and promoting peace. The Court cannot be blind to political concerns if it seeks to be influential and effective. At the same time, it must be guided by reasonable interpretations of existing law and state consent to retain its legitimacy.

Unless states explicitly inform the Court of their desire to have a case decided ex aequo et bono or international law on a particular issue requires or allows a compromise judgment, states have not authorized the Court to adopt a Solomonic approach. To the extent the Court decides cases in accordance with principles not consented to by the litigating parties, it acts ultra vires and thereby threatens its own normative legitimacy. Although the Court must be sensitive to political concerns in its decision making, the Court's reasoning must be consistent with reasonable interpretations of the relevant legal norms.

The judgment in *Peru v. Chile* is a powerful example of the Court exceeding the authority delegated to it, and thereby potentially harming its own normative legitimacy. The judgment appears to skirt around the law and selectively choose a couple of tangentially relevant facts to achieve a compromise result, a dispute-resolution method litigating states did not agree to ab initio. Rather than adopting the position of one of the parties – either an agreement existed reaching to 200 nautical miles or there was no agreement out to any length – the Court split the baby. Chile got what it wanted out to 80 nautical miles, and Peru got what it wanted from 80 to 200 nautical miles.

Although the Court acknowledged that "[t]he establishment of a permanent maritime boundary is a matter of grave importance," and the law requires that "[e]vidence of a tacit legal agreement must be compelling,"[36] it spent many pages seeking to uncover the nature and extent of that very agreement. Judge Donoghue, though she voted in favor of the judgment, acknowledged in her Declaration that the parties "did not address the existence or terms of such an agreement."[37]

---

[35] *United States Consular and Diplomatic Staff in Tehran (United States v. Iran)* ICJ Reports (1980) 22, para. 40.

[36] *Maritime Dispute (Peru v. Chile)* 37, para. 91.

[37] Ibid. Declaration of Judge Donoghue.

NIENKE GROSSMAN

Others expressed similar concerns.[38] The evidence the Court pointed to in determining the length of the tacitly agreed boundary was flimsy at best. The Court made only little mention of 80 nautical miles in its reasoning. It noted that the "biological limit" of the Humboldt Current, which supports marine life, was 80–100 nautical miles off the coast in the summer (and 200–250 nautical miles in the winter!).[39] And species being taken in the 1950s were up to around 60 nautical miles from the coast.[40] Yet it acknowledged the parties' references to 200 nautical miles in various documents, in anticipation of marine life to be found in those areas, and to protect against third-party long-distance fishing. Without explanation, the Court declared: "It does not see as of great significance their knowledge of the likely or possible extent of the resources out to 200 nautical miles ..."[41]

In response to this problematic reasoning, then-ICJ president Judge Peter Tomka wrote separately: "In my view, there is insufficient evidence to conclude that the agreed maritime boundary extends only to 80 nautical miles. The evidence rather points to a different conclusion."[42] In fact, several of the judges who voted both for and against the 80-nautical-mile turning point questioned the sufficiency of the evidence on this issue. For example, Judge Skontikov, who voted in favor, asserted that "the determination of the figure of 80 nautical miles ... does not seem to be supported by the evidence which the Court found relevant."[43] Judge Donoghue noted that neither party proposed that only an initial segment of the boundary had been settled by agreement and that the remainder would be delimited in accordance with customary international law,[44] arguably making it difficult to justify a segmented delimitation line. Judges Xue, Gaja, Bhandari, and Judge ad hoc Orrego-Vicuña wrote that the majority "labours to argue" for an 80-nautical-mile end point to the agreed maritime boundary.[45]

---

[38] *See, e.g.,* ibid. Dissenting Opinion Judge Sebutinde, para. 3 (noting that "neither Party asserts the existence of a tacit agreement"); *see also* Separate Opinion of Judge Owada, para. 6 ("the Judgment states quite categorically that the Parties acknowledge in the 1954 Agreement the existence of a maritime boundary for all purposes between them, without showing how and when such agreement came about and what concretely this agreement consists in;").
[39] *Maritime Dispute (Peru v. Chile)* 40, para. 105.   [40] Ibid., 40, para. 108.
[41] Ibid., 42, para. 109.   [42] Ibid., Separate Opinion of Judge Peter Tomka, para. 3;
[43] Ibid., Declaration of Judge Skotnikov.   [44] Ibid., Declaration of Judge Donoghue.
[45] Ibid., Joint Dissenting Opinion of Judges Xue, Gaja, Bhandari, and Judge Orrego-Vicuña, para. 2.

One strains without success to find any well-supported legal justification for the 80-nautical-mile turning point in the maritime boundary in the Court's reasoning. Rather, it appears that the majority of the Court sought to please and displease the parties about equally. If the Court's analysis of the law and facts aimed at achieving a compromise judgment rather than following established legal principles, it exceeded the scope of its delegated authority. Chile and Peru did not ask the Court to decide the case ex aequo et bono, yet it is at least arguable that the Court did.

II Bias

A biased court is illegitimate. For a court to possess justified authority, it must give both sides equal opportunity to make their arguments, and it must consider them without preexisting bias toward any litigating party.[46] *Audi alteram partem*, literally "listen to the other side,"[47] is essential to legitimate adjudication. According to the ICJ, such principles "are integral constituents of the rule of law and justice."[48] In the same vein, the provisions of the ICJ Statute and Rules of Procedure on evidentiary matters are "devised to guarantee the sound administration of justice, while respecting the equality of the parties."[49]

When a claimant has particularly weak or strong claims, Solomonic courts are inherently biased. If the ICJ seeks to please and displease the litigating parties equally in such cases, it does not faithfully apply the law. For example, if state X sues state Y, but state X has weak claims, a Solomonic court will always award state X more than it deserves. Alternatively stated, a court that splits the baby, despite what the law requires,

---

[46] *Application for Review of Judgment No. 158 of the United Nations Administrative Tribunal* ICJ Reports (1973) 179, para. 34 (quoting *Judgments of the Administrative Tribunal of the ILO Upon Complaints Made Against Unesco, Advisory Opinion* ICJ Reports (1956) 77) ("The principle of equality of the parties follows from the requirements of good administration of justice."); Martin Shapiro, *Courts: A Comparative and Political Analysis* (Chicago: University of Chicago Press, 1981), p. 1 (discussing the "ideal type" of courts, "involving (1) an independent judge applying (2) pre-existing legal norms after (3) adversary proceedings in order to achieve (4) a dichotomous decision in which one of the parties was assigned the legal right and the other found wrong").

[47] Fellmeth and Horwitz, *Guide to Latin in International Law*, p. 41.

[48] *Order on Request for an Examination of Situation in Accordance with Paragraph 63 of the Court's Judgment of 20 December 1974 in the Nuclear Tests (New Zealand v. France)* ICJ Reports (1995) 325 (Dissenting Opinion of Judge Weeramantry).

[49] *Military and Paramilitary Activities in and against Nicaragua (Nicaragua v. US)* ICJ Reports (1986) 39, para. 59.

is biased against a respondent whenever a claimant raises a weak claim. A strong respondent will always be worse off before such a court than the status quo ante. Conversely, a Solomonic court is partial to state Y whenever state X has a strong claim. State X will get less than what it deserves before a Solomonic court.

Are there times when a Solomonic judgment is not biased against one of the litigating parties? In the common law domestic context, Joseph Jaconelli queried whether Solomonic judgments may be beneficial when the evidence and arguments advanced are in equipoise.[50] In a winner-take-all scenario, the Court has a 50 percent chance of getting the case entirely wrong, but in a compromise judgment split down the middle, the Court has a 100 percent certainty of getting the case half right.[51] Perhaps it is preferable to get a case half right than entirely wrong? The problem with this approach is that states have not authorized the ICJ to use it pursuant to the ICJ Statute. Neither the Statute nor the case law of the Court indicates that in cases where the legal arguments and facts are in equipoise, the Court should simply rule down the middle. Alternatively, one could argue that when the Court is faced with what appear to be arguments of equal weight, the judicial role requires it, instead, to consider who bears the burden of proof and the burden of persuasion in a particular case. If the arguments advanced are of equal weight or the facts adduced are insufficient, then the burden of proof "break[s] the impasse" by requiring a court to decide against the party who bears the burden.[52] Splitting the pie evenly is not an authorized approach to adjudicating a claimant's weak case.

A Solomonic approach may endanger the ICJ's legitimacy because it is inherently biased and unfair in cases where one party's legal arguments are particularly weak or strong. Through the lens of the *Peru v. Chile* case, if the Court sought a compromise judgment, it was inherently biased against Chile if Chile had a much stronger legal case, or against Peru if Peru had a much stronger legal case. The party with the better status quo ante, here Chile, would have more to lose from the get-go, while the party with the worse status quo ante, here Peru, would have the

---

[50] Jaconelli, "Solomonic Justice and the Common Law," 484–5. [51] Ibid., 485.

[52] Mojtaba Kazazi, *Burden of Proof and Related Issues: A Study on Evidence before International Tribunals* (Leiden, The Netherlands: Martinus Nijhoff, 1996), pp. 30, 85 ("The rule generally applied by the Court with respect to the burden of proof is the basic rule according to which the party who asserts a fact is responsible for providing proof thereof. This rule has consistently been applied by the Court in cases before it...") (citations omitted).

most to gain, regardless of the power of a particular state's legal arguments. Using a Solomonic approach, the Court would always award more than what is due to the weaker party and less than what is due to the stronger one.

III Sound Legal Argumentation

Solomonic judgments threaten the legitimacy of the ICJ when they lack the hallmarks of sound legal reasoning. For a court to be perceived as legitimate, its rulings must both generally accord with the interests and values of those normatively addressed (states), as well as reflect the predominant legal discourse.[53] Both "political and discursive constraints" play an important role in cabining judicial decision making on international courts.[54] Reasoning that does not stay within accepted bounds or refuses to engage with them substantively may raise doubts about whether the Court is acting within its delegated authority, impartially, and in a competent manner, thereby threatening its legitimacy.

In *The Power of Legitimacy among Nations*, Tom Franck described characteristics of rules that affect their legitimacy, or ability to pull states to compliance.[55] Although his focus is on the rules themselves, if courts consistently issue rulings without these characteristics, they risk losing their authority over time. These characteristics include "determinacy" and "coherence." Determinacy refers to a rule's "clarity of meaning," as well as "the extent to which the rule's communicative power exerts its own dynamic pull toward compliance."[56] The ICJ can help to enhance the determinacy of a rule by serving as a "credible interpreter."[57] "Coherence legitimates a rule, principle, or implementing institution because it provides a reasonable connection between a rule, or the application of a rule, to 1) its own principled purpose, 2) principles previously employed to solve similar problems, and 3) a lattice of principles in use to resolve different problems."[58] The idea is that the application of a rule to a set of facts should be principled and consistent.

---

[53] Grossman, "Legitimacy and International Adjudicative Bodies," 149.

[54] A. M. Slaughter and L. Helfer, "Why States Create International Tribunals: A Response to Professors Posner and Yoo," *California Law Review*, 93 (2005), 930.

[55] Thomas Franck, *The Power of Legitimacy among Nations* (Oxford, UK: Oxford University Press, 1990).

[56] Ibid., 84–5.   [57] Ibid., 86–7.   [58] Ibid., 147–8.

Solomonic courts are hard-pressed to issue determinate and coherent judgments. The Court does not admit that it is issuing a compromise judgment. Instead, it seeks to couch its compromise judgments in the language of relevant positive law. What results is the weak, misguided, or muddied interpretation or application of the underlying binding positive law in the service of a Solomonic judgment. As a result, compromise judgments neither clarify the underlying positive legal norm, nor do they result in consistent judgments. The Court's legal reasoning and the underlying norms may suffer to reach a compromise judgment.

Some might argue that coherence is less important at the ICJ because Article 59 of the ICJ Statute specifies that the Court's decisions are binding only on the parties in a particular case.[59] But the statements of law articulated in each case are expected by most, including former ICJ presidents, to have a much more enduring and clarifying impact. For example, former ICJ judge and president, Manfred Lachs, commented:

> [Y]ou do not only decide the dispute between state A and state B, you perform an educational function. You indicate to states A and B how their dispute should be solved, but you also give a wider background to all nations so that similar issues, or related issues, should be solved in a similar way.[60]

Nagendra Singh, another of the Court's former presidents, asserted that judges "generalise and enunciate principles of jurisprudence which would serve as a guide to prevent future disputes and to the establishment of a regime of law."[61] And other courts and policymakers in states are aware of and may consider the ICJ's statements on international law as they rule on important international legal issues. The point is that a court that muddies rules rather than clarifying them both weakens the compliance pull of the relevant rule and makes a poor case for its own authority as a law declaring body.

Returning to *Peru v. Chile*, the judgment arguably muddied legal rules, rather than clarifying and promoting coherent application of the law. It takes great pains to attempt to discover the nature and extent of a tacit agreement, when evidence of such agreements must be "compelling." And the fragile basis on which the Court found that the agreement

---

[59] Article 59 of the Statute of the International Court of Justice ("The decision of the Court has no binding force except between the parties and in respect of that particular case.").

[60] Garry Sturgess and Philip Chubb, *Judging the World: Law and Politics in the World's Leading Courts* (Sydney, Australia: Butterworths, 1988), p. 89.

[61] Ibid., p. 90.

SOLOMONIC JUDGMENTS AND THE LEGITIMACY OF THE ICJ   57

reached only 80 nautical miles does little to guide future litigants concerning how much evidence is necessary to establish the content of a tacit maritime boundary agreement. Also, the judgment calls into question, at least to some extent, the deference that the Court will have to preexisting maritime boundary agreements, or to the requirement of *pacta sunt servanda*, treaties are observed, of course assuming a preexisting treaty was at issue in this case. Perhaps pacta sunt servanda now applies with less force when one of the parties argues that the status quo disfavors it.

IV   A Razian Critique

Solomonic judging threatens the Court's legitimacy when the Court fails to do a better job of assisting states in complying with their legal obligations than they would in its absence. Joseph Raz's service conception of authority provides a normative account of when authority is justified.[62] In recent years, scholars have examined Raz's scholarship in the context of the legitimacy of international law and international courts.[63] Although his is only one normative theory of legitimacy, it is an influential one.

Raz proposes that authority is justified only when (1) it takes into account reasons that independently apply to the subjects of its directives and are relevant in the circumstances ("dependence thesis") and (2) the subjects are more likely to comply with reasons that apply to them independently by accepting and implementing the authority's directives than by attempting to follow these reasons on their own ("normal justification thesis").[64] In other words, an authority is justified when its subjects do a better job of complying with their obligations by doing what the authority says than they would in the authority's absence.

A Solomonic approach to judging may be inconsistent with the service conception of authority. By issuing Solomonic judgments when not required or allowed by law, the ICJ is not helping states better to comply

---

[62] Joseph Raz, *The Morality of Freedom* (Oxford, UK: Oxford University Press, 2012), p. 63.

[63] E.g., L. H. Meyer and P. Sanklecha, "Introduction," in L. H. Meyer (ed.), *Legitimacy, Justice and Public International Law* (Cambridge, UK: Cambridge University Press, 2009), pp. 5–8; J. Tasioulas, "Parochialism and the Legitimacy of International Law," in M. N. S. Sellers (ed.), *Parochialism, Cosmopolitanism, and the Foundations of International Law* (Cambridge, UK: Cambridge University Press, 2012), pp. 100–11; N. Grossman, "The Normative Legitimacy of International Courts," *Temple Law Review*, 86 (2013), 61, 97.

[64] Raz, *The Morality of Freedom*, pp. 47, 53.

with their legal obligations than they would in its absence, even if it might help states reach a politically palatable resolution in a specific dispute. If the Court ignored or watered down preexisting positive law in *Peru v. Chile*, it cannot be said to have helped the litigating states better to comply with it. Instead, Solomonic judgments can skirt around the law inside the Peace Palace and may discourage states from strict adherence to law outside its doors. To the extent that states perceive the Court as Solomonic, they have fewer incentives to comply with international law at all. Instead, it may be to states' strategic benefit to stretch and even break law in an effort to establish the boundaries of legal argumentation in anticipation of a case being filed. In the same vein, in their framing of issues in written and oral pleadings before the Court, states have incentives to exaggerate their claims or include essentially meritless claims along with strong claims to give the Court something to rule against them on.

Similarly, a Solomonic ICJ may encourage states to refrain from subjecting themselves to the Court's jurisdiction in the first place, vigorously to contest jurisdiction, and possibly to withdraw from the Court's compulsory jurisdiction, further undermining its authority. Simply, potential respondents who believe the law is on their side are better off staying out of, challenging, or leaving the Court's jurisdiction than subjecting themselves to Solomonic decision making.[65] States may have

---

[65] For example, Colombia withdrew from the Pact of Bogotá, a treaty providing the ICJ with compulsory jurisdiction over its dispute with Nicaragua, in response to the ICJ's judgment in *Nicaragua v. Colombia*, issued in November 2012, a judgment that was also characterized as Solomonic by many. *La Nación*'s headline the day the judgment was issued was "ICJ in Solomonic judgment gives more sea to Nicaragua and all the keys to Colombia." *CIJ en fallo salomónico dio más mar a Nicaragua y todos los cayos a Colombia*, La Nación Mundo (19 November 2012) (author's translation) at www.nacion.com/mundo/CIJ-fallo-salomonico-Nicaragua-Colombia_0_1306269542.html. A Chilean former president, Eduardo Frei, characterized that decision as "solomonic" shortly after it was issued. *Rebeldía de Colombia salpica diferendo Perú-Chile*, El Universal (30 November 2012), at www.eluniversal.com/internacional/121130/rebeldia-de-colombia-salpica-diferendo-peru-chile. Frei added, "'En nuestro caso, nosotros no podemos aceptar un fallo que no se funde en los tratados y los acuerdos internacionales que Chile ha firmado'..." ("'In our case, we cannot accept a ruling which is not founded on treaties and international agreements that Chile has signed'...")(author's translation). Ibid. *See also Eduardo Frei muestra preocupación por fallo "salomónico" de La Haya en caso Nicaragua-Colombia: El ex presidente dijo que esto puede significar que "todos los países" van al tribunal internacional "porque siempre les va a tocar algo" tras un fallo*, La Tercera (26 November 2012)("Eduardo Frei shows concern for the 'Solomonic' judgment of the Hague in the Nicaragua-Colombia case: The ex-president said this could mean that 'all the countries' go to the international tribunal 'because they will always get something'

many reasons to consent to jurisdiction, even if it means they may lose cases from time to time. The Court provides adjudicatory services should political negotiations fail. If states are committed to the implementation of a particular legal regime, regardless of their interests in a particular case, submitting to judicial oversight makes sense. But states have little incentive to subject themselves to the Court's jurisdiction if their legal case is strong and their opponent's is weak. And if the Court's rulings do not serve to promote and protect specific legal regimes, a normative commitment to a particular area of law is not served by membership in the Court. Because Solomonic decisions are highly contextual, they rarely provide principles to guide state behavior prospectively or serve to develop the law.

From a Razian perspective, Solomonic courts fail the service conception of authority test, unless the law itself mandates or allows a Solomonic approach. A Solomonic ICJ does not help the litigating parties better to comply with the law because the Court is either not being faithful to it or diluting its force in favor of splitting the pie. Further, Solomonic courts may fail to articulate useful legal principles to guide state behavior prospectively and may even encourage disobedience of international legal norms outside the courtroom.

V Perceptions of Solomonism and Sociological Legitimacy

What impact does the perception of Solomonic judging have on the sociological legitimacy of the ICJ? To the extent states and others believe the Court is sacrificing law in favor of splitting the pie, Solomonism may threaten perceptions of justified authority, regardless of the accuracy of those beliefs. If the Court's constituencies are convinced that the Court is making decisions divorced from legal rules to please and displease the litigating parties in relatively equal amounts, sociological legitimacy is likely to decline, even if normative legitimacy remains intact. States may question a Solomonic court's fairness and whether it is serving an adjudicatory or conciliatory function. Rather than being hailed before a lawless Court, states with strong claims and defenses may prefer to challenge or limit the Court's jurisdiction in the future, or to refrain from opting for the Court's compulsory jurisdiction in the first place. On

through a judgment") (author's translation), available at www.latercera.com/noticia/politica/2012/11/674-495350-9-eduardo-frei-muestra-preocupacion-por-fallo-salomonico-de-la-haya-en-caso.shtml.

the other hand, to the extent the Court's Solomonic judgments fall within a set of reasonable legal outcomes, such decisions may enhance the Court's sociological legitimacy. For domestic political purposes, states may value the Court's attempts to appease both sides in a dispute, which may lead to greater compliance with its judgments and, thereby, increased effectiveness – assuming the two concepts are linked.[66] More research is needed to improve our understanding of the relationship between Solomonic judging and sociological legitimacy.

The Court can take concrete steps to avoid charges that its decision making is unduly or inappropriately Solomonic, even if its judges do not believe it is. For example, the Court can tie its reasoning more explicitly and more concretely to underlying legal rules and to its previous decisions. It can be more transparent and public about what motivates its decision making, and it can engage both scholars and states more deeply about what it means to be the "principal judicial organ" of the United Nations and how decision making takes place at the Court. These measures could help to strengthen the sociological legitimacy of the Court by responding to concerns about judgments that appear to prize splitting the pie over relevant law.

VI Conclusion

This chapter raises new questions about the many judgments labeled "Solomonic" in the International Court of Justice. Although some Solomonic judgments may be divorced from law, others may be deeply embedded in it. The *Peru v. Chile* judgment is just one in a plethora of judgments issued by the ICJ. Whether Solomonic judgments unmoored from law or perceived as such are an aberration or a common occurrence in the Court's jurisprudence is a question that deserves more thought and analysis, taking into account a wide range of the Court's decisions over time. And there may be implications for legitimacy even when a Solomonic judgment is justified or allowed by law.

This chapter is a first step in understanding the impact of Solomonic judgments on the Court's legitimacy. Solomonic decisions may present a threat to the ICJ's legitimacy, yet they are underexplored and undertheorized in the scholarship about the Court. This chapter identifies a number of ways that Solomonic judgments may affect the Court's legitimacy. If the

---

[66] *See*, in this volume, Chapter 13, Yuval Shany's discussion of the complex and dynamic relationship between legitimacy and effectiveness.

Court chooses to pursue a Solomonic route when states do not consent to it or when the law does not require or allow it, the Court acts ultra vires. It is neither appropriately exercising its judicial function, nor deciding in accordance with international law. A Solomonic Court is inherently biased against the litigant with a significantly stronger legal argument, and does no better – and perhaps even worse – at getting states to comply with law than they would on their own. Also, the stretching of positive law and logical reasoning to achieve compromise judgments can render the law vague and incoherent. If judgments are unique to the particular facts at hand, the articulated law loses much of its force. When states believe the Court's judgments are divorced from law in the service of Solomonism, even when they may not be, its sociological legitimacy is endangered. On the other hand, to the extent that Solomonic judgments rooted in law enhance compliance and effectiveness, they may positively impact sociological legitimacy. The relationship between compliance, effectiveness, and sociological legitimacy requires further theorizing and empirical testing.

Future scholarship on this topic must continue to recognize that Solomon's suggestion to "split the baby" was a device intended to achieve proper application of the law. It was a provisional judgment, not a final one. King Solomon sought to determine which woman was the mother of the baby because the law demanded that the baby be returned to her. To protect and enhance its legitimacy, the ICJ too must take care to be faithful to the true intent of Solomon by applying law within the bounds of justice, rather than seeking to achieve a particularized notion of justice outside the bounds of the law. And it must be understood to be doing so.

3

The Global–Local Dilemma and the ICC's Legitimacy

MARGARET M. DEGUZMAN*

I Introduction

Commentary on the legitimacy of the International Criminal Court (ICC or Court) usually identifies one or more perceived flaws in the institution's constitution or work as impediments to its legitimacy. Some commentators consider the flaws to be fatal and recommend closing the Court.[1] More often, writing about the ICC's legitimacy advocates reforms to the Court's statute, practices, or procedures, which the author claims will improve the ICC's legitimacy. Scholars have argued that the ICC could increase its legitimacy by, for instance, adopting more transparent selection procedures,[2] requiring more trustworthy evidence,[3] ensuring greater victim participation,[4] and improving sentencing

---

* I am grateful to Zane Johnson for exceptional research assistance.
[1] See, e.g., D. Hoile, Time to 'defund' the International Criminal Court, Should the ICC be disbanded?, available at www.globalresearch.ca/time-to-defund-the-international-crim inal-court-should-the-icc-be-disbanded/5490817 (arguing that the ICC should be closed for a variety of reasons, including that '[t]he ICC's claims to international jurisdiction and judicial independence are institutionally flawed and the court's reputation has been irretrievably damaged by its racism, blatant double standards, hypocrisy, corruption and serious judicial irregularities').
[2] A. M. Danner, Enhancing legitimacy and accountability of prosecutorial discretion at the International Criminal Court. *American Journal of International Law* 97 (2003), 515.
[3] M. Findlay and S. Ngane, Sham of the moral court? Testimony sold as the spoils of war. *Global Journal of Comparative Law*, 1 (2012), 100 ('Rather it is the failure to ensure truth through the adversarial process which may challenge moral court legitimacy in the eyes of the global community and particularly of its victim constituency. Counter-intuitively a more vigorous attitude to procedural protection in the form of the contempt prosecutions of untruthful victim witnesses may as a consequence challenge victim cooperation with the court, and resultant legitimacy for victim communities.').
[4] M. Pena and G. Carayon, Is the ICC making the most of victim participation? *International Journal of Transitional Justice*, 7 (2013), 518.

practices.[5] As this chapter seeks to demonstrate, such prescriptions tend to ignore a fundamental impediment to strong ICC legitimacy: the unresolved tension between the Court's global and local agendas.

This global–local dilemma often goes unacknowledged because accepted wisdom holds that the ICC can and should serve both global and local constituencies. The Court should promote global goals, particularly global crime prevention, while simultaneously advancing local justice agendas in the communities where the crimes occurred. In reality, however, the Court's limited resources often require it to privilege either global or local goals. For instance, in deciding what situations and cases to prosecute, the Court can direct its resources toward worldwide crime prevention, or focus more specifically on meeting the needs of particular affected groups. Some selection decisions may promote both agendas, but in many cases the goals of the two communities conflict. For example, global crime prevention may mitigate in favor of a small number of prosecutions in a given situation, even in the absence of complementarity prosecutions at the local level. In contrast, the needs for retribution or deterrence of the communities most affected by the crimes may require a broader scope of prosecutions.[6]

The ICC's founding document, the Rome Statute, provides little guidance regarding how the Court should resolve tensions between global and local objectives. The Statute's preamble asserts that the Court was established to address crimes that 'threaten the peace, security and well-being of the world'.[7] Such language can be read to suggest that the Court should be viewed primarily as an instrument of crime prevention at the global level. On the other hand, the Statute's complementarity regime, whereby the ICC may act only when national courts are inactive or unwilling or unable to act,[8] can be interpreted as an indication that the Court's central function is to act as a surrogate for local courts.

---

[5] N. Combs, Seeking inconsistency: Advancing pluralism in international criminal sentencing. *Yale Journal of International Law*, 41 (2016), available at papers.ssrn.com/sol3/papers.cfm?abstract_id=2630317; S. Glickman, Victim's justice: Legitimizing the sentencing regime of the International Criminal Court. *Columbia Journal of Transnational Law*, 43 (2004), 229 (arguing that 'for the ICC to bring new legitimacy to international humanitarian law, it must adopt mechanisms to ensure that war criminals receive certain minimal punishments and serve out their full sentences').

[6] *See* C. Aptel, Prosecutorial discretion at the ICC and victims' right to remedy. *Journal of International Criminal Justice*, 10 (2012), 1357.

[7] Rome Statute of the International Criminal Court, Rome, 17 July 1998, in force 1 July 2002, 2187 UNTS 38544; UN Doc A/CONF.183/9 Preamble.

[8] Ibid., art. 17.

64 MARGARET M. DEGUZMAN

This global–local dilemma is an important impediment to the ICC's efforts to develop greater legitimacy. The term *legitimacy* as applied to international institutions connotes the 'right to rule'[9] or 'justified authority'.[10] The bases for justified authority and thus legitimacy are complex and cannot be fully expounded here.[11] However, one useful distinction this chapter employs is that between normative and sociological legitimacy.[12] Normative legitimacy relates to justifications for authority derived from either moral norms ('moral legitimacy') or legal norms ('legal legitimacy').[13] Sociological legitimacy, on the other hand, refers to the extent to which relevant audiences perceive an institution's authority to be justified.[14]

These categories often overlap: moral and legal norms can derive from social customs; and perceptions of justified authority often depend on the strength of beliefs in the underlying legal and moral norms. Nonetheless, the distinction can be analytically important, particularly for institutions such as the ICC, which purport to represent multiple constituencies simultaneously. The ICC might be highly normatively legitimate in the sense that it pursues normatively appropriate goals in normatively desirable ways, and yet some audiences might nonetheless view it as illegitimate because they do not share those goals. In the analysis that follows, the term *legitimacy* is used to encompass both normative and sociological aspects of the concept except when the distinction is specifically noted. In

---

[9] *See, e.g.,* A. Buchanan and R. O. Keohane, The legitimacy of global governance institutions. *Ethics and International Affairs,* 20 (2006), 405; J. d'Aspremont and E. De Brabandere, The complementary faces of legitimacy in international law: The legitimacy of origin and the legitimacy of exercise. *Fordham International Law Journal,* 34 (2011), 190.

[10] D. Bodansky, The legitimacy of international governance: A coming challenge for international environmental law. *The American Journal of International Law,* 93 (1999), 596, 601.

[11] For an excellent literature review see D. Bodansky, Legitimacy in international law and international relations. In J. Dunoff and M. Pollack, eds., *Interdisciplinary Perspectives on International Law and International Relations: The State of the Art* (Cambridge, UK: Cambridge, 2013), pp. 324–8.

[12] *See* ibid.

[13] The distinction between moral and legal norms is controversial. *See* N. Purvis, Critical legal studies in public international law. *Harvard International Law Journal,* 32 (1991), 112 (arguing that legitimacy theories 'reflect a positivist or naturalist first premise' and that debates about legitimacy 'are destined to the same indeterminacy as other international legal debates').

[14] Bodansky, Legitimacy in international law and international relations. 324–8; Buchanan and Keohane, The legitimacy of global governance institutions, 405 (defining sociological legitimacy as when an institution is 'widely believed to have the right to rule').

particular, the conclusion focuses on sociological legitimacy, arguing that whatever goals the ICC prioritizes it will inevitably alienate some audiences, at least until greater global consensus is achieved as to its appropriate priorities.

The concept of legitimacy is closely connected to that of effectiveness.[15] Indeed, as Yuval Shany argues in Chapter 13, legitimacy and effectiveness are often mutually reinforcing.[16] The central claim of this chapter – that enhancing the ICC's legitimacy requires greater consensus about whether the ICC should act primarily as a vehicle for global or local justice – could also be framed in terms of effectiveness. According to Shany's definition, effectiveness requires that an institution pursue well-accepted and clear goals in an efficient manner.[17] For the ICC to be highly effective, therefore, its goals, including the priorities among them, must be clearer and more widely accepted. The global–local dilemma is thus an important impediment to the ICC's effectiveness as well as to its legitimacy.[18]

The chapter begins by explaining the global–local dilemma. It then demonstrates that the dilemma has been underexplored in the commentary on the ICC's legitimacy and explains why it is important to rectify this omission. The chapter concludes by suggesting that whatever approach the ICC adopts to resolving the global–local dilemma it will

---

[15] The direction of influence between legitimacy and effectiveness is debatable. Some argue that sociological legitimacy is a potential basis of effectiveness because 'the more an institution is perceived as legitimate, the more stable and effective it is likely to be.' Bodansky, The legitimacy of international governance. 603. Others suggest that legitimacy depends in part on an institution's relative effectiveness. See, e.g., Buchanan and Keohane, The legitimacy of global governance institutions. 422 ('If an institution cannot effectively perform the functions invoked to justify its existence, then this insufficiency undermines its claim to the right to rule'.). Therefore, it appears legitimacy and effectiveness are interdependent.

[16] See Y. Shany, Stronger together: Legitimacy and effectiveness of international courts as potentially mutually reinforcing notions. In N. Grossman, H. G. Cohen, A. Follesdal, and G. Ulfstein, eds., Legitimacy and International Courts (2015), pp. 11–13 (discussing the 'goal-based' system of international court organization and its effect on legitimacy).

[17] This chapter adopts the goal-based approach to effectiveness described in Yuval Shany, Assessing the Effectiveness of International Courts (Oxford, UK: Oxford University Press, 2014). Scholars sometimes define effectiveness in terms of compliance. For an explanation of why the goal-based approach is more appropriate for international courts see ibid., p. 14.

[18] It is important to remember that both legitimacy and effectiveness exist along a spectrum. It is rarely true that an institution is completely illegitimate, and it is perhaps even less likely that any institution can claim 100 percent legitimacy. Instead, an institution's legitimacy is strong to the extent that its authority is strongly justified and weak to the extent the reverse is true.

66 MARGARET M. DEGUZMAN

alienate some audience, and its sociological legitimacy will suffer in the short term as a result. Over time, however, if the ICC succeeds in convincing the world of the appropriateness of its mission, the adverse effect on its sociological legitimacy will be reversed.

While the global–local dilemma is far from the only challenge to the ICC's legitimacy,[19] it is an important one that is often overlooked. By foregrounding the relationship between the global–local dilemma and the ICC's legitimacy, the chapter hopes to expand the debates on the ICC's legitimacy to include a greater emphasis on mission clarity.

II The Global–Local Dilemma

It is widely agreed that the drafters of the Rome Statute failed to endow the institution with a clearly defined mission. The Statute's preamble proclaims that the Court was established 'to put an end to impunity' for 'the most serious crimes of concern to the international community as a whole.'[20] This anti-impunity rhetoric helped to motivate states to establish and join the Court. At the same time, the intuitive appeal of the anti-impunity campaign served to obscure important questions about the ICC's goals and priorities. State and nongovernmental actors alike chose to focus on promoting the fight against impunity rather than on the details of how the fight should be fought.

The goals ascribed to the ICC are many and diverse, from promoting peace and enhancing security to reconciling groups, healing victims, and establishing a historical record.[21] It would be difficult for any institution to pursue such broad goals simultaneously, and it is all the more difficult for the ICC to do so in light of its very limited resources. As such, the ICC's decision making often requires it to privilege the goals of one of its key constituencies over the other. A decision about whether to prosecute a particular crime or individual may depend on whether the ICC gives priority to the needs for redress of affected local communities or focuses instead on giving voice to particular norms of the international

---

[19] Other challenges include, for instance, the absence of consistent support from the United Nations Security Council and the Court's limited funding.

[20] The preamble to the Rome Statute asserts that grave international crimes threaten the world's peace and security, affirms the need for national-level prosecution of such crimes, and articulates the determination of the international community that there should be no impunity for their perpetrators. Preamble to the Rome Statute.

[21] *See* M. R. Damaska, What is the point of international criminal justice? *Chicago-Kent Law Review*, 83 (2008), 331.

community. Similar considerations animate decisions about which situations to investigate. Even decisions about what procedures to follow and how severely to sentence can hinge on whether the ICC privileges global or local agendas. To be clear, the ICC's global and local goals are not always in tension. Often, ICC prosecution in a particular situation or case serves both global and local communities. But in situations where the interests of the communities conflict, or where they compete for scarce resources, the ICC must choose which to privilege.

Although few commentators have addressed this dilemma directly,[22] many implicitly adopt either a global or a local vision of the ICC's priorities. Commentators who view the ICC through a primarily global lens tend to consider the Court's central task to be the prevention of international crimes across the globe,[23] while those who adopt a local justice lens see the ICC as serving the needs of the communities most affected by the crimes at issue.[24] These lenses can have important consequences both for assessments of the Court's legitimacy and for prescriptions aimed at promoting such legitimacy. For instance, a commentator with a local justice approach to the Court's work might criticize the Court for intervening in a situation where the local population prefers nonprosecutorial responses to crime, such as a truth commission or lustrations. On the other hand, a commentator with a global justice approach might argue that the Court has an obligation to the international community to prosecute international crimes, even when the local population opposes such prosecution. As the next section seeks to demonstrate, much of the literature about the ICC's legitimacy either ignores the global–local dilemma or implicitly adopts one lens or the other in critiquing the Court and making reform recommendations.

---

[22] Dustin Sharp has written about the global–local dilemma in the context of transitional justice. D. N. Sharp, Addressing dilemmas of the global and the local in transitional justice. *Emory International Law Review*, 29 (2014).

[23] *See, e.g.*, Bruce Broomhall, *International Justice and the International Criminal Court: Between Sovereignty and the Rule of Law* (Oxford, UK: Oxford University Press, 2003), p. 189 (viewing the ICC as entrenching 'the concepts of rule of law, accountability, and legality' in international discourse).

[24] *See, e.g.*, L. Moffett, 'Realising Justice for Victims Before the International Criminal Court,' *International Crimes Database Brief*, 6 (September 2014), available at www.internationalcrimesdatabase.org; L. M. Keller, Seeking justice at the International Criminal Court: Victims' reparations. *Thomas Jefferson Law Review*, 29 (2007), 189–90 ('The goal of the ICC is to provide a foundation for rebuilding society after mass violence, through prosecution of the perpetrators and reparations for the victims'.).

III The Absence of the Global–Local Dilemma from Discussions of the ICC's Legitimacy

This section reviews the commentary on the ICC's legitimacy to demonstrate the failure to address the global–local dilemma. The discussion is organized around the types of claims that are frequently made about the ICC's legitimacy. Various legitimacy typologies are advanced in the literature.[25] Without endorsing any particular typology, this analysis employs some of the categories commonly found in the literature as a convenient way to organize the major arguments concerning the ICC's legitimacy. The first section addresses arguments routed in the legitimacy of the ICC's creation – its 'legitimacy of origin'.[26] The second section examines arguments about the 'personal legitimacy'[27] of the major actors at the ICC: its prosecutors and judges. The third section addresses one of the most common ways of assessing the ICC's legitimacy, which looks to its operational practices and procedures. This legitimacy lens is often termed 'legitimacy of exercise' in contrast with 'legitimacy of origin'.[28] Alternatively this process-based legitimacy is sometimes called 'input legitimacy'.[29] The final section examines arguments related to the results or 'outputs' the ICC produces.[30] With regard to each type of legitimacy, this section seeks to demonstrate that the failure to address the global–local dilemma undermines the usefulness of the analytic and prescriptive claims being made.

---

[25] *See, e.g.*, S. Vasiliev, Between international criminal justice and injustice: Theorising legitimacy. In N. Hayashi and C. M. Bailliet, eds., *The Effectiveness and Legitimacy of International Criminal Tribunals* (Cambridge, UK: Cambridge University Press, 2017), available at papers.ssrn.com/sol3/papers.cfm?abstract_id=2665821 (proposing various categories of legitimacy); A. Kiyani, The antimonies of legitimacy: On the (im)possibility of a legitimate International Criminal Court. *African Journal of Legal Studies*, 8 (2015), 12 (discussing David Easton's typology of ideological, structural, and personal legitimacies).

[26] d'Aspremont and De Brabandere, Complementary Faces of Legitimacy, 190.

[27] David Easton, *A Systems Analysis of Political Life* (New York: John Wiley & Sons, 1965), p. 302.

[28] d'Aspremont and De Brabandere, Complementary faces of legitimacy, 190.

[29] For a discussion of input versus output legitimacy, see F. W. Scharpf, Legitimacy and the multi-actor polity. In M. Egeberg and P. Lægreid, eds., *Organizing Political Institutions: Essays for Johan P. Olsen* (Oslo: Scandinavian University Press, 1999), p. 26; C. Kelly, Institutional alliances and derivative legitimacy. *Michigan Journal of International Law*, 29 (2008), 608.

[30] Ibid.

A *Legitimacy of Origin*

Arguments concerning an institution's 'legitimacy of origin' address whether the institution was established pursuant to appropriate legal and moral norms (normative legitimacy of origin) and whether it is perceived as having such normatively appropriate origins (sociological legitimacy of origin). The literature on the ICC's legitimacy of origin largely addresses the roles that the related concepts of state consent and democratic representativeness play in determining the institution's legitimacy. Authors who have considered these issues tend to reach one of three conclusions. Some scholars argue that the manner in which the ICC was established renders it illegitimate; others assert that those processes contribute positively to the institution's legitimacy; and a third group claims that the manner in which the ICC was established is not a significant determinant of its legitimacy. Missing from the discussions is an acknowledgment that the ICC's legitimacy of origin depends in part on whether it is intended to serve primarily global or local audiences.

Some authors focus on state consent as a determinant of the ICC's legitimacy of origin. State consent is often considered an important determinant of the legitimacy of international organizations.[31] State consent is deemed to promote legitimacy because states are assumed to represent the people within their borders such that the state's consent reflects the consent of the people.[32] Of course, many states, particularly nondemocratic states, do not represent the will of their citizens, making the usefulness of their consent in conferring legitimacy questionable.[33]

Nonetheless, many authors cite state consent – or its absence – in assessing the ICC's legitimacy. For instance, Linda Carter believes that the high number of ratifications of the Rome Statute (123 to date) is an indication of the Court's legitimacy. Carter asserts that 'the impressive number of ... member states is evidence of the acceptance and support for the Court' and that '[t]he greater the number of states parties, the

---

[31] *See* d'Aspremont and De Brabandere, Complementary faces of legitimacy, 216 ('[S]ince an international organization is created by states, the source and legitimacy of the exercise of powers by international organizations is derived from the consent validly expressed by the different states party to the constitutional treaty of the organization.').

[32] Ibid.

[33] *See* Buchanan and Keohane, 'The legitimacy of global governance institutions', 413 ('[I]t is hard to see how state consent could render global governance institutions legitimate, given that many states are nondemocratic and systematically violate the human rights of their citizens and are for that reason themselves illegitimate'.); N. Grossman, The normative legitimacy of international courts. *Temple Law Review*, 86 (2013), 77.

70   MARGARET M. DEGUZMAN

more legitimacy the ICC will have'.[34] For other commentators, the failure of some of the world's most powerful and populous states to ratify the statute is an indication of weak legitimacy of origin.[35]

Another line of argument addressing the ICC's legitimacy of origin concerns the Court's ability to exercise jurisdiction over crimes committed in states, or by nationals of states, that have not consented as a determinant of its legitimacy. For authors such as Madeline Morris, the extension of jurisdiction beyond member states renders the institution illegitimate. According to Morris, by allowing for jurisdiction over nationals of nonparty states, the ICC 'displaces the state as the conduit for democratic representation, and provides no alternative mechanism for democratic governance'.[36] Morris suggests that this 'democratic deficit' is fatal to the ICC's legitimacy.[37]

Shlomit Wallerstein counters that the ICC is sufficiently democratically representative to be legitimate.[38] According to Wallerstein, with respect to states parties, the ICC derives democratic legitimacy from the fact that states delegate their primary jurisdiction to adjudicate international crimes to the Court.[39] With regard to nonparty states, Wallerstein asserts that as members of the United Nations, states have delegated to the Security Council the power to refer situations to the ICC.[40] For Wallerstein, therefore, all states have in some way consented to ICC jurisdiction, which affirms the institution's legitimacy.[41]

Some scholars reject the idea that democratic representativeness helps to determine the ICC's legitimacy. David Luban asserts that, as a matter of

---

[34] L. E. Carter, The future of the International Criminal Court: Complementarity as a strength or a weakness? *Washington University Global Studies Law Review*, 12 (2013), 495.

[35] *See, e.g.*, J. Goldsmith, The self-defeating International Criminal Court. *University of Chicago Law Review*, 70 (2003), 100.

[36] M. Morris, The democratic dilemma of the International Criminal Court. *Buffalo Criminal Law Review*, 5 (2002) 599, see note 131.

[37] Ibid., 600.

[38] *See* S. Wallerstein, Delegation of powers and authority in international criminal law. *Criminal Law and Philosophy*, 9 (2015).

[39] Ibid.; *see also* M. J. Struett, The transformation of state sovereign rights and responsibilities under the Rome Statute for the International Criminal Court. *Chapman Law Review*, 8 (2005), 183 (discussing the establishment of the ICC as a function of delegation); *see also* William A. Schabas, *The UN International Criminal Tribunals: The Former Yugoslavia, Rwanda, and Sierra Leone* (Cambridge, UK: Cambridge University Press, 2006), p. 56 (arguing that there is little support in the literature for the view that 'states cannot delegate all of their criminal law powers to an international criminal tribunal').

[40] Wallerstein, The delegation of powers and authority, 135.   [41] Ibid.

moral norms, states cannot delegate their criminal law authority.[42] He further argues that only a world political community would be capable of authorizing international adjudication and that such a community does not exist.[43] On this basis, Luban concludes that the ICC's legitimacy cannot be derived from its origin, democratic or otherwise, and must instead relate to the procedures it follows.[44] Aaron Fichtelberg agrees.[45] He criticizes Morris's focus on democratic governance, arguing that democracy is simply a vehicle for the protection of more essential rights.[46] For Fichtelberg, it is respect for such rights that confers legitimacy.[47]

Michael Struett adds an interesting dimension to this debate by pointing out that aspects of the Court's formation other than its democratic pedigree may be important to its legitimacy.[48] Struett's work highlights the extensive and effective involvement of nongovernmental organizations in crafting the institution's normative framework, as well as the far-reaching international discourse surrounding the Court's formation. Struett argues that the ICC gains at least some of its legitimacy from these normatively desirable aspects of its establishment.[49]

These and other discussions of the ICC's legitimacy of origin overlook the impact of the global–local dilemma on such legitimacy. Yet the importance to the ICC's legitimacy of democratic representativeness or of the involvement of nongovernmental organizations depends on what purpose the institution is meant to serve. If the ICC is primarily intended to operate as a substitute for unavailable national courts, its legitimacy should be just as dependent on democratic representativeness as that of national courts. Therefore, if Luban is correct that states cannot delegate their criminal jurisdiction, the ICC's legitimacy as an institution of local justice is in serious question.

---

[42] D. Luban, Fairness to rightness: Jurisdiction, legality, and the legitimacy of international criminal law. In S. Besson and J. Tasioulas, eds., *The Philosophy of International Law* (Oxford, UK: Oxford University Press, 2010), p. 569. Wallerstein provides a detailed refutation of this claim. *See* Wallerstein, The delegation of powers and authority.

[43] Luban, Fairness to rightness, 579.   [44] Ibid.

[45] A. Fichtelberg, Democratic legitimacy and the International Criminal Court: A liberal defense. *Journal of International Criminal Justice*, 4 (2006), 765; *see also* M. Glasius, Do International Criminal Courts require democratic legitimacy? *The European Journal of International Law*, 23 (2012), 63 (asserting that a democratic basis is not essential to international criminal courts).

[46] Fichtelberg, Democratic legitimacy, 776.   [47] Ibid.

[48] Michael J. Struett, *The Politics of Constructing the International Criminal Court: NGOs, Discourse, and Agency* (New York: Palgrave Macmillan, 2008).

[49] Ibid.

On the other hand, if the ICC's central task is to promote global norms prohibiting international crimes, the importance of democratic representativeness is much less evident. The global norms at issue, like those underpinning the human rights regime, can be understood as universal norms that do not depend on state consent for legitimacy. In that case, the involvement of many states and nongovernmental organizations in establishing the Court helps to demonstrate the universal character of the norms; but the consent of large numbers of states, or of any given state, to the ICC's jurisdiction is not necessary to legitimate its work.

In sum, it makes little sense to reach conclusions about the ICC's legitimacy of origin without reference to the ICC's central goals and priorities.

B Personal Legitimacy of the ICC's Prosecutors and Judges

Commentators sometimes focus on the personal legitimacy of the ICC's prosecutors and judges as determinants of the institution's sociological legitimacy. Personal legitimacy refers to an individual decision maker's potential to act as the source of legitimacy for the institution as a whole.[50] Some commentators have argued that the ICC's first prosecutor, Luis Moreno Ocampo, failed to establish his own legitimacy and thereby undermined that of the institution.[51] Conversely, when Fatou Bensouda was selected as Moreno Ocampo's successor, Aminta Ossom asserted that the decision to select a prosecutor from Africa was likely to increase the Court's sociological legitimacy in light of the institution's extensive work in Africa.[52] More generally, many commentators subscribe to the view that the ICC's normative and sociological legitimacy requires its prosecutors and judges to be independent of political bodies and to be seen as such.[53]

---

[50] See Easton, A Systems Analysis of Political Life, p. 302. Max Weber's idea of charisma represents one form of personal legitimacy. See ibid., p. 303.

[51] See, e.g., K. Sheffield, Speak softly and carry a sealed warrant: Building the International Criminal Court's legitimacy in the wake of Sudan. Appeal, 18 (2013), 163; J. Rozenberg, Why the World's Most Powerful Prosecutor Should Resign: Part 2. The Telegraph, 17 July 2008, available at www.telegraph.co.uk/news/newstopics/lawreports/joshuarozenberg/2446064/Why-the-worlds-most-powerful-prosecutor-should-resign-Part-2.html.

[52] A. Ossom, An African solution to an African problem? How an African prosecutor could strengthen the ICC. Virginia Journal of International Law Digest, 52 (2011), 68.

[53] See, e.g., R. Mackenzie and P. Sands, International courts and tribunals and the independence of the international judge. Harvard International Law Journal, 44 (2003); J. Fowler, The Rome Treaty for an International Criminal Court: A framework of international justice for future generations. Human Rights Brief, 6 (1998), 20.

THE GLOBAL–LOCAL DILEMMA AND THE ICC'S LEGITIMACY   73

Commentary on the personal legitimacy of ICC actors, and the impact of such personal legitimacy on the institution's legitimacy, rarely takes account of the global–local dilemma. Yet the relationship between the personal legitimacy of ICC actors and the institution's legitimacy depends on the ICC's goals and priorities. If the Court's primary purpose is to act as a stand-in for unavailable local justice systems, it is very important that ICC prosecutor and judges be perceived as legitimate among local audiences and that they be attuned and responsive to local needs. Indeed, it would perhaps make most sense for the ICC to employ, or at least cooperate with, local prosecutors and judges, at least when such actors enjoy a reasonable degree of local legitimacy.

A local justice vision of the ICC's role also suggests, contrary to the views of most commentators,[54] that it may sometimes be appropriate for the ICC to take instructions, or at least guidance, from the government of the society most affected by the crimes. Where that government is democratically elected and is widely considered to be legitimate within the society, the government's views of which cases should be pursued and what penalties should apply could help to ensure that the local population's vision of justice is achieved. Although such political involvement in the justice process would decrease the ICC's independence, it would increase its ability to serve local goals.

In contrast, a global justice vision of the ICC's work suggests that prosecutors and judges should be selected to ensure the most effective communication of global norms to a worldwide audience.[55] For instance, according to a global justice approach, particular attention should be paid to ensuring adequate representation of women judges at the ICC.[56] Such representation telegraphs that the global community values the justice perspectives of women and men equally.[57] Likewise, a global justice

---

[54] *See, e.g.*, Mackenzie and Sands, International courts and tribunals; Fowler, 'The Rome Treaty'.

[55] *Cf.* Grossman, The normative legitimacy of international courts, 79 ('[I]nternational courts do not solely decide one-time disputes but rather are involved in creating norms over time'.).

[56] The current procedures for selecting ICC judges, which seek to ensure various kinds of representation, including representation based on geographic and gender diversity, support a global justice approach to the Court's work. *See* Article 36 of the Rome Statute.

[57] *Cf.* N. Grossman, Sex on the bench: Do women judges matter to the legitimacy of international courts? *Chicago Journal of International Law*, 12 (2012), 668 ('[S]ex representation strengthens the legitimacy of international courts by reflecting the population subject to their authority'.).

74 MARGARET M. DEGUZMAN

approach strengthens the argument that the prosecutor and judges should be independent from the influence of any government or organization.

C Legitimacy of Exercise/Input

Perhaps the most significant focus of scholarly attention concerning the ICC's legitimacy is on the procedural aspects of the Court's work – how the court performs its functions. As noted earlier, this is often labeled 'legitimacy of exercise' or 'input legitimacy'. There are many different aspects of the ICC's procedures that can be examined for legitimizing effects. Three of the most widely studied are the procedures related to the selection of situations and cases, fairness, and victim participation. In each of these areas, the global–local dilemma is important yet largely overlooked.

1 Selection of Situations and Cases

Some scholars identify the manner in which the ICC selects situations and cases as an important contributor to its legitimacy. Allison Marston Danner argues that the ICC's legitimacy depends on the ability of the prosecutor to select situations and cases for prosecution based on law and justice, rather than politics or power.[58] To enhance the ICC's legitimacy, Danner believes that the Court should adopt guidelines for the prosecutor to follow in making decisions about when to open investigations and whom to prosecute.[59] A number of other authors make similar claims, sometimes asserting that the ICC's current selection practices undermine its legitimacy.[60] For instance, Phil Clark argues that the ICC's decision to prosecute rebels but not government perpetrators in Uganda and the Democratic Republic of Congo has undermined the ICC's legitimacy.[61] According to Clark, the ICC made these decisions based on 'self-interested pragmatic concerns', in particular the desire to maintain government cooperation, rather than principles of law or justice.[62] Adam Branch agrees, accusing the ICC of allowing the Ugandan government

---

[58] Danner, Enhancing legitimacy and accountability, 515. [59] Ibid.

[60] *See, e.g.*, J. A. Goldston, More candour about criteria: The exercise of discretion by the prosecutor of the International Criminal Court. *Journal of International Criminal Justice*, 8 (2010), 386–7 (citing critics).

[61] P. Clark, Law, politics and pragmatism: The ICC and case selection in Uganda and the Democratic Republic of Congo. In N. Waddell and P. Clark, eds., *Courting Conflict? Justice, Peace, and the ICC in Africa* (London: Royal African Society, 2008), p. 44.

[62] Ibid.

THE GLOBAL–LOCAL DILEMMA AND THE ICC'S LEGITIMACY   75

to use it as a pawn in a political contest with its opponents.[63] Similarly, Kai Sheffield believes that former prosecutor Moreno Ocampo failed to follow accepted prosecutorial practices in deciding to prosecute the president of Sudan, and that this decision has negatively affected the ICC's legitimacy.[64]

The premise inherent in these critiques – that the ICC should select situations and cases without regard to political considerations – is not universally shared. Thomas Hansen argues that 'the ICC is often "trapped" between the demands of legalism and the demands arising out of the broader political and social contexts in which it operates'.[65] For Hansen, the ICC's legitimacy depends not on its ability to overcome political pressures, but rather on the skill with which it navigates the tension between law and politics.[66] Joseph Hoover takes the argument further, asserting that in purporting to be apolitical, the ICC actually undermines its legitimacy.[67]

Debates about how the ICC should select situations and cases, including the role of political considerations in that process, have largely failed to take into account the underlying question of what goals and priorities the ICC should pursue. Yet the normative legitimacy of selection decisions is, in significant part, a function of the extent to which they enable the institution to pursue its goals effectively and efficiently.[68] Consider the situation the ICC is investigating in Uganda. If the ICC's goal is to serve as a stand-in for unavailable national court systems, its decision to investigate and prosecute members of the Lord's Resistance Army (LRA) can be seen as illegitimate. The government of Uganda by most accounts is perfectly able to prosecute LRA leaders and would do so were it able to capture them.[69] Given that the ICC has no enforcement arm, it lacks the ability to assist the Ugandan government in the way the government needs. The ICC action also appears unlikely to advance national justice

---

[63] A. Branch, Uganda's Civil War and the politics of ICC intervention. *Ethics and International Affairs*, 21 (2007), 179.

[64] Sheffield, Speak softly, 163.

[65] T. Hansen, The ICC and the legitimacy of exercise. In P. Andersen et al., eds., *Law and Legitimacy* (Copenhagen: DJOEF Publishers, 2014), p. 2.

[66] Ibid., p. 15.

[67] J. Hoover, Moral practices: Assigning responsibility in the International Criminal Court. *Law and Contemporary Problems*, 76 (2013), 263.

[68] *See* Buchanan and Keohane, The legitimacy of global governance institutions 422.

[69] W. A. Schabas, 'Complementarity in practice': Some uncomplimentary thoughts. *Criminal Law Forum*, 19 (2007), 13.

76 MARGARET M. DEGUZMAN

goals within Uganda. Indeed, some commentators claim that prosecuting only one side of the conflict could exacerbate the conflict.[70]

On the other hand, if the ICC's goal in prosecuting a small number of rebel leaders in Uganda is to promote global justice, the selection decisions may be more normatively legitimate. Some commentators, including the present author, posit that the ICC's global justice mission is to express global norms to a global audience.[71] In prosecuting rebel leaders for underprosecuted crimes such as the recruitment of child soldiers and crimes of sexual violence, the ICC can contribute to such norm expression. Even if the goal is simply to signal the importance of prosecuting crimes committed in internal armed conflicts, which often go unprosecuted, the ICC's selection decisions can be seen as legitimate.

The degree of sociological legitimacy the ICC enjoys as a result of its selection decisions likewise depends on whether one subscribes to a primarily global or local vision of the Court's work. The different visions imply different priorities in terms of the most important audiences for legitimacy determinations. A local justice approach suggests that local audiences are the most important evaluators of the ICC's legitimacy, whereas a global justice vision of the ICC's work requires a broader inquiry into the views of people around the world. While the ICC's selection decisions have been unpopular with some local audiences,[72] the global community, or at least global civil society, has been generally supportive.[73]

2 Fairness

A number of scholars assert that a key determinant of the ICC's legitimacy is the fairness of its procedures, particularly those related to defendants' rights. As noted earlier, David Luban is a strong proponent of this view, arguing that because the ICC cannot derive legitimacy from the political bodies that created the institution, its legitimacy hinges instead on the extent to which it follows fair procedures in adjudicating and

---

[70] *See* ibid. (discussing the possibility of the prosecutions serving as an obstacle to peace); J. Ku and J. Nzelibe, Do international criminal tribunals deter or exacerbate humanitarian atrocities? *Washington University Law Review*, 84 (2006), 820 (articulating belief that ICC prosecutions in Uganda have "jeopardized the peace process").

[71] M. M. deGuzman, Choosing to prosecute: Expressive selection at the International Criminal Court. *Michigan Journal of International Law*, 33 (2012), 314–19.

[72] J. Ramji-Nogales, Designing bespoke transitional justice: A pluralist process approach. *Michigan Journal of International Law*, 32 (2010), 45–50.

[73] Although it is difficult to demonstrate 'global' support and African governments have criticized the ICC's selection decisions, the ongoing financial and logistical support the ICC enjoys from many states is one indicator of such support.

THE GLOBAL–LOCAL DILEMMA AND THE ICC'S LEGITIMACY   77

punishing defendants.[74] Mark Findlay and Sylvia Ngane also take this view.[75] They argue that the heavy dependence of international criminal courts on witness testimony that is sometimes unreliable undermines the institutions' claims to moral legitimacy.[76]

Although fairness is undoubtedly an important determinant of the ICC's legitimacy, the quality, and perhaps even quantity, of fairness required should be considered in conjunction with the goals the ICC seeks to achieve. A local justice vision of the ICC's purpose suggests the ICC should apply the local fairness standards in the situations it adjudicates. For instance, in states that do not require the presence of the accused at trial or provide counsel to indigent defendants, it is not clear that the ICC should do so either.

Indeed, some scholars have argued for a pluralist approach to the ICC's procedures, whereby at least some of the procedures the Court employs should draw on local norms and standards.[77]

These observations should be qualified in one respect, however. Because the ICC's existence and work depends on the cooperation of governments around the world, its fairness standards should never dip so low as to offend a large segment of the global community. In other words, even assuming a local justice vision of the Court's role, the institution should abide by at least a minimum level of universally recognized norms of fairness to maintain its sociological legitimacy.

On the other hand, if the central purpose of the ICC is to promote global norms, it stands to reason that the Court should employ global norms related to fairness. Such global norms would include not only minimum standards, but also evolving notions of fairness that have significant support around the world. In this way, the Court communicates to the global community both norms related to the crimes at issue in a given case and norms pertaining to the appropriate procedures for adjudicating those crimes.[78]

---

[74] Luban, Fairness to rightness, 1–24; *see also* Fichtelberg, Democratic legitimacy, 782 (arguing that 'the legitimacy of the ICC and similar institutions depends primarily upon the fairness of its procedures').

[75] Findlay and Ngane, Sham of the moral court? 73.   [76] Ibid.

[77] *See, e.g.*, Ramji-Nogales, Bespoke transitional justice, 3; A. K. A Greenawalt, The Pluralism of International Criminal Law. *Indiana Law Journal*, 86 (2011), 1099 (arguing that sentencing practices of international criminal courts should take local norms regarding punishment into consideration).

[78] For a related argument see Grossman, The normative legitimacy of international courts, 101 (arguing that to enhance their legitimacy, international courts should help states to comply better with their human rights obligations than they otherwise would).

3 Victim Participation

A third area in which commentators make process-based claims about the ICC's legitimacy involves the extent to which victims participate in the Court's work. Unlike most other international courts, the ICC permits victims to participate directly in the proceedings and establishes a trust fund aimed at securing reparations for victims.[79] Some commentators are critical of the way the ICC has implemented these victim-centered provisions, arguing that it has been insufficiently attentive to victims' needs.[80] After convening discussions among civil society groups and others on the role of victims at the ICC, a respected nongovernmental organization issued a report stating: 'The main message of the discussions is that victims should be brought back to have a more central role in the operations of the ICC to ensure its legitimacy and its capacity to have a deterrent effect in the communities, or as a participant stated, for the Court "*to recover its humanity*"'.[81] Others caution that the Court should avoid giving victims too great a role in its proceedings.[82]

The global–local dilemma has obvious implications for the question of how much, and what kinds, of victim participation will enhance the legitimacy of the ICC. Victim participation may advance some global justice goals, such as truth telling as a means of global crime prevention or promoting victims' rights norms globally. However, such goals can likely be achieved with relatively limited victim participation. On the other hand, if the central mission of the ICC is to advance the local justice agendas of the communities most affected by the crimes, more extensive victim participation may be needed to ensure the Court's moral and sociological legitimacy. Extensive victim participation can help to ensure that trials focus on the victims' interests, rather than on those of the global community.

---

[79] Articles 68 and 79 of the Rome Statute.

[80] *See, e.g.,* E. Haslam and R. Edmunds, Common legal representation at the International Criminal Court: More symbolic than real? *International Criminal Law Review*, 12 (2012); Pena and Carayon, Most of victim participation; M. Stewart, The Lubanga reparations decision: A missed opportunity? *Polish Yearbook of International Law*, 32 (2012).

[81] *See, e.g.,* Antoine Bernard (ed.), *Enhancing Victims' Rights before the ICC: A View from Situation Countries on Victims' Rights at the International Criminal Court* (Paris: International Federation for Human Rights, 2013), p. 6.

[82] S. Mouthaan, Victim Participation at the ICC for Victims of Gender-Based Crimes: A Conflict of Interest. *Cardozo Journal of International and Comparative Law*, 21 (2013), 651 ('[T]he system of victim participation as it has evolved is too burdensome to cope with the increase of potential participating victims, its modalities are applied inconsistently, and it contributes to lengthening judicial procedures unnecessarily'.).

THE GLOBAL–LOCAL DILEMMA AND THE ICC'S LEGITIMACY   79

In sum, the ICC's normative and sociological legitimacy derives, at least in part, from the procedures it employs, but any assessment of this 'input' legitimacy must take account of the ends to which the Court employs those procedures.

D   Output Legitimacy

A final aspect of institutional legitimacy relates to the outputs the institution produces. For the ICC, the most important outputs are the punishments it inflicts and any benefits (or detriments) that accrue from its work to victims, the societies where the crimes occurred, or the global community. In these contexts, like those discussed earlier, commentators often make recommendations about how the ICC can enhance its legitimacy without addressing the global–local dilemma.

1   Punishment

Because the ICC has only recently begun to sentence defendants, scholars have yet to focus significant attention on the legitimacy of the Court's sentencing practices. However, a substantial literature exists critiquing the sentencing practices of other international criminal courts, some of which includes prescriptive suggestions for the ICC.[83] Some scholars argue that international sentences should be harsher,[84] while others suggest leniency is more in line with human rights norms.[85] Many commentators urge international courts to be more consistent in their sentencing practices, often favoring the adoption of sentencing

---

[83] *See, e.g.*, R. D. Sloane, The expressive capacity of international punishment: The limits of the national law analogy and the potential of international criminal law. *Stanford Journal of International Law*, 43 (2007); A. M. Danner, Constructing a hierarchy of crimes in international criminal law sentencing. *Virginia Law Review*, 87 (2001); R. Henham, Developing contextualized rationales for sentencing in international criminal trials. *Journal of International Criminal Justice*, 5 (2007); J. D. Ohlin, Proportional sentences at the ICTY. In B. Swart et al., eds., *The Legacy of the International Criminal Tribunal for the Former Yugoslavia* (Oxford, UK: Oxford University Press, 2011), p. 322.

[84] *See, e.g.*, J. D. Ohlin, Towards a unique theory of international criminal sentencing. In G. Sluiter and S. Vasiliev, eds., *International Criminal Procedure: Towards a Coherent Body of Law* (London: Cameron May, 2009), p. 381, 390; Ohlin, Proportional sentences, p. 322; Glickman, Victim's justice.

[85] M. M. deGuzman, Harsh justice for international crimes. *Yale Journal of International Law*, 39 (2014), 2; W. A. Schabas, Sentencing by international tribunals: A human rights approach. *Duke Journal of Comparative and International Law*, 7 (1997), 498–505.

guidelines.[86] In contrast, at least one scholar argues for a pluralist approach to international sentencing that takes account of the sentencing norms of the states where the crimes occurred.[87]

Such critiques of international sentencing practice, including at the ICC, have generally not taken into account the global–local dilemma. Yet whether the ICC should inflict harsh, lenient, or moderate sentences, and whether it should adopt a uniform or pluralist sentencing practice, surely depends at least in part on whether the institution aims primarily at global or local justice. A local justice agenda militates in favor of adopting the punishment norms of the societies most affected by the crimes. Harsh retributive sentencing would appeal to people in some states, but would be seen as cruel in other parts of the world. On the other hand, a global justice agenda suggests that the ICC should develop a unique sentencing practice that aims to promote global norms effectively and efficiently.[88]

2 Impact on Victims, Communities, and the Global Community

One of the most common critiques of the ICC's output legitimacy is that the institution is failing adequately to address the needs of crime victims and affected communities.[89] Laurel Fletcher notes that the discourse concerning the ICC's legitimacy tends to make victims key arbiters of that legitimacy.[90] Victims are portrayed as deserving justice and the ICC as a tool for fulfilling this entitlement.[91] According to Fletcher, a key impediment to the ICC's legitimacy is that the Court equates justice with retributive justice, whereas victims of international crimes may desire other forms of justice, such as restorative justice.[92]

---

[86] D. B. Pickard, Proposed sentencing guidelines for the International Criminal Court. *Loyola of Los Angeles International and Comparative Law Review*, 20 (1997), 124.

[87] Nancy Combs, Seeking inconsistency.

[88] I have developed this argument in Proportionate sentencing at the International Criminal Court. In C. Stahn, ed., *The Law and Practice of the International Criminal Court* (Oxford, UK: Oxford University Press, 2014).

[89] *See, e.g.*, L. Moffett, Meaningful and effective? Considering victims' interests through participation at the International Criminal Court. *Criminal Law Forum*, 26 (2015), 255 (arguing that the ICC does not give adequate weight to victims' interests and claiming that improvement in this area would increase the Court's legitimacy).

[90] L. E. Fletcher, Refracted justice: The imagined victim and the International Criminal Court. In C. De Vos, S. Kendall, and C. Stahn, eds., *Contested Justice: The Politics and Practice of International Criminal Court Interventions* (Cambridge, UK: Cambridge University Press, 2014).

[91] Ibid.   [92] Ibid.

Marlieus Glasius takes a similar view, arguing that the legitimacy of an international organization like the ICC depends on its entering into a communicative relationship with the societies most affected by the crimes at issue.[93] Lauren Marie Balasco asserts that the moral justification for the ICC's authority rests in significant part on its ability to protect and empower victims and argues that the Court's failure to achieve this goal has damaged its legitimacy.[94] Balasco urges the ICC to work harder to fulfill its role as a 'human security agent'.[95] Similarly, Jeremy Sarkin encourages the ICC to play a greater role in local transitional justice.[96]

Again, whether greater attention to the needs of victims and their communities will enhance the ICC's legitimacy depends on how the institution's central purpose is conceived. The critics discussed earlier implicitly adopt a local justice vision of the ICC's work.[97] A global justice approach, in contrast, would focus less on meeting victims' needs and more on ensuring that the ICC identifies and fulfills the justice objectives of the global community. As noted earlier, these two goals are not always in tension. Some ICC decisions can both meet victims' needs and promote global norms. Indeed, promoting victims' needs sometimes helps to promote global justice, by, for instance, expressing the victims' value in the face of contrary expression by offenders. Nonetheless, an ICC primarily oriented toward global justice objectives would almost certainly invest fewer resources in pursuing victims' justice objectives than one with a central focus on local justice.

IV Conclusion

The lack of clarity about whether the ICC should privilege local or global justice goals is a central impediment to the institution developing

---

[93] Glasius, Democratic legitimacy?

[94] L. M. Balasco, The International Criminal Court as a human security agent. *The Fletcher Journal of Human Security*, 28 (2013).

[95] Ibid.

[96] J. Sarkin, Enhancing the legitimacy, status, and role of the International Criminal Court globally by using transitional justice and restorative justice strategies. *Interdisciplinary Journal of Human Rights Law*, 6 (2011).

[97] D. Tolbert, Taking Stock of the Impact of the Rome Statute and the International Criminal Court on Victims and Affected Communities. International Center of Transitional Justice, available at http://docplayer.net/11912251-Taking-stock-of-the-impact-of-the-rome-statute-and-the-international-criminal-court-on-victims-and-affected-communities .html ('Ultimately, the success of the Court will hinge on whether it is perceived as an effective option in terms of delivering justice for the victims of the world's worst crimes'.).

stronger legitimacy. Rather than limiting their critiques to isolated aspects of the Court's work, scholars should address this underlying challenge. Once greater consensus is achieved around the ICC's core mission, the institution will be better placed to develop procedures and to shape outputs that build its normative and sociological legitimacy.

In the short term, as the Court seeks to hone its core mission, its sociological legitimacy will likely continue to suffer. The institution's initial reserve of good will, based on its laudable but ambiguous mission of 'ending impunity for serious crimes', has begun to dwindle. Taking a clearer stand – whether in favor of a global or local emphasis – will surely alienate some audiences further. Victim populations in states with situations currently before the Court will likely feel betrayed if the Court declares a primarily global mission, and some states parties may be less inclined to support a Court that devotes its resources primarily to helping victims in other states.

Nonetheless, continuing to purport to pursue both missions equally is not a good option for the ICC. Without greater clarity about whether the ICC is centrally a global or local justice institution, each audience will continue to experience unmet expectations and frustrations with the Court's procedures and outputs. Instead, the ICC, with the help of states parties, scholars, civil society organizations, and other supporters of the international criminal justice project, should work to identify and articulate a mission that includes clearer priorities between global and local justice objectives. As the ICC's mission becomes clearer and more widely accepted, its legitimacy – both normative and sociological – is likely to improve.

4

Justice as Legitimacy in the European Court of Human Rights

MOLLY K. LAND[*]

I Introduction

How far should an international human rights court go to protect unpopular groups from the tyranny of the domestic majority? At first glance, the legitimacy challenges faced by the European Court of Human Rights (ECtHR) after its prisoner voting cases would seem to reflect a relatively limited ability of human rights courts to protect unpopular minorities when faced with substantial opposition among important compliance communities. Outcry in the United Kingdom in response to the Court's decisions finding the UK ban on prisoner voting inconsistent with the European Convention on Human Rights was unusually vociferous, with several in the government even calling for withdrawal from the Convention. Although the Court has refused to reconsider its prior judgments, it has gone to great lengths since then to narrow these decisions – even upholding an Italian law that can be viewed as more restrictive of prisoners' rights than the original law at issue in the United Kingdom.

Yet the controversy over prisoner voting is not only, or even necessarily, a story about limits on the Court's ability to protect vulnerable populations. For human rights courts such as the ECtHR, interpreting their mandates expansively to protect unpopular groups can be an affirmative source of legitimacy. Moral decisions by such courts are both normatively legitimate and also foster perceptions of legitimacy. Thus, expanding the reach of the European Convention on Human Rights to protect vulnerable and unpopular groups can also contribute to the

---

[*] Professor of Law and Human Rights, University of Connecticut School of Law and Human Rights Institute. Many thanks to Richard Kay and to the participants in the Legitimacy and International Courts Symposium at the University of Baltimore for helpful comments and feedback. Dorothy Diaz-Hennessey, Tatyana Marugg, and Stacey Samuel provided excellent research assistance.

legitimacy of the Court. Indeed, the Court's retroactive narrowing of its earlier decisions on prisoner voting may be a greater threat to its legitimacy than the original reaction its judgment provoked in the United Kingdom. When a court that derives its legitimacy from its moral compass bows to political pressure, it risks doing violence to the perception that it is a moral actor, which may be a critical part of the foundation of its legitimacy. In other words, in some cases, human rights courts may have to be principled to survive.

Using the example of the ECtHR, this chapter builds on existing literature regarding the legitimacy of judicial institutions to consider the role of justice as a component of the normative and sociological legitimacy of international human rights courts. In so doing, the chapter identifies the pursuit of just outcomes as an important independent influence on the legitimacy of the Court and perhaps of human rights courts more broadly. The chapter first provides an overview of the ways in which justice, as a form of moral legitimacy, has been examined in the literature on legitimacy and international courts. Then, it uses the case law of the ECtHR to illustrate the way in which justice appears to be functioning as an independent basis for the Court's legitimacy. As the Court expands the rights protected by the Convention and applies them to new situations, the legitimacy of reaching just outcomes seems to be doing considerable work in building the legitimacy of the Court.

In considering the role justice plays in the work of the Court, the chapter also contributes to the ongoing discussion about how to promote compliance with the judgments of human rights courts. The chapter argues that the perceived justice of the Court's decisions fosters a culture of obedience that promotes state compliance. As a result, the potential injustice of the Court's retreat from its earlier decisions on prisoner voting may in fact pose a greater risk to the continued compliance pull of the Court's judgments than the initial backlash. The experience of the ECtHR indicates that for human rights courts, their ability to successfully demand compliance with their decisions may depend at least in part on whether they act in ways that are consistent with their image as moral actors, even if it is at the expense of other modes of legitimacy.

II   Justice and Legitimacy

It seems that there are as many definitions of legitimacy as there are scholars writing about it. Broadly, however, most distinguish between two different ways of thinking about the legitimacy of an institution.

The first is a sociological or empirical approach, which asks whether the institution is perceived as legitimate by relevant constituencies.[1] The second is a normative approach, typically used in philosophy and political theory, that asks whether the institution in fact possesses justified authority, such as in terms of law or expertise.[2] Fundamentally, the distinction between normative and sociological legitimacy is one between fact and belief about facts – that is, whether the institution "has *the right to rule*" (normative legitimacy) and "is widely *believed* to have the right to rule" (sociological or empirical legitimacy).[3]

Although empirical and normative approaches to legitimacy are different in terms of what they measure, when, and by whom,[4] the distinction between the two is often blurred in practice. Moreover, the two approaches are complementary, interdependent, and mutually constitutive. They are complementary because normative and sociological legitimacy can be understood as different ways to measure justified authority.[5] The concepts are interdependent because they depend on one another for meaning; we cannot understand beliefs about legitimate authority unless we also examine the normative grounds on which those beliefs are built.[6] Finally, normative and sociological legitimacy are also mutually constitutive because acting in a normatively legitimate way can promote public perceptions of legitimacy.[7] This chapter uses both conceptions of legitimacy to evaluate the role of justice in the legitimacy of

---

[1] See, e.g., Yuval Shany, *Assessing the Effectiveness of International Courts* (Oxford University Press, 2014), p. 138.

[2] D. Bodansky, "The concept of legitimacy in international law" in R. Wolfrum and V. Röben (eds.), *Legitimacy in International Law* (Berlin: Springer, 2008), p. 313; R. Wolfrum, "Legitimacy in international law from a legal perspective: Some introductory considerations," in Wolfrum and Röben (eds.), *Legitimacy in International Law*, p. 6.

[3] A. Buchanan and R. Keohane, "The legitimacy of global governance institutions" in Wolfrum and Röben (eds.), *Legitimacy in International Law*, p. 25 (emphasis in original); see also Aida Torres Pérez, *Conflicts of Rights in the European Union: A Theory of Supranational Adjudication* (Oxford University Press, 2009), p. 99 (distinguishing between whether an institution is obeyed and ought to be obeyed).

[4] Bodansky, "Concept of legitimacy," 313, 315.

[5] M. Loth, "Courts in a quest for legitimacy: A comparative approach" in N. Huls, J. Bomhoff, and M. Adams (eds.), *The Legitimacy of Highest Courts' Rulings: Judicial Deliberations and Beyond* (The Hague: T.M.C. Asser Press, 2009), pp. 268–9.

[6] B. Çalı, A. Koch, and N. Bruch, "The legitimacy of human rights courts: A grounded interpretivist analysis of the European Court of Human Rights," *Human Rights Quarterly*, v. 35 (2013), 955, 957–8.

[7] A. Follesdal, "The legitimacy deficits of the human rights judiciary: Elements and implications of a normative theory," *Theoretical Inquiries in the Law*, v. 14 (2013), 339, 346; Pérez, "Conflicts of Rights," 99.

the ECtHR. It considers justice as an aspect of normative legitimacy, like legality or efficacy,[8] and evaluates the extent to which acting in a just manner increases the extent to which the Court is perceived as legitimate.

Justice as an independent dimension of the legitimacy of international tribunals has been less well developed in the literature. Nienke Grossman has called for an alternative approach to legitimacy that includes both procedural and substantive justice as independent determinants of a tribunal's legitimacy.[9] Substantive justice, in this view, relates to the "just-ness" of the outcomes of the tribunal's decision-making process, separate and apart from the extent to which these outcomes correspond to the law.[10] Thus, a decision could be just even if it would not be legal. At the same time, although justice and legality are different concepts, they are nonetheless closely related. The legitimacy of law depends on the extent to which it conforms with "broadly held notions of justice."[11] Moreover, it may be difficult for courts to be seen as legitimate if they render decisions in tension with the law given their position as guardians and interpreters of the law.[12]

Justice is independent of judicial effectiveness, which also contributes to a court's legitimacy. As Yuval Shany notes in Chapter 13, judicial effectiveness can be viewed along three dimensions – "the degree [to] which organizations actually attain the goals set for them by important constituencies, . . . the impact of organizations on their social environment and . . . the ability of organizations to attract the resources necessary for their survival and growth."[13] In the abstract, justice and effectiveness are separate and independent concepts; a decision could be just but still be ineffective in furthering a court's mandate, influencing its

---

[8] N. Grossman, "Legitimacy and International Adjudicative Bodies," *George Washington International Law Review*, v. 41 (2009), 107, 124–42; Shany, *Assessing the Effectiveness*, p. 6.

[9] N. Grossman, "The normative legitimacy of international courts," *Temple Law Review*, 86 (2013), 61, 64. For additional discussion of procedural justice, see also Grossman, "Legitimacy and international adjudicative bodies," 124; J. P. Costa, "On the legitimacy of the European Court of Human Rights' Judgments," *European Constitutional Law Review*, 7 (2011), 173, 175. See generally Tom Tyler, *Why People Obey the Law* (Princeton, NJ: Princeton University Press, 1990), p. 5 (connecting procedural fairness and compliance).

[10] See Grossman, "Legitimacy and international adjudicative bodies," 115–17; T. Treves, "Aspects of legitimacy of decisions of international courts and tribunals," in Wolfrum and Röben (eds.), *Legitimacy in International Law*, 170.

[11] Shany, *Assessing the Effectiveness*, p. 140.   [12] Treves, "Aspects of legitimacy," 178.

[13] Shany, Chapter 13.

environment, or attracting resources. For human rights courts, however, justice and effectiveness are likely closely related in most cases because the mandate of a human rights court is to protect human rights, and thus just decisions will promote that mandate. Nonetheless, even a human rights court might act to protect a vulnerable group in ways that exceed its mandate. Indeed, one might argue that the prisoner voting cases are examples of precisely this.

This chapter builds on Grossman's work to consider justice as a factor that by itself can foster a tribunal's normative and sociological legitimacy. Typically, when justice is discussed with reference to an international court's legitimacy, it is as a necessary but not a sufficient condition of legitimacy. The presence of *injustice* can undermine the legitimacy of an institution,[14] but it is unclear whether and if so how *doing justice* can affirmatively promote such an institution's legitimacy. Indeed, in most accounts, affirmatively doing justice is seen as illegitimate, thus depleting a court's legitimacy reserves, especially if the court disregards law in the process.[15] This chapter argues, in contrast, that for human rights courts, achieving just outcomes can in the right circumstances also bolster their general legitimacy.[16]

This is not to say that "justice" by itself can legitimize otherwise illegitimate conduct, except perhaps in extreme cases.[17] Nor is it to argue

---

[14] See, e.g., Shany, *Assessing the Effectiveness*, p. 144 (the legitimacy of a decision is limited if it "sharply conflicts with basic notions of justice"); Grossman, "Normative legitimacy," 103 (failing to protect human rights undermines the legitimacy of human rights courts); Treves, "Aspects of legitimacy," 177 (the legitimacy of an international tribunal can be negatively affected if it fails to reach issues due to jurisdictional limits).

[15] These perspectives assume that a tribunal must have sufficient general legitimacy to sustain its efforts to do justice when doing so will be unpopular. See Shany, *Assessing the Effectiveness*, p. 147; see also S. Dothan, "How international courts enhance their legitimacy," *Theoretical Inquiries in the Law*, 14 (2013), 455, 456; G. Letsas, "The ECHR as a living instrument: Its meaning and legitimacy" in A. Follesdal, B. Peters, and G. Ulfstein (eds.), *Constituting Europe: The European Court of Human Rights in a National, European and Global Context* (Cambridge University Press, 2013), p. 125.

[16] It is unclear whether justice could function in a similar manner for other kinds of international tribunals. It may be that justice has a special meaning and role for human rights courts given their mandate to protect and promote human rights. Justice may be relevant to a non–human rights court to the extent it is viewed as having moral authority or vested with a responsibility to pursue moral aims. In such a situation, the pursuit of just outcomes might similarly bolster the court's authority even in the absence of a clear legal basis for its decision.

[17] Shany, *Assessing the Effectiveness*, p. 144 ("second-order considerations relating to the epistemological uncertainty surrounding questions of justice support reference to morality as a counterweight to formal authority only in exceptional cases where the conflict

88 MOLLY K. LAND

in favor of justice-oriented legitimacy over any other particular measure. As Shany notes, legitimacy is not an "on/off" switch, and the legitimacy of any given institution is at any one point in time a product of many different factors.[18] The purpose is merely to interrogate the extent to which achieving just outcomes plays a role in fostering the perception of legitimacy of one particular international human rights court. The chapter focuses on a human rights court because of the unique mandate of such courts to protect individual rights. The different demands placed on different kinds of adjudicatory bodies call for different theories of legitimacy,[19] and for human rights tribunals, justice may have a uniquely important role to play.

Although substantive justice refers to just outcomes, what constitutes a "just" outcome may depend on the court and the context in question. Those who have considered the role of just outcomes in promoting the legitimacy of institutions have defined such outcomes as those that reflect and embody general principles of morality[20] or human rights.[21] In arguing that justice should be understood as an independently legitimating factor for international tribunals, Grossman, for example, defines substantive justice as respect for a minimum core of human rights.[22] At the same time, although respect for a minimum core of human rights would seem to be an appropriate baseline for evaluating the justice of the decisions of international courts as a whole, justice for human rights courts – with their special and unique obligations and mandate – must mean something more. In addition, while failure to protect human rights would certainly deprive a human rights court of its justified authority,[23] this does not necessarily answer the question of what it means for such a court to act in a just manner.

This chapter defines just outcomes for human rights courts as outcomes that expand human rights protection and, in particular, the

---

between law and morality is clear and strong"). Even in extreme cases, a variety of factors may lead judges to enforce positive law at odds with their moral convictions. See Robert Cover, *Justice Accused: Antislavery and the Judicial Process* (New Haven, CT: Yale University Press, 1975) (antislavery judges enforcing the Fugitive Slave Acts); Tyler, *Why People Obey*, p. 68 (noting that people may comply with the law because it is the law, even if it is unjust).

[18] Shany, *Assessing the Effectiveness*, p. 143.
[19] Bodansky, "Concept of legitimacy," 315–16.
[20] R. Müllerson, "Aspects of legitimacy of decisions of international courts and tribunals: comments" in Wolfrum and Röben (eds.), *Legitimacy in International Law*, p. 191.
[21] Buchanan and Keohane, "Legitimacy of global governance institutions," 43–4.
[22] Grossman, "Normative Legitimacy," 97.   [23] Ibid., 103.

protections available for those in society who are most vulnerable. This definition draws inspiration from two sources. First, it evokes the progressive nature of human rights law, which evolves both to meet new challenges and to continually increase levels of protection. Buchanan and Keohane, for example, define minimum moral acceptability as achieving ever higher human rights standards as those rights evolve.[24] Second, this definition of justice draws on both the unique role of courts in general and human rights courts in particular. Human rights courts can be viewed as trustees that are empowered to exercise their authority on behalf of victims of human rights violations,[25] and it is this emphasis on the interests of the least powerful that distinguishes the use of a human rights framework.[26] Finally, courts in general are also often viewed as having a special role in protecting the powerless from the tyranny of the majority.[27]

What it means for a court to act in a just manner under this definition will depend on the particular court in question and the context in which the decision occurs. For a young human rights court, even reaching a decision may be a significant step toward consolidating its authority and thereby moving progressively forward toward greater rights protection. In some of its earliest cases, for example, the ECtHR solidified its position by refraining from issuing judgments that would have significantly

---

[24] Buchanan and Keohane, "Legitimacy of global governance institutions," 44.

[25] Karen Alter, *The New Terrain of International Law: Courts, Politics, Rights* (Princeton, NJ: Princeton University Press, 2014), p. 9 (key insight of the trustee model is that "judges exercise their power on behalf of the trust's beneficiaries"); *see also* K. Alter, "Delegation to international courts and the limits of re-contracting political power" in D. Hawkins, D. Lake, D. Nielson, and M. Tierney (eds.), *Delegation and Agency in International Organizations* (Cambridge University Press, 2006), p. 316 (human rights courts as trustees).

[26] E. Benvenisti, "Margin of appreciation, consensus, and universal standards," *New York University Journal of International Law and Politics*, 31 (1998–1999), 843, 850 ("One of the main justifications for an international system for the protection of human rights lies in the opportunity it provides for promoting the interests of minorities."). Other theories of justice may counsel different definitions; this chapter uses a human rights approach as the animating frame for understanding justice in the context of human rights tribunals.

[27] See *United States v. Carolene Prods. Co.*, 304 U.S. 144, 152 n.4 (1938) (finding it unnecessary to determine "whether prejudice against discrete and insular minorities may be a special condition, which tends seriously to curtail the operation of those political processes ordinarily to be relied upon to protect minorities, and which may call for a correspondingly more searching judicial inquiry"). This chapter considers only the potential effect of just outcomes on the normative and perceived legitimacy of human rights courts. It does not address the related countermajoritarian, antidemocratic objection to international courts overruling the decisions of national legislatures. See generally Follesdal, "The legitimacy deficits of the human rights judiciary."

90 MOLLY K. LAND

challenged state sovereignty.[28] In the 1970s, after it was more established, the Court progressively moved the law forward with a series of decisions that signaled a more assertive approach.[29] The justice of a particular outcome will also depend on the case and the trade-offs that the outcome involves – for example, whether the decision involves limits on the human rights of others – as well as the geopolitical context in which the court operates.

The decisions of the ECtHR today, particularly in cases involving the United Kingdom, have reflected a definition of justice focused on the protection of unpopular groups – namely, prisoners and suspected terrorists.[30] The Court has expanded the rights of prisoners to vote in public elections[31] and, for those sentenced to life in prison, to review of the possibility of early release.[32] The Court's judgments have also limited the ability of the government to detain and deport terrorism suspects, constrained the use of secret evidence, and required suspects to have avenues for legal recourse.[33] For the ECtHR, achieving just outcomes that expand the protection of human rights and protect the interests of society's most vulnerable is strongly legitimate.

Further, although beyond the scope of this chapter, it is reasonable to think that an orientation on the protection of the least powerful would likely be legitimizing for human rights courts in general. As Follesdal notes, "[t]he first reason why the human rights judiciary may be justifiable and hence normatively legitimate is that a well-functioning *international* human rights judiciary provides further protection of vulnerable domestic groups."[34] As a practical matter, however, the ability of a court to act in this normatively justified way depends in part on whether its pursuit of just outcomes is perceived as legitimate.

---

[28] N. Krisch, "The open architecture of European human rights law," *The Modern Law Review*, 71 (2008), 183, 205.

[29] M. Madsen, "Explaining the power of international courts in their contexts: From legitimacy to legitimatization" in A. Dreyzin de Klor, M. Poiares Maduro, and A. Vauchez (eds.), *Courts, Social Change and Judicial Independence* (San Domenico di Fiesole, Italy: RSCAS, 2012), p. 27.

[30] Courtney Hillebrecht, *Domestic Politics and International Human Rights Tribunals: The Problem of Compliance* (Cambridge University Press, 2014), pp. 102–12.

[31] *Hirst v. United Kingdom (no. 2)* [GC], no. 74025/01, ECHR 2005-IX; *Greens and M.T. v. United Kingdom*, nos. 60041/08 and 60054/08, ECHR 2011.

[32] *Vinter and Others v. United Kingdom* [GC], nos. 66069/09, 130/10 and 3896/10, ECHR 2013.

[33] *A. and Others v. United Kingdom* [GC], no. 3455/05, ECHR 2009.

[34] Follesdal, "The legitimacy deficits of the human rights judiciary," 355.

That is the question this chapter addresses in the context of the prisoners' rights cases before the ECtHR.

III   Legitimacy Challenges at the ECtHR

The ECtHR currently faces two different types of legitimacy challenges. The first relates to its very large caseload, which has impeded its ability to deliver procedural fairness. Despite substantial reforms designed to reduce the backlog of cases, the Court still had over 64,000 pending applications as of March 31, 2015.[35] The second legitimacy challenge relates to its balance of concern for sovereignty and human rights – specifically, the concern that the Court unduly limits the first to protect the second.[36] These legitimacy challenges are not necessarily unrelated; some have argued that the Court's caseload would be smaller if it adopted more restrictive interpretive approaches that deferred more to member states, although this is not likely given that most of its caseload relates to issues that are relatively well settled under the Court's jurisprudence.[37]

This chapter focuses on the second of these legitimacy challenges to consider the role of just outcomes in the legitimacy of the Court. This section argues that the Court's judgments appear in many instances to be driven by the logic of justice rather than law. The Court's adoption of a teleological approach that is in some instances only weakly tethered to

---

[35] European Court of Human Rights, Statistics 30/11/2015, www.echr.coe.int/Documents/Stats_month_2015_ENG.pdf.

[36] See A. Bradley, "Introduction: The need for both international and national protection of human rights – The European challenge" in S. Flogaitis, T. Zwart, and J. Fraser (eds.), *The European Court of Human Rights and Its Discontents: Turning Criticism Into Strength* (Cheltenham: Edward Elgar Publishing Limited, 2013), pp. 4–5; S. Greer, "The legal and constitutional impact of the European Convention on Human Rights in the United Kingdom," *Ius Gentium*, 16 (2012), 189, 194.

[37] J. Gerards, "The scope of ECHR rights and institutional concerns: The relationship between proliferation of rights and the case load of the ECtHR" in E. Brems and J. Gerards (eds.), *Shaping Rights in the ECHR: The Role of the European Court of Human Rights in Determining the Scope of Human Rights* (Cambridge University Press, 2013), p. 91. Most attribute the Court's rising caseload to the introduction of the right of individual petition and the expansion of the Council of Europe, as well as greater awareness of the Court and distrust of national institutions in many of the new member states. See A. Sweet, "The European Convention on Human Rights and national constitutional reordering," *Cardozo Law Review*, 33 (2012), 1859, 1860; L. Caflisch, "Reform of the European Court of Human Rights: Protocol No. 14 and Beyond," *Human Rights Law Review*, 6 (2006) 403, 403–5.

92   MOLLY K. LAND

the Convention's text and drafting history evidences a preoccupation with achieving just outcomes – namely, ever greater protection of rights, with special attention to the vulnerable.

A Expansionist Methodologies

Although much of the criticism of the Court today claims it overreaches into state sovereignty, early critiques saw it as too respectful of sovereignty, relying on deferential doctrines such as the margin of appreciation to provide states with latitude in protecting the rights enumerated in the Convention. The margin of appreciation is a doctrine that the Court employs in different ways; among other things, the Court uses it as a doctrine of deference that considers the practice of other European states in evaluating whether a challenged state action is within the range of activity that would be consistent with the Convention.[38] As demonstrated in its 2010 decision in *A, B and C v. Ireland*, addressing restrictive laws in Ireland governing access to abortion,[39] the margin of appreciation continues to fulfill this function today, at least in part. Nonetheless, the Court has clearly expanded the scope of the Convention's protections over time.[40] Some argue that this shift toward more expansive lawmaking occurred with the introduction of Protocol No. 11 in 1998,[41] while others

[38] See K. Dzehtsiarou, "European consensus and the evolutive interpretation of the European Convention on Human Rights," *German Law Journal*, 12 (2011), 1730. The margin has been critiqued as providing insufficient methodological rigor and creating tension with concepts of universality of human rights. See generally Y. Arai-Takahashi, "The margin of appreciation doctrine: A theoretical analysis of Strasbourg's variable geometry" in Follesdal, Peters, and Ulfstein (eds.), *Constituting Europe*, pp. 78–81; Benvenisti, "Margin of appreciation," 843–44; O. Gross and F. Aoláin, "From discretion to scrutiny: Revisiting the application of the margin of appreciation doctrine in the context of Article 15 of the European Convention of Human Rights," *Human Rights Quarterly*, 23 (2001), 625, 628–9; J. Brauch, "The margin of appreciation and the jurisprudence of the European Court of Human Rights: Threat to the rule of law," *Columbia Journal of European Law*, 11 (2004/2005), 113, 125–47.

[39] *A, B and C v. Ireland* [GC], no. 25579/05, ¶¶ 241, 267, ECHR 2010. Although the Court ultimately found a procedural violation of the Convention, it relied on the margin of appreciation to hold that Ireland's restriction of access to abortion within Ireland to cases in which the health of the mother is in danger, was consistent with the Convention. The state was to be afforded a broad margin of appreciation given the "acute sensitivity of the moral and ethical issues" involved. Ibid. ¶¶ 233–36.

[40] L. Helfer, "Consensus, coherence and the European Convention on Human Rights," *Cornell International Law Journal*, 26 (1993), 133, 134.

[41] See Letsas, "The ECHR as a living instrument," 125.

locate the timing of the shift in the mid-1970s.[42] Shany and Lovat cite in particular the Court's decisions in *Golder, Tyrer, Marckx*, and *Airey* as marking the Court's turn to a more assertive mode of interpretation.[43]

In addition to extending the Convention to new areas such as procedural and economic rights,[44] the Court also expands the protections of Convention through the use of interpretive doctrines such as the living instrument approach, the doctrine of effective protection, the principle of autonomous interpretation, and in some instances, the margin of appreciation itself.

The living instrument approach is founded on the idea that the Convention must be interpreted in light of conditions existing at the time of interpretation, rather than what the drafting parties may have intended.[45] This approach, also called "evolutive" or "dynamic" interpretation,[46] allows the Court to privilege its own interpretation of the rights protected by the Convention and to revise its position if it finds that rights once within the margin of appreciation now constitute violations of the Convention.

The principle of practical and effective protection counsels adoption of interpretations of Convention rights that have practical impact.[47] It provides a vehicle for the Court to reject formalistic interpretations that, although perhaps complying with the letter of the law, would have little to no practical impact.[48] In other instances, the principle of effective protection is invoked when the Court is faced with a choice between two

---

[42] Shany (with H. Lovat), *Assessing the Effectiveness*, p. 266; K. Dzehtsiarou, "Interaction between the European Court of Human Rights and member states: European consensus, advisory opinions and the question of legitimacy," in Flogaitis, Zwart, and Fraser (eds.), The European Court of Human Rights and Its Discontents, p. 119.

[43] Shany (with H. Lovat), *Assessing the Effectiveness*, p. 266.

[44] See, e.g., I. Leijten, "Defining the scope of economic and social guarantees in the case law of the ECtHR" in Brems and Gerards (eds.), *Shaping Rights in the ECHR*, p. 109; E. Brems, "Procedural protection: An examination of procedural safeguards read into substantive convention rights," in Brems and Gerards (eds.), *Shaping Rights in the ECHR*, p. 137.

[45] *Tyrer v. United Kingdom* [GC], no. 5856/72, ¶ 31, ECHR 1978-A26.

[46] George Letsas, *A Theory of Interpretation of the European Convention on Human Rights* (New York: Oxford University Press, 2007), p. 65.

[47] J. G. Merrills, *The Development of International Law by the European Court of Human Rights* (New York: Manchester University Press, 1993), pp. 98–9.

[48] For example, in *Artico v. Italy*, the Court rejected the state's position that its obligation to provide a lawyer was fulfilled by the initial appointment even though the attorney then withdrew. *Artico v. Italy*, no. 6694/74, ¶ 33, ECHR 1980-A37.

different interpretations to justify the choice of the interpretation that is more protective of Convention rights.[49]

Developed in *Engel v. Netherlands*, the principle of autonomous interpretation states that the Court is not required to use the classifications of rights given to them by a state[50] but must exercise independent judgment to ascertain the meaning of Convention rights.

Finally, the margin of appreciation also supports expansionist lawmaking in some cases. Although the margin has historically been associated with deference, the Court also invokes the margin of appreciation to find that a European consensus precludes the national action in question. In *Hirst (no. 2)*, for example, the Court invoked the margin but found that there was in fact a European consensus against automatic, undifferentiated disenfranchisement of prisoners.[51]

The application of these expansionist tools has resulted in ever higher standards of protections under the Convention. I use Helfer and Alter's definition of expansionist lawmaking as a court's identification of "new legal obligations or constraints not found in treaty texts or supported by the intentions of their drafters, and when these obligations or constraints narrow states' discretion."[52] The Court clearly uses its interpretive methodologies to constrain state discretion in ways that are not tied to text or intent. In a recent case, for example, the Court explicitly disavowed reliance on the text of the Convention, finding that trafficking ran counter to the "spirit and purpose" of Article 4 regardless of whether it constituted "slavery," "servitude," or "forced or compulsory labour."[53] In addition, although drafting history is only a supplementary means of treaty interpretation[54] and there are reasons to be cautious about the use

---

[49] *Soering v. United Kingdom*, no. 14038/88, ¶ 90, ECHR 1989-A161 (choosing an interpretation of Article 3 that required consideration of the harm the applicant would suffer if he were extradited to the United States).

[50] For example, in *Engle and Others v. Netherlands*, the Court was not bound by the determination by the state as to whether a proceeding was criminal in nature. *Engel and Others v. Netherlands*, nos. 5100/71, 5101/71, 5102/71, 5354/72, 5370/72, ¶ 81, ECHR 1976-A22.

[51] *Hirst (no. 2)* [GC], ¶ 81.

[52] L. Helfer and K. Alter, "Legitimacy and lawmaking: A tale of three international courts," *Theoretical Inquiries in Law*, 14 (2013), 479, 482 (citation omitted); Letsas, "The ECHR as a Living Instrument," 123 (noting a "gradual severing of interpretive links" with the text and the intent of the parties).

[53] *Rantsev v. Cyprus and Russia*, no. 25965/04, ¶¶ 279, 282, ECHR 2010. See also *Golder v. The United Kingdom*, no. 4451/70, ¶ 36, ECHR 1975-A18 (finding a right of access to court inherent in the fair trial guarantee of Article 6 of the Convention).

[54] Vienna Convention on the Law of Treaties, Vienna, 23 May 1969, in force 27 January 1980, 1155 UNTS 331; (1969) 8 ILM 679; UKTS (1980) 58, art. 32.

of drafting history to interpret a multilateral human rights treaty,[55] the Court's disregard of the drafters' intent can also be troubling. In *Young, James and Webster*, for example, the Court has recognized a right to be free from compelled association that the drafting history clearly indicated had been intentionally omitted from the Convention.[56]

Although expansionist interpretations of the Convention have a reasonable legal basis given the object and purpose of the Convention, it does seem that something other than law is motivating the Court when it uses these methodological approaches. As Wheatley notes: "In developing a dynamic and teleological interpretation of Convention rights, the ECtHR has brought into being an autonomous legal order that is subject neither to the individual will of a state party nor the collective wills of state parties."[57] The untethering of its interpretive methodologies from text and intent has the function of allowing the Court far more discretion with respect to the outcome – including the ability to ensure its outcomes are just.[58]

B The Prisoner Voting Cases

The Court has most recently faced significant criticism in connection with its decisions regarding prisoner voting in the United Kingdom. Those decisions have led to charges of unchecked expansionist lawmaking and fueled opposition to the Court within the United Kingdom.

---

[55] *See* A. Mowbray, "Between the will of the contracting parties and the needs of today: Extending the scope of convention rights and freedoms beyond what could have been foreseen by the drafters of the ECHR," in E. Brems and J. Gerards (eds.), *Shaping Rights in the ECHR*, p. 20 (discussing the drafters' lack of consensus on key issues); G. Letsas, "Intentionalism and the Interpretation of the ECHR" in M. Fitzmaurice, O. Elias, and P. Merkouris (eds.), *Treaty Interpretation and the Vienna Convention on the Law of Treaties: 30 Years On* (Leiden: Brill, 2010), p. 272 (contending that the object and purpose of the Convention justifies departure from what the drafters may have concretely intended in 1950).

[56] *Young, James and Webster v. The United Kingdom*, nos. 7601/76 and 7806/77, ¶ 57, ECHR 1981-A44.

[57] S. Wheatley, "The construction of the constitutional essentials of democratic politics by the European Court of Human Rights Following Sejdić and Finci" in R. Dickinson, E. Katselli, C. Murray, and O. Pedersen, *Examining Critical Perspectives on Human Rights* (Cambridge University Press, 2012), p. 164.

[58] Letsas, *A Theory of Interpretation*, p. 3 (describing critiques of the Court's use of "illegitimate judicial discretion"); T. Zwart, "More human rights than court: Why the legitimacy of the European Court of Human Rights is in need of repair and how it can be done," in Flogaitis, Zwart, and Fraser (eds.), *The European Court of Human Rights and Its Discontents*, p. 79 (arguing that "the Court makes policy judgments while using standards like European consensus to rationalize them").

This subsection provides background on the prisoner voting cases; the next section will consider the role that justice has played in the debate.

In 2004, the Fourth Section issued a decision in a case brought by applicant John Hirst challenging a law in the United Kingdom that barred him from voting in parliamentary or local elections as inconsistent with Article 3 of Protocol No. 1.[59] Article 3 governs elections but has been interpreted by the Court to also protect the individual rights to vote and to stand for election.[60] The UK law at issue withdrew the franchise from prisoners for the duration of an individual's incarceration. The Fourth Section left open the question about whether disenfranchisement could serve a legitimate purpose, finding the UK's law incompatible with Article 3 of Protocol No. 1 because "[i]t applies automatically to all such prisoners, irrespective of the length of their sentence and irrespective of the nature or gravity of their offence."[61] The Court noted in particular that continued disenfranchisement of the applicant did not seem to be warranted because he had served his sentence and was only being held in custody on the grounds that he was a danger to society.[62] The Fourth Section referred the decision to the Grand Chamber.

In 2005, the Grand Chamber of the Court issued a decision confirming that the United Kingdom could not, consistently with the Convention, deny prisoners the right to vote in this way. The Court emphasized that the removal of the right to vote must be tailored in two ways. First, it must be proportional to the gravity of the offense, noting that the "[s]evere measure of disenfranchisement must not ... be resorted to lightly."[63] Second, states must establish a "discernible and sufficient link between the sanction and the conduct and circumstances of the individual concerned."[64] In discussing this link, the Court explained that the right to vote could be limited to protect against acts that would destroy Convention rights and freedoms, and cited as permissible limitations the removal of the right to vote from an "an individual who has, for example, seriously abused a public position or whose conduct threatened to undermine the rule of law or democratic foundations."[65]

The Court agreed that punishment and incentivizing citizen-like behavior were permissible purposes under the Convention for limiting the right to vote.[66] It concluded, however, that the United Kingdom's ban nonetheless fell outside the margin of appreciation because it applied

---

[59] *Hirst v. United Kingdom (no. 2)*, no. 74025/01, ¶ 11, ECHR 2004 (referred to Grand Chamber).
[60] Ibid. ¶ 36.   [61] Ibid. ¶ 49.   [62] Ibid.   [63] *Hirst (no. 2)* [GC], ¶ 71.   [64] Ibid.
[65] Ibid.   [66] Ibid. ¶¶ 74–75.

"automatically to such prisoners, irrespective of the length of their sentence and irrespective of the nature or gravity of their offence and their individual circumstances."[67] According to the Court, "Such a general, automatic and indiscriminate restriction on a vitally important Convention right must be seen as falling outside any acceptable margin of appreciation, however wide that margin might be, and as being incompatible with Article 3 of Protocol No. 1."[68]

The UK government was slow in implementing *Hirst* from the start.[69] Domestic legal challenges were unsuccessful; national courts acknowledged that Section 3(1) of the 1983 Representation of the People Act, the provision that removed the right to vote from incarcerated individuals, was inconsistent with the Convention and the UK's Human Rights Act, but determined it was for the legislature to resolve the conflict.[70] The government engaged in a process of consultation but delayed in bringing proposals to the legislature; this delay was critiqued by the Joint Committee on Human Rights and identified as a subject of concern in a resolution by the Council of Ministers.[71] Several additional decisions of the Council of Ministers followed, condemning the United Kingdom's failure to implement the *Hirst* decision and allowing the 2010 elections to occur with the blanket ban in effect.[72]

Continued delay in the United Kingdom eventually brought another case to the Court. In *Greens and M.T. v. United Kingdom*, two incarcerated individuals challenged their inability to vote in the 2009 European parliamentary elections and a general election in the United Kingdom in 2010.[73] The Court's decision in this case, handed down in November 2010, noted that Section 3(1) had not been amended and determined that the United Kingdom was in continued noncompliance with the Convention.[74] In *Greens*, the Court also used the pilot judgment procedure to give the United Kingdom six months to amend the blanket voting ban, although it refrained from indicating what amendments would be acceptable.[75]

The Court's decision in *Greens* sparked intense domestic resistance. The *Daily Mail* tabloid used the case as an opportunity to launch a

---

[67] Ibid. ¶ 82.   [68] Ibid.

[69] See, e.g., A. Bradley, "Introduction: The need for both international and national protection of human rights – The European challenge," in Flogaitis, Zwart, and Fraser (eds.), *The European Court of Human Rights and Its Discontents*, p. 5; E. Myjer, "Why much of the criticism of the European Court of Human Rights is unfounded" in Flogaitis, Zwart, and Fraser (eds.), *The European Court of Human Rights and Its Discontents*, p. 43.

[70] *Greens*, ¶¶ 27–40.   [71] Ibid. ¶¶ 41, 44.   [72] Ibid. ¶¶ 45–7.   [73] Ibid. ¶ 73.

[74] Ibid. ¶¶ 78–9.   [75] Ibid. ¶¶ 114–15.

full-fledged attack on the Court as a whole.[76] Debates on proposed amendments took place in early 2011, but the British House of Commons voted in February of that year to reject the proposed amendments and uphold the voting ban.[77] In connection with that debate, Member of Parliament Philip Hollobone asked, "[H]ow has it come about that we, in a sovereign Parliament, have let these decisions be taken by a kangaroo court in Strasbourg, the judgments of which do not enjoy the respect of our constituents?"[78] Reflecting on this time period, Michael O'Boyle observes that "[t]he Court has never, in its 50-year history, been subject to such a barrage of hostile criticism as that which occurred in the United Kingdom in February 2011."[79] These criticisms even prompted calls for the United Kingdom to withdraw from the Convention.[80]

Further action on *Greens* was postponed to await the Court's 2012 decision on a similar issue in a case brought against Italy. In *Scoppola v. Italy (no. 3)*, handed down in May 2012, the Court affirmed its holding in *Hirst* but distinguished the Italian law in ways that allowed it to uphold Italy's restriction on prisoner voting.[81] Rather than a blanket ban, Italy only prohibited voting by prisoners who were sentenced to more than three years in prison. In addition, it varied the length of the ban based on the gravity of the offense; those sentenced to three to five years in prison lost the right to vote for five years, while those sentenced to greater than five years in prison lost the right permanently, with the ability to apply for rehabilitation under certain conditions.[82] In finding the law consistent with the Convention, the Court noted that it "show[ed] the legislature's concern to adjust the application of the measure to the particular circumstances of the case in hand" and, as a result, did not

---

[76] Ian Loveland, *Constitutional Law, Administrative Law, and Human Rights: A Critical Introduction*, 7th ed. (Oxford University Press, 2015), pp. 705–6.

[77] D. Davis, "Britain must defy the European Court of Human Rights on prisoner voting as Strasbourg is exceeding its authority" in Flogaitis, Zwart, and Fraser (eds.), *The European Court of Human Rights and Its Discontents*, p. 65.

[78] Dzehtsiarou, "Interaction between the European Court of Human Rights and member states, 123.

[79] M. O'Boyle, "The future of the European Court of Human Rights," *German Law Journal*, 12 (2011) 1862, 1862.

[80] See, e.g., "UK 'should withdraw from European Court of Human Rights'," *The Telegraph*, February 7, 2011, www.telegraph.co.uk/news/worldnews/europe/8307782/UK-should-withdraw-from-European-Court-of-Human-Rights.html.

[81] *Scoppola v. Italy (no. 3)* [GC], no. 126/05, ¶¶ 96, 110, ECHR 2012.

[82] Ibid. ¶¶ 105–6, 109. The permanent ban on voting was a result of the fact that those sentenced to five years or more in prison are ineligible to hold public office, and a ban on holding public office is accompanied by a forfeiture of the right to vote. *See* ibid. ¶¶ 33–4.

have the same "general, automatic and indiscriminate character" that mandated the result in *Hirst*.[83]

IV The Legitimacy of Justice

Although the reaction to the prisoners' rights cases in the United Kingdom would seem to indicate the presence of a significant legitimacy crisis, "[a] court that is controversial is not the same as one whose legitimacy is suspect."[84] The question is whether the reaction in the United Kingdom indeed indicates a challenge to the court's overall legitimacy.[85] The answer to this question turns at least in part on the extent to which the Court's decision to engage in expansionist lawmaking in order to protect the rights of highly unpopular[86] but vulnerable groups contributes to or detracts from its perceived legitimacy.

This section argues that the prisoner voting cases illustrate two ways in which the pursuit of just outcomes can augment the legitimacy of a court. First, a court's legitimacy is fostered when compliance constituencies view its decisions as just. Although the public and politicians in the United Kingdom opposed the Court's position on prisoner voting, the decision enjoyed the support of other important groups. Second, even when decisions conflict with national policy preferences, the existence of a robust domestic human rights culture raises the costs of noncompliance. As long as the Court appears to be a moral actor, divergence between domestic policies and the court's pronouncements creates a kind of cognitive dissonance that promotes compliance and thereby bolsters legitimacy.

A Justice as Perceived Legitimacy

A human rights court's legitimacy is strengthened when compliance constituencies view its decisions as just. Compliance constituencies are

---

[83] Ibid. ¶¶ 106, 108.   [84] Helfer and Alter, "Legitimacy and lawmaking," 502.

[85] Shany, *Assessing the Effectiveness*, p. 139; Dothan, "How international courts enhance their legitimacy," 456 (distinguishing between diffuse and specific support).

[86] Daily Mail coverage of the debate provides insight into the depths of unpopularity of the applicants in these cases. See, e.g., J. Slack and G. Peev, "Toasting victory with cannabis and bubbly, the axe killer who won convicts the vote," *Daily Mail*, November 3, 2010, www.dailymail.co.uk/news/article-1325930/Axe-killer-toasts-prison-vote-victory-canna bis-Champagne-Youtube.html ("Drinking champagne and smoking a cannabis joint, evil axe killer John Hirst smirkingly toasts David Cameron for giving the vote to the UK's worst criminals.").

partners or supporters involved in promoting compliance with the decisions of an international court. Compliance constituencies include both compliance partners, who can directly influence implementation of an international court's decisions domestically, and compliance supporters, who can mobilize to pressure compliance partners to take action.[87] For the ECtHR, compliance partners include not only domestic lawmakers such as judges and politicians but also, for example, the Joint Committee of Human Rights, the national institution charged with considering human rights matters and drafting orders under the 1988 Human Rights Act. Compliance supporters include among others nongovernmental human rights organizations, advocates, and coalitions that mobilize around decisions of the Court.

Empirical evidence indicates that as a general matter, the Court's expansionist approach promotes perceptions of legitimacy among many of these compliance constituencies. In a study measuring attitudes toward the ECtHR, Çalı, Koch, and Bruch found that interviewees, which included judges, lawyers, politicians, and advocates, cited the protection of human rights as an important factor influencing the Court's legitimacy.[88] Although some considered the Court's decisions limiting national sovereignty in favor of human rights to be "legitimacy eroding, others described them as legitimacy boosting."[89] The extent to which the Court has been effective in promoting reforms in national law to protect human rights also augments its perceived legitimacy.[90]

The role of justice in promoting perceptions of legitimacy is more complicated, however, when a decision enjoys only relative legitimacy. Relative legitimacy is when an institution or decision is accepted by some groups but not others.[91] Without taking a position on how precisely to assess relative legitimacy,[92] it is important to note there is variation between (and likely also within) different communities in terms of their

---

[87] Alter, *The New Terrain of International Law*, pp. 20–1.

[88] Çalı, Koch, and Bruch, "The legitimacy of human rights courts, 966; see also O'Boyle, "The future of the European Court of Human Rights," 1867 (noting that the Court derives legitimacy from its "collective guarantee of human rights").

[89] Çalı, Koch, and Bruch, "The legitimacy of human rights courts," 968.

[90] Loth, "Courts in a Quest for Legitimacy," 277.

[91] Shany, *Assessing the Effectiveness*, p. 139.

[92] Dothan argues that in cases of relative legitimacy, we should look for a "prevailing view" generated by "aggregate[ing] the views of all the different actors within the public" while also "giv[ing] the views of different actors varying weight depending on their power to affect the court's interests and the intensity of their beliefs." Dothan, "How international courts enhance their legitimacy," 457.

support for the Court's judgments, particularly those that take progressive positions. Human rights advocates, for example, appear to view the Court's decisions more positively than the general public.[93] Lawyers and opposition politicians also view the Court's expansionist approach as significantly enhancing the Court's legitimacy.[94] Expansionist approaches likely foster the Court's legitimacy with advocates, lawyers, and opposition politicians because these groups share at least in part the Court's view on appropriate outcomes from a policy perspective.

Judges in the United Kingdom also work to promote compliance with the Court's judgments. Judges refer to these judgments "with a frequency and diligence hardly matched anywhere else in Europe" and have manifested "close attention and loyalty to Strasbourg judgments."[95] Even when judges take a position that is difficult to reconcile with Court precedent, "they usually go to great lengths to achieve reconciliation through detailed exegesis and thus maintain the authority of the Strasbourg court."[96] This may be because national judges see the Court as promoting normative harmonization across Europe. As Çalı, Koch, and Bruch explain, "Apex court judges see harmonizing human rights standards across Europe as a value in and of itself and regard the Court as the legitimate interpretive instrument for achieving this."[97] For this group, the legitimacy of the Court is associated with the idea of the rule of law because the Court promotes "equal application of human rights in all countries."[98]

Consistent with this data, descriptive accounts of the debate around prisoner voting in the United Kingdom indicate that while the public and politicians were outraged by the prisoner voting cases (encouraged in no small part by the *Daily Mail* campaign), judges, lawyers, and human rights advocates were more receptive. The Joint Committee of Human Rights, for example, took strong positions on the importance of compliance with the Court's judgment, "not only declaring that future elections could be declared illegal but also demanding that the government explain its reticence and lack of cooperation."[99] Justice Minister Michael Wills

---

[93] Zwart, "More human rights than court," 79 (arguing that activist decisions have triggered a decline in the perceived legitimacy among the general public, but noting that at the same time, the Court's decisions are popular "in human rights circles" and that expansionist decisions are favorably received "as they are perceived as strengthening human rights").

[94] Çalı, Koch, and Bruch, "The legitimacy of human rights courts," 972–3.

[95] Krisch, "Open architecture," 202–3.   [96] Ibid. 203.

[97] Çalı, Koch, and Bruch, "The legitimacy of human rights courts," 972.   [98] Ibid.

[99] Hillebrecht, *Domestic Politics and International Human Rights Tribunals*, p. 110.

also spoke out in favor of the decision.[100] Although it ultimately declined to issue a decision on the merits, the Supreme Court of the United Kingdom accepted the applicability of the European Court's prisoner voting jurisprudence in a 2013 judgment. Hearing two appeals from prisoners who had been denied the right to vote, the Supreme Court rejected the explicit invitation of the Attorney General to refuse to follow the European Court's decisions,[101] although it in the end decided not to make a declaration of incompatibility.[102] Thus, it seems that even on this controversial issue, there was more diversity of opinion than a quick media survey might initially indicate.

The particular characteristics of the Court and the context in which it operates affect the extent to which the pursuit of just outcomes bolsters its perceived legitimacy. First, achieving just outcomes may be both less risky and more legitimizing for mature courts like the ECtHR because they enjoy significant general legitimacy.[103] Legitimacy for mature courts can be a virtuous circle in which the decisions of such courts are automatically seen as more legitimate and have as a result greater influence on conceptions of justice among relevant groups.[104] On the other hand, tribunals such as the ECtHR that issue decisions that have domestic political consequences may encounter greater resistance to their decisions and thereby need to be more sensitive to the risks of doing justice.[105] Comparing the records of the Court of Justice of the European Union, the Andean Tribunal of Justice, and the ECOWAS Community Court of Justice, Larry Helfer and Karen Alter have argued that legitimacy crises are often triggered not by judicial activism but by the extent to which decisions have domestic political consequences. A decision that has domestic political consequences is more likely to encounter resistance regardless of whether the decision is characterized by expansionist lawmaking.[106]

---

[100] Ibid.

[101] *Regina (Chester) v. Secretary of State for Justice and Another* [2013] UKSC 63, ¶¶ 34–5.

[102] There were several reasons given for this decision: first, a declaration of incompatibility had already been made in another case by a lower court, rendering an additional declaration unnecessary; second, the seriousness of the crimes committed by the appellants would render them ineligible to vote even were the law more tailored; and third, it was in the first instance a task for the Parliament rather than the Court to determine how best to reform the prisoner voting laws. Ibid. ¶¶ 39–42.

[103] See Shany, *Assessing the Effectiveness*, p. 156.

[104] See ibid. (noting that more legitimate courts may be in a better position to influence "competing conceptions of justice").

[105] Helfer and Alter, "Legitimacy and Lawmaking," 482.   [106] Ibid.

B Justice as Moral Dissonance

Just outcomes can also contribute to a court's legitimacy by promoting compliance through shaming. A decision that protects the rights of the powerless can contribute to a human rights court's sociological legitimacy – even when the decision is not perceived as just – if it creates dissonance with the community's perception of itself as a moral actor. In such situations, the sociological legitimacy of the court is measured not in terms of what the constituencies say, but rather by reference to what they do – namely, the extent to which the court's decisions exert a compliance pull on those constituencies.[107] Just outcomes can promote compliance when they create cognitive dissonance with strongly held faith in the justice of domestic institutions, as long as the court issuing the decision is itself seen as a moral actor.

The historical pattern of the United Kingdom's response to decisions of the Court illustrates this dynamic. The United Kingdom's record with the Court has been one of "begrudging compliance," in which national authorities protest vociferously but in the end comply with the Court's decisions.[108] Although many in the United Kingdom may be skeptical of the Court as an institution, they share a strong commitment to human rights and a belief in their domestic human rights culture.[109] According to Hillebrecht, the United Kingdom's strong record of compliance with Court decisions is attributable to both domestic institutions and "the country's history and identity as a staunch supporter of human rights."[110] This strong support for and belief in the legitimacy of domestic institutions can foster resistance to decisions of the Court that are perceived to weaken those institutions.[111] At the same time, the affinity of domestic elites to cosmopolitan ideas acts as a counterbalance to

---

[107] Sociological legitimacy can be measured not only with reference to actual perceptions but also by rates of compliance. Shany, *Assessing the Effectiveness*, p. 139.

[108] Thus, despite the "skepticism and inflammatory language" often triggered by Court decisions, the United Kingdom has one of the highest rates of compliance in Europe. Hillebrecht, *Domestic Politics and International Human Rights* Tribunals, pp. 98, 101.

[109] Ibid. p. 101 ("Although Britons do not care much for the ECtHR, they do care about the protection of their rights. In a 2008 poll commissioned by Liberty, a British human rights organization, 96 percent of the respondents stated that legal protection for rights in Great Britain was important.").

[110] Ibid. p. 98.

[111] Çalı, Koch, and Bruch, "The legitimacy of human rights courts," 975. But see E. Voeten, "Public Opinion and the Legitimacy of International Courts," *Theoretical Inquiries in Law*, 14 (2013), 411, 414 (arguing that individuals in countries that trust domestic institutions are more likely to extend this trust to international institutions).

Euro-skepticism and forces compromises in the form of acceptance of the Court's judgments.[112] This commitment also delegitimizes intentional lawbreaking. As Lord Wolf, the Lord Chief Justice, explained in talking about national security cases, the temporary unpopularity of the judiciary for upholding the rights of terrorism suspects "is a price well worth paying if it ensures that this country remains a democracy committed to the rule of law."[113]

This pattern of begrudging compliance illustrates the second way in which justice can play a role in fostering compliance and thus legitimacy. Just outcomes issued by a court perceived as a moral actor promote compliance because they can shame the state into changing its practices, even when the change is undesired and believed unnecessary.[114] In this way, resistance to the Court's decisions may illustrate not the vulnerability of the Court, but rather one of the means by which its norms can be incorporated domestically. Nico Krisch argues that the Court's decisions are implemented through a process of dialogue that leads to ever greater harmonization over time.[115] In this process of dialogue, "temporary crises and controversies" indicate not defeat but evolution.[116]

So viewed, debate over the decisions of Strasbourg is part of the inevitable political struggle that follows an articulation of rights.[117] The Court issues an authoritative statement of rights, which is then used domestically to delegitimize interpretations of the law raised by opponents.[118] Whether or not the Court should be thought of as a "constitutional" court,[119] this process can over time contribute to the emergence

---

[112] Çalı, Koch, and Bruch, "The legitimacy of human rights courts," 980.

[113] Hillebrecht, *Domestic Politics and International Human Rights Tribunals*, p. 112.

[114] The United Kingdom's response to the Court may illuminate at least in part an observation made by Tom Tyler in his study of the relationship between fairness and legitimacy. Tyler observed that both distributive and procedural justice influence compliance, but in different ways: Procedural fairness more strongly influences perceptions of legitimacy, which then promotes compliance, while distributive fairness influences behavior directly. Tyler, *Why People Obey*, pp. 103–4. Due process primarily affects perceptions of fairness, while just outcomes create pressure to comply through either example or shame.

[115] Krisch, "Open architecture," 215.

[116] Madsen, "Explaining the power of international courts in their contexts," 24.

[117] Stuart Scheingold, *The Politics of Rights: Lawyers, Public Policy, and Political Change* (New Haven, CT: Yale University Press, 1974), p. 123.

[118] Alter, *The New Terrain of International Law*, p. 22.

[119] Compare Wheatley, "The construction of the constitutional essentials," 158, 164 (noting that the Court has described itself as a "constitutional instrument of European public order" and has reviewed national constitutions for their compatibility with the

of what Karen Alter calls a "constitutional culture" – a "culture of constitutional obedience where domestic actors see violations of higher order laws as ipso facto illegitimate."[120] Resistance to the Court is itself part of the process by which the Court is legitimated.[121]

Clearly, however, any such dissonance was not enough to cause the United Kingdom to comply in the context of prisoner voting. In part, this may be because these cases involved radically different visions of the justice of allowing prisoners to vote.[122] Although some compliance communities supported the Court, others viewed the Court's position as in fact contrary to principles of justice. Former Prime Minister Cameron made this point most vividly when he said that providing prisoners with voting rights made him "physically ill," and he vowed that he would not comply with the Court's judgments.[123] This indicates that shaming might promote compliance only when the decision in question presents at least a plausible claim of justice to most of the relevant compliance constituencies.

Yet for the Court's judgments to make contrary interpretations of the Convention more costly, the Court must be seen as not only a legal but also a moral actor. As Kim Lane Scheppele explains in her work on constitutional courts in Russia and Hungary, "Judicial power has a moral basis because constitutions and laws are typically normative documents as well as strictly legal ones, and courts must be seen as engaging in something bigger and more important than mere legalism."[124] The moral force of a court's decision increases the cost of noncompliance because failure to

---

Convention), with Krisch, "Open architecture," 185 (arguing that the European human rights system is better thought of as pluralist rather than constitutional).

[120] Alter, *The New Terrain of International Law*, p. 284.

[121] Madsen, "Explaining the power of international courts in their contexts," 23 (calling for greater attention to the processes by which international courts "develop means of legitimization in their interface with democratic politics and other environments key to their practices").

[122] Shany, *Assessing the Effectiveness*, p. 144. A recent article by Paul Johnson focused on debates about marriage equality in the United Kingdom posits that UK parliamentarians use negative rhetoric regarding the Court to legitimize particular political arguments. P. Johnson, "Beliefs about the European Court of Human Rights in the United Kingdom Parliament," in A. Amatrudo and R. Rauxloh (eds.), *Law in Popular Belief: Myth and Reality* (Manchester: Manchester University Press, 2017).

[123] See, e.g., Zwart, "More human rights than court," 76; Shany, *Assessing the Effectiveness*, p. 144.

[124] K. Scheppele, "Guardians of the constitution: Constitutional court presidents and the struggle for the rule of law in post-Soviet Europe." *University of Pennsylvania Law Review*, 154 (2006), 1757, 1759–60.

comply is then not only illegal but also immoral. Correspondingly, courts can undermine their authority when they are seen as acting in an explicitly political as opposed to moral manner.[125] When a court loses its standing as a moral actor, it is easier or less costly for domestic actors to disregard the decisions and the discrepancy between the judgment and national practice, and thus decreases the compliance pull of the court's decisions.

In part, the moral authority of human rights courts stems from the fact that they declare the existence and violations of rights; their power, in other words, derives in part from the authority of rights themselves. Although rights are also political constructs that can be deployed in ways that have distributional consequences, the "myth of rights" posits rights as removed from politics. Rights are "the ideological manifestation of law," timeless manifestations of social justice that serve to guide society through processes of change.[126] As such, rights are powerful symbols that are often invoked as higher-order principles that take precedence over law.[127] Indeed, it may be that human rights courts are able to rely on justice narratives more than other courts because of both their special mandate to protect human rights and the "natural law" resonance of the human rights framework.[128]

These insights about the legitimacy of justice counsel that an international human rights court like the ECtHR must be sensitive not only to the risks of ignoring political pressures, but also to the risks of responding to them. It is not unusual for an international court to be sensitive to the political context in which it operates and in some instances to refrain from reaching decisions that would be viewed as exceeding its mandate. At the same time, an understanding of justice as legitimacy should lead human rights courts in particular to be cautious about deferring too obviously to political pressure because revealing itself as a political actor may also undermine its perceived legitimacy.

C Competing Illegitimacy in the Prisoner Voting Cases

In the prisoner voting cases, the Court is caught between two competing sources of illegitimacy. The first and most obvious is the United

---

[125] Ibid.   [126] Scheingold, *The Politics of Rights*, p. 203.

[127] See ibid. p. 13 ("We believe that politics *is and should be* conducted in accordance with patterns of rights and obligations established under law.").

[128] Cf. Letsas, "Intentionalism and the Interpretation of the ECHR," 271–2 (arguing that human rights violations, even if democratically supported and supported by state consent, would still be invalid).

Kingdom's continued noncompliance, coupled with the credible albeit low risk of the United Kingdom's withdrawal from the Convention. The purpose of this section is to argue that the Court, in attempting to navigate this first challenge, should not neglect a second source of illegitimacy – namely, the risk that bowing to this political pressure could reveal it as a political as opposed to moral actor and thus decrease the compliance pull of its decisions. The course the Court has charted has been to moderate its position in ways that would enable the United Kingdom to more easily comply, while maintaining a robust legal doctrine that can be expanded later as needed. Only time will tell whether this will be a successful strategy, or whether the Court's retroactive narrowing of its decision in *Hirst* has undermined the extent to which prisoner voting is viewed as an issue of justice.

Hirst itself was a principled and strong decision, and individual sections of the Court in subsequent cases began applying this decision in robust ways. In *Frodl v. Austria*, for example, the First Section heard a challenge to an Austrian law that removed the right to vote from prisoners convicted of intentional offenses carrying a sentence longer than one year.[129] The Court emphasized the importance of three factors in evaluating prisoner disenfranchisement laws:

> Disenfranchisement may only be envisaged for a rather narrowly defined group of offenders serving a lengthy term of imprisonment; there should be a direct link between the facts on which a conviction is based and the sanction of disenfranchisement; and such a measure should preferably be imposed not by operation of a law but by the decision of a judge following judicial proceedings.[130]

Thus, according to the Court in *Frodl*, tailoring the penalty to the severity of the offense in order to avoid removing such an important civil right for minor infractions is only the first step. In addition, there must also be a substantive relationship between the nature of the offense and the

---

[129] *Frodl v. Austria*, no. 20201/04, ¶ 21, ECHR 2010.

[130] Ibid. ¶ 28. These elements had also been identified by the Third Section in *Calmanovici v. Romania*, no. 42250/02, ¶ 153, ECHR 2008 ("[P]ar ailleurs, le principe de proportionnalité exige l'existence d'un lien discernable et suffisant entre la sanction et le comportement ainsi que la situation de la personne touchée. . . . Si une telle interdiction n'était pas à exclure d'emblée dans le cas d'un délit commis en tant que fonctionnaire public, la Cour ne saurait l'accepter eu égard aux circonstances de l'espèce, et notamment aux dispositions du droit interne, au caractère automatique et indifférencié de l'interdiction et à l'absence de tout examen de la proportionnalité de la part des tribunaux internes en raison de leur défaut de compétence sur ce point.").

punishment of disenfranchisement – for example, a state might decide to remove the right to vote from someone who had abused a public position.[131] Finally, the punishment should be judicial and not legislative. Although the Austrian law, which was limited to prisoners convicted of intentional offenses receiving sentences of more than one year, was narrower than the one at issue in *Hirst*,[132] the Court found it nonetheless incompatible with the Convention because there was no substantive link between offense and sanction, and the judiciary had no ability to tailor the sanction.[133]

Continued noncompliance on the part of the United Kingdom eventually led the Court to engage in a retroactive narrowing of *Hirst* in an Italian case called *Scoppola (no. 3)*. In *Scoppola*, the Court offered an interpretation of *Hirst* that was much narrower than the interpretation put forward in *Frodl* and which appeared to limit *Hirst* to its facts. In *Scoppola*, the Court found that Italy's law passed muster because it was tailored to the circumstances of the crime. Prisoners who were sentenced to fewer than three years did not lose the right to vote; those who had been sentenced to between three and five years of imprisonment lost the right to vote temporarily; and those who were sentenced to five or more years lost the right to vote permanently.[134] The Court found that "defining the circumstances in which individuals may be deprived of the right to vote show the legislature's concern to adjust the application of the measure to the particular circumstances of the case in hand, taking into account such factors as the gravity of the offence committed and the conduct of the offender."[135] The Italian system did not have the "general, automatic and indiscriminate" character that led the Court to reject the United Kingdom's law in *Hirst*.[136]

The decision in *Scoppola* was a retroactive narrowing of the Court's jurisprudence on prisoner voting for several reasons. First, it explicitly repudiated the idea that a court must be involved in tailoring the penalty. Disagreeing with *Frodl*, in which the absence of judicial involvement in assessing proportionality had been decisive,[137] the Grand Chamber in

---

[131] *Hirst (no. 2)*, ¶ 71.

[132] *Frodl*, ¶ 31. The Court declined to consider the effect of a provision that allowed the judge discretion in determining whether to impose the consequence because it was not in effect at the time the applicant's sentence was handed down. Ibid. ¶ 32.

[133] Ibid. ¶¶ 35–6.

[134] *Scoppola (no. 3)*, ¶ 105. Those who permanently lost the right to vote could regain it by applying for rehabilitation. Ibid. ¶ 109.

[135] Ibid. ¶ 106.   [136] Ibid. ¶ 108.   [137] *Frodl*, ¶¶ 35–6.

Scoppola noted that what is critical is that the measures be tailored and that this tailoring could be accomplished either by a court or by legislation.[138] Second, the Court in *Scoppola* discussed only the importance of tailoring the sentence based on the severity of the offense and did not address whether there was a substantive link between the nature of the offense and the penalty of disenfranchisement – that is, whether this was the *kind* of offense for which removal of the right to vote would further a legitimate purpose of the state.

Third, *Scoppola* narrowed the rule in *Hirst* to its facts, thereby transforming it from an exceptionally severe example of disenfranchisement into a rule against blanket bans on prisoner voting. In *Hirst*, the Court emphasized that the automatic and indiscriminate nature of the United Kingdom law at issue "must be seen as falling outside any acceptable margin of appreciation, however wide that margin might be."[139] Thus, under *Hirst*, a blanket restriction on prisoner voting was only the clearest example of a national law contravening the Convention. By emphasizing that the United Kingdom's fell "outside *any* acceptable margin," it implicitly indicated that measures short of a blanket ban could also fall afoul of the Convention if the penalty was not proportional to the crime in both severity and nature.

In *Scoppola*, in contrast, the Court abandoned its proportionality analysis, upholding the Italian law because it was tailored, even though the consequences of that law were arguably more severe than in *Hirst*; while the UK law deprived individuals of the right to vote only while incarcerated, the Italian law resulted in *permanent* loss of the right to vote for those serving five or more years.[140] Although the Court noted that the Italian system was not "excessively rigid" because prisoners subject to permanent disenfranchisement could apply to have their voting rights restored,[141] it assessed neither the impact of a permanent loss of these rights nor the burden associated with seeking rehabilitation. In disregarding proportionality, the Court appeared to send the message that as long as a law was not a blanket ban, devoid of any limiting factor, it would pass muster under the Convention. Indeed, a dissenting judge

---

[138] *Scoppola (no. 3)*, ¶¶ 99, 102.   [139] *Hirst (no. 2)* [GC], ¶ 82.

[140] As the dissenting opinion of Judge Björgvinsson notes, the Italian legislation "it deprives prisoners of their right to vote beyond the duration of their prison sentence and, for a large group of prisoners, for life." *Scoppola (no. 3)*, para. 17 (dissenting opinion of Judge Björgvinsson).

[141] Ibid. ¶ 109.

argued that in disregarding the relative severity of the two laws, the *Scoppola* decision "stripped the *Hirst* judgment of all its bite as a landmark precedent for the protection of prisoners' voting rights in Europe."[142]

Reaction to *Scoppola* has portrayed it as a necessary partial retreat in the face of overwhelming political pressure. Commentators have characterized the decision as a reasonable response to the legitimacy challenges the Court faced due to the United Kingdom's refusal to comply with *Hirst* and *Greens*.[143] The United Kingdom's continued noncompliance with the Court's decisions was a threat to the Court's effectiveness and its legitimacy, especially given the United Kingdom's significant political influence.[144] The Court needed to find a way out of the standoff it was in with the United Kingdom, but without overruling *Hirst* and *Greens* – which also would have done considerable damage to the Court's legitimacy. Upholding the Italian ban, even based on a distinction difficult to defend as either logical or just, allowed the Court to signal that any policy change, even a minor or formalistic one, would likely be acceptable. This move, although not principled,[145] was a pragmatic response to a significant legitimacy challenge.

In this debate about prisoner voting, the Court is caught between two sources of illegitimacy. On the one hand, the United Kingdom's continued resistance presents a problem for the Court. Courts in crisis often do reach decisions that are politically rather than legally or morally motivated.[146] Further, even when not in crisis, courts – especially international courts – are highly aware of the political context in which they operate, and they respond to that context. The dialogue that occurs between international courts and member states is in many ways an appropriate and natural part of the way international law is created and internalized.[147]

---

[142] Ibid. para. 19 (dissenting opinion of Judge Björgvinsson).

[143] M. Milanovic, "Prisoner voting and strategic judging," *EJIL: Talk!* (2012); K. Corrie, "European court takes a pragmatic approach on prisoner voting rights," *Case Watch* (2012).

[144] K. Corrie, "Case watch: European court takes a pragmatic approach on prisoner voting rights," *Open Society Foundations*, July 19, 2012, www.opensocietyfoundations.org/voices/case-watch-european-court-takes-pragmatic-approach-prisoner-voting-rights.

[145] Milanovic, "Prisoner voting and strategic judging" (calling *Scoppola* "hardly a decision born out of principle").

[146] S. Dothan, "Judicial Tactics in the European Court of Human Rights," *Chicago Journal of International Law*, 12 (2011), 115, 136–7 (discussing the Court's backtracking from *Osman v. the United Kingdom* in *Z and Others v. United Kingdom* after the first decision "provoked severe academic criticism").

[147] See Krisch, "Open architecture," 208 (arguing that the relationship between the European Court of Human Rights and member states is not a "one-way street" but a "mutual

Yet there is also a risk that the Court might undermine its moral authority by responding to political pressure. The authority of rights – and of the courts that declare them – depends at least in part on maintaining the illusion that the courts are removed from politics. The power of courts can be augmented when they are perceived as advancing independently derived and apolitical understandings of law; revealing courts and judges as explicitly political actors may undermine the extent to which they are perceived as authoritative.[148] Pursuing outcomes framed in terms of morality or which correspond to moral judgments can strengthen perceptions that a court is acting independent of politics.

Subsequent cases addressing violations of Article 3 of Protocol No. 1 indicate that the Court may be attempting to roll back aspects of *Scoppola*. First, the Court has not in fact found *any* tailoring compatible with the Convention. In *Anchugov and Gladkov v. Russia*, for example, the Court did not accept Russia's argument that the law in question was valid because it only applied to prisoners who had been sentenced to a custodial term.[149] In *Söyler v. Turkey*, the Court rejected Turkey's argument that limiting the law to intentional crimes was reconcilable with Article 3 of Protocol No 1.[150] More recently, in *Kulinski and Sabev v. Bulgaria*, the Court rejected Bulgaria's arguments that its law did not violate the Convention because it applied only to individuals serving sentences on the basis of a final judgment, affected only a low number of individuals, and provided a means for restoring voting rights automatically on release.[151]

Second, the Court seems to be reviving the substantive link first discussed in *Hirst* and later emphasized in *Frodl*. In *Söyler*, the Court critiqued the decision to deprive the applicant of his ability to vote because it was "unable to see any rational connection between the sanction and the conduct and circumstances of the applicant," who had

---

process in which signals from political actors, including courts, feed back into the ECtHR jurisprudence").

[148] Scheppele, above note 124, at 1848 (discussing the authority of the first two Presidents of the Hungarian and Russian Constitutional Courts as a function of their "explicitly disavowing political influence").

[149] *Anchugov and Gladkov v. Russia*, nos. 11157/04 and 15162/05, ¶ 105, ECHR 2013.

[150] *Söyler v. Turkey*, no. 29411/07, ¶ 42, ECHR 2013; see also *Murat Vural v. Turkey*, no. 9540/07, ¶¶ 79–80, ECHR 2015.

[151] *Kulinski and Sabev v. Bulgaria*, no. 63849/09, ¶ 30, ECHR 2016. The Court characterized the law as a "blanket ban" that was "therefore comparable to [the law] examined in the case of *Anchugov and Gladkov*." Ibid. ¶ 37.

been convicted of passing bad checks.[152] The Court "reiterated in this connection that the severe measure of disenfranchisement must not be resorted to lightly and that the principle of proportionality requires a discernible and sufficient link between the sanction and the conduct and circumstances of the individual concerned."[153] Finally, the Court may even be reviving the importance it had placed in having a judicial determination of proportionality.[154]

V Conclusion

This chapter has argued that doing justice can indeed play a role in establishing and maintaining the legitimacy of international human rights courts. It is both a necessary condition of legitimacy and, in at least some cases, perhaps also a sufficient one. Doing justice can promote the extent to which a human rights court is perceived as legitimate both when it is explicitly seen as doing justice, and when it is not. The perception on the part of a court's compliance constituencies that the court is acting in a just way can increase its legitimacy. Yet a court can also bolster its sociological legitimacy in reaching just decisions if it is perceived as a moral actor, even if constituencies disagree about the morality of the particular decision in question.

By handing down a more limited decision in *Scoppola* while maintaining a robust legal foundation that could later be expanded, the Court did its best to minimize both sources of potential harms to its legitimacy – not only the risk of ignoring political pressure, but also the risk associated with responding to it. The "justice" of its position on prisoner voting was not having an effect in the United Kingdom, so sending a message that emphasized the limited nature of the burden associated with its decisions was reasonable, even if such a move could also be seen as political.

Yet this compromise was not, in the end, successful. Unfortunately, *Scoppola* weakened the moral position the Court had staked out in *Hirst* – without obtaining the desired result. In October 2012, former Prime Minister Cameron reiterated that he did not believe the United Kingdom

---

[152] *Söyler*, ¶ 45.   [153] Ibid.

[154] In *Cucu v. Romania*, the Court found Romania's law incompatible with the Convention citing its earlier decision in *Calmanovici*, including the emphasis in that case on the need for judicial involvement in the determination of penalty. *Cucu v. Romania*, no. 22362/06, ¶ 111, ECHR 2012 ("The Court has already found in respect of Romania a violation of Article 3 of Protocol No. 1 on account of an automatic withdrawal of the right to vote as a secondary penalty to a prison sentence and of the lack of competence of the courts to proceed with a proportionality test on that measure.").

should change its law,[155] and the Court has continued to find against the United Kingdom on this issue in several judgments since then.[156] Given the long-term cost to its perceived legitimacy from acting politically, perhaps the Court must for the time being simply hold its course. On the other hand, it seems unlikely that domestic resistance will fade over time. Prime Minister Theresa May, who came to power in the wake of the Brexit vote, recently announced plans to pull out of the European Convention on Human Rights as soon as the United Kingdom's withdrawal from the European Union is complete.[157] May, who has expressed frustration with the Court since her term as Home Secretary between 2010 and 2016, noted that the delay until after Brexit might be "disappointing for the British public because they are the ones who are sick to the back teeth of the abuse of the human rights act and finding it difficult to kick terrorists out of the country and give prisoners the vote."[158]

Generalizing from the experience of the ECtHR to other human rights courts is challenging because the scope and impact of any "justice effect" likely depends on particular features, history, and context of the tribunal in question. Nonetheless, focusing on the concept of justice in the prisoner cases at the ECtHR generates some insights for human rights courts navigating periods of political crisis. The experience of the European Court in these cases indicates that pragmatic but unprincipled stands in response to political pressure pose the risk of undermining the compliance pull of a human rights court's decisions. In some instances, taking an unpopular position may even be a source of strength for these courts. Sometimes stretching the law and displeasing states is precisely what human rights courts are supposed to do – and in so doing, they may end up strengthening their position in the long term.

[155] M. Milanovic, "No détente on prisoner voting and the ECHR in the UK," *EJIL: Talk!* (2012).
[156] *Millbank and Others v. United Kingdom*, nos. 44473/14, 58659/14, 70874/14, 71699/14, 73574/14, 73638/14, 73771/14, 73783/14, 73909/14, 73911/14, 74403/14, 74409/14, 75735/14, 75846/14, 2294/15, 18149/15, 24868/15, 26031/15, 26045/15, 28688/15, 32681/15 and 32685/15, ¶ 10, ECHR 2016; *McHugh and Others v. United Kingdom*, no. 51987/08, ¶ 11, ECHR 2015; *Firth and Others v. United Kingdom*, nos. 47784/09, 47806/09, 47812/09, 47818/09, 47829/09, 49001/09, 49007/09, 49018/09, 49033/09 and 49036/09, ¶ 15, ECHR 2014.
[157] W. Worley, "Theresa May will campaign to leave the European Convention on Human Rights in 2020 election," *Independent*, December 29, 2016; C. Hope, "Theresa May to fight 2020 election on plans to take Britain out of European Convention on Human Rights after Brexit is completed," *The Telegraph*, December 28, 2016.
[158] Hope, "Theresa May to fight 2020 election."

5

Legitimacy and Jurisdictional Overlap

The ICC and the Inter-American Court in Colombia

ALEXANDRA HUNEEUS

Judicialization is among the most distinctive features of international law in our era: from six international courts in 1985, today there are roughly two dozen international courts adjudicating disputes between states, between states and other legal subjects, or between private actors.[1] As these courts proliferate and their memberships grow, their work increasingly overlaps: with greater frequency they find themselves interacting with the same actors and institutions over the same policy areas. In contrast to national judicial systems, however, there is no agreed-upon hierarchical ordering among international courts: each commands obedience to its rulings regardless of the others. What happens, then, when the work of two or more international courts coincides or, put more contentiously, collides? When courts from different international orders interact with the same domestic actors over the same policy matters, is their legitimacy fortified or undermined?

An anxiety that permeates the scholarship on international law is that the absence of hierarchy and the ever-growing overlap between international regimes yields confusion, forum-shopping, and turf wars and will ultimately undermine the legitimacy of these legal regimes.[2] It could

---

[1] Cesare P. R. Romano, Karen J. Alter, and Yuval Shany (eds.), *The Oxford Handbook of International Adjudication* (Oxford University Press, 2014), pp. 28–32.

[2] J. Charney, "Is international law threatened by multiple international tribunals?" in *Collected Courses*, 271 (Hague Academy of International Law, 1998), pp. 101–382; P.-M. Dupuy, "Unification rather than fragmentation of international law? The case of international investment law and human rights law" in P.-M. Dupuy, E.-U. Petersmann, and F. Francioni (eds.), *Human Rights in International Investment Law and Arbitration* (Oxford University Press, 2009); Nikolaos Lavranos, *Jurisdictional Competition: Selected Cases in International and European Law* (Groningen, NL: Europa Law Publishing, 2009); V. Lowe, "Overlapping jurisdictions in international courts and tribunals," *Australian Year Book of International Law*, 20 (1999), 191; C. P. Romano, "The proliferation of international judicial bodies: The pieces of the puzzle," *New York University Journal of*

be, for example, that domestic actors pit international courts against each other: They might argue that conflicting standards make it impossible to be in compliance with both, undermining each. In this scenario, each court's legitimacy is diminished or canceled by the presence of the other in a dynamic of destructive interference (to borrow a concept from wave physics).[3] Alternatively, a more optimistic view on international law's growing complexity points to the tactics and methods whereby such overlapping regimes accommodate to and reinforce each other absent a higher authority.[4] Through experimentation, dialogue, and repeated interaction, institutions learn from and adjust to each other. We can even imagine that, like similarly phased waves that grow in amplitude on meeting, international courts with overlapping jurisdiction heighten each other's legitimacy beyond what each could have achieved on its own.

To deepen our understanding of which dynamic comes into play when, this chapter undertakes a case study of international courts involved in the same matters, in the same country. The Colombian peace process, a multiparty effort to end the Western Hemisphere's longest-running conflict, is one of the first to take shape under the shadow of two international courts: the International Criminal Court (ICC) and the Inter-American Court of Human Rights (IACtHR).[5] Their presence has

---

International Law and Politics, 31 (1999), 709; Yuval Shany, "The competing jurisdictions of international courts and tribunals," *International Courts and Tribunals* (Oxford University Press, 2005); P. Webb, "Scenarios of jurisdictional overlap among international courts," *Revue Quebecoise de Droit International*, 19.2 (2006); Brandeis Institute for International Judges, *The International Rule of Law: Coordination and Collaboration in Global Justice* (Waltham, MA: Brandeis University, 2012).

[3] Negative interference refers to the meeting "of two waves of equal frequency and opposite phase, resulting in their cancellation where the negative displacement of one always coincides with the positive displacement of the other." Constructive interference refers to the opposite dynamic, where two waves of equal frequency and phase meet.

[4] Above. *See also* G. de Búrca, R. O. Keohane, and C. Sabel, "New modes of pluralist global governance," *New York University Journal of International Law and Politics*, 45.1 (2013); R. Michaels and J. Pauwelyn,"Conflict of norms or conflict of law? Different techniques in the fragmentation of international law," *Duke Journal of Comparative and International Law*, 22 (2012), 349; A. Reinisch, "The proliferation of international dispute settlement mechanisms: The threat of fragmentation vs the promise of a more effective system? Some reflections from the perspective of investment arbitration" in *International Law between Universalism and Fragmentation* (Leiden, NL: Martinus Nijhoff Publishers, 2008).

[5] Colombia is not the first state to try to resolve issues of peace, reconciliation, and criminal accountability while under the jurisdiction of two or more international courts. The former Yugoslav states were under the jurisdiction of both the International Criminal Tribunal for the Former Yugoslavia and the International Court of Justice, and some of the African states also find themselves under the watch of the International Criminal Court

loomed large: the Colombian president who leads the peace process, the ex-president who opposes it, the guerrilla leadership, and the Colombian Constitutional Court are among many key actors that have frequently referred to the ICC and the Inter-American Court as they engage with the peace process, and in particular as they sought to resolve the question of liability for atrocity crimes committed during the conflict.[6]

By analyzing the trajectory of these courts in Colombia during the time leading up to the final peace agreement, the chapter reveals the ways in which their work coincided, and evaluates the implications of this coincidence for the courts' legitimacy. Overall, the overlap of the courts' work has benefitted the sociological legitimacy of each in a dynamic of constructive interference.[7] Both courts work with state and civil society to spur the justice system to respond to atrocity crimes. Most often they do so in reference to different bodies of law, using different methods of interaction, and in dialogue with different state and civil society actors. However, there was also a moment when the overlap between the two raised the question of whether one court, by blurring the lines between itself and the other, began to overstep its proper ambit, undermining its normative legitimacy.[8]

The case study makes several contributions to the current volume on the legitimacy of international courts and to the field of inquiry into international court power more generally. First, it suggests that courts with coincident or shared goals may benefit from each other's presence. Although the ICC and the Inter-American Court are by no means the first courts to expand their mandates in a bid for greater relevance, the study reveals the dynamics by which international courts can become

---

and a regional or subregional court. But Colombia is unique and perhaps more exemplary of things to come, in that both the ICC and IACtHR have mandatory jurisdiction, and both have been actively engaged over many years.

[6] Following David Scheffer, I adopt the term *atrocity crimes* as the single term that refers to genocide, war crimes, and crimes against humanity. D. Scheffer, "Genocide and atrocity crimes," *Genocide Studies and Prevention: An International Journal*, 1.3 (2006), 229–50.

[7] Drawing on Nienke Grossman, I define sociological legitimacy as the belief by relevant audiences that "particular claims to authority deserve respect or obedience for reasons not restricted to self-interest."

N. Grossman, "Legitimacy and international adjudicative bodies," *George Washington International Law Review*, 41.1 (2009), 116; D. Bodansky, "The legitimacy of international governance: A coming challenge for international environmental law?" *The American Journal of International Law*, 93.3 (1999), 596–600.

[8] L. R. Helfer and K. J. Alter, "Legitimacy and lawmaking: A tale of three international courts," *Theoretical Inquires in Law*, 14 (2013), 479 (arguing that activism can, at times, enhance legitimacy).

activist in concert and reflects on the consequences of this coupling for the sociological and normative legitimacy of each. More generally, although the lens here remains trained on the ICC and the Inter-American Court, the study suggests there is another unit of analysis that should concern us – that of the international judiciary as a whole. Legitimacy might be an attribute not just of individual courts, but also of international courts in general. Perhaps the greatest impact of the ICC and the Inter-American Court in the Colombian peace process will not be on the deal brokered on the ground, but rather on perceptions of the usefulness of international courts in peace-making and other international affairs.

Further, the chapter contributes a focus on the work of courts outside their adjudicatory capacity, beyond particular cases, on those not party to the case – what Law and Society scholars call "the shadow of the law."[9] As international courts evolve, they have, like national courts, taken on roles beyond dispute resolution. Indeed, even though we often speak of the ICC Office of the Prosecutor (OTP) as part of the International Criminal Court, the OTP is a *sui generis* actor on the international stage, and in Colombia it works wholly outside the context of adjudication as it reviews state responses to atrocity crimes. For its part, the Inter-American Court has interpreted its mandate to include monitoring of state actions: After it issues a final judgment, it opens a supervisory stage through which it reviews states as they implement the judgment over long periods of time. Both courts, then, spend many resources on and exert influence through supervision of state actions in the realm of prosecution. The chapter also examines the ways courts have influence through judicial dialogue with domestic courts. Although supervision and judicial dialogue are distinct from the core judicial activity of triadic dispute resolution, they play a hand in shaping international court legitimacy.

Theoretically, the argument aligns with the new institutionalist school of judicial politics, emphasizing the relationships that international courts forge with national audiences.[10] To bring these relationships to light, the case study draws not only on court judgments but also

---

[9] For the seminal article on this term *see* R. N. Mnookin and L. Kornhauser, "Bargaining in the shadow of the law: The case of divorce," *Yale Law Journal*, 88.5 (1979), 950.

[10] Karen Alter, *The New Terrain of International Courts* (Princeton, NJ: Princeton University Press, 2014), pp. 32–67 (emphasizing the importance of the relationship of international courts to distinct national audiences that are charged with fostering compliance).

interviews with domestic actors, media accounts, and court-generated documents such as annual reports and press releases.

Part 1 introduces the Colombian conflict, and shows how the work of the two courts has converged. Part 2 examines three ways in which the courts' work has coincided and the repercussions of each for the courts' legitimacy. Part 3 raises concerns about the courts' increasingly confluent work. Part 4 considers the implication of this dynamic of constructive interference for the legitimacy of the evolving and increasingly judicialized international system.

I The Colombian Conflict and International Courts

The Colombian conflict predates by many years the establishment of the Inter-American Court (1979) and the ICC (2002). It began in the mid-1960s when the Revolutionary Armed Forces of Colombia – People's Army (FARC) first organized as an armed force. Even as many other conflicts with leftist guerrilla movements in the region were pacified, the Colombian conflict has endured, fueled in part by its participants' engagement in the drug trade. It has undergone different iterations, and different armed groups have stepped into and out of the battle arena. The participants today include the state, the FARC (with whom the state now has a peace treaty), and the *Ejercito Libertador National* (ELN), the second-largest guerrilla organization with whom the state was also negotiating a treaty when this book went to press. Paramilitaries have played an important role in the past, and despite a process of demobilization beginning in the mid-2000s, may be reemerging as an important actor.

Although described as a "low-intensity" war, the Colombian conflict has had devastating effects. All sides have committed international crimes, including forced disappearance, extrajudicial execution, torture, kidnapping, sexual crimes, and forced displacement; however, the paramilitary have committed the greatest percentage of these crimes.[11] Colombia's National Centre for Historical Memory reports that 220,000 people died in the conflict between 1958 and 2013. Of these, the majority were civilians. Further, over 5.7 million civilians have been

---

[11] Grupo de Memoria Historica, "¡Basta Ya! Colombia: Memorias De Guerra Y Dignidad," Centro Nacional de Memoria Historica, 2013.

forced from their homes since1985.[12] Today Colombia has the world's second-largest population of internally displaced persons, topped only by Syria.[13]

Throughout the conflict there have been moments when the government and nonstate armed groups have tried to forge peace. One effort took place between 1982 and 1985, during which one of the armed groups, M-19, formed a political party and relinquished the use of force. M-19 became a successful participant in the political process. A different experience was that of the members of FARC and other guerrilla groups who helped form *Union Patriotica (UP)*, a leftist political party in 1985. *UP* candidates did well in elections, even as the guerrillas continued their armed struggle. However, *UP* politicians were then subject to a campaign of targeted killings that essentially decimated the party. Another important attempt to create peace was initiated by conservative President Pastrana in 1998. This effort, too, unraveled in the face of ongoing guerrilla attacks.

Soon after assuming the presidency in 2002, conservative Alvaro Uribe opened negotiations with the United Self-Defense Forces of Colombia (AUC), an organization that represents Colombia's different paramilitary organizations. Uribe was able to forge a deal in which the paramilitary would demobilize and cooperate in judicial processes in return for lower sentences for their crimes. In 2005, Congress passed the Peace and Justice Law, which put the bargain into effect, establishing a special jurisdiction in the courts and a dedicated unit in the National Prosecutor (*Fiscalía General de la Nación*). The judicial processes have moved forward, albeit slowly, and continue to this day.

In 2010, five years after the Peace and Justice Law, President Santos approached the FARC to propose opening a dialogue toward ending the conflict. The FARC agreed, and the two sides began to hold talks in Havana, Cuba. In August 2012, the government and FARC signed a General Agreement for the Termination of the Conflict and Building of a Stable and Long-Lasting Peace, which laid the groundwork and sequencing for a series of dialogues on five different topics: agrarian reform, ending the illicit drug trade, responding to victims of the conflict, political participation of the guerillas, and demilitarization. President Santos officially made public the government's decision to move forward

---

[12] Internal Displacement Monitoring Centre (IDMC), "Global Figures: Internal displacement by country in 2015," www.internal-displacement.org/global-figures (last checked February 16, 2017).
[13] Ibid.

with a peace process in September of 2012, and the first formal round of talks was held in Oslo just two months later. In September 2015, the government and FARC announced that they had reached an accord on the question of punishment and the rights of the victims, one of the most contentious areas of negotiation. A year later, on September 26, 2016, the Colombian president and the FARC held a triumphant signing ceremony to solidify the accord they had at last agreed to. Just a month later, however, the Colombian people rejected the accord in a popular referendum, by a razor-thin margin of 50.23%. The government blamed low voter turnout and a strong opposition movement guided by former president and now Senator Alvaro Uribe. Despite continued resistance from the conservative Right, however, the government forged ahead. The *Acuerdo Final para la Terminación del Conflicto y la Construcción de una Paz Estable y Duradera* was signed and approved by the Colombian Congress in November and is currently being implemented.[14]

The peace process has generated hope in Colombia, and in the world, that one of the world's longest-running conflicts may at last come to an end. But the process continues to be slow, rocky, and greatly contested, with Uribe maintaining that it yields too much to the FARC, particularly by allowing individuals to escape punishment for atrocity crimes. Throughout, one of the most contentious issues has been the question of criminal liability for members of the FARC for war crimes and crimes against humanity. In an ironic twist, it has been the conservative Right that has emphasized the importance of punishment for atrocity crimes, with the Left emphasizing leniency. As will be discussed later, the ICC and the Inter-American Court have been frequently cited in the ongoing debate.

II The ICC and the Inter-American Court in the Colombian Conflict

Like many Latin American states, Colombia is an active participant in the new world of international courts. It has accepted the compulsory

---

[14] R. Jervis, "Colombia's president, rebels announce breakthrough in talks," *USA Today*, September 23, 2015, www.usatoday.com/story/news/2015/09/23/colombias-president-rebels-announce-breakthrough-talks/72708430/; T. Betin, "Cámara aprobó 130 votos a 0 la refrendación del nuevo Acuerdo de Paz," *El Heraldo*, December 1, 2016, www .elheraldo.co/colombia/camara-aprobo-130-votos-0-la-refrendacion-del-nuevo-acuerdo-de-paz-307224; J. Lafuente, "Los argumentos de los partidarios del no en el plebiscito de Colombia," *El Pais*, August 24, 2016, www.internacional.elpais.com/internacional/2016/08/20/actualidad/1471706901_557856.html.

jurisdiction of the International Court of Justice, the Andean Court of Justice, and the World Trade Organization Dispute Resolution System, as well as the ICC and the Inter-American Court of Human Rights. On paper, each of these courts has a distinct jurisdictional ambit. Thus, the Inter-American Court is a regional court that adjudicates cases arising under the American Convention of Human Rights. The ICC, by contrast, is an international court created by the Rome Statute, with jurisdiction over three international crimes: genocide, war crimes, and crimes against humanity. The two courts draw from different legal sources (a human rights treaty versus an international criminal law treaty); have power over different subjects (20 states in the Americas versus natural persons the world round); and impose different outcomes (reparation of those wronged versus punishment of wrongdoers). From a strictly legal perspective, their jurisdictions do not conflict or overlap.

These distinctions fall away, however, when we consider not the formal jurisdiction of the two courts, but what they actually strive to achieve on the ground and the various paths by which they exert impact. In particular, both courts have sought to foster criminal investigation of atrocity crimes committed in the course of the internal conflict.

A   The Inter-American Court and Atrocity Crimes in Colombia

The Inter-American Court, one of the two main organs of the human rights system of the Organization of American States, was created in 1979. Under its contentious jurisdiction, it adjudicates petitions claiming state violations of the American Convention on Human Rights.[15] Twenty states are currently under its jurisdiction. In recent years, it has become an important presence in certain Latin American States, issuing judgments that shape domestic judicial interpretation of rights, and achieving compliance with over half of its remedial orders.[16]

Throughout its history, the Inter-American Court has been deeply involved in the question of how states should respond to legacies of state-sponsored atrocity. While the American Convention of Human Rights covers the traditional spectrum of civil and political rights as well as social and economic rights, over half of its judgments have focused on

---

[15] American Convention on Human Rights, "Pact of San Jose, Costa Rica," San Jose, November 22, 1969, in force July 18, 1978, 1144 UNTS 123.

[16] Courtney Hillebrecht, *Domestic Politics and International Human Rights Tribunals: The Problem of Compliance* (Cambridge University Press, 2014), p. 51.

the state's duty to investigate, punish, and compensate for state-sponsored atrocity crimes. Through a series of judgments, it has developed a jurisprudence intolerant of laws that block criminal investigation or lift sentences for atrocity crimes.[17] Some argue that it has outlawed amnesty laws.[18] The Court has also developed an influential jurisprudence on reparations for victims of atrocity crimes that has shaped how states respond to human rights violations, even in the absence of a judgment. It is known for its creative use of equitable remedies and, in particular, for ordering specific actions such as state apologies, creation of memorials, and creation of DNA databases – it even regularly orders states to provide courses in human rights to local officials.[19]

One of the striking aspects of the Inter-American Court's emphasis on atrocity crimes is how willing it has been to oversee and monitor criminal processes. Although it is not a criminal court, the Inter-American Court typically orders states to prosecute as a remedial measure. It is the only human rights court to do so. Further, it has interpreted its powers to include the ability to monitor compliance to its orders, which means that it becomes involved in monitoring the advance of domestic criminal investigations.[20] In this capacity, it asks the different parties to the case to provide reports on compliance to its judgment, and it holds closed compliance hearings in which judges take on the role of mediator, pushing the parties to work together to overcome obstacles to

---

[17] *Barrios Altos* v. *Peru*, Monitoring Compliance with Judgment Inter-Am. Ct. H.R. (September 7, 2012), *at* www.corteidh.or.cr/docs/supervisiones/barrios_07_09_12.pdf; *Castillo Paez* v. *Peru*, Reparations & Costs, Inter-Am. Ct. H.R. (November 27, 1998); *Almonacid Arellano* v. *Chile*, Preliminary Objections, Merits, Reparations & Costs, Inter-Am. Ct. H.R. (ser. C) No. 154 (September 26, 2006); *Gelman* v. *Uruguay*, Reparations & Costs, Inter-Am. Ct. H.R. (February 24, 2011) *at* www.corteidh.or.cr/docs/casos/articulos/seriec_221_esp1.pdf; *Gomes Lund et al.* v. *Brazil*, Preliminary Objections, Merits, Reparations & Costs, Inter-Am. Ct. H.R. (November 24, 2010) *at* www.corteidh.or.cr/docs/casos/articulos/seriec_219_esp.pdf; *El Mozote and nearby places* v. *El Salvador*, Reparations & Costs, Inter-Am. Ct. H.R. (October 25, 2012) *at corteidh.or.cr/docs/casos/articulos/seriec_252_esp.pdf.*

[18] C. Binder, "The prohibition of amnesties by the IACtHR of human rights," *German Law Journal*, 12 (2011), 1203; L. J. Laplante, "Outlawing amnesty: The return of criminal justice in transitional justice schemes," *Virginia Journal of International Law*, 49.4 (2009), 915.*IACtHR.*

[19] T. Antkowiak, "Remedial approaches to human rights violations: The Inter-American Court of Human Rights and Beyond," *Colombia Journal of Transnational Law*, 46 (2008), 351–419.

[20] A. Huneeus, "International criminal law by other means: The quasi-criminal jurisdiction of the human rights courts," *American Journal of International Law*, 107.1 (2013), 1–44.

implementation of the Court's orders. Throughout the judgment and compliance phases, the Court is not shy of delving into criminal files and opining on different aspects of the criminal investigation, including advising prosecutors to interrogate specific witnesses and to investigate particular theories of the case.[21]

In Colombia, the majority of the Inter-American Court's work has focused on atrocity crimes committed in the course of the internal conflict.[22] Colombia accepted the jurisdiction of the Court in 1986, but the Court did not adjudicate a Colombian case until 1997. Since then, it has issued a string of sixteen judgments examining atrocity crimes, including several massacres conducted by the paramilitary with the acquiescence or knowledge of the Colombian military. In these cases, the Court has typically demanded that the state conduct a criminal investigation of the underlying acts, and that it punish all of those responsible. Further, in all cases against Colombia, the Court has decided to supervise the state's implementation of its orders, putting it in the position of supervising compliance with fifteen judgments against Colombia. As each judgment orders the state to prosecute for complex atrocity crimes, this means that the Court is supervising the advance of over 100 domestic prosecutions for acts that can be classified as war crimes or crimes against humanity.[23] So far, it has issued over thirty-three compliance reports in which it monitors their advance, and, as full compliance is elusive, it is likely that Court will continue to be mired in monitoring their progress, even as more new cases involving the internal conflict arrive on its docket.

B   The ICC's Preliminary Investigation in Colombia

Colombia deposited its instrument of ratification of the Rome Statue on August 5, 2002, the year the treaty came into effect. The president

---

[21] See, for example, *La Rochela Massacre v. Colombia*, Merits, Reparations & Costs, Inter-Am. Ct. H.R. (ser. C) No. 163 (May 11, 2007) *at* www.corteidh.or.cr/docs/supervisiones/rochela_26_08_10_ing.pdf (in which IACtHR advises Colombia what theories of the case to follow in the investigation of a massacre).

[22] Colombia has belonged to the Organization of American States since it ratified the OAS Charter in 1951. It ratified the American Convention on Human Rights in 1973. However, it did not accept the jurisdiction of the IACtHR until 1985, six years after the Convention came into effect and the first slate of judges took office.

[23] Inter-American Court of Human Rights, Jurisprudence Finder *at* www.corteidh.or.cr/cf/Jurisprudencia2/index.cfm?lang=en (last accessed February 17, 2017).

included with the instrument of ratification a reservation that suspended ICC jurisdiction over war crimes for seven years.[24] Less than two years later, in June 2004, the Office of the Prosecutor (OTP) placed Colombia under a "preliminary examination," the process whereby it decides whether it will open its own criminal investigation.[25] Colombia thus became one of the ICC's early preliminary investigations, and one of the cases through which the term's meaning would be defined. In particular, Colombia would be a test of the doctrine of proactive complementarity, which holds that the ICC should use preliminary investigations as a way of monitoring and pushing states to conduct their own investigations to avoid ICC prosecution.[26]

Colombia held promise as a case for vindicating proactive complementarity because, even as it was mired in a four-decade war, it had developed fairly strong judicial institutions and boasted a long, if constrained, democratic tradition. It was one of the few states under the ICC's watch with institutional capacity to respond to pressure to prosecute. Perhaps through this case Prosecutor Luis Moreno Ocampo could make good on his famous claim that the success of the ICC would be measured by the *absence* of cases on its docket (because it had managed to foster domestic prosecution and deter crimes).[27] Colombia also had the advantage that it took the ICC outside of Africa for the first time. Its drawback was that it was the first case in the proverbial "backyard" of the United States, encompassing a conflict in which U.S. financial and military involvement was deep.

How, then, should the ICC engage Colombia's government? The OTP was not investigating a specific case, and the Rome Statute is silent on the means by which the ICC should foster local prosecutions; indeed, proactive complementarity is a prosecutorial invention and not formally an

---

[24] A. Chehtman, "The impact of the ICC in Colombia: Positive complementarity on trial," DOMAC Reports, October 2011, www.domac.is/media/domac-skjol/Domac-17-AC.pdf.

[25] The Office of the Prosecutor, "Situation in Colombia: Interim report," International Criminal Court, November 2012, www.icc-cpi.int/NR/rdonlyres/3D3055BD-16E2-4C83-BA85-35BCFD2A7922/285102/OTPCOLOMBIAPublicInterimReportNovember2012.pdf.

[26] W. W. Burke-White, "Proactive complementarity: The International Criminal Court and National Courts in the Rome System of International Justice," *Harvard International Law Journal*, 49 (2008), 53.

[27] L. Moreno-Ocampo, "Ceremony for the solemn undertaking of the Chief Prosecutor of the International Criminal Court," (2003) *at* www.iccnow.org/documents/MorenoOcampo16June03.pdf.

LEGITIMACY AND JURISDICTIONAL OVERLAP 125

aspect of the Rome Statute.[28] The methods by which the ICC ultimately chose to foster domestic prosecution fell short of what some scholars had envisioned as a robust complementarity regime that would include capacity building.[29] Rather, the OTP embarked on what could be described as an ongoing dialogic process with diverse state and nonstate actors. The OTP's main object seems to be to project an image of itself as a looming supervisory presence ready to step in should local justice falter. Through in-person meetings, official interim reports, statements to the press, and private letters to government officials, the OTP has kept Colombians informed of its opinion on various judicial and legislative matters relevant to the prosecution of atrocity crimes committed during the internal conflict. On official missions, OTP officers meet not only with authorities from the executive branch, but also the *Fiscalía General de la Nación*, or National Prosecutor, the Attorney General (or *Procurador*), the regular judiciary, the Constitutional Court, and members of the military justice system. Through these meetings the OTP gathers information about the prosecutorial processes, even as it communicates its areas of concern and priorities and reminds the state actors of its presence. Further, the OTP has held biannual roundtables with local and international nongovernmental organizations and has participated in events on relevant matters.[30] Finally, the OTP at times communicates its opinion on pending matters by private letters with Colombia's authorities.[31]

This communicative strategy has changed in intensity and emphasis over the decade.[32] The first focus was the Justice and Peace Law, the 2005 law that put into effect the bargain reached between the government and paramilitaries on the demobilization of the paramilitary. The OTP also put emphasis on the prosecutions for the "false-positives" cases, in which the military targeted civilians and then reported them as guerillas killed in combat to meet military goals. Two other areas of focus have been the prosecution of sexual crimes and the prosecution of politicians for their involvement with the paramilitaries. Finally, as the peace

---

[28] Sarah M. H. Nouwen, *Complementarity in the Line of Fire: The Catalyzing Effect of the International Criminal Court in Uganda and Sudan* (Cambridge University Press, 2013).

[29] See note 28.   [30] See note 26.

[31] See Part 3. *See also* Carta del Fiscal de la CPI, Luis Moreno Ocampo, dirigida al Embajador colombiano acreditado ante la CPI, Guillermo Fernández de Soto, 2 de marzo de 2005.

[32] R. Urueña, "Prosecutorial politics: The ICC's influence in Colombian peace processes, 2003–2017," *American Journal of International Law*, 111(1) (2017), 104–25. doi:10.1017/ajil.2016.3.

process began in 2012, the OTP intensified its presence, increasing the frequency of trips and using press statements, private letters, and yearly reports to articulate its position on the question of the lifting or lightening of penal responsibility in return for peace.

For over a decade, then, these two international courts have been increasingly engaged in monitoring and guiding the government in its response to atrocity crimes committed during the armed conflict. The ICC has never opened its own criminal investigation in Colombia. But like the Inter-American Court in its self-styled supervisory capacity, the OTP monitors the advance of domestic prosecutions for atrocity crimes in Colombia and pressures different state actors toward action, in a unique communicative strategy rooted in the doctrine of complementarity. We now turn to this study's animating question: Has the two courts' overlapping work amplified or diminished their legitimacy? Have they worked in tandem or in tension?

III   Court Convergence and Legitimacy

An examination of how the two courts have influence and are perceived by national actors on the ground reveals three dynamics of confluence: that of working in parallel toward consonant but distinct ends; that of working through distinct means toward the same end; and finally, that of blurring the boundaries between them, borrowing from each other, as they work toward the same end. As will be argued next, each has different repercussions for the courts' legitimacy.

A   Working toward Complementary Goals

The first dynamic, that of working in parallel toward consonant goals, is perhaps how we usually imagine the coexistence of human rights and criminal law courts – while each works generally toward improved human rights on the ground, they have distinct particular goals, and they have different working tools and methods. Their goals differ because they are part of very distinct international legal regimes: whereas the Rome Statute commits states to cooperate with international prosecution of three international crimes, the American Convention commits states to protect and provide enjoyment of a broad spectrum of rights. Their means differ because one is a criminal court, the other a civil court.

One salient example of this complementary dynamic occurs through judicial dialogue with domestic courts. Domestic courts frequently cite the international human rights treaties as they interpret the scope of domestic rights. This dynamic is particularly pronounced in Colombia, where the constitutional court reviews domestic legislation under international human rights treaty law as part of constitutional review. Under the doctrine of the "constitutional bloc" Colombian constitutional judges are bound not only by the text of the constitution, but also by a broader "constitutional block," which includes, in the words of Góngoro Mera,

> a set of norms and principles with constitutional rank that … encompasses 1) the Constitution *stricto sensu*, 2) international declarations of human rights, such as the Universal Declaration and the American Declaration and 3) human rights treaties ratified by the States.[33]

Thus, the American Convention and the Rome Statute are binding and directly applicable in Colombian court: Indeed, the Constitutional Court of Colombia (CCC) regularly reviews national legislation for conformity to these instruments and strikes down legislation that is in conflict.

A main source of the constitutional block is the American Convention, and the CCC views the judgments of the Inter-American Court as an authoritative source on the meaning of the Convention, frequently referring to them to establish whether Colombia's laws and governmental actions are in conformity.[34] When the Constitutional Court reviewed the Justice and Peace Law for conformity to the Constitution, for example, it relied heavily on the jurisprudence of the Inter-American Court on amnesty, citing the Inter-American System over 150 times, even though this jurisprudence was mostly developed in cases against states other than Colombia.[35]

While the ICC is not yet as deeply embedded in the domestic judicial system as is the Inter-American System, Colombia's domestic courts also

---

[33] Manuel Eduardo Gongora Mera, *Inter-American Judicial Constitutionalism: On the Constitutional Rank of Human Rights Treaties in Latin America through National and Inter-American Adjudication*, (San Jose: Inter-American Institute of Human Rights, 2011), pp. 161–3 (explaining the difference between the constitutional block doctrine in Europe, where it originated, and in Latin America).

[34] Constitutional Court of Colombia, Sentence C-010 (2000) *at* www.corteconstitucional .gov.co/relatoria/2000/c-010-00.htm ("La Corte coincide con el interviniente en que en esta materia es particularmente relevante la doctrina elaborada por la Corte Interamericana de Derechos Humanos, que es el órgano judicial autorizado para interpretar autorizadamente la Convención Interamericana."); *see generally* H. A. O. García, "El Bloque de Constitucionalidad en Colombia," *Estudios Constitucionales*, 3 (2006), 231 (describing the constitutional block in Colombia).

[35] Constitutional Court of Colombia, Sentence C-370 (2006) *at* www.corteconstitucional .gov.co/relatoria/2006/C-370-06.htm.

have it in view in their adjudication of atrocity crimes.[36] The Constitutional Court has declared that certain articles of the Rome Statute form part of the Constitutional Bloc, which means that it can strike down legislation under the Rome Statute.[37] For example, the CCC struck down a law that sought to expand the statute of limitations on war crimes from twenty to thirty years on the grounds that such crimes were prescribed under the Rome Statute.[38] Further, the Constitutional Court has cited the ICC as a constraint on the implementation of the Justice and Peace Law, which created a special jurisdiction for the prosecution of the paramilitary, and in its review of the Framework for Peace Law, which set the legal groundwork for the current peace dialogues.

Beyond the constitutional block, international courts can also have influence by modeling approaches to legal questions that may appear in both the international and domestic setting. In the context of the internal conflict, each court has been able to create approaches and standards that serve as models for different domestic actors trying to solve very different problems. In its judgments, the Inter-American Court regularly assigns monetary reparations for victims of atrocity, and it has developed a robust jurisprudence on these matters. Colombia's *Consejo Superior del Estado* regularly draws on this jurisprudence as a guide to its own remedial practice in the context of victims of the armed conflict.[39]

The Inter-American Court is not a criminal court, and thus its practice is less relevant to domestic criminal courts: it does not have its own set of criminal procedures, and it does not issue penal sentences. However, the Colombian Supreme Court in its criminal cassation role does at times turn to the Rome Statute and the ICC's jurisprudence for guidance and doctrinal support as it reviews national prosecutions of crimes against

---

[36] The CCC and Supreme Court databases show that these two peak courts have referred to and cited the ICC in hundreds of cases. Colombian Supreme Court, Search Engine *at* http://181.57.206.12/busquedadoc/FULLTEXT.ASPX. Simple search using "corte interamericana" resulted in 1980 documents (last checked February 17, 2017).

[37] Constitutional Court of Colombia, Sentence C-290 (2012) at www.corteconstitucional.gov .co/RELATORIA/2012/C-290-12.htm.

[38] Ibid.

[39] E. G. Botero, "El principio de reparación integral en Colombia a la luz del Sistema Interamericano de Derechos" in H. O. Alonso and S. C. Curbello (eds.), *Perspectiva Iberoamericana sobre la Justicia Penal Internacional* (2012) p. 319; R. Uprimny, "Bloque De Constitucionalidad, Derechos Humanos y Nuevo Procedimiento Penal," http://www .cejamericas.org/BoletinNexos/publicaciones/Dia1Impactodelcontroldeconvencionalidad LibroBloquedeConstitucionalidadyProcesoPenal.pdf. (Botero was judge on the Consejo and is now a member of the Commission.)

humanity and war crimes. In one case, for example, it referred extensively to the Rome Statute's treatment of the limits of res judicata as a guide to its own decision.[40] Finally, Colombian courts cite the ICC not only as a source of law and norms, but also as a threat. The Supreme Court has bolstered its own pro-prosecutorial rulings by emphasizing the need "to show the international community that intervention by the international criminal justice system is not necessary because Colombia is able to try those responsible for such crimes and to impose the punitive consequences established under national criminal law."[41]

Through this judicial dialogue, then, each international court has influenced the state's response to atrocity crimes, but their influence works through distinct bodies of law, is used by different national actors, and achieves different types of changes in state behavior. In this dynamic of parallel work, the fact that both courts are involved in similar matters does not seem to heighten or lessen their legitimacy. If the *Consejo Superior* refers to the Inter-American Court, for example, it neither bolsters nor undermines the work of the ICC, except perhaps in the weak sense that it normalizes citation to international jurisdictions.

B   Working toward the Same Goals

The ICC and the Inter-American Court do not only work toward consonant goals; at times they also work toward the same goal. In particular, both seek, as a priority, to foster domestic investigation and punishment of atrocity crimes. Both courts have read their mandates to include not just litigation over specific violations covered in their respective treaties, but also processes for pushing the state to open prosecutions for atrocity crimes and supervising ongoing prosecutions for conformity to international standards. Indeed, they are supervising the prosecution of many of the same underlying criminal acts. Further, in light of their converging roles, actors on the ground who are making decisions about the internal conflict or advocating a particular solution to the question of criminal liability for atrocity crimes keep both courts in view, referring to them both as guides and constraints on these matters.

---

[40]   Colombian Supreme Court Division of Criminal Appeals, October 22, 2014, AP6557-2014 Radicación No. 41.490 Act No. 349 at 181.57.206.37:8080/WebRelatoria/FileReferenceServlet?corp=csj&ext=pdf&file=308303.
[41]   Colombian Supreme Court Division of Criminal Appeals, No. 30510 (March 11, 2009) (translated from Spanish original). (Cited in ICTJ briefing for Kampala conference.)

130   ALEXANDRA HUNEEUS

Both courts, for example, have played a role in shaping and overseeing prosecutions that take place pursuant to the Justice and Peace Law (2005). When President Uribe assumed power in 2002, he began negotiations to decommission the paramilitary, one of the several actors in the Colombian conflict that had regularly committed atrocity crimes, including massacres of noncombatants. The Justice and Peace Law created a special judicial process, which lightened the sentences of paramilitaries who put down arms and cooperated with ongoing investigations.

Eight of the Inter-American Court's judgments have addressed the question of how the state should respond to violations committed by the paramilitaries in the context of the Justice and Peace Law.[42] In several of these cases, the Commission and the representatives of the victims have asked the Court to review the Justice and Peace law and find that it was an impediment to prosecution and in violation of the American Convention. In response, the Court has examined the progress of each relevant case and argued that the state has violated the right to justice due to lack of investigation. However, it has not declared that the Justice and Peace Law itself violates the Convention. A 2014 judgment carefully evaluates the work of these special jurisdictions in response to forced displacement and other organized attacks against civilians that took place in an Afro-descendant community in the department of Choco in 1997.[43] Although it concedes that the law itself is not in violation of the Convention and could thus be read as supporting this transitional justice measure, the Court asserts its power to monitor the prosecutions that fall under its jurisdiction until they reach conclusion. In this way, the Inter-American Court will continue to consider the course of these cases under the Peace and Justice Law. The Inter-American Court has also indicated that it is not enough to investigate the cases as individual crimes: they

---

[42] *19 Tradesmen v. Colombia*, Reparations & Costs, Inter-Am. Ct. H.R. (ser. C) No. 109 (July 5, 2004); *Mapiripán Massacre v. Colombia*, Merits, Reparations & Costs, Inter-Am. Ct. H.R., (September 15, 2005); *Pueblo Bello Massacre v. Colombia*, Merits, Reparations & Costs, Inter-Am. Ct. H.R. (ser. C) No. 140 (January 31, 2006); *Ituango Massacres v. Colombia*, Reparations & Costs, Inter-Am. Ct. H.R. (ser. C) No. 148, (July 1, 2006); *La Rochela Massacre v. Colombia*, Reparations & Costs, Inter-Am. Ct. H.R. (ser. C) No. 163 (May 11, 2007); *Valle Jaramillo et al. v. Colombia*, Reparations & Costs, Inter-Am. Ct. H.R. (ser. C) No. 192 (July 7, 2009); *Cepeda Vargas v. Colombia*, Merits, Reparations & Costs, Inter-Am. Ct. H.R. (ser. C) No. *213* (2010); *Afro-descendant Communities Displaced from the Cacarica River Basin (Operation Genesis) v. Colombia*, Series C No. 270 (November 20, 2013).

[43] *Afro-descendant Communities Displaced from the Cacarica River Basin (Operation Genesis) v. Colombia*, see note 41.

must also be analyzed in the larger context of organized violence to bring into view the structural dimensions of the crime.[44]

Within the criminal justice system, judges and prosecutors are aware of and responsive to the Inter-American Court's demands. The *Fiscalia General*, the national prosecutor, has a high-level office devoted to its international relations that acts as the locus of communication with other branches and international entities. When the Inter-American Court issues a judgment against Colombia in which it requests criminal investigation, or when the Court requests information about particular investigations, the office gets in touch with the prosecutor on the case. From the prosecutor's perspective, this is a signal to prioritize a particular case and move it forward so that the next time a superior requests information, there will be something to report. These requests for information also prompt prosecutors to read the Inter-American Court's judgments.

The ICC has also monitored the progress of the Justice and Peace Law. Although ICC Prosecutor Luis Moreno Ocampo formally announced that he was opening a preliminary investigation in 2005, he did not lead a fact-gathering mission to Colombia until 2007. During that trip, he met with state and nonstate actors to discuss the various matters that were of concern to the OTP. High among matters of concern to the ICC was the Justice and Peace Law. In statements to the press during the first trip, Luis Moreno Ocampo lauded the advance of prosecutions under the Law, conveying that Colombia was on the vanguard of transitional justice and had the potential to provide an example to the world.[45]

In May 2007, however, the OTP's public position shifted when Colombia extradited the first of several top leaders of the paramilitaries to the United States, where they were wanted for drug dealing. This was perceived by human rights advocates as a severe setback to the Justice and Peace process.[46] In the United States, the paramilitaries could be only be prosecuted for drug trafficking crimes, and they would be shielded from the ICC. Further, it was at first unclear if the United States would allow them to continue to collaborate with the JPL process and what incentives they would have to do so. The extraditions prompted

---

[44] Ibid.

[45] J. T. Martinez, "'Ningún país hace tanto en justicia transicional como Colombia': Luis Moreno dice que el país ha hecho un esfuerzo por esclarecer los crímenes de los paramilitares," *El Tiempo*, September 15, 2013, www.eltiempo.com/archivo/documento/CMS-13064207.

[46] Redacción Política, "Corte Responde a la CPI," *El Espectador*, August 16, 2008, www.elespectador.com/impreso/politica/articuloimpreso-corte-responde-cpi.

Prosecutor Ocampo to write a letter expressing concern to Colombia's ambassador in The Hague in June.[47] The prosecutor traveled to Colombia the following month, which was perceived as a way to pressure the government to end the extraditions and return to the Justice and Peace process. The Colombian government's responses to the criticisms of the OTP and other human rights bodies, including the Inter-American Court, was that it would have access to the paramilitaries in the United States, and the Truth and Justice Law processes would continue unhindered.

Alongside this public intervention, the OTP also continued to monitor the advance of Justice and Peace cases, regularly requesting information from state officials. To this day, the OTP's trips to Colombia include visits to the Justice and Peace Courts and the Justice and Peace unit in the national prosecutor's office.[48] Further, OTP officials regularly meet with the Justice and Peace judges and the national prosecutor when they travel to Colombia, and they, too, request updates on the advance of *all* the Peace and Justice cases (as opposed to just the cases before the Inter-American Court. In its 2012 interim report the ICC finds that the advance of the cases under the Justice and Peace Law was satisfactory and therefore would not trigger ICC jurisdiction.[49] Like the Inter-American Court, however, the ICC approved the Justice and Peace Law processes with the caveat that it will continue to monitor the advance of cases under this special jurisdiction.

In this way, the two courts keep a close eye on the Colombian justice system as it processes the prosecutions of the former paramilitaries. Both have worked to push the Colombian government to prosecute. However, the *means* by which they push for this shared end differ in significant ways, reflecting their distinct mandates and structure. Overall, the Inter-American Court has acted in a more court-like manner: It is constrained

---

[47] See note 31. In the letter, Ocampo asks: "How will you assure the judgment of the most responsible for crimes that would be under ICC jurisdiction ...? In particular, I would like to know if the investigations that have been conducted to date indicate the commission of acts that the Rome Statue penalizes and if the extradition of the leaders of the paramilitaries presents an obstacle to the effectiveness of the investigation of said politicians."

[48] The Peace and Justice Law created a special Justice and Peace jurisdiction within the judiciary devoted to the paramilitary cases and a special unit within the National Prosecutor as well. *See* L. J. Laplante and K. Theidon, "Transitional justice in times of conflict: Colombia's Ley de Justicia y Paz," *Michigan Journal of International Law*, 28.1 (2006).

[49] See note 31.

to examination of the facts of the cases that arrive on its docket; it interacts only with the parties to the case before it; and it speaks only through its judgments and compliance reports. The ICC, by contrast, acts through the Office of the Prosecutor, and not in its adjudicative role. Through the preliminary investigation, it has embarked on a process whereby it seeks to influence prosecutorial policy through various types of communications. These communications do not have the legal force of judgments, nor are they limited to the facts and timing of individual cases. Rather, they have often been timed for impact, in response to political decisions being made on the ground, and they refer to prosecutorial policies and laws in general, rather than in specific cases. Thus, while the Inter-American Court monitors compliance to its judgments by reviewing the advance of the specific prosecutions relevant to the cases that come before it, the ICC compiles overall statistics of the processes conducted by the attorney general (*Fiscalía General*). And while the Inter-American Court officially speaks only to the state parties that represent the state in international litigation, the Office of the Prosecutor of the ICC directly schedules meetings with high-level officials key to prioritization of the advance of certain cases overall and sends the occasional letter reminding different Colombian officials of its looming threat.

Another significant difference of means is the type of consequences the courts can impose: As the Inter-American Court pushes for compliance, the only threat it can wield is the reputational cost to the state of Colombia of ongoing noncompliance with its different judgments. The ICC carries a bigger stick: It can threaten to make Colombia its first situation outside of Africa. Not only does this threat entail a greater reputational cost to the state; crucially, it also impacts individuals in their personal capacity. The ICC's power to open an investigation carries a threat of imprisonment that directly concerns high-ranking individuals who have acted within the state, as well as the paramilitaries and guerrilla organizations. Further, in a place such as Colombia where the state is not in control of the entire territory,[50] the ICC potentially poses a threat even to individuals who escape the state's grasp, residing in those areas where the state is absent. By contrast, the Inter-American Court can work only *through* the state.[51] But the threat of opening a situation is also a blunter

---

[50] Mauricio Garcia Villegas and Jose Rafael Espinosa, *El Derecho al Estado: Los Efectos del Apartheid Institucional en Colombia* (Bogota: Colección de Justicia, 2013), pp. 91–3.

[51] Of course, as many scholars have noted, the paradox of the ICC is that it ultimately relies on the unable or unwilling state to conduct its own investigation.

instrument: it does not respond to the course of individual cases, but to the Colombian situation in its entirety. Further, it is a threat that arguably wanes in impact as the preliminary investigation enters its second decade.[52]

Through different strategies and means, then, the two courts helped resolve different aspects of the same problem: accountability for the crimes of the paramilitary. In this mode of complementary work, the legitimacy of the work of one is boosted by the work of the other in a dynamic of constructive interference: We can imagine that where not one but two international courts push toward the same end, the end toward which they push becomes harder to question. When a prosecutor has before her a case that is being monitored by the Inter-American Court, and she learns from her superiors that the ICC prosecutor is also pushing for that particular type of case to move forward, that case is doubly prioritized. We can further imagine that that as the goal becomes more legitimate, the institutional legitimacy of each court is bolstered.

C Working as One?

That two international courts complement each other, taking different legal and political pathways to shared goals, seems laudable – an example of the international legal system working harmoniously. But the Colombian peace process has also revealed ways in which the ICC and the Inter-America Court begin to blur the distinctions between their legal mandates, raising questions of both normative and sociological legitimacy.

One episode in particular captures this dynamic. In 2012, the Congress enacted the Framework for Peace Law, which reformed the 1991 Constitution to include a transitional justice provision designed to pave the way for an eventual peace accord with the irregular armed groups in the internal conflict.[53] The emphasis of the law was on striking a balance between punishment and victims' rights. As in the Peace and Justice Law, one of the most controversial aspects of the Framework for Peace was its proposal to create a more flexible transitional justice regime.[54]

---

[52] See note 24.
[53] Colombian Congress, Marco Juridico para la Paz, Acto Legislativo 01, (2012) *at* wsp .presidencia.gov.co/Normativa/actos-legislativos/Documents/2012/ACTO%20LEGISLA-TIVO%20N%C2%B0%2001%20DEL%2031%20DE%20JULIO%20DE%202012.pdf.
[54] Ibid.

Many criticized it for allowing the possibility of international crimes going unpunished. It was soon challenged before the Constitutional Court.[55]

While the Framework Law was pending on the Constitutional Court's docket, the media leaked two closed letters sent by the OTP to the CCC.[56] The letters, addressed to the president of the Constitutional Court and signed by Chief Prosecutor Fatou Bensouda, articulate the OTP's position on two matters regarding criminal liability in the peace process that were being debated before the CCC. In the first, the OTP considers as a matter of first impression whether, after a judicial process that is genuine, the state could forego the sentence, allowing the defendant to avoid incarceration. In its interim report of 2012 the OTP had declared that Colombia's prosecutions of the crimes of the FARC had been "genuine," and thus were not being considered by the OTP, even if some of the processes had taken place 'in absentia." Now, the Framework Law could be read as allowing for those convicted to avoid incarceration altogether. Bensouda's letter was a warning to the Constitutional Court that such a reading of the law would again make Colombia vulnerable to the ICC opening a case against FARC actors.

In supporting her reading of the Rome Statute, Bensouda seemed to acknowledge that the *travaux preparatoires* do not provide clear guidance, citing instead an early policy statement of the OTP. The problem is that the Rome Statute does not articulate a standard and, some argue, does not actually impose an obligation on states to prosecute, as it is an instrument aimed at defining the role of the ICC, not the state.[57] The sources of the state's obligations in this matter arguably lie elsewhere. Further, there is no ICC jurisprudence that she can cite; this is, she noted, a matter of first instance for the ICC. She relied for support instead on the jurisprudence of the Inter-American Court of Human Rights. The Inter-American Court has a rich line of jurisprudence developing what its critics label a neopunitivist stance on the obligation

---

[55] Constitutional Court of Colombia, C-577 (2014) *at* www.corteconstitucional.gov.co/RELATORIA/2014/C-577-14.htm

[56] Bensouda to Constitutional Court, 26 July 2013, Ref. 2013/0/FB/JCCD-evdu, http://www.derechos.org/nizkor/colombia/doc/cpicol7.html/. In the second letter, Bensouda turns to the question of whether the state can adopt a policy of prosecuting only the most responsible, as does the OTP. Bensouda to Constitutional Court, 18 August 2013, "Bensouda to Constitutonal Court," *at* www.semana.com/nacion/articulo/una-carta-bomba/354430-3.

[57] See note 29.

136 ALEXANDRA HUNEEUS

of states to investigate and punish under the American Convention. The Colombian Constitutional Court is well aware of this jurisprudence, with which it is bound to comply under the doctrine of the constitutional bloc, and which it cited over ninety times when it reviewed the Justice and Peace Law. But here the OTP seemed to say that not only does that jurisprudence define Colombia's obligations under the American Convention, but it also defines the obligations of Colombia under the Rome Statute.[58]

Just a few weeks later, the Constitutional Court upheld the Legal Framework for Peace.[59] However, it emphasized that the law should not be implemented in such a way that those responsible for crimes within the jurisdiction of the ICC be excused from punishment. The judgment cites to the Inter-American Court's jurisprudence, the American Convention, the ICC, and the Rome Statute. But it makes no mention of the ICC's letters.

The two international courts' roles in the Constitutional Court's review of the Framework for Peace Law again suggests the possibility of a dynamic whereby the joint presence of the Inter-American Court and the ICC enhance their shared goals. In the preceding section, we discussed how the courts at times work toward the same goal but using distinct means. Here, the ICC seemingly begins to merge means: it hitches itself to Inter-American Court jurisprudence in such a way that the Inter-American Court's goals are enforced through ICC means, as will be further discussed later. This convergence is a positive development for those persuaded that heightened pressure toward prosecution will lead to better, more just outcomes as Colombia struggles to resolve its internal conflict. In terms of the inquiry of this chapter, however, which seeks to analyze the legitimacy of overlapping jurisdictions in an ever more judicialized international world order, the coupling of IAS jurisprudence with the ICC's big-stick threat raises an important issue.

IV Blurred Lines

Each international agreement strikes a balance between substance and form and can be altered by changes to either. As Andrew Guzman has argued, "The burden of an agreement can be affected by changing the substance, but the same change can be achieved through changes to the

---

[58] See note 56.   [59] See note 54.

form of the agreement."[60] The ICC/IACtHR convergence described earlier arguably increases the burden of the state by changing the form of enforcement of the American Convention and the substance of the Rome Statute.

In the balance between the substance of a commitment and its structural form, the Inter-American System imposes a high substantive level of commitment. Since its founding, the Inter-American Court has developed a broad, progressive jurisprudence on a full spectrum of human rights contained in the American Convention. However, this long list of strong substantive commitments comes coupled with weak forms of implementation. First, the Inter-American Court is passive; it can only respond to violations that arrive on its docket through the petition system. Second, the American Convention formally places enforcement in the hands of the OAS General Assembly, a political rather than juridical body, and a body in which Colombia has greater political clout than it does, say, in the UN General Assembly, or the Assembly of State Parties of the Rome Statute.[61]

Finally, a salient feature of the Inter-American System is its slowness. Petitioners must first exhaust local resources and then wait for the Inter-American Commission to try to resolve a case, which can take up to five years.[62] Only then can their case be referred to the Inter-American Court. Arguably one of the reasons the Inter-American Court has been able to successfully take a strong stand on the matter of amnesties is that by the time it rules, the leaders who protected themselves through the amnesty law have usually stepped down, and their power has waned. The Inter-America Court's exacting amnesty jurisprudence is coupled with a slow, lenient implementation process that waits out recalcitrance.

The Rome Statute, by contrast, has far fewer substantive norms: It covers three crimes, and these are defined in greater detail, giving judges less interpretive license. But it has more powerful mechanism of enforcement. Not only is the reputational cost to a state of having the ICC open a case high, but also the threat of an ICC prosecution may threaten leaders in their personal capacity. Further, the ICC has an office unique in the world of international courts – the world prosecutor, who in her

---

[60] A. T. Guzman, "How international law works," *International Theory*, 1.2 (2009), 285–93.

[61] *Medellín* v. *Texas*, 552 U.S. 491 (2008).

[62] A. Dulitzky, "Too little, too late: The pace of adjudication of the Inter-American Commission on Human Rights," *Loyola of Los Angeles International and Comparative Law Review*, 35 (2013), 131.

investigatory capacity, works unconstrained by the forms and times of adjudication and can even initiate an investigation *proprio motu*. Finally, while the ICC has been criticized for moving slowly when it prosecutes, the Office of the Prosecutor can move quickly into the preliminary examination stage. The ICC is thus able to enter the arena even as a conflict is still roiling and its leaders still in power.[63]

Each judicial regime, then, was designed by states to have particular features and to have a distinct balance of strengths and weaknesses. But these distinctions are lost when the ICC threatens Colombia with opening a case if it does not comply with the Inter-American Court's standards. Indeed, the ICC seems to be changing the stakes, enhancing the substantive norms it protects, or, alternatively, changing the forms by which the American Convention is judicialized. In ratifying the American Convention and accepting the jurisdiction of the Inter-American Court, Colombia was accepting the jurisdiction of a small, underfunded court with weak and slow-moving mechanisms of enforcement. Now noncompliance to the Inter-American Court's standards leads to a different, more high-stakes outcome: an ICC prosecution. This was not part of the original bargain, and it could dramatically alter the stakes attached to the options available to the peace negotiators.

That the ICC uses the Inter-American Court's jurisprudence to expand the substantive norms it enforces might seem another example of the international system working as it should. By citing to the Inter-American Court, it likely enhances its own sociological legitimacy as well as that of the ICC, and it ascertains that the work of the ICC does not conflict with the Inter-American standards. In any case, it is often the case that courts alter their original mandate by their actions through the years. This can lead to greater legitimacy when they rule in a way that generates support among key audiences.[64] The courts, in other words, may be gaining sociological legitimacy at the cost of their normative legitimacy.[65]

However, it is also clear that the ICC, by coupling its forms of working with the substantive norms developed by the Inter-American Court,

---

[63] M. Kersten, *Justice in Conflict: The Effects of the International Criminal Court's Interventions on Ending Wars and Building Peace* (Oxford University Press, 2015), pp. 1–8 (on how one of the unique features of the ICC is that it almost always becomes involved in ongoing conflicts, as opposed to conflicts that have passed).

[64] See note 8.

[65] See note 8 (arguing that activism can, at times, enhance legitimacy). The European Court of Justice, the European Court of Human Rights, the IACtHR of Human Rights, and the International Criminal Court are all often accused of mission creep.

could reduce the options available to OAS states as they attempt to negotiate peace. It would be awkward if as a result of this coupling, the ICC imposed higher standards on American states than African states.

A   Timely Retreat

With not a moment to lose, the ICC seems to have stepped back from its maximalist interpretation of the Rome Statute by way of the Inter-American Court's jurisprudence. In September 2016, the government of Colombia and the FARC at last signed a peace treaty. The Treaty left open the possibility that certain actors who have committed international crimes may be able to serve alternative sentences: In other words, they might avoid prison time altogether, although they would suffer some restriction of their liberty as a form of punishment. The OTP again opined on developments on the ground. This time, however, it issued a public statement (as opposed to closed letter) in which it was more deferential to the Colombian government's discretion:

> The paramount importance of genuine accountability – which by defin-ition includes effective punishment – in nurturing a sustainable peace cannot be overstated ... I note, with satisfaction, that the final text of the peace agreement excludes amnesties and pardons for crimes against humanity and war crimes under the Rome Statute. The peace agreement acknowledges the central place of victims in the process and their legit-imate aspirations for justice. These aspirations must be fully addressed, including by ensuring that the perpetrators of serious crimes are genu-inely brought to justice.[66]

Again, the Rome Statute does not actually specify what punishment means. But now the OTP seems less concerned with the mode of punishment. It softened its position, offering support as the government tried to campaign for the treaty in a national referendum.

The government failed in this campaign: a month after the treaty was signed, Colombians surprised the world by voting against the peace in the plebiscite. Proponents of peace were outraged and quick to blame the loss on illegitimate factors, including the weather, a powerful campaign by Uribe, and Human Rights Watch, which opined that the Peace Treaty

---

[66] Fatou Bensouda, "Statement of ICC Prosecutor, Fatou Bensouda, on the conclusion of the peace negotiations between the Government of Colombia and the Revolutionary Armed Forces of Colombia – People's Army," International Criminal Court, September 1, 2016 at www.icc-cpi.int/Pages/item.aspx?name=160901-otp-stat-colombia.

was too lenient on punishment.[67] The OTP's supportive letter could not have been more timely. A critical statement on the peace accord would have made the ICC a scapegoat for the failed plebiscite vote. Several news articles instead took aim at Human Rights Watch (HRW), in one instance arguing that HRW had acted as Uribe's useful idiot.[68] It is easy to imagine that the ICC would have drawn even more indignation and ire.

If this turn of events shows the legitimacy risks to the ICC, it is noteworthy that the ICC was deft enough to avoid them in the end. Despite pressure from the opponents of Santos's piece, including a long complaint by the *procurador,* who is charged with monitoring legality of government actions,[69] the OTP seemed to have been able to perceive the risk to its legitimacy and to retreat. The dangers of self-aggrandizing are real. But this vignette suggests that perhaps there are mechanisms in place that allow the ICC to be politically responsive. In particular, the OTP, not bound by precedent or legal argument, can be politically nimble. The specter of an overbearing ICC joining ranks with the Inter-American Court is thus tempered by its ability to perceive and respond to legitimacy risks.

V Conclusion

We invite our counterparty in the Peace Process ... to retire the juridical weeds that they have crossed, like a dead mule, on the road to peace.

– FARC-EP Peace Negotiation Team, March 26, 2015

The ICC and the Inter-American Court have acted in concert to reshape how Colombia contends with its armed conflict and how it makes peace. Ultimately, their coincidence and interaction has bolstered their impact even as it has narrowed the spectrum of choices available for the actors involved in the peace talks. For the study of fragmentation and legitimacy in international law, the significance of the Colombian case is twofold. First, Colombia provides an example of a growing phenomenon: one or

---

[67] José Miguel Vivanco, "Letter to President Santos on the New Peace Agreement with the FARC," *Human Rights Watch* (2016), www.hrw.org/news/2016/11/23/letter-president-santos-new-peace-agreement-farc (last visited July 27, 2016) (expressing concern that war criminals will not undergo punishment).

[68] G. Grandin, "Did Human Rights Watch sabotage Colombia's peace agreement?" *The Nation*, October 3, 2016.

[69] Carta Alejandro Ordonez a Fatou Bensouda, January 19, 2016, www.procuraduria.gov.co/portal/media/file/portal_doc_interes//216_190116COMUNICACION.pdf.

more international courts interacting with the same state over the same policy area. It shows us how international courts with distinct mandates can converge on similar goals and work as complements in similar policy areas, enhancing their mutual influence and legitimacy. The case study also suggested that the coupling of court power holds risks. In particular, their interaction can lead to judicial effects beyond what the state committed to in submitting to the jurisdiction of each. In the end, the ICC avoided this outcome by supporting the peace agreement.

It is important to note that the dynamic of constructive interaction revealed here is only one of many different ways that this coincident jurisdiction may play out and captures a moment in an ongoing process. We can also imagine a dynamic of competition or discord, in which international courts together undermine the effect each would have on its own.[70] Or, we can imagine that one court gains and the other loses legitimacy. A next step is to develop a more comprehensive typology of how these interactions are playing out, laying the ground for empirical analysis of what conditions lead to which outcome and to what effect.

It is also important, going forward, to consider whether legitimacy attaches to one court at a time, or to the international judiciary as a whole. Of course, formally speaking, there is no international judiciary. Each international court belongs to a distinct international order, just as national courts from different states belong to different legal orders. But where courts are interacting with the same domestic actors over the same matters, the actions of one international court might affect perceptions of international courts in general. This is likely especially the case where international courts are newer and less deeply entrenched (as in Latin America as opposed to Europe). It seems fitting, therefore, to close by suggesting as a next step in the study of international court legitimacy research that views international courts, or a subset of international courts, together. The Colombian case study, for example, may impact the legitimacy of international courts in conflict resolution. Although international courts were originally conceived as a way to avoid war through adjudication, new or recently established international courts are reviewing an ever broader set of situations of peace-making, post-conflict reconstruction, and even active conflict. The European Court of Human Rights, the African Court of Human and Peoples' Rights, the Economic Community of West African States Community Court of

---

[70] See note 4.

Justice, and the International Court of Justice have all been asked to adjudicate situations of conflict or postconflict.[71] It is possible that the outcome of the Colombian experience will color perceptions of the legitimacy of such interventions. It would also be of interest to consider how perceptions of the domestic judiciary shapes perceptions of international courts, and vice versa, and how the interaction of national and international courts affects their legitimacy. In Colombia the judiciary and the Constitutional Court in particular enjoy relatively high prestige, especially in comparison to the elected branches. The CCC likely imbues the Inter-American Court and ICC with its own prestige when it weaves them into domestic dispute resolution through the constitutional block, even as it bolsters its own jurisprudence.

---

[71] This will be the case especially in Africa when and if the African Union adds a criminal jurisdiction to its human rights and general court. *See* M. Sirleaf, "Regionalism, regime complexes and the crisis in international criminal justice," *Columbia Journal of Transnational Law*, 54 (2016).

6

The Legitimacy of the European Court of Justice

Normative Debates and Empirical Evidence

MARK A. POLLACK

International courts (ICs) occupy a precarious perch in international law and politics. Creatures of their member states and the treaties and statutes that created them, ICs lack the power to compel respect for or compliance with their rulings. Even the most powerful international courts ultimately enjoy neither the power of the purse nor that of the sword, relying entirely on "the goodwill of their constituents for both support and compliance."[1] International courts, in other words, rely on their legitimacy vis-à-vis their audiences, yet they suffer from a twofold disadvantage: As *courts,* they are suspect for their lack of direct selection by and accountability to mass publics; and as *international* courts, they lack grounding in domestic law and politics, their rulings appearing as foreign impositions on national communities.

This chapter examines both normative debates and empirical evidence about the legitimacy of one of the oldest, busiest, and most powerful international courts in the world: the Court of Justice of the European Union (CJEU).[2] The CJEU, it must be conceded at the outset, is not a typical international court, given its long life span, its large caseload, and

---

[1] J. L. Gibson, G. A. Caldeira, and V. A. Baird, "On the legitimacy of national high courts," *American Political Science Review,* 92(2) (1998), 343–58. In this regard international courts are similar to national constitutional courts, which lack the material force to compel governments and legislators to obey their rulings; see J. K. Staton and W. H. Moore, "Judicial power in domestic and international politics," *International Organization,* 65(3) (2011), 553–87. Both international and constitutional courts, in other words, face the same problem: getting people with guns to obey people with gavels.

[2] As a formal matter, the CJEU is the judicial institution of the EU and is made up of three courts: the Court of Justice, the General Court (the former Court of First Instance), and the Civil Service Tribunal. My focus in this chapter is on the Court of Justice, often referred to as the ECJ.

143

its direct links to domestic courts and legal systems of its member states. Any findings about the Court can therefore be generalized only with great care to other international courts. Nevertheless, in the context of this pioneering, comparative volume on the legitimacy of international courts, the CJEU is of considerable interest because scholars have engaged in more extensive and sustained normative debate and empirical study of the Court's legitimacy than perhaps any other international court, offering potential lessons about how to theorize and empirically study international judicial legitimacy. In normative terms, European law scholars spent decades lauding the CJEU's pioneering jurisprudence and its "constitutionalization" of the treaties, only to engage in recent years in a vigorous debate about the legitimacy of the Court and its jurisprudence. In empirical terms, a handful of widely cited scholarly studies have explored the extent, and the causes, of diffuse support for the Court among mass publics, and these studies are worth examining closely, not only for their findings about the CJEU, but also with an eye to the strengths and weaknesses of these studies as models for the empirical study of legitimacy of other ICs.

The chapter is organized in four parts. The first provides a basic theoretical framework, defining legitimacy and distinguishing its two variants (normative and sociological). The second part of the chapter examines the normative legitimacy of the CJEU, identifying and applying three criteria for international court legitimacy: that courts should be fair and unbiased, that their rulings should be politically acceptable and legally sound, and that they should operate openly and transparently. Although the CJEU has historically enjoyed a high degree of normative legitimacy, I find, recent decades have witnessed the emergence of a vigorous debate featuring overlapping charges of bias, of judicial activism and poor legal reasoning, and of opacity at the Court. The third part of the chapter turns to the sociological legitimacy of the CJEU among its various audiences, and in particular among mass publics. The study of public attitudes toward the Court, I argue, is highly sensitive to measurement issues, but in general paints a picture of a public support that has been historically widespread but shallow and quite fragile, and I demonstrate that this support has decreased in the past decade, as the Court has been caught up in a broader crisis of EU legitimacy. A brief fourth section concludes by arguing that the Court, although still broadly supported, is subject to both greater normative criticism and lower levels of public support than in the past.

I Framework for Analysis

As the editors point out in their introduction to this volume, meanings of the term *legitimacy* vary considerably across disciplines and across levels of analysis, but most definitions of the term revolve around the "justification and acceptance of political authority," or more simply, "the right to rule."[3] From this core definition, many scholars proceed to distinguish between two distinct conceptions of legitimacy. *Normative legitimacy* refers to a philosophical question about whether a particular actor "has a right to rule as a matter of moral theory," whereas *sociological legitimacy* refers to an empirical question about "whether its authority is accepted by relevant audiences, such as states and civil society groups; whether it enjoys a reservoir of support that makes people willing to defer even to unpopular decisions and helps sustain the institution through difficult times."[4] This core distinction between normative and sociological legitimacy is fundamental, and the respective literatures on normative and sociological legitimacy also introduce several core concepts that have influenced the study of CJEU legitimacy.

The discussion of normative legitimacy, for example, has yielded the influential distinction between what Fritz Scharpf refers to as "*input*" and "*output*" legitimacy. Input legitimacy, or government *by* the people, refers to features of government including electoral accountability of representative institutions to the people, transparency, and public participation; while output legitimacy, or government *for* the people, refers to the quality of government policies, including features such as efficiency, fairness, stability, and respect for human rights.[5]

The discussion of sociological legitimacy, in turn, directs our attention to other conceptual and empirical questions, including most notably the question of the *audience*. Sociological legitimacy is a relational concept, a subjective assessment of an institution by the members of its audience.[6]

---

[3] D. Bodansky, "Legitimacy in international law and international relations" in J. L. Dunoff and M. A. Pollack (eds.), *Interdisciplinary Perspectives on International Law and International Relations: The State of the Art* (New York: Cambridge University Press, 2013), pp. 321–41, at 324.

[4] Ibid., at 326–7.

[5] Fritz W. Scharpf, *Governing in Europe: Effective and Democratic?* (Oxford: Oxford University Press, 1999); c.f. V. A. Schmidt, "Democracy and legitimacy in the European Union revisited: Input, output and 'throughput,'" *Political Studies*, 61(1) (2013), 2–22.

[6] I. Hurd, "Legitimacy and authority in international politics," *International Organization*, 53(2) (1999), 379–408, at 381, cited in Y. Lupu, "International judicial legitimacy: Lessons from national courts," *Theoretical Inquiries in Law*, 14(2) (2013), 437–54, at 442.

In studies of domestic institutions, the audience is often considered unproblematically to consist of the mass public, although some studies focus more narrowly on "attentive publics" with some knowledge of an institution and its activities.[7] In the case of international courts, however, the attentive public may include not only mass publics, whose knowledge of international institutions may be minimal, but also and primarily various elite actors, including the national governments, courts, or the legal communities of the court's member states. Nevertheless, lacking systematic data about the attitudes of such elite actors, the literature on the sociological legitimacy of international courts has focused primarily on public opinion, as I will demonstrate in this chapter.

Another key concept arising from the literature on sociological legitimacy is the crucial distinction between what David Easton called *specific* and *diffuse support* for an institution. As crystallized by Yonatan Lupu, "Specific support for an institution is the extent to which individuals find that the institution has fulfilled their demands for policy (or policy preferences)."[8] In the case of a court, specific support is manifest in audiences' substantive satisfaction with the decisions of that court. Most scholars of judicial legitimacy, however, focus on diffuse support, defined as a willingness to support and defend a court and its jurisdiction even in the face of decisions with which audience members disagree, which is seen as the better (and more demanding) measure of legitimacy.[9]

The question of the CJEU's normative legitimacy has thus far been the province primarily of legal scholars and philosophers, while the descriptive or sociological legitimacy of the CJEU has been the subject of a handful of empirical studies conducted primarily by political scientists. I address each of these two literatures, and their findings, in Sections II and III of this chapter.

---

[7] See, e.g., J. L. Gibson and G. A. Caldeira, "The legitimacy of transnational legal institutions: Compliance, support, and the European Court of Justice," *American Journal of Political Science*, 39(2) (1995), 459–89, at 470–1; G. A. Caldeira and J. L. Gibson, "The legitimacy of the Court of Justice in the European Union: Models of institutional support," *American Political Science Review*, 89(2) (1995), 356–76; J. L. Gibson and G. A. Caldeira, "Changes in the legitimacy of the European Court of Justice: A post-Maastricht analysis," *British Journal of Political Science*, 28(1) (1998), 63–91; and Gibson, Caldeira, and Baird, "On the legitimacy of supranational high courts," at 345.

[8] Lupu, "International judicial legitimacy," at 440–1.   [9] Ibid., at 441.

II The Normative Legitimacy of the CJEU: Criteria and Critiques

Concern about the legitimacy of international governance has exploded in recent years, tracking the growth of international law and institutions and their impact on nonstate actors. This literature has been largely normative, characterized by a search for the appropriate standards of legitimacy for international institutions. With the increasing penetration of domestic politics by international law and institutions, the traditional international standard of legitimacy, state consent, is no longer seen as adequate. Instead, to the extent that international human rights, criminal, trade, and other rules impact individuals, the demand for democratic accountability of international institutions has increased dramatically.[10] I make no effort in this section to summarize this vast literature, but proceed instead in three steps. First, I briefly review the debate over the democratic legitimacy of the EU, noting the contested and generally marginal role of the CJEU in that debate. Second, I therefore look to the broader literature on the legitimacy of international courts qua courts and identify three criteria for international court legitimacy, namely that courts should be fair and unbiased, that their rulings should be politically acceptable and legally sound, and that they should operate openly and transparently. Third and finally, I apply these criteria to the CJEU and review a trio of interrelated and overlapping charges against the CJEU, namely charges of bias, of judicial activism and poor legal reasoning, and of opacity. As we shall see, the Court is generally held in high repute among legal scholars, yet all three normative critiques of the Court and its legitimacy have multiplied in recent years.

A The CJEU in Debates over the EU's "Democratic Deficit"

The debate over the legitimacy of the EU erupted early, more than a decade before the flowering of the broader literature on the legitimacy of international institutions. Beginning in the late 1980s, when the EU's internal market program began to legislate increasingly in areas that had previously been reserved to national legislatures, a growing number of critics began to identify a "democratic deficit" within the EU.[11]

---

[10] The literature on the legitimacy of international governance has mushroomed in recent years; Bodansky, "Legitimacy," provides an excellent overview.

[11] S. Williams, "Sovereignty and accountability in the European community" in R. O. Keohane and S. Hoffmann (eds.), *The New European Community* (Boulder, CO: Westview Press, 1991), pp. 155–76.

148   MARK A. POLLACK

Simplifying only slightly, one can identify in this literature three broad strands: (1) a "standard" critique[12] of the EU's lack of democratic accountability, (2) a social democratic critique of a Union biased toward neoliberal trade liberalization, and (3) a defense of the EU as an efficient nonmajoritarian institution (NMI).

The first of these strands, the standard critique, can be summarized in two key claims. First, it is argued, the EU is eroding national democracy by supplanting, though EU legislation or through CJEU decisions, national laws adopted by democratically elected national legislatures.[13] Second, the EU legislative process, which is increasingly displacing its domestic counterparts, is democratically unaccountable, owing to the distant and opaque nature of EU institutions and decision making, the strong role of indirectly elected politicians in the Council of Ministers and the unelected members of the Commission and the Court, and the historic weakness of the European Parliament.[14]

The second strand is what one might call the social democratic critique, which emphasizes the purported neoliberal bias of EU law and institutions. Most extensively articulated by Fritz Scharpf, this critique argues that the EU – from the structure of the treaties' objectives through the behavior of the legislative, executive, and judicial branches – prioritizes the free movement of goods, services, labor, and capital over other competing aims of social policy and social regulation.[15] In the words of Claus Offe, the *acquis communautaire* (the body of legislation accumulated by the EU and devoted primarily to market liberalization) now threatens the West European *acquis nationale* of strong liberal democracy and well-developed welfare states.[16]

By contrast with the first two, a third strand of the literature questions the use of parliamentary democracy as the appropriate metric for the EU, noting the increasingly widespread use of NMIs as instruments of

---

[12] A. Follesdal and S. Hix, "Why there is a democratic deficit in the EU: A response to Majone and Moravcsik," *Journal of Common Market Studies*, 44(3), 533–62.

[13] See, e.g., Williams, "Sovereignty and accountability"; and M. Th. Greven, "Can the European Union finally become a democracy?" in M. Greven and L. Pauly (eds.), *Democracy Beyond the State? The European Dilemma and the Emerging World Order* (New York: Rowman and Littlefield), pp. 35–61.

[14] Greven, "Can the European Union?"

[15] See, e.g., F. W. Scharpf, "The asymmetry of European integration, or why the EU cannot be a 'social market economy'," *Socioeconomic Review*, 8(2) (2010), 211–50.

[16] C. Offe, "The democratic welfare state in an integrating Europe" in M.Th. Greven and L. Pauly (eds.), *Democracy Beyond the State? The European Dilemma and the Emerging World Order* (New York: Rowman and Littlefield, 2000), pp. 63–90, at 73.

governance at both the domestic and international levels.[17] Contemporary democratic governments, it is argued, delegate far-reaching powers to NMIs, either to take advantage of those institutions' specialized expertise or to insulate them from majoritarian pressures so that they can defend important values such as the rule of law, human rights, a stable money supply, and so on. The EU, in this view, constitutes a variant of this domestic trend, in which governments delegate complex and technical tasks to nonmajoritarian actors such as the Commission and the European Central Bank.[18]

One striking feature of the "democratic deficit" literature is the generally peripheral place of the CJEU in the debate, which has focused in large part on the making, rather than the interpretation, of EU law. Equally striking, however, are the very different normative assessments of the CJEU across the three strands. The CJEU generally plays a minor and generally negative role in the "standard" critique, commonly criticized as one of several EU institutions lacking democratic accountability.[19] The Court plays a more central, and essentially negative, role in the social democratic critique, frequently accused of neoliberal bias in its dismantling of national regulations and welfare states. By contrast, the nonmajoritarian defense of the EU presents the Court in a positive light, suggesting that a politically insulated Court can play a role in safeguarding constitutional principles and individual rights. This disagreement about the role of the Court suggests that we need to look elsewhere for clues to the normative standards for the CJEU as a *court*.

B   The Normative Legitimacy of International Courts qua Courts: Three Criteria

Courts are, in most constituencies, *designed* to be NMIs, and hence their legitimacy is likely to rest on criteria and standards of legitimacy distinct from those of democratic, majoritarian institutions. A complete survey of the literature on the criteria for judicial legitimacy is beyond the scope of this chapter. For our purposes here, I therefore take as a template the

---

[17] See, e.g., A. Moravcsik, "In defense of the democratic deficit: Reassessing legitimacy in the European Union," *Journal of Common Market Studies*, 40(4) (2002), 603–24; and R. W. Grant and R. O. Keohane, "Accountability and abuses of power in world politics," *American Political Science Review*, 99(1) (2005), 29–43.

[18] Moravcsik, "In defense of the democratic deficit."

[19] See, e.g., Greven, "Can the European Union," p. 50.

most extensive exploration of IC legitimacy, by Nienke Grossman.[20] In her analysis, Grossman proposes three specific sets of factors that might be expected to influence the sociological legitimacy of an international court. An IC, she posits, "is legitimate when it is (1) fair and unbiased, (2) interpreting and applying norms consistent with what states believe the law is or should be, and (3) transparent and infused with democratic norms."[21] Although Grossman puts these three qualities forward as possible criteria for sociological legitimacy, they also provide an excellent set of *normative* standards whereby numerous scholars have judged the CJEU's legitimacy – and, in many instances, found it wanting.[22] For this reason, I first review and adopt Grossman's three criteria, in this section, before assessing the CJEU against those criteria in the next section.

1   Fair and Unbiased

Taking these three criteria in turn, Grossman first hypothesizes that courts are likely to be seen as *fair and unbiased* if they possess "a core set of provisions guaranteeing (1) fair process; (2) impartial, competent, and independent individual adjudicators; (3) impartial and independent benches and panels; and (4) unbiased secretariats and registries."[23] Taking a largely institutional approach, Grossman argues that courts with certain statutory rules and structures are most likely to guarantee (and be seen to guarantee) procedural fairness as well as qualified and unbiased judges, panels, secretariats, and registries.

Yet, looking beyond the institutional features of the court to the behavior of its judges, Grossman also notes, "No matter how stringent a body's procedural rules might be, however, if the public or international actors perceive them to be applied in an inconsistent or biased manner,

---

[20] N. Grossman, "Legitimacy and international adjudicative bodies," *George Washington International Law Review*, 41(1) (2009), 107–80.

[21] Grossman, "Legitimacy and international adjudicative bodies," at 115.

[22] In a related, more recent paper, Grossman offers a revised, normative theory of IC legitimacy, identifying three related grounds for legitimacy: (1) procedural fairness, extended beyond litigants to include all stakeholders whose rights are affected by IC rulings; (2) adherence to "certain universal standards of justice," including prohibitions against torture, slavery, racial discrimination, and genocide; and (3) implementation of the objective for which the court was established. See N. Grossman, "The normative legitimacy of international courts," *Temple Law Review*, 86(1) (2013), 61–105. I nevertheless adopt Grossman's original three criteria of legitimacy because they resonate closely with the common normative critiques of the CJEU reviewed in this chapter.

[23] Grossman, "Legitimacy and international adjudicative bodies," at 123–24.

THE LEGITIMACY OF THE EUROPEAN COURT OF JUSTICE   151

the tribunal itself may lose legitimacy."[24] Bias, it is worth pointing out, can take place at the level of an entire court or at the level of individual judges.[25] Bias can also take place along different dimensions, including possible biases in favor of strong or weak states, greater integration or respect for national sovereignty, the rights of workers or those of employers, and so on.

2 Political Acceptability and Legal Soundness

Moving to her second criterion, Grossman argues that the normative "currency" of a court depends on two characteristics: political acceptability and legal soundness.[26] With respect to political acceptability, she argues, "If a tribunal consistently makes decisions that do not coincide with international actors' interests and values, they will likely cease to perceive the tribunal as possessing justified authority."[27]

With respect to "legal soundness," Grossman suggests that, to be considered legitimate, court rulings "must utilize a kind of legal reasoning or discourse that is commonly accepted by litigants and members of the treaties establishing tribunals."[28] Adapting concepts from Thomas Franck, she argues that IC rulings may be perceived as legitimate to the extent that they satisfy Franck's criteria of determinacy, symbolic validation, coherence, and adherence.[29] In a similar vein, Joseph Weiler cites Koen Lenearts, the recently elected president of the CJEU, to the effect that the "internal legitimacy" of the Court "turns on the need for judgments to be 'sound' in their legal reasoning; their need to be 'transparent' and easy to understand rather than 'cryptic.' The grounds of the judgment must be strong and convincing and meet the arguments put by the parties. Decisions must be coherent with the rest of the jurisprudence, and based on criteria known in advance."[30] While

---

[24] Ibid., at 129.
[25] On the latter, see, e.g., E. Posner and M. de Figueiredo, "Is the International Court of Justice biased?" *Journal of Legal Studies*, 34(2), 599–630.
[26] Grossman, "Legitimacy and international adjudicative bodies," at 144.
[27] Ibid., at 145.   [28] Ibid., at 149.
[29] Thomas M. Franck, *The Power of Legitimacy among Nations* (Oxford: Oxford University Press, 1990), cited in Grossman, "Legitimacy and international adjudicative bodies," at 120. For an application to the CJEU, see A. Alemanno and O. Stefan, "Openness at the Court of Justice of the European Union: Toppling a taboo," *Common Market Law Review*, 51(1) (2014), 97–140, at 106–7.
[30] J. H. H. Weiler, "Epilogue: Judging the judges: Apology and critique," in M. Adams, H. de Waele, J. Meeusen, and G. Straetmans (eds.), *Judging Europe's Judges: The Legitimacy of*

Lenaerts defends the CJEU's legal reasoning along all of these criteria, other observers have been more critical, as we shall see.

3 Openness and Transparency

Grossman's third criterion is openness and transparency, such that "interested parties, both inside and outside the judicial process, can observe its processes and outcomes."[31] Transparency, she suggests, is valuable both indirectly, as a means for audiences to assess judicial behavior, possible bias, and the quality of legal reasoning, and directly, as a democratic norm that promotes accountability.[32] In concrete terms, states can design a number of specific features to enhance the transparency of tribunals:

> A transparent tribunal might hold open hearings with translation into the languages of the litigating parties and produce minutes of its proceedings for public access in relevant languages. It might make pleadings of pending and past cases and the names of adjudicators and parties publicly available. A tribunal might also issue written decisions listing the names of adjudicators and including explicit reasoning, dissenting, concurring, and separate opinions, vote tallies, and signatures.[33]

International courts vary substantially in terms of these various design features and behaviors, each of which is designed to promote "judicial candor," according to which judges "should neither omit their reasoning nor conceal their motives."[34] As we shall see, the CJEU has frequently been found wanting along this third criterion.

C Normative Critiques of CJEU Legitimacy

By all accounts, the early scholarship on the CJEU was nearly uniform in its normative praise for the Court and its teleological, integrationist jurisprudence, which famously "constitutionalized" the Treaties, declaring and extending the core doctrines of direct effect and supremacy of EU law, and working with national courts to create not only an economic

---

the *Case Law of the European Court of Justice* (Oxford: Hart Publishing, 2013), pp. 235–53, at 237.

[31] Grossman, "Legitimacy and international adjudicative bodies," at 153.

[32] Ibid., at 153.   [33] Ibid., at 154.

[34] Ibid., at 134–5, quoting S. C. Idleman, "A prudential theory of judicial candor," *Texas Law Review*, 73(6) (1995), 1307–418, at 1309.

THE LEGITIMACY OF THE EUROPEAN COURT OF JUSTICE   153

community but also a "community of law."[35] Beginning with the publication of Hjalte Rasmussen's landmark critique in 1986, however, the tone of EU scholarship turned more critical of the Court, whose jurisprudence and legitimacy has been challenged by a growing number of scholars.[36] These academic criticisms, moreover, have increased in tandem with other criticisms launched by political leaders and by the popular press. Taken together, these critiques can be taken as a collective challenge to the normative legitimacy of the Court, along all three of Grossman's proposed criteria: fairness and impartiality, political acceptability and legal soundness, and transparency. Inverting these criteria yields three strands of criticism against the CJEU, namely: (1) charges of bias, (2) charges of "judicial activism" and poor legal reasoning, and (3) charges of opacity. Let us discuss each of these, briefly, in turn.

1   Charges of Bias

First, if we assume that states seek to delegate dispute settlement powers to international courts that are neutral, fair, and unbiased among potential litigants, then bias among international judges would constitute a challenge to IC legitimacy. As noted earlier, Grossman indicates that the test of an unbiased court is not only institutional, namely procedural fairness, but also behavioral, such that a court that consistently rules in favor of one class of interests is likely to be perceived as biased. This author is aware of few if any charges that the CJEU is characterized by procedural unfairness, yet charges of bias in *outcomes* are common in normative critiques of the Court. Such bias can, in principle, take three basic forms: *national* bias (in favor of a particular state), *integrationist*

---

[35] The legal literature on the CJEU is, of course, voluminous. For useful surveys, see, e.g., A. S. Sweet, "The European Court of Justice and the judicialization of EU governance," *Living Reviews in European Governance*, 5(2) (2010), www.livingreviews.org/lreg-2010-2; and A. Arnull, "Judicial activism and the Court of Justice: How should academics respond?" *Maastricht Working Papers, Faculty of Law*, Working Paper 2012/3 (January 2012).

[36] See, e.g., Hjalte Rasmussen, *On Law and Policy in the European Court of Justice* (Boston: Martinus Nijhoff, 1986). On the increasing normative challenges to the Court among legal academics, see, e.g., J. H. H. Weiler, "The Court of Justice on trial," *Common Market Law Review*, 24(3) (1987), 555–89; "Editorial comments: The Court of Justice in the limelight – again," *Common Market Law Review*, 45(6) (2008), 1571–9; Arnull, "Judicial activism and the Court of Justice"; and E. Muir, M. Dawson, and B. de Witte, "Introduction: The European Court of Justice as a political actor" in M. Dawson, B. de Witte, and E. Muir (eds.), *Judicial Activism at the European Court of Justice* (Cheltenham: Edward Elgar, 2013), pp. 1–10, at 2.

bias (in favor of centralization of power at the expense of national sovereignty), and *neoliberal* bias (in favor of business and deregulation at the expense of labor and national social regulation).

Among international courts, perhaps the most obvious potential source of bias is *national*: One could, for example, posit that international courts as a whole are biased in favor of the most powerful states in the system[37], or that individual judges are biased in favor of their home states.[38] In the case of the CJEU, charges of bias in favor of powerful states have been largely falsified by studies showing that the CJEU regularly rules against the most powerful EU member states, including Germany, and that the Court's rulings most strongly track the preferences of the Commission.[39] As for charges of favoritism by individual judges in favor of their home states, the judges have benefited from the Court's practice of suppressing any and all concurring or dissenting opinions or votes of the judges. This practice, which I examine later under the rubric of transparency, makes it impossible to assess the existence of national bias, if any, among the judges.

Nevertheless, charges of CJEU bias have been made, and become increasingly widespread, in recent decades, falling primarily into the second category of *integrationist* bias. Across multiple disciplines, scholars have argued that the Court has demonstrated a decades-long bias in favor of European integration, interpreting the treaties in a teleological fashion that goes far beyond what the member states intended in their drafting of the original Treaties, and undermining national sovereignty.[40]

---

[37] A charge made by Garrett and Weingast against the CJEU; see G. Garrett and B. Weingast, "Ideas, interests, and institutions: Constructing the European community's internal market" in J. Goldstein and R. O. Keohane (eds.), *Ideas and Foreign Policy* (Ithaca, NY: Cornell University Press 1993), pp. 173–206, at 173.

[38] A charge made against ICJ judges by Posner and de Figueiredo, "Is the International Court of Justice biased?"

[39] A. S. Sweet and T. L. Brunell, "Constructing a supranational constitution: Dispute resolution and governance in the European community," *American Political Science Review*, 92(1) (1998), 63–81.

[40] Rasmussen, *On Law and Policy in the European Court of Justice*, at 3. See also the otherwise diverse views of judges and scholars like P. Pescatore, "Les Travaux du Groupe Juridique dans la Négociation des Traités de Rome," *Studia Diplomatica*, 34 (1981), 159–92; Trevor C. Hartley, *The Foundations of European Community Law* (New York: Oxford University Press, 1998), at 79; F. Mancini, "The Making of a Constitution for Europe" in R. O. Keohane and S. Hoffmann (eds.), *The New European Community* (Boulder: Westview Press, 1991), pp. 177–94; and M. Bobek, "Legal reasoning of the

THE LEGITIMACY OF THE EUROPEAN COURT OF JUSTICE   155

Although many EU law scholars have applauded the Court's pro-integration decisions, they increasingly raise Michal Bobek's sharply pointed question, whether "a body consistently deciding in one direction" can "be perceived as an independent and impartial court."[41] Bobek's answer is equally sharp:

> A supreme court in a larger federal unity ought to decide even-handedly in favour as well as against the federation. Such court draws its legitimacy from the impartial judicial process itself, not from one-sided "corruption by rights" for the individuals coupled with messianic promises of a "Community of Destiny" to come.[42]

In this view, the Court's legitimacy is called fundamentally into question due to its pro-integration bias and its failure to protect the integrity of sovereign national legal orders.

Finally, we find a third, increasingly frequent charge that the CJEU has demonstrated a bias in favor of market liberalization and against national social regulations and practices that might operate as impediments to free movement. In a trio of controversial rulings in the late 1990s, for example, the CJEU ruled that strikes by Scandinavian trade unions, as well as a decision by a German state government to terminate a contract with a firm whose Polish workers earned substantially less than the collectively bargained German wage, constituted illegal interferences with the EU-guaranteed freedoms of establishment and service provision.[43] These rulings, and others since, have prompted a critique of the Court – and indeed of the EU constitutional order more broadly – as systematically biased in favor of the market, and as a threat to national social policies and to the European social model.[44]

2   Charges of Judicial Activism and Poor Legal Reasoning

A second, widely expressed set of critiques focuses on the obverse of Grossman's double criterion of political acceptability and legal soundness, namely (1) judicial activism and (2) poor legal reasoning. Neither of these critiques is new, but both have become increasingly commonplace

---

Court of Justice of the EU" (27 May 2014), *European Law Review*, 39, 418, Forthcoming. Available at SSRN: https://ssrn.com/abstract=2442235.

[41] Bobek, "Legal reasoning," 10.   [42] Ibid., at 11.

[43] See, e.g., A. C. L. Davies, "'One step forwards, two steps back?' The Viking and Laval cases in the ECJ," *Industrial Law Journal*, 37(2) (2008), 126–48.

[44] Scharpf, "The asymmetry of European integration."

in recent years, constituting perhaps the primary normative challenges to the jurisprudence of the CJEU.

The cry of judicial activism was most famously and forcefully articulated by Hjalte Rasmussen in his 1986 book, *On Law and Policy in the European Court of Justice*. Rasmussen accused the Court of judicial activism in favor of further integration and in defiance of the EU's member governments.[45] The canonical 1963 decision in *Van Gend en Loos*, for example, which proclaimed the doctrine of direct effect of EC law in national legal orders, was described as a "goal-oriented" decision, which achieved by "judicial fiat" an outcome that had not been intended by the founders and could not be found in the text of the Treaties.[46] "To many a European lawyer," Rasmussen charged, "this is revolting judicial behavior," which was likely, in the long term, to undermine the authority and legitimacy of the Court.[47]

Notwithstanding the largely hostile scholarly reception to Rasmussen's book, charges of CJEU judicial activism have proliferated in the intervening years. While definitions of judicial activism vary,[48] critics of the Court regularly suggest that the judges act improperly by taking decisions that should properly be left to the EU legislator or to the member states; that the Court has improperly adopted a teleological method of interpretation that finds no basis in either the treaties or in the practice of other international courts;[49] and that the Court has repeatedly engaged in results-oriented jurisprudence, deciding cases to achieve the judges' favored political outcomes.[50] A thorough discussion of all these claims of judicial activism is, of course, beyond the scope of this

---

[45] Rasmussen, *On Law and Policy in the European Court of Justice,* at 17.

[46] Rasmussen, *On Law and Policy,* at 12.   [47] Ibid., at 13.

[48] In a useful contribution, Anthony Arnull, drawing on previous work by Keenan Kmiec, identifies five distinct meanings of "judicial activism" and assesses the behavior of the Court of Justice, and the responses of the scholarly community, along all five. Arnull, "Judicial activism and the Court of Justice," 9–13, citing K. Kmiec, "The Origin and current meanings of 'judicial activism,'" *California Law Review*, 92(5) (2004), 1441–77, at 1451.

[49] On teleological interpretation in the CJEU, see, e.g., K. Lenaerts, "Interpretation and the Court of Justice: A basis for comparative reflection," *The International Lawyer*, 41(4) (2007), 1011–32.

[50] See, e.g., Rasmussen's infamous discussion in *On Law and Policy*, and Gunnar Beck's recent critique of the Court's decision in *Pringle*, which Beck attributes to "the overriding political commitments to try to save the single currency irrespective of what the Treaties say or do not say." Gunnar Beck, *The Legal Reasoning of the Court of Justice of the EU* (Oxford: Hart, 2013), p. 447.

THE LEGITIMACY OF THE EUROPEAN COURT OF JUSTICE   157

chapter,[51] but what is clear is that the Court has faced and will likely continue to face accusations of each of the various types of judicial activism discussed.

Closely related to charges of judicial activism, but focusing less on the outcome than on the method of reaching it, are charges of poor legal reasoning by the Court. In recent years, a growing chorus of critics has characterized the Court's reasoning as "magisterial,"[52] "clipped,"[53] "cryptic,"[54] and "uneven and unpredictable."[55] The Court, it is often argued, is prone to delivering terse, thinly reasoned decisions that fail either to explain the logic underlying its rulings or to engage systematically with the arguments put forward by the parties and intervenors (e.g., the Commission and the member governments).[56]

Defenders of the Court, including the judges themselves, insist that this style of legal reasoning is, in fact, appropriate to a Union of diverse legal cultures and traditions, and that speaking with a single voice serves to *enhance* the legitimacy of the Court.[57] Critics, however, argue that the Court's terse style results in unclear, poorly reasoned decisions and an impoverished dialogue with the national courts,[58] and even judges occasionally concede that the Court's legal reasoning in specific cases leaves much to be desired.[59] Once again, space precludes a more thorough discussion of the often vigorous critiques of, and debates over, the Court's reasoning in some of its most controversial rulings, such as *Francovitch, Mangold,* and *Ruiz Zambrano*, but what is perhaps most

---

[51] For a far-reaching exploration, see the essays in Dawson, de Witte, and Muir, *Judicial Activism at the European Court of Justice*.

[52] Mitchel de S.-O.-l'E. Lasser, *Judicial Deliberations: A Comparative Analysis of Judicial Transparency and Legitimacy* (Oxford: Oxford University Press, 2004), p. 16.

[53] Ibid., p. 104.

[54] J. H. H. Weiler, "The judicial après Nice" in G. de Búrca and J. H. H. Weiler (eds.), *The European Court of Justice* (Oxford: Oxford University Press, 2001), pp. 215–26, at 225.

[55] Muir et al., "Introduction," p. 2–3.   [56] Lasser, *Judicial Deliberations*, p. 107.

[57] See, e.g., K. Lenaerts, "The court's outer and inner selves: Exploring the external and internal legitimacy of the European Court of Justice" in M. Dawson, B. de Witte, and E. Muir (eds.), *Judicial Activism at the European Court of Justice* (Oxford: Hart, 2013), p. 46.

[58] Weiler, "The judicial après Nice," p. 225.

[59] See, e.g., the off-the-bench writings of Judge David Edwards and Advocate General Eleanor Sharpston. D. Edward, "How the Court of Justice works," *European Law Review*, 20 (1995), 539–58, at 557 ("A camel is said to be a horse designed by a committee, and some judgments of the Court of Justice are camels"); and E. Sharpston, "Transparency and clear legal language in the European Union: Ambiguous legislative texts, laconic pronouncements and the credibility of the judicial system," *Cambridge Yearbook of European Legal Studies*, 12 (2009–2010), 409–23, at 409.

striking in these cases is the tendency for scholars to focus, not (only) on claims of judicial activism in terms of outcome but (also) on the Court's failure, in major cases, to adequately explain its reasoning or engage with the arguments of the parties and intervenors.[60]

To some extent, critics have argued, the putative failings of the judges' brief, collective decisions are ameliorated by the more elaborate Opinions of Advocates General, who are much more likely to engage at length with the arguments of the parties as well as the views of legal scholars.[61] For others, however, these Opinions are at best an imperfect substitute for more detailed rulings from the Court itself, or for the kinds of rich judicial dialogue that might be sparked if the judges engaged in the publication of individual concurring or dissenting opinions.[62]

3 Charges of Opacity

This last consideration brings us, finally, to the question of the openness or transparency of the Court. Grossman, in her broad survey of ICs, notes that the CJEU lacks a number of provisions and practices that we associate with open, transparent judicial decision making:

> [A]ccess to preliminary decisions and judgments, their reasoning, and separate, concurring, and dissenting opinions allows interested parties to determine whether individual adjudicators or benches and panels made their decisions based on legally sound reasoning in the predominant legal discourse, pure bias, or by flipping a coin.[63]

For this reason, Grossman advocates judicial openness as a key criterion of judicial legitimacy, and the CJEU itself, in its substantial body of jurisprudence on the principle and practice of openness in EU governance, has echoed these arguments, embracing openness and transparency as fundamental principles of the EU legal order.[64]

---

[60] On the quality of legal reasoning in *Ruiz Zambrano*, see, e.g., N. N. Shuibhne, "Seven questions for seven paragraphs," *European Law Review*, 36(2) (2011), 161–2; and Weiler, "The judicial après Nice," p. 249.

[61] Lasser, *Judicial Deliberations*, Chapters 4, 7.

[62] M. Bobek, "A fourth in the court: Why are there advocates general in the Court of Justice," *Cambridge Yearbook of European Legal Studies*, 14 (2011-2012), 529–61, at 543 and 557–8.

[63] Grossman, "Legitimacy and international adjudicative bodies," 155.

[64] *Openness, Transparency and Access to Documents and Information in the European Union*, European Parliament, Directorate General for Internal Policies Report (2013), at 9.

By the same token, however, both EU law and the Court recognize a distinction between the *administrative* functions of the Court, which are subject to the principles of openness and transparency, and the Court's *judicial* functions, for which exceptions to this general principle are granted "to ensure that the act of delivering judgments is protected from external interference."[65] Indeed, as Alberto Alemanno and Oana Stefan argue, the Court "has shown circumspection with regard to extending the application of the principle [of openness] to its own activities in the name of the specificity of the judicial process."[66]

In a recent contribution, Thore Neumann and Bruno Simma have engaged in a comparative assessment of the transparency of various international courts, along four stages of the judicial process: access to written proceedings; public accessibility of hearings; deliberation and drafting; and communication of the judicial output.[67] If we follow these authors by engaging in a brief analysis of CJEU practice vis-à-vis other international courts at each of these four stages, we see that the CJEU generally operates openly as a public court, with a publicly accessible docket, hearings, and judgments; yet the Court has also restricted access to those proceedings in ways that have attracted considerable normative critique.

First, with respect to public access to the written submissions of the parties, all international courts face a trade-off between the principle of transparency on the one hand, and the legitimate interests of the court or the parties in maintaining confidentiality about some or all parts of the case file on the other hand. Different courts address this trade-off in different ways. The European Court of Human Rights, for example, takes a particularly open approach, making the parties' submissions public as a general rule, with occasional and narrowly construed exceptions. By comparison, the CJEU has taken a more restrictive approach, as "only the parties to the proceedings and the interveners have access to the case file," and third parties, including the general public, do not have a right of access to written submissions in pending cases.[68] Confronted with this question in the *API* case, in which plaintiffs sought the disclosure of the

---

[65] Alemanno and Stefan, "Openness at the ECJ," 138.
[66] Alemanno and Stefan, "Openness at the ECJ," 98–9.
[67] T. Neumann and B. Simma, "Transparency in international adjudication" in A. Bianchi and A. Peters (eds.), *Transparency in International Law* (New York: Cambridge University Press, 2013), pp. 436–76.
[68] Alemanno and Stefan, "Openness at the ECJ," at 122.

160 MARK A. POLLACK

Commission's observations before the Court, the Court famously ruled that public disclosure of written submissions "would have the effect of exposing judicial activities to external pressure, albeit only in the perception of the public, and would disturb the serenity of the proceedings."[69] Although the protection of the serenity of the Court's proceedings and the independence of its judges both qualify as normatively compelling considerations, the net effect of this ruling is a lower level of transparency at this stage than most other international courts.

By contrast, when it comes to the second stage of oral hearings, the CJEU appears more open than many other international courts, the general rule being that oral hearings are conducted in public, unless "serious reasons" justify their exclusion.[70] Critics point out, however, that public access to the hearings is limited to those who are able to attend in person in Luxembourg, as the Court does not release the transcripts of oral hearings, nor provide public access to video of the hearings over the Internet.[71]

At the third stage of deliberation and drafting judicial decisions, the statute of the CJEU, like those of most international courts, indicates clearly that the deliberations of the Court shall be and shall remain secret, and the judges take an oath to protect the secrecy of deliberations.[72] The common rationale for this secrecy of deliberations is to protect the independence of the judges and the legitimacy of the court, and the CJEU is therefore well in the mainstream of courts in safeguarding judicial deliberations behind a "purple curtain" of secrecy.[73] Indeed, by comparison with other courts, one could argue that the CJEU is relatively open because the Court identifies the Judge Rapporteur in each decision and because most important decisions are preceded by the publication of the individual Opinion of the Advocate General in the case.[74]

---

[69] Judgment of the Court (Grand Chamber) of 21 September 2010. *Kingdom of Sweden v Association de la presse internationale ASBL (API) and European Commission* (C-514/07 P), *Association de la presse internationale ASBL (API) v European Commission* (C-528/07 P) and *European Commission v Association de la presse internationale ASBL (API)* (C-532/07 P). Joined cases C-514/07 P, C-528/07 P and C-532/07 P.

[70] Neumann and Simma, "Transparency," at 448–50; Alemanno and Stefan, "Openness at the ECJ," 127–130.

[71] Neumann and Simma, "Transparency," at 454, and Alemanno and Stefan, "Openness at the ECJ," at 132.

[72] Neumann and Simma, "Transparency," at 457.

[73] K. Kelemen, "Dissenting opinions in constitutional courts," *German Law Journal*, 14(8) (2013), pp. 1346–71, at 1362.

[74] Lasser, *Judicial Deliberations*.

THE LEGITIMACY OF THE EUROPEAN COURT OF JUSTICE   161

This takes us to the fourth stage of the judicial process, the communication of "judicial outputs," namely decisions and opinions of the court. The Court's openness in this final stage is a mixed bag. On the one hand, the collective decision of the Court is delivered openly in public session and placed on the Court's website in the various official languages of the EU, rendering that opinion freely accessible to the members of the European public in their own languages. On the other hand, CJEU judges have long made a practice of suppressing any public disclosure of judicial votes, or of concurring or dissenting opinions. In doing so, the judges have clearly sought to speak with a single voice, which they believe increases the legitimacy of the Court's decisions as well as the independence of the judges.[75] Critics, however, argue that the Court's suppression of concurring and dissenting opinions undermines not only the transparency but also the legitimacy of the Court, which, it is argued, is sufficiently mature and well established as to allow dissenting opinions.[76]

In sum, although Alemanno and Stefan conclude their survey by concluding that "the EU Courts score quite well from an openness point of view,"[77] the fact remains that, in comparative perspective, the CJEU is arguably less open and transparent than other international courts, in terms of access to written submissions (a presumption of closure), oral hearings (public but not broadcast), and above all deliberation and output (all signs of voting and all concurring and dissenting opinions suppressed). Defenders of the Court's practices can and do argue that this lack of openness is justified in terms of other normative desiderata such as judicial independence, litigant confidentiality, and the serenity of judicial proceedings, but the end result is a court whose workings and reasoning are at least partially opaque to legal experts and to the general public alike.

More generally, while the Court and its judges have been lionized by many scholars for building a supranational community of law, they have also been subject to increasingly strident charges that the Court is biased,

---

[75] See, e.g., J. Azizi, "Unveiling the EU courts' internal decision-making process: A case for dissenting opinions?" 12 *ERA Forum*, 49 (2011), 49–68; Damian Chalmers, Gareth Davies, and Giorgio Monti, *European Union Law: Cases and Materials*, 2nd edition (Cambridge: Cambridge University Press, 2010) at 145; Weiler, "The judicial après Nice," at 225–6; and Weiler, "Judging the judges," at 252.

[76] See, e.g., J. Laffranque, "Dissenting opinion and judicial independence," *Juridica International*, 8 (2003), 162–72; V. Perju, "Reason and authority in the European Court of Justice," *Virginia Journal of International Law*, 49(2) (2009), 307–78; and Weiler, "The judicial après Nice," at 225.

[77] Alemanno and Stefan, "Openness at the ECJ," at 138.

activist, and opaque. These normative debates are interesting and important, but also inconclusive, and they raise a more basic empirical question: to what extent is the Court actually *seen* as legitimate by its various audiences? It is to this question that we turn in the next section.

III The Sociological Legitimacy of the CJEU: Empirical Evidence

> If we adopt a sociological approach to legitimacy, an approach which tries to gauge empirically the measure of acceptability of institutions and regimes, there is no legitimacy crisis in the European Court of Justice. It is widely respected, and rightly so, and its decisions are, we tend to believe, mostly followed – or at least open revolt is rare.
>
> – Joseph H. H. Weiler[78]

By contrast with the vast literature on the normative legitimacy of the EU as a whole, and the CJEU in particular, we know much less about the empirical or sociological legitimacy of the Court among its multiple audiences, which include national courts (which play a key role in the preliminary reference procedure), EU member governments (which often litigate before the Court and are called on to implement its judgments), the "invisible college" of the European legal profession, and finally the general public.

Because of the unusual nature of the preliminary reference procedure, whereby the CJEU relies on references from national courts for the majority of its cases, much of the existing literature emphasizes the Court's reliance on national courts to refer questions to it and loyally implement the Court's rulings in the various member states.[79] Despite this consensus about the reliance of the CJEU on national courts, we find a tension in the literature about whether the Court actually enjoys legitimacy in the eyes of this most crucial and attentive public. Much of the literature, typified by the preceding quote by Joseph Weiler, holds that the jurisdiction and the jurisprudence of the Court are widely

---

[78] Weiler, "Judging the judges," p. 235. For a similar view, see Muir et al., "Introduction," p. 2.

[79] See, e.g., J. H. H. Weiler, "A quiet revolution: The European Court of Justice and its interlocutors," *Comparative Political Studies*, 24(4) (1994), 510–34; A.-M. Slaughter, J. H. H. Weiler, and A. S. Sweet, (eds.), *The European Court and National Courts: Doctrine and Jurisprudence: Legal Change in Its Social Context* (Oxford: Hart Publishing, 1998); and Weiler, "The judicial après Nice," at 220.

THE LEGITIMACY OF THE EUROPEAN COURT OF JUSTICE   163

accepted by national courts – and indeed also by national governments – and that there is therefore no "crisis of legitimacy" for the CJEU vis-à-vis national courts and governments. Other scholars, however, point to both historic and persistent tensions in the Court's ongoing relationship and dialogue with national courts, including inter alia the early reluctance of national high courts to accept the supremacy of EC law in the 1960s and 1970s[80]; the efforts by national courts to "contain" the unwelcome effects of CJEU rulings in national legal orders[81]; the reluctance of national courts in the UK, Scandinavia, and elsewhere to submit preliminary references[82]; and the sometimes contentious constitutional dialogue between the CJEU, the German Constitutional Court, and other national high courts about the protection of fundamental rights and the limits of the EU's legal competence.[83]

Whether the CJEU enjoys sociological legitimacy in the eyes of national courts or member governments – its most attentive audiences – therefore remains a matter of contention, in part because debates over the issue rely on indirect evidence. In the absence of systematic information about the attitudes and beliefs of national judges and/or governments about the Court, scholars in this debate have relied on data about the *behavior* of national judges (do they submit preliminary references to the Court, and/or loyally implement the Court's rulings?) and of national governments (do they comply with CJEU decisions, or do they try to overturn those rulings or curb the Court as a whole?) as proxies for their actual views about the Court. Such behaviors can provide important *clues* about the Court's legitimacy with these audiences, but the fact remains that national courts can refer (or not refer)

---

[80] See, e.g., Karen J. Alter, *Establishing the Supremacy of European Law: The Making of an International Rule of Law in Europe* (New York: Oxford University Press, 2001); and Bill Davies, *Resisting the European Court of Justice: West Germany's Confrontation with European Law, 1949–1979* (New York: Cambridge University Press, 2012).

[81] Lisa Conant, *Justice Contained: Law and Politics in the European Union* (Ithaca, NY: Cornell University Press, 2002).

[82] See, e.g., D. Chalmers, "The application of community law in the United Kingdom, 1994–1998," *Common Market Law Review*, 37(1) (2000), 83–128; M. Wind, D. S. Martinsen, and G. P. Rotger, "The uneven legal push for Europe: Questioning variation when national courts go to Europe," *European Union Politics*, 10(1) (2009), 63–88.

[83] On the long and contentious constitutional dialogue between the CJEU and the German Constitutional Court, see, e.g., Davies, *Resisting the European Court of Justice*; D. Grimm, "The European Court of Justice and National Courts: The German constitutional perspective after the *Maastricht* decision," *Columbia Journal of European Law*, 3 (1997), 229–42.

questions and national courts and governments can comply (or not comply) with CJEU judgments for instrumental reasons distinct from their views about the Court's legitimacy. We thus have the least systematic data about the legitimacy of the Court in the eyes of its most attentive and important audiences.

By contrast, data regarding public trust in and support for the CJEU are most readily available at the level of mass publics, thanks primarily to two decades of Eurobarometer surveys measuring public attitudes toward the Court. The empirical literature on CJEU legitimacy therefore focuses almost exclusively on public opinion data. I therefore devote the rest of this section to a detailed analysis of the *public* legitimacy of the CJEU in the eyes of EU citizens. As we shall see, the measurement of CJEU "legitimacy" in public opinion raises important measurement questions, but the overall picture is one of relatively stable legitimacy over the course of many decades, declining precipitously in recent years.

A Public Legitimacy: Pioneering Studies by Caldeira and Gibson

The study of court legitimacy in domestic contexts focuses overwhelmingly on public legitimacy, defined as "the beliefs among the mass public" that a court "has the right to exercise authority in a certain domain."[84] As a practical matter, the theories and methods of *domestic* studies have strongly influenced the handful of empirical studies of CJEU and international court legitimacy, including the landmark early 1990s studies by Gregory Caldeira and James L. Gibson.[85] In a widely cited 1995 paper reporting on survey research undertaken in 1992, Caldeira and Gibson sought to extend previous studies of U.S. Supreme Court legitimacy to the CJEU. Given that this is the only extensive study seeking both to measure and to explain public legitimacy of the CJEU, Caldeira and Gibson's study is worth examining carefully.

Following earlier studies of court legitimacy in the United States, Caldeira and Gibson define and operationalize legitimacy in terms of both specific and diffuse support.[86] Specific support for Caldeira and

---

[84] E. Voeten, "Public opinion and the legitimacy of international courts," *Theoretical Inquiries in Law*, 14 (2013), 411–33.

[85] See Caldeira and Gibson, "The legitimacy of the Court of Justice"; Gibson and Caldeira, "The legitimacy of transnational legal institutions"; and Gibson and Caldeira, "Changes in the Legitimacy of the European Court of Justice."

[86] Caldeira and Gibson, "The legitimacy of the Court of Justice," at 357 ("Scholars often equate legitimacy and political support, and we have found it useful to do so as well").

Gibson "refers to a set of attitudes toward an institution based on the fulfillment of expectations of policies or actions," while

> *Diffuse support* is a more difficult concept, since every citizen will at times disagree with the policies, dislike or distrust the incumbents, or criticize the procedures of political institutions. Normally, however, discontent with officials, policies or procedures does not translate into alienation from an institution. Citizens may disagree with what an institution does but nevertheless continue to concede its authority as a political decision maker. This firmer and more durable set of attitudes toward the legitimacy of the institution is what we mean by diffuse support.[87]

From this starting point, the authors seek to measure basic variables such as public awareness and salience of the Court, specific support for its outputs, and above all diffuse support, which they associate with legitimacy.

In order to do so, the authors commissioned a special set of questions about the Court in the Eurobarometer public opinion survey of the then-12 member states of the EU, administered in October 1992. Caldeira and Gibson's methods closely followed earlier studies of the U.S. Supreme Court, but they are significantly different from the regularly reported Eurobarometer survey questions utilized by subsequent authors, so again their methods bear close examination for those seeking to draw lessons about how to study the legitimacy, not only of the CJEU, but also of any international court.

Beginning with public knowledge of the Court, Caldeira and Gibson asked a series of questions designed to measure both the public *salience* of the CJEU and other EU institutions as well as *awareness* of the Court. Results on these questions were mixed. With respect to salience, only 34.4% of EU-wide respondents reported having heard recently about the CJEU, far lower than the corresponding figures for the then-European Community as a whole (81.6%), the Commission (51.3%), the European Parliament (55.3%), or national courts (59.0%).[88] In terms of awareness, only 4.4% of respondents said that they were very aware of the CJEU, while 67.5% were somewhat or very aware, and 28.2% were not at all aware of the Court.[89] Caldeira and Gibson interpret these results as suggesting that, "the Court has become something of a public institution,

---

[87] Ibid., at 357.
[88] Ibid., at 362. These figures, like those that follow, differ quite significantly across member states.
[89] Ibid., at 362.

one that no longer works entirely in anonymity and obscurity."[90] Nevertheless, faced with large numbers of respondents who reported no awareness at all of the Court, the authors exclude this "inattentive" public, which constitutes more than one-third of the sample, from their analysis of the so-called "attentive public."[91]

Caldeira and Gibson then go on to measure diffuse support for the CJEU within this culled sample of the attentive public. Defining "*diffuse support* as institutional commitment – a willingness to defend the institution against structural and functional alterations that would fundamentally alter the role of the institution in society," they measure this commitment through responses to three questions about the continued existence, jurisdiction, and independence of the Court, respectively. In the first question, respondents were prompted with a statement designed to measure their willingness to defend the Court against attempts to abolish it: "If the European Court of Justice started making a lot of decisions that most people disagree with, it might be better to do away with the Court altogether." In this case, respondents who disagreed with the statement were considered to show diffuse support for the Court. A second question sought to measure institutional commitment to the Court by asking respondents whether its jurisdiction should be reduced; once again, a negative response could be taken to indicate diffuse support. Third and last, respondents were challenged to defend the independence of the Court: "The political independence of the European Court of Justice is essential. Therefore, no other European institution should be able to override Court opinions even if it thinks they are harmful to the European Community." Here, agreement with the statement was taken as diffuse support for the Court.[92]

Using an index of these three questions as their measure of diffuse support, Caldeira and Gibson report sobering findings about the public legitimacy of the CJEU: "Overall, about 7% of the respondents endorsed all three statements, 16% gave supportive responses to two of the three items, about 33% expressed support on only one item, and *45% of the respondents expressed support on not a single item.*"[93] It is on the basis of these findings that the authors draw their much-quoted conclusion that "*the Court of Justice seems to have more enemies than friends within the mass publics of the EU*"[94] and that "the ECJ does not possess a surplus of legitimacy."[95]

---

[90] Ibid., at 361.   [91] Ibid., at 363.   [92] Ibid., at 363.
[93] Ibid., at 363, emphasis in original.   [94] Ibid., at 363, emphasis in original.
[95] Gibson and Caldeira, "Changes in the legitimacy," at 63.

I emphasize this methodological point here because subsequent and more optimistic discussions of the public legitimacy of the CJEU (discussed later) have relied on different measures of support, and in particular on the regularly asked question whether respondents "tend to trust" the Court. Clearly, Caldeira and Gibson's three-item measure of diffuse support, although arguably capturing important dimensions of legitimacy, is a demanding one and helps to explain differences between Caldeira and Gibson and later authors about the Court's public legitimacy.[96]

Having thus measured (disappointing levels of) diffuse support, the authors seek to test four hypotheses that might explain variations in individuals' levels of diffuse support. Briefly, they first hypothesize that individuals who express specific support for the performance of the Court will over time develop diffuse support for it as well.[97] Second, they hypothesize that, "[b]ereft of information about specifics, members of the mass public who do not pay attention to politics might well form orientations toward particular institutions from general impressions of the political system. Citizens' views would likely move from the general to the particular rather than the other way around. That is, citizens deduce their views of particular institutions from their more general affect toward the polity." This yields a second hypothesis, that EU attitudes toward the CJEU will reflect their more general attitudes about the EU as a whole.[98] Third, they hypothesize that individuals are more likely to support the Court as a function of their general values, including values such as support for the rule of law and individual liberty that are seen to be "generally compatible and associated with courts as institutions."[99] Fourth and finally, they hypothesize that individuals with higher levels of "cognitive mobilization," as measured by variables such as education and attentiveness to the media, might be more likely to support the Court.[100]

Regressing these independent variables against their measure of diffuse support, Caldeira and Gibson produce, once again, mostly sobering findings. With respect to specific support, measured in response to the question, "Has what you heard or read given you a genuinely favorable or unfavorable impression of the European Court of Justice?" they find that

---

[96] These questions were repeated in other surveys the following year, 1993, reported in Gibson and Caldeira, "Changes in the legitimacy," but not since then, hence we lack data on any possible changes in this particular measure of public support over time.

[97] Caldeira and Gibson, "The legitimacy of the Court of Justice," at 359.   [98] Ibid., at 359.

[99] Ibid., at 359–60.   [100] Ibid., at 360.

168 MARK A. POLLACK

the modal response is uncertainty.[101] Even among respondents expressing specific support for the Court, moreover, diffuse support for the CJEU remained low, reaching a simple majority only in the Netherlands, and only in four countries of the sample did the relationship between specific and diffuse support reach the level of statistical significance.[102] "These findings reinforce our earlier conclusion that the reservoir of diffuse support for the Court is remarkably shallow; satisfaction with the Court's outputs has not yet been transformed into institutional commitments."[103] Instead, the authors found, the strongest predictors of public support for the EU were two other attitudinal variables, namely support for the EU as a whole and support for the rule of law and individual liberty.[104]

On the basis of these findings, Caldeira and Gibson again reach rather pessimistic conclusions:

> For relatively obscure institutions such as the Court of Justice, a strategy of building support through satisfying the demands of various constituencies is unlikely to be successful. Too few of the citizenry have even a vague idea of the general course of the Court's decisions. In the absence of information about the Court of Justice, ordinary citizens depend on this institution's connection with the EU, as well as its association with broad political and legal values such as the rule of law and individual liberty. In other words, lacking specifics, people make inferences based on their general values and preferences.[105]

B Contemporary Studies of CJEU Public Legitimacy

Caldeira and Gibson's analysis of CJEU legitimacy is widely cited, yet it is a striking feature of the scholarship on the CJEU that, two decades later, not a single scholar has replicated their study, and so we are forced to rely primarily on analyses of the very different, regularly administered Eurobarometer survey questions to assess subsequent developments in public support for the CJEU.

For example, in a recent paper, R. Daniel Kelemen examined survey data from 1999 through 2010 on public support for the CJEU.[106]

---

[101] Ibid., at 365.   [102] Ibid., at 370.   [103] Ibid., at 365.

[104] Ibid., at 367–8. By contrast, a number of other factors, including various measures of cognitive mobilization, awareness of the Court, left–right ideological self-placement, gender, and union membership, all showed weak or no correlations with diffuse support for the Court. Ibid., at 367–72.

[105] Ibid., at 356.

[106] R. D. Kelemen, "The Political Foundations of Judicial Independence in the European Union," *Journal of European Public Policy*, 19(1) (2012), 43–58, at 47–9.

THE LEGITIMACY OF THE EUROPEAN COURT OF JUSTICE   169

Specifically, examining Eurobarometer data on public trust in the Court and other EU institutions between 1999 and 2010, Kelemen found that net public trust (the percentage of those tending to trust in an institution minus those tending not to trust) in the CJEU was consistently positive throughout more than two decades. Indeed, the Court enjoys a higher level of public trust than the bodies (national governments, courts, and parties) most likely to challenge it.[107] Descending from the EU to the national level, moreover, Kelemen shows that trust in the CJEU remained broadly stable even in the face of controversial court decisions, demonstrating that support for the Court remained robust in Germany, Finland, and Sweden, even in the face of adverse rulings such as the *Laval* (C-341/05), *Viking* (C-438/05), and *Rüffert* (C-346/06) cases affecting those countries.[108] Kelemen interprets these data as falsifying Caldeira and Gibson's gloomy predictions:

> In short, average levels of public trust in the ECJ across Europe are far higher than levels of trust in other governmental institutions, they are relatively stable over the last decade and evidence does not seem to suggest that they decrease in response to controversial Court rulings.[109]

We must, however, be cautious about interpreting Kelemen's data in relation to Caldeira and Gibson's earlier studies because Kelemen draws on a narrower and less demanding measure of support for the CJEU. Furthermore, the fact that public opinion appears not to respond to controversial CJEU rulings might be interpreted to support Caldeira and Gibson's argument that public trust in the CJEU is at best weakly related to the actual behavior of the judges and derives instead from more general attitudes toward the EU and the rule of law.

In another recent study, Erik Voeten interrogated the small amount of existing data on the public legitimacy of international courts, including the CJEU.[110] Examining Eurobarometer data on the reported public trust in the CJEU from 1993 through early 2010, Voeten found that, after a drop between 1993 and 1999, "levels of trust have remained relatively stable and high," with the exception of the UK, which he identified as an outlier, where those who distrust the court outnumber those who express trust.[111] Seeking to explain these generally high levels of trust, Voeten analyzed the correlations between individuals' tendency to trust the court as a dependent variable and two other independent variables, namely trust in the EU as a whole and trust in national legal systems, finding that

---

[107] Ibid., 48–9.   [108] Ibid., 49–50.   [109] Ibid., 49.   [110] Voeten, "Public Opinion."
[111] Ibid., at 423.

trust in the CJEU correlates strongly and positively *both* with trust in the EU *and* with trust in national legal systems, at the individual as well as the country level, and when controlling for other factors such as left–right placement, knowledge of the EU, age, and gender.[112]

The first of these findings confirms Caldeira and Gibson's claim about the link between support for the CJEU and the EU more broadly. This finding suggests that international courts such as the CJEU can "borrow" legitimacy from the organizations such as the EU of which they form a part – yet it also leaves them vulnerable should those broader institutions themselves suffer a legitimacy crisis.[113] The second finding, about the correlation between trust for national courts and ICs, appears to falsify a common claim in the literature, which is that individuals are more likely to trust ICs when they distrust their own domestic courts, on the logic that the former operates as a substitute for the latter. Instead, Voeten found that across 25 of 27 member states in his sample, those who trust their domestic courts are more likely to also trust the CJEU.[114] Finally, looking beyond the CJEU to other courts such as the ECtHR and the ICC, Voeten found that "international courts quickly lose support when they get embroiled in public controversy."[115] Taken together, he argued, these findings "support ... Caldeira and Gibson's conclusions that high levels of trust may not be based on actual experience and thus may be vulnerable to new information."[116]

C   Public Support for the CJEU after the Financial Crisis: Discouraging Data

Taken together, Kelemen's and Voeten's studies suggest that public trust in the CJEU has been relatively high and robust over time, at least outside the UK, seemingly contradicting the pessimistic claims of Caldeira and Gibson's widely cited studies – yet recent Eurobarometer data from the period of the Eurozone financial crisis allow us to speak directly to Voeten's question about the resilience of diffuse public support for the CJEU in the face of the EU's own legitimacy crisis.

Looking at Kelemen's and Voeten's core measure of diffuse support for the CJEU, namely a tendency to trust the institution, data for the period since 2010 demonstrate a considerable erosion of trust in the Court in recent years (Figure 6-1). Unlike the Commission, the European Parliament, the

---

[112] Ibid., at 424.   [113] Ibid., at 435.   [114] Ibid., at 426.   [115] Ibid., at 435.
[116] Ibid., at 436.

THE LEGITIMACY OF THE EUROPEAN COURT OF JUSTICE   171

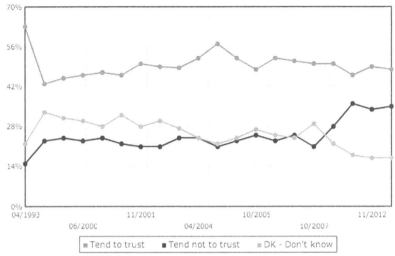

Figure 6-1:   EU Public Trust in CJEU, 1993–2013
Source: Eurobarometer

Council, and the European Central Bank, for which EU-wide net trust has turned from positive to negative in the period since 2010, net trust in the CJEU remains narrowly positive since 2010 – a modestly encouraging sign. Yet expressions of trust in the CJEU have decreased dramatically, from a high of 63% in 1993 to a low of 48% in 2013 among all EU respondents, while distrust more than doubled over the same period, from 15% in 1993 to 35% in 2013. Given the absence of any major EU-wide controversies over the Court's legal rulings during this period, it seems likely that the decline in support for the Court is attributable not to the performance of the judges, but rather to the dramatic decline in support for the EU as a whole during the recent Eurozone sovereign debt crisis.

This interpretation, moreover, is given greater credence by the striking cross-national patterns of support, and movement in that support, before and after the global financial crisis of 2008–2009. Prior to the crisis, trust in the CJEU was high in nearly all EU countries, with the notable exception of Great Britain, where scepticism about the CJEU long predates the 2016 Brexit referendum.

Since the financial crisis, levels of trust in the CJEU have declined in nearly every member state, but variation across member states is dramatic. In most northern European countries, support for the CJEU remained high and largely stable over time. Among the new member states that joined in 2004 and 2007, moreover, a majority (Czech Republic, Estonia, Hungary, Lithuania, Malta, Poland, Slovakia, Slovenia) show somewhat lower but consistently positive levels of net trust in the CJEU over time, and several other new members (Bulgaria, Croatia, and Latvia) began their membership with low and net-negative levels of trust but have since seen trust in the CJEU rise, becoming net-positive in each country. By contrast, support for the CJEU – along with other EU institutions – has virtually collapsed among publics along the southern periphery of the EU. The countries of Greece, Italy, Spain, and Portugal began with fairly strong levels of trust in the 1990s and early 2000s, only to see trust in the Court plummet, and "don't trust" responses predominate, in the years following the 2008 financial crisis, suggesting that generalized resentment of EU-mandated austerity in those countries has "infected" popular views of the Court.

The data discussed here are simple descriptive statistics, relying entirely on a single, regularly administered Eurobarometer question, and we should be cautious about drawing overly broad conclusions – yet they offer a strong cautionary message. Although optimists like Kelemen might point to the fact that EU-wide support for the CJEU remains stronger than that for other EU institutions and modestly net-positive, the fragility of support for the CJEU and its clear link to support for the EU more broadly appear to support Caldeira and Gibson's view that public support for the EU is shallow and largely parasitical on declining public support for the EU project as a whole.

IV Conclusions

The CJEU is one of the oldest, busiest, most deeply embedded, and most powerful international courts in the world. It hears and decides hundreds of cases a year, brought by supranational actors, member governments, national courts, and individual litigants; its decisions are generally complied with; and its powers and jurisdiction have grown dramatically over time. As such, it is tempting to argue that the Court enjoys a high level of both normative and sociological legitimacy.

Yet – and here is the burden of this chapter – a careful review of extant scholarship and public opinion data suggests that both the normative and the sociological legitimacy of the Court are more fragile and contested than they might first appear. In normative terms, generations of scholars with a strong normative commitment to supranationalism have lionized the Court for its constitutionalization of the treaties and its creation of a supranational rule of law. In recent decades, however, these accounts have been joined by others, which plausibly accuse the Court of bias, judicial activism, poor legal reasoning, and opacity vis-à-vis the EU's citizenry.

In terms of the Court's descriptive or sociological legitimacy, finally, we have seen that the measurement of public attitudes toward the Court is highly sensitive to the use of metric. Studies drawing on the regularly asked question of whether individuals tend to trust the Court suggest that it is, over time and across the EU, one of the most trusted institutions in Europe; yet Caldeira and Gibson's more demanding measure shows public support to be sparse and largely decoupled from the behavior of the judges themselves. Indeed, both scholarly studies and the most recent Eurobarometer data suggest that the public legitimacy of the Court rests on a very thin base of public knowledge about the Court, which appears to borrow much of its legitimacy from more general attitudes toward Europe and the rule of law. If these studies and data are to be believed, the Court of Justice is vulnerable both to a broader crisis of legitimacy of the EU, of the kind that is already playing out along the Union's southern periphery and within the departing United Kingdom, independent of the actions and decisions of the Court and its judges.

7

The International Tribunal for the Law of the Sea

Seeking the Legitimacy of State Consent

ANASTASIA TELESETSKY

The International Tribunal of the Law of the Sea (ITLOS) is celebrating its twentieth birthday in 2017. It is a young but seasoned judicial institution that has faced its share of legitimacy tribulations. For supporters, the Tribunal is regarded as a group of experts who are "the chief guardian of the 1982 Convention."[1] For detractors, the Tribunal is a distractor from the UN system of justice focused on the International Court of Justice (ICJ), which now shares its formerly exclusive authority to decide matters involving the UN Law of the Sea Convention (UNCLOS).[2] ITLOS has negotiated a delicate path in seeking recognition by states by courting states to choose ITLOS as their dispute resolution body of choice for ocean law issues and being cautious in its interpretations of international and regional ocean law. In particular, the desire to attract additional state support has been central to the work of the ITLOS judges as they order provisional measures and issue judgments. This chapter explores why despite great care being taken by panels of judges for almost two decades, ITLOS has not been chosen by many states as the judicial forum of choice for marine-related disputes. In Part I, this chapter introduces ITLOS's statutory authority and then briefly explores the legitimacy challenges associated with the limited number of states actively supporting ITLOS's operations and the lack of compliance with orders. In Part II, the chapter describes how ITLOS judges through their

---

[1] *The Monte Confurco Case, Seychelles v. France*, ITLOS Application for Prompt Release, Dissenting Opinion of Judge Laing (2000): para. 3.

[2] J. Noyes, "International Tribunal for the Law of the Sea," *Cornell International Law Journal*, 32 (1998), 111 fn. 9. The ICJ and its predecessor, the Permanent Court of International Justice, have been adjudicating marine disputes for decades. Many of the matters concluded particularly by the ICJ are substantive cases involving continental shelf disputes and fishery rights.

174

provisional orders and judgments are systematically working to enhance perceptions of the Tribunal as a legitimate judicial body. Finally, in Part III, the chapter concludes with some thoughts about the future challenges to ITLOS's authority to interpret the Law of the Sea given its ongoing competition with the ICJ for cases.

I Bases of ITLOS Legitimacy and Inherent Challenges of Relying on State Consent

Although there is no single shared definition of legitimacy as applied to judicial institutions, legitimacy is understood, for purposes of this essay, as referring to the perception that the ITLOS authority is justified and justifiable.[3] In the case of treaty-based dispute resolution bodies such as ITLOS, finding that authority has been justified requires a review of treaty negotiation materials legalizing the Tribunal and defining its functions. As described later in this part, there is little controversy that state parties to the UNCLOS III negotiations concluded a treaty creating a new dispute resolution body with power to offer interpretations of UNCLOS and other marine law. The more interesting question that ITLOS grapples with as a young institution is whether the continued exercise of its powers are justifiable in light of the ICJ as a competing judicial institution with an august reputation and of the perceived flexibility of arbitrator selection for Annex VII tribunals. As will be explained in greater detail in Part 2, ITLOS has made substantial investments in creating a decision-making methodology that affirms state sovereignty to reinforce respect for states that have given their consent to ITLOS as a dispute resolution body and to persuade states that have not given their consent to ITLOS that the Tribunal continues to have justifiable authority.

From the perspective of states who negotiate treaties like UNCLOS that create new institutions to resolve mostly state-to-state disputes, the legitimacy of a new judicial institution will depend, in large part, on whether states have given their explicit consent to constitute a new institution to interpret international rights and obligations, whether states actively support the formation of the institution, and then whether the institution that emerges after the treaty comes into force will be trusted to protect both the process of international rule of law and core

---

[3] N. Grossman, "Legitimacy and international adjudicative bodies," *George Washington International Law Review*, 41 (2009), 110.

sovereign interests.[4] Judicial bodies that do not receive state support in the form of having disputes referred to them and are not trusted to be respectful of sovereign rights and fair in deliberations will not survive. In practice, the survival of a judicial tribunal such as ITLOS will depend on states both actively participating in constituting the institution and then referring cases to be heard by the judicial institution. As discussed in Part 2, the judges of ITLOS are acutely aware of the need to build a larger constituency of states so that the organization can evolve from being a new judicial institution to becoming a more active player in dispute resolution.

ITLOS is a treaty-designed judicial institution. The source of state consent to constitute ITLOS is clearly articulated in UNCLOS, as states have given their blessing to the legal creation of the institution as an alternative to the ICJ or other dispute resolution mechanisms. Under Article 287 of UNCLOS, state parties must choose by declaration one of four dispute settlement mechanisms or be assigned by default to arbitration before a tribunal constituted under Annex VII of UNCLOS.[5] The first dispute settlement option mentioned in Article 287 is ITLOS, whose organizational powers are defined in the "Statute of the International Tribunal of the Law of the Sea" located in Annex VI of UNCLOS. By creating ITLOS, states agreed that there was a necessity for a neutral institution with a broad scope of judicial powers including resolving contentious disputes and offering advisory opinions involving marine matters.[6] The design for ITLOS seems largely inspired by the operation of the ICJ. There are few surprises in the statute in terms of the structure

---

[4] R. Wolfrum, "Legitimacy of international law from a legal perspective: Some introductory considerations" in R. Wolfrum and V. Roben (eds.), *Legitimacy in International Law* (Berlin: Springer, 2008), p. 171. (Referring to three recognized bases for legitimacy associated with judicial decisions: source-based theories [e.g., how a judicial body is established], procedure-based theories [e.g., basis of jurisdiction and how judges follow rules to make judgments], and outcome-based theories [e.g., substantive content of decision and implementation]); For purposes of this chapter, Part 1 focuses on source-based legitimacy and outcome-based legitimacy of the ITLOS deriving from state referrals to ITLOS and state adherence to ITLOS decisions. Part 2 focuses on concepts of procedure-based legitimacy associated with ITLOS's judgments and orders.

[5] United Nations Convention on Law of the Sea (adopted 1982, in force 1994) 1833 UNTS 3; 21 ILM 1261 (1982) (UNCLOS).

[6] Ibid., at Annex VI, Art. 21 (Describing ITLOS's jurisdiction as comprising "all applications submitted to it in accordance with this Convention and all matters specifically provided for in any other agreement which confers jurisdiction on the Tribunal."); Rules of the International Tribunal of the Law of the Sea, ITLOS/8 (March 1999), Art. 130–138 (Describing advisory proceedings).

of ITLOS and many similarities to existing global judicial bodies. Like the ICJ, the twenty-one elected judges are expected to represent a variety of legal systems and geographical regions. As with other international judicial bodies, the judges enjoy certain privileges and immunities and must recuse themselves where there is a conflict of interest.[7] Also like the ICJ, an ITLOS judge "must make a solemn declaration in open session that he will exercise his powers impartially and conscientiously."[8] Mirroring the ICJ, the judges are expected to have "the highest reputation for fairness and integrity."[9] In addition, because ITLOS was designed to be a specialized tribunal rather than a court of general practice, each judge must have a "recognized competence in the field of the law of the sea."[10]

ITLOS will usually sit as a full panel requiring an eleven-member quorum unless the matter involves a dispute specific to the seabed of the high seas ("the Area") to be resolved by the Seabed Dispute Chamber or if a special chamber is requested.[11] As of 2015, ITLOS also has four standing special chambers. The Chamber of Summary Procedure consists of five judges who may at the request of parties hear and determine cases by summary procedure or issue provisional measures if the Tribunal is not in session or there is a lack of quorum. The Chamber for Fisheries Disputes is a subset of nine judges assigned to address disputes concerning the conservation and management of marine living resources arising under UNCLOS or other agreements conferring jurisdiction on ITLOS. The Chamber for Marine Environment Disputes is a subset of nine judges designed to address disputes involving the protection and preservation of the marine environment arising under UNCLOS or other agreements conferring jurisdiction on ITLOS. Finally, the Chamber for Maritime Delimitation Disputes is a subset of eleven judges who can be assigned to decide maritime delimitation matters. None of the Standing Special Chambers have been requested to issue decisions on the merits.[12]

---

[7] UNCLOS, see note 5 at Annex VI, Art. 8 and 10.   [8] Ibid., at Art 11.
[9] Ibid., at Arts. 2.1.   [10] Ibid.
[11] Ibid., at Arts. 13–16; UNCLOS, *supra* note 5 Part XI, Sec. 5 and Rules of the Tribunal, Arts. 27–31 (Describing ad hoc chambers of the Seabed Disputes Chamber and Special Chambers).
[12] Information about the special chambers is available at www.itlos.org/en/the-tribunal/chambers/. A Special Chambers was convened in 2000 to consider the case of conservation of swordfish stocks between Chile and the European Union but was disbanded in 2009. A Special Chambers was convened in January 2015 to deliberate on the *Dispute Concerning Delimitation of the Maritime Boundary between Ghana and Côte d'Ivoire in*

Ordinarily, ITLOS is only available to resolve state-to-state disputes, though it also has the power to issue advisory opinions.[13] In disputes that might be characterized as civil or administrative suits, ITLOS's Seabed Dispute Chamber may also exercise its jurisdiction over the International Seabed Authority (Authority), national seabed mining enterprises, private parties to a contract involving seabed floor mineral resources beyond the limits of national jurisdiction, also known as "the Area," and prospective contractors.[14] The assigned powers of the Seabed Dispute Chamber includes deciding interpretation disputes between state parties, compliance disputes between state parties and the Authority, contract disputes between any parties to a seabed mining within the Area, general disputes between the Authority and a prospective contractor, and compliance disputes between the Authority and parties with powers to prospect, explore, and exploit.

ITLOS is not restricted to exercise jurisdiction only over UNCLOS disputes but may also assert jurisdiction over "all matters specifically provided for in any other agreement which confers jurisdiction on the Tribunal."[15] Disputes that arise under other international agreements that involve Law of the Sea matters may also be referred to ITLOS.[16] In all cases, ITLOS is empowered to apply its own rules of procedures.[17]

Like the ICJ, ITLOS has additional powers beyond simply interpreting and applying the Convention to resolve disputes when it delivers provisional measures as a form of injunctive relief.[18] The statute offers transparency to the international community by requiring the tribunal to conduct its business through public hearings and to issue a judgment that "shall state the reasons on which it is based."[19]Reflecting the states' willingness at the institutional creation stage to design an authoritative body, the statute provides all decisions by ITLOS are "final and shall be complied with by all the parties to a dispute."[20] There is no controversy among states that ITLOS was legitimately founded as a recognized treaty entity with its own statute. More surprising, given the auspicious birth of the Tribunal as a body designed to survive in perpetuity, states seem to be either neglecting or in some instances rejecting ITLOS as a dispute settlement body.

---

the Atlantic Ocean (Ghana v. Côte d'Ivoire). The Special Chambers for this dispute is not the Standing Chambers for Maritime Delimitation Disputes but a small chamber of five judges with two of the judges being ad hoc judges selected by the two parties.

[13] UNCLOS, see note 5 at Annex VI, Art. 20 and Art. 21.

[14] Ibid., at Art. 20(2); UNCLOS, above note 5 at Article 187.

[15] UNCLOS Annex VI, Art. 21.   [16] Ibid., at Art. 22.   [17] Ibid., at Art. 16.

[18] Ibid., at Art. 25.   [19] Ibid., at Art. 26 and Art. 30.   [20] Ibid., at Art. 33(1)

THE INTERNATIONAL TRIBUNAL FOR THE LAW OF THE SEA 179

More problematic for ITLOS has been the lack of "state consent" after the initial constituting of the Tribunal to support ITLOS as an *active* dispute resolution institution. Bodansky distinguishes between two types of consent that are relevant to ITLOS: "general consent to an ongoing system of governance" and "specific consent to particular obligations or decisions."[21] As explained later ITLOS seems to be challenged by the lack of "general consent," which the ITLOS judges themselves attempt to address by self-consciously using their decisions to demonstrate the tribunal's respect of both sovereign rights and detailed jurisprudence. Given the extensive ratification of UNCLOS and other conventions that indirectly reference ITLOS such as the UN Fish Stocks Agreement, ITLOS has received at least general consent from most states.[22] This contributes to what Rudiger Wolfrum terms "source-based" legitimacy.[23] States have endorsed the idea of a judicial institution with specific expertise on law involving disputes under UNCLOS and other related treaties. More concerning for ITLOS as an institution is the lack of interest from states in referring either UNCLOS cases or other related cases to the Tribunal and, at least in one recent case, failure to comply with the Tribunal's decision.[24] The lack of referrals and questions of compliance are two separate but potentially related problems when evaluated in the context of judicial legitimacy.

[21] D. Bodansky, "The legitimacy of international governance: A coming challenge for international environmental law?" *American Journal of International Law*, 93 (1999), 596, 603.; He further refines these ideas in D. Bodansky, "The concept of legitimacy in international law" in R. Wolfrum and V. Roben (eds.), *Legitimacy in International Law* (Berlin: Springer, 2008), p. 315. (Distinguishing between normative legitimacy and social legitimacy where normative legitimacy concerns itself with *ex ante* perspectives on procedures and institutionalization and social legitimacy concerns itself with *ex post* perspectives on whether a decision is considered by stakeholders to be fair and just.)
[22] UN Fish Stocks Agreement, A/CONF.163/37 www.un.org/depts/los/convention_agree ments/texts/fish_stocks_agreement/CONF164_37.htm. (For purposes of applying the Fish Stocks Agreement, Article 30(3) of the UNFSA reaffirms a Party's selection of a dispute resolution mechanism under Article 287 of UNCLOS unless parties opt to apply a different Article 287 mechanism to disputes arising in regard to the UNFSA.)
[23] Wolfrum, see note 4 at p. 6; Yuval Shany, *Assessing the Effectiveness of International Courts* (Oxford University Press, 2008), p. 206.
[24] There are far more disputes over maritime issues and marine issues than are ever referred to either the ICJ or ITLOS. Some of these issues are resolved politically through negotiated treaties involving maritime boundaries. Other disputes over proper allocations for fishery areas are resolved institutionally by regional fisheries management organiza-tions.

180 ANASTASIA TELESETSKY

A Limited State Referrals

As indicated earlier, ITLOS has some degree of source-based legitimacy among UNCLOS parties. Yet the extent of this legitimacy seems bounded. Regarding the submission of cases to the Tribunal, one of the recurring critiques of ITLOS has been directed at the quantity of decisions that it has issued rather than what one might expect from dissatisfied states – the quality of the decisions. ITLOS has received twenty-five cases in its docket, but has made very few decisions on the merits.[25]

Of the twenty-five cases, eight of the cases involved provisional measures usually requiring either the prompt release of a vessel or the requested future cooperation of two parties.[26] ITLOS has only been asked to convene two specialized chambers, one of which has been disbanded,

---

[25] In contrast, the ICJ in the time that ITLOS has been operating (1996–2015) has decided eleven cases involving issues related to Law of the Sea issues. See note 35.

[26] *M/V Saiga (No. 2) (Saint Vincent and the Grenadines v. Guinea)*, Provisional Measures, Order of 11 March 1998, ITLOS Reports 1998, p. 24 (Ordering Guinea to refrain from taking or enforcing any judicial or administrative measure against the *M/V Saiga*); *Southern Bluefin Tuna (New Zealand v. Japan; Australia v. Japan)*, Provisional Measures, Order of 27 August 1999, ITLOS Reports 1999, p. 280 (Ordering parties to avoid antagonizing each other, to limit annual catches to previously agreed-upon tonnage until, to incorporate fish tons from experimental fish programs as part of the annual catch, to resume negotiation among the three parties, and to reach out to other fishing parties to conserve and manage Bluefin tuna); *MOX Plant (Ireland v. United Kingdom)*, Provisional Measures, Order of 3 December 2001, ITLOS Reports 2001, p. 95 (Ordering England and Ireland to cooperate and consult on the exchange of information regarding the English MOX plant, risk monitoring plans, and efforts to prevent pollution of the marine environment.); *Land Reclamation in and around the Straits of Johor (Malaysia v. Singapore)*, Provisional Measures, Order of 8 October 2003, ITLOS Reports 2003, p. 10 (Ordering Malaysia and Singapore to establish a group of independent experts to evaluate the impacts of Singapore's reclamation efforts, to exchange information on a regular basis; and to submit a report to ITLOS. Ordering Singapore to not "conduct its land reclamation in ways that might cause irreparable prejudice to the rights of Malaysia or serious harm to the marine environment."), *M/V Louisa (Saint Vincent and the Grenadines v. Kingdom of Spain)*, Provisional Measures, Order of 23 December 2010, ITLOS Reports 2008–2010, p. 58 (Declining to issue provisional measures); *ARA Libertad (Argentina v. Ghana)*, Provisional Measures, Order of 15 December 2012, ITLOS Reports 2012, p. 332 (Ordering Ghana to release the *ARA Libertad* frigate and for both Argentina and Ghana to submit a report to the Tribunal); *Arctic Sunrise (Kingdom of the Netherlands v. Russian Federation)*, Provisional Measures, Order of 22 November 2013, ITLOS Reports 2013 (Ordering the Russian Federation to immediately release the vessel upon the posting of a 3.6 million Euro bond or other financial security by the Netherlands and for the Russian Federation and the Netherlands to both submit reports); *Enrica Lexie Incident (Italy v. India)*, Provisional Measures, Order of 24 August 2015, ITLOS Reports 2015 (Ordering Italy and India to desist legal matters related to two Italian nationals accused of improper force).

and has only once convened a Seabed Disputes Chamber to deliberate on an advisory opinion.[27] As explained later, ITLOS exercised default jurisdiction over most of these cases. This means that ITLOS was only actively selected as the tribunal for a handful of cases averaging out to less than one referral a year for the lifetime of the tribunal.

One possible explanation for why the referral rates have been so low is that marine matters are not the subject of many disputes. Although it is true that there are not a large number of marine disputes submitted to international judicial bodies, the ICJ has received since the founding of ITLOS approximately ten marine-related matters, mostly of a substantive nature involving maritime boundaries and marine use rights. Another explanation could be that parties submitting matters to the ICJ are not UNCLOS parties, but all of the parties to the ICJ cases are also UNCLOS parties. The most probable explanation for the low rate of referral is that states on some level do not trust ITLOS to reflect their interests as closely as the ICJ might. This explanation seems to have been particularly true, until quite recently, regarding significant maritime boundaries.[28]

This general lack of trust is manifested in the paucity of state parties who have opted under Article 287 to accept ITLOS jurisdiction. Only thirty-three states have explicitly accepted any ITLOS jurisdiction beyond the default jurisdiction of the tribunal, which covers disputes arising over the exploration and exploitation of seabed minerals and provisional measures while an arbitral tribunal is being formed and all prompt release cases.[29] Of these thirty-three states, approximately twenty-three have left

---

[27] An ITLOS specialized chambers heard the initial applications for *Conservation and Sustainable Exploitation of Swordfish Stocks (Chile/European Community)*, Order of 20 December 2000, ITLOS Reports 2000, p. 148; ITLOS's Seabed Chamber delivered an opinion for the matter involving "*The Responsibilities and Obligations of States Sponsoring Persons and Entities with Respect to Activities in the Area.*" See Advisory Opinion, 1 February 2011, ITLOS Reports 2011, p. 10.

[28] See, e.g., E. Posner and J.C. Yoo, "Judicial independence in international tribunals," *California Law Review*, 93 (2005), 1, 14.

[29] Declarations of States Parties Relating to Settlement of Disputes in Accordance with Article 287. www.itlos.org/fileadmin/itlos/documents/basic_texts/287_declarations_041111_english .pdf; ITLOS has jurisdiction over UNCLOS seabed disputes and UNCLOS Article 290 provisional measure cases when an arbitral tribunal is in the process of being convened. ITLOS has de facto compulsory jurisdiction over Article 292 prompt release cases. Although parties could agree to submit a prompt release case to the ICJ or an arbitral tribunal, in practice the parties submit to ITLOS. This practice may have emerged because prompt release cases are often the result of individual vessel owners putting pressure on the flag state to resolve as rapidly as possible what amounts to a property dispute from the perspective of the vessel owner and a detention dispute from the

their adjudication options open and have agreed to submit to dispute resolution before more than one international court or tribunal. Of these, thirteen states have indicated no preference for ITLOS over other dispute resolution mechanism, and ten have prioritized ITLOS.[30] Only seven states provide exclusive jurisdiction to ITLOS to resolve Law of the Sea related disputes.[31] In some cases, such as Bangladesh's Declaration on Article 287 jurisdiction, ITLOS's power to adjudicate disputes involving Bangladesh is explicitly limited to particular subject matters.[32]

Some states such as the United Kingdom remain undecided about whether they will avail themselves of the Tribunal's services. In its Article 287 declaration, the United Kingdom submitted that "The International Tribunal for the Law of the Sea is a new institution, which the United Kingdom hopes will make an important contribution to the peaceful settlement of disputes concerning the law of the sea. In addition to those cases where the Convention itself provides for almost compulsory jurisdiction of the Tribunal, the United Kingdom remains ready to consider the submission of disputes to the Tribunal as may be agreed on a case-by-case basis."[33] The United Kingdom has yet to submit any matters to ITLOS or appear before ITLOS in a contentious case.[34]

What these limited declarations in favor of exclusive jurisdiction suggest is that ITLOS is frequently positioned to be the bridesmaid but not the bride when it comes to settling marine disputes. In a number of recent instances involving maritime boundaries and other marine issues, states have opted to submit their disputes to the ICJ rather than ITLOS.[35]

---

perspective of the crew. These decisions have been decided within 22 days after filing an application. ITLOS, Press Release, Tribunal Delivers Judgment in the *Camouco* case: 4. www.itlos.org/fileadmin/itlos/documents/press_releases_english/press_release_35_en.pdf.

[30] ITLOS Declarations, see note 29 (the following states prioritize ITLOS: Argentina, Austria, Cape Verde, Chile, Croatia, Germany, Hungary, Montenegro, Trinidad and Tobago, and Tunisia).

[31] Ibid. (Exclusive jurisdiction has been provided by Angola, Fiji, Madagascar, St. Vincent and the Grenadines, Switzerland, Tanzania, and Uruguay.)

[32] Ibid. Bangladesh has expressed its willingness to submit its maritime delimitation disputes with Myanmar and India to ITLOS review. Belarus, Ukraine, and Russian Federation only recognize ITLOS's review of prompt review cases. This recognition is not exceptional because prompt release cases can be considered under ITLOS' exclusive compulsory jurisdiction.

[33] Ibid.

[34] The UK has appeared before an Annex VII arbitral tribunal in 2015 in *In the Matter of the Chagos Marine Protected Area Arbitration, (Mauritius v. UK)*, www.pca-cpa.org/MU-UK%2020150318%20Awardd4b1.pdf?fil_id=2899.

[35] *Maritime Delimitation in the Indian Ocean (Somalia v. Kenya)* (2014); *Maritime Delimitation in the Caribbean Sea and the Pacific Ocean (Costa Rica v. Nicaragua)* (2014);

THE INTERNATIONAL TRIBUNAL FOR THE LAW OF THE SEA 183

Even though thirty-three states have accepted the possibility of ITLOS jurisdiction, unless both parties to a given dispute have selected ITLOS dispute settlement in their Article 287 declarations or have opted voluntarily for an ITLOS decision, ITLOS will not be able to hear a case. Instead, an arbitration panel will be convened under Annex VII of UNCLOS.[36] With the low probability of hearing any case due to only seventeen states assigning to ITLOS either exclusive jurisdiction or priority jurisdiction, ITLOS's expert resources are underutilized with ITLOS either repeatedly hearing the same types of cases (e.g., prompt release cases and provisional measure cases) or having the case conclude at an early phase.[37] Of the remaining five cases before ITLOS that are not prompt release or provisional measures cases, two were important advisory opinions,[38] one was a significant maritime boundary case,[39] one is a potential second maritime boundary case,[40] and one case is a review of prompt release but also raises questions about the right of freedom of

Alleged Violations of Sovereign Rights of Maritime Space in the Caribbean Sea (Nicaragua v. Columbia) (2013); *Question of the Delimitation of the Continental Shelf between Nicaragua and Colombia beyond 200 nautical miles from the Nicaraguan Coast (Nicaragua v. Colombia)* (2013); *Obligation to Negotiate Access to the Pacific Ocean (Bolivia v. Chile)* (2013); *Whaling in the Antarctic (Australia v. Japan: New Zealand intervening)* (2010); *Maritime Dispute (Peru v. Chile)* (2008); *Dispute regarding Navigational and Related Rights (Costa Rica v. Nicaragua)* (2005); *Maritime Delimitation in the Black Sea (Romania v. Ukraine)* (2004); *Territorial and Maritime Dispute (Nicaragua v. Colombia)* (2001); *Territorial and Maritime Dispute between Nicaragua and Honduras in the Caribbean Sea (Nicaragua v. Honduras)* (1999).

[36] UNCLOS, see note 5 at Article 287(5) (Providing that "If the parties to a dispute have not accepted the same procedure for the settlement of the dispute, it may be submitted only to arbitration in accordance with Annex VII, unless the parties otherwise agree.") and Annex VII (Providing for five-member binding arbitration panels.)

[37] Eighteen of the twenty-five cases considered by ITLOS were prompt release cases and provisional measure cases. Two of the cases were terminated at the request of the parties before ITLOS weighed in on the merits of the cases. (*Conservation and Sustainable Exploitation of Swordfish Stocks (Chile/European Union)*, Order of 16 December 2009, ITLOS Reports 2008–2010, p. 13; *"Chaisiri Reefer 2" (Panama v. Yemen)*, Order of 13 July 2001, ITLOS Reports 2001, p. 82)

[38] *Responsibilities and obligations of States with respect to activities in the Area*, supra note 27; *Request for an Advisory Opinion Submitted by the Sub-regional Fisheries Commission*, 2 April 2015, ITLOS Reports 2015.

[39] *Dispute concerning delimitation of the maritime boundary between Bangladesh and Myanmar in the Bay of Bengal (Bangladesh v. Myanmar)*, 14 March 2012, ITLOS Reports 2012.

[40] *Dispute Concerning Delimitation of the Maritime Boundary between Ghana and Côte d'Ivoire in the Atlantic Ocean (Ghana v. Côte d'Ivoire)* (filed under a special agreement in 2014).

184 ANASTASIA TELESETSKY

navigation.[41] ITLOS recognizes this quantity dilemma, and as will be discussed in Part 2, the Tribunal is taking affirmative steps in each of its individual judgments to bolster its reputation as a fair, conscientious, and predictable tribunal to build trust from individual states. ITLOS perceives support from states as foundational for its source-based legitimacy. This ongoing lack of state consent challenges the long-term legitimacy of ITLOS because when disputes arise under UNCLOS and related agreements that are not resolved politically, these disputes will not be referred to ITLOS. Without cases, ITLOS will become a marginalized institution. Although one might argue that there is a commitment of general consent for those seven states who have given the tribunal exclusive jurisdiction over marine disputes, the lack of support including financial support from other states is also problematic.[42] Without ongoing support from state parties who indicate a willingness to submit a matter to the tribunal and in light of competition with the ICJ for the same cases and institutional financing challenges, the sustainability of ITLOS as an international judicial institution is jeopardized. This suggests at least one core aspect of international judicial legitimacy is the operational sustainability of a judicial body

B Compliance with Orders and Judgment

A separate problem from the lack of general consent to refer matters to the tribunal is the willful disregard of ITLOS decisions, which raises questions about aspects of outcome or result-oriented legitimacy. A lack of good faith compliance with final ITLOS decisions by specific states who reject ITLOS's authority to rule over their individual disputes is potentially delegitimizing. In the recent *Arctic Sunrise* case when the Russian Federation seized a Greenpeace boat and imprisoned the activists onboard because of alleged violations of Russian domestic laws including piracy laws, the Russian Federation never appeared before ITLOS but indirectly challenged ITLOS's authority by refusing to comply with an ITLOS order. Russia, a state party to UNCLOS, asserted that ITLOS lacked jurisdiction to decide provisional measures that concerned Russian law-enforcement measures.[43] Meanwhile,

---

[41] *MV "Norstar," Republic of Panama v. The Italian Republic* (filed in November 2015).

[42] As of 2014, Japan was contributing 15% of ITLOS's annual budget. www.mofa.go.jp/press/release/press4e_000502.html.

[43] *Arctic Sunrise Case, Kingdom of the Netherlands v. Russian Federation*) Public Sitting (6 November 2013), 1.

THE INTERNATIONAL TRIBUNAL FOR THE LAW OF THE SEA   185

after locating jurisdiction in UNCLOS,[44] ITLOS proceeded under Article 28 of its statute to issue a default decision ordering the Russian Federation to immediately release both the boat and the crew in exchange for The Netherlands posting a 3.6 billion Euro bond.[45] As part of the decision, both the Netherlands and the Russian Federation were requested to submit compliance reports to ITLOS. The Netherlands posted the bond on November 29, 2013, but neither the crew members nor the boat were immediately released.[46] While the Russian compliance report was due by December 2, 2013, it was not until December 19, 2013, that Russia released the crew members under

---

www.itlos.org/fileadmin/itlos/documents/cases/case_no.22/ITLOS_PV13_C22_1_Eng.pdf (Including language from the Note Verbale from the Russian Federation to the Tribunal indicating that it would not submit to jurisdiction because it had indicated at the time of UNCLOS ratification that it would not submit to third-party dispute resolution on disputes involving "law-enforcement activities in regard to the exercise of sovereign rights or jurisdiction."); "Arctic Sunrise is not within UN Court's Jurisdiction-Russia," *Voice of Russia* (22 November 2013) http://voiceofrussia.com/news/2013_11_22/Arctic-Sunrise-situation-is-not-within-International-Tribunal-Russian-FM-2076/ (Quoting a Russian foreign ministry statement that "The Russian side proceeds on the basis that the situation with the Arctic Sunrise does not fall under the jurisdiction of the International Tribunal for the Law of the Sea" and citing the presence of a domestic court case as a barrier to accepting ITLOS jurisdiction); UNCLOS, see note 5 (Annex VI Article 25 authorizes ITLOS to issue provisional measures on the basis of Article 290, which provides that a tribunal can issues the provisional measures if the dispute has been "duly submitted" and the tribunal considers that "*prima facie* it has jurisdiction." and Article 290(6) further provides that "The parties to the dispute shall comply promptly with any provisional measures prescribed under this article.")

44 Even though the Russian Federation had entered a declaration indicating it would not submit to jurisdiction on the basis of its law-enforcement activities, ITLOS could issue provisional measures as part of its exclusive compulsory jurisdiction to issue provisional measures while an arbitral tribunal is being convened. "Arctic Sunrise" Provisional Measures, see note 26 at paras. 71 and 82. The rationale relied on by the Tribunal was that UNCLOS's Article 298 language providing for an exception from dispute resolution only applied with respect to "disputes ... excluded from the jurisdiction of a court or tribunal under article 297, paragraph 2 or 3." Article 297(2) and 297(3) only cover disputes involving marine scientific research and fisheries. Russia's declaration as applied to disputes that do not involve marine scientific research and fisheries would be considered a violation of UNCLOS 309 prohibiting reservations unless expressly permitted. Presuming that Russia did not intend to be in violation of UNCLOS by interpreting its declaration, ITLOS found that it had jurisdiction to evaluate the provisional measures.

45 *Arctic Sunrise* Provisional Measures, see note 26.

46 A. Jones, "Arctic 30: Russia 'defies international ruling' and tells protesters they cannot leave," *The Independent* (13 December 2013) www.independent.co.uk/news/world/europe/arctic-30-russia-defies-international-ruling-and-tells-protesters-they-cannot-leave-9002572.html.

a parliamentary amnesty and not until June 2014 that Russia released the vessel.[47] The Russian Federation has never provided a compliance report.

The lack of compliance with the ITLOS provisional order by the Russian Federation marked a clear and deliberate disavowal of general state consent to ITLOS authority by a powerfully positioned maritime actor.[48] The events in the *Arctic Sunrise* case directly challenged ITLOS's power to practically resolve marine-related disputes and raised questions about outcome legitimacy. While the choice of the Russian Federation to defy the deadline in the ITLOS order and wait over seven months to release the *Arctic Sunrise* can probably be ascribed to political grandstanding, the failure of other UNCLOS states to respond to the willful disregard of the *Arctic Sunrise* ITLOS order raises bigger questions of whether other UNCLOS states are willing to protect ITLOS's authority as a judicial institution. ITLOS is acutely aware that its sustainability as an institution capable of exercising its powers under UNCLOS depends on ongoing state consent. The next section explores how the Tribunal, through its substantive judgments and orders for provisional measures over the past twenty years, is self-consciously pursuing recognition by states as a legitimate international judicial institution capable of resolving disputes methodically, neutrally, and equitably while still protecting state interests.

---

[47] "Duma declares amnesty on occasion of 20th anniversary of Constitution," ITAR-TASS New Agency (19 December 2013) http://en.itar-tass.com/russia/712026; "Greenpeace International says Arctic Sunrise ship released," ITAR-TASS (6 June 2014) http://en.itar-tass.com/world/735129 (ITAR-TASS is the official news service of the Russian Federation.); The only mention of the ITLOS order by ITAR-TASS in its English archives is a one-sentence article that indicates "The United Nations International Tribunal for the Law of the Sea has taken the side of the Netherlands in its dispute with Russia ..." "International Tribunal for the Law of the Sea makes a decision on Prirazlomnaya case," ITAR-TASS News Agency (22 November 2013) http://en.itar-tass.com/world/708632.

[48] The Russian Federation's choice to refuse any participation in the ITLOS process is somewhat surprising in light of earlier comments by Konstantin Dobrynin, deputy chairman of the upper house Federation Council Committee on Constitutional Legislation, Legal and Judicial Affairs who believed that the Dutch could not prevail before ITLOS and stated, "I welcome the Netherlands' appeal with the international tribunal for one simple reason: they will likely fail to win in court. Any way of solving a dispute, except legal and judicial, would be counter-productive." Mr. Dobrynin went on to encourage Dutch authorities to give "closer consideration to both Russian and international law." "Russian official: No future for Dutch appeal with Maritime Court" (23 October 2013) http://en.itar-tass.com/greenpeace-ship-arctic-sunrise-case/702657.

II Institutionalizing Legitimacy

This part evaluates how ITLOS has through the vehicle of its judgments and orders actively constructed itself as a tribunal that reliably supports state sovereignty while also curbing arbitrary state action that threatens global cooperation. This part emphasizes the process-based component of generating international legitimacy, a task that is critical for ITLOS as a young judicial institution. The efforts by ITLOS judges to highlight the process are motivated in part by a shared institutional goal to bolster external support for ITLOS.[49] These are self-conscious efforts designed to improve the longevity of ITLOS because as Daniel Bodansky observes, "Deference to an institution develops gradually as the institution proves itself worthy of support."[50]

Given the relatively small docket and the recurring criticism that ITLOS has contributed to fragmentation within the international adjudication system, ITLOS has been eager to improve its reputation among states as a reliable specialized judicial body. The first component of sustaining ITLOS is for ITLOS to make decisions that demonstrate that it can be entrusted with dispute resolution over marine matters. Decisions become vehicles not just to decide the immediate dispute presented to the Tribunal but also to project to other states outside the dispute that ITLOS is an institution that can be trusted to protect state interests while assigning state responsibility when appropriate. The second component of sustaining ITLOS's legitimacy looks inward at the judges' interaction with each other as members of an independent judicial body. Many of the Separate Opinions and Dissenting Opinions in the cases before the Tribunal appear to have been drafted to gently critique not just the substantive portions of the decisions of the Tribunal but also how the Tribunal applies its decision-making powers. The effort Judges put into drafting their Separate Opinions and Dissenting Opinions reflects keenly a desire by some judges to focus on institution building that imparts an internal value to the court independent of the opinion of UNCLOS state members. The internal work to strengthen the reasoning of opinions and the judicial methodology is important for the potential longevity of the Tribunal. Hailing from a variety of legal traditions and normative

---

[49] Y. Shany, "Assessing the effectiveness of international courts: A goal-based approach," *The American Journal of International Law*, 106(2) (April 2012), 243. (Observing that "[i]dentifying the internal goals of international courts may therefore help us to identify and comprehend their external goals.").

[50] Bodansky, "The concept of legitimacy in international law," see note 21 at p. 315.

perspectives on the rule of law, many of the Tribunal members seem to understand that the long-term institutional success of the Tribunal will depend in the short-term on the confidence of the Tribunal itself that it is delivering equitable and methodologically sound decisions. Part of the sustainability of the tribunal is the judges' confidence in the value of the Tribunal as a rule of law institution.

A   Crafting Legitimacy for External Stakeholders

ITLOS is conscious that it "competes" for jurisdiction with other international dispute resolution bodies. Its approach to its cases is to deliberate carefully and make coherent contributions to general maritime law by articulating specific UNCLOS rights and obligations while also being cognizant to explicitly respect state sovereignty. The Tribunal in delivering its judgments has made pointed efforts to provide certain reassurances to states, ITLOS's primary external stakeholders, that it is a competent dispute resolution body. The Tribunal has incorporated three important practices into its decision making. First, the Tribunal provides careful justification of the basis on which it is assuming jurisdiction in a given matter. Second, in a number of cases, the Tribunal offers a clear description of what issues it will be deciding in a particular case. Third, the Tribunal incrementally builds its jurisprudence by relying on its interpretation in former cases. This practice is particularly significant as it creates a predictable standard for states that might refer a matter to the Tribunal. Finally, ITLOS cites the decisions of other international courts and tribunals, particularly the ICJ, to identify ITLOS jurisprudence with a larger, long-respected body of international law.

In addition to being perceived as a fair and predictable institution by states, the Tribunal is also concerned with being identified as an effective settler of disputes. Sometimes resolving a dispute will require the Tribunal to interpret law progressively to respond to contemporary legal concerns that were not considered at the time that the treaty language being interpreted was originally adopted. This may raise concerns over the perception of legitimacy in terms of who should have the power to extend the reach of a given law. Should it only be states who can shape the law or can ITLOS share in this effort? If ITLOS can share in this effort because states have consented to ITLOS's analysis of the law, then ITLOS will enhance its own legitimacy as an international judicial body capable of resolving a broad range of contemporary disputes.

1 Jurisdiction: The Tribunal Provides a Detailed Jurisdictional Analysis in Its Judgments before Exercising Its Jurisdiction

The assertion of judicial power for the Tribunal begins and sometimes ends with a jurisdictional analysis. As Judge Paik observed in his declaration on the *M/V Louisa* case where the Tribunal declined to exercise jurisdiction, "[t]he matter of jurisdiction should always be considered with great care, as it hinges on the consent of States."[51] Even when there is no disagreement between the parties over jurisdiction, "the Tribunal must satisfy itself that it has jurisdiction to deal with the case as submitted."[52] This practice reflects the practices of other international judicial decision-making bodies such as the International Court of Justice and panels authorized by the International Convention on the Settlement of Investment Dispute (ICSID).[53]

Before weighing in on a dispute before it, "The Tribunal will commence by considering the question of its jurisdiction."[54] To do so, the Tribunal confirms that the parties to the dispute are state parties to the LOS Convention and then determines what section of the Convention allows the Tribunal to exercise jurisdiction. In all of its prompt release cases, the Tribunal sets out the full text from the Convention of Article 292 so that readers of the decision will be able to immediately ascertain what jurisdictional standards are being applied by the Tribunal.[55] In the case of a prompt release matter, the Tribunal will only take jurisdiction if an application for prompt release is submitted by the flag state to the Tribunal and the parties by agreement have not already referred the question to another court or tribunal within ten days of the time of detention.[56]

---

[51] *M/V Louisa Saint Vincent and the Grenadines v. Kingdom of Spain)*, Judgment, (28 May 2013), Declaration of Judge Paik, ITLOS Reports 2013.

[52] *M/V Saiga (No. 2) Judgment (Saint Vincent and the Grenadines v. Guinea)*, (1 July 1999), 1999 ITLOS Reports, p. 10, para. 40; *The Grand Prince Case (Belize v. France)*, Judgment, (20 April 2001), 2001 ITLOS Reports, p. 17, para. 77.

[53] See, e.g., ICSID opinions quote Article 25(1) of the ICSID Convention providing specific language on the jurisdictional powers of panels.

[54] *M/V Saiga (Saint Vincent and the Grenadines v. Guinea)*, Order of 13 November 1997, ITLOS Reports 1997, p. 4, para. 37.

[55] See, e.g., *Camouco (Panama v. France)*, Order of 17 January 2000, ITLOS Reports 2000, p. 4, para. 44.; *Monte Confurco (Seychelles v. France)*, Order of 27 November 2000, ITLOS Reports 2000, p. 80: para. 57.

[56] *M/V Saiga (No. 2)*, see note 52 at para. 40.

The Tribunal does not presume that it will take jurisdiction. In a prompt release case where the Tribunal declined to take jurisdiction, the Tribunal ascertained that even though both parties were LOS parties and an application seemed to be properly filed, there were still outstanding jurisdictional questions that the Tribunal needed to evaluate "whether or not they have been expressly raised by the parties."[57] Specifically the Tribunal was concerned that the application had not been made on behalf of the flag state of the vessel. It then evaluated a number of specific documents that were not in dispute that had been submitted to the Tribunal to substantiate Belize's claim that it was the flag state for the *Grand Prince*.[58] Although not all members of the Tribunal were in agreement with ultimately rejecting jurisdiction,[59] the Tribunal's decision did reflect a concern to impartially evaluate the documents submitted by Belize before arriving at its conclusion regarding the contents of the documents.[60]

The Tribunal seems acutely aware that its legitimacy depends on explicitly identifying consent by litigating states before it delivers an opinion. In the case of M/V '*Saiga*' No. 2, the Tribunal was quick to acknowledge that even though objections had been raised to its jurisdiction by Guinea early in the proceedings, ITLOS could proceed because both states accepted in their submissions to the Tribunal that a 1998 Agreement between the Parties was the basis for the Tribunal's jurisdiction.[61] Even where one party rejects ITLOS jurisdiction and the Tribunal still asserts jurisdiction, as in the *Juno Trader* case, the Tribunal is careful to acknowledge actions taken by the domestic courts of the state rejecting jurisdiction.[62]

The necessity of carefully exercising jurisdiction becomes particularly apparent in hotly contested cases such as the maritime delimitation case between Bangladesh and Myanmar. In this case, the Tribunal began its section on jurisdiction by presenting the two divergent positions on jurisdiction by the parties followed by general observations regarding

---

[57] *The Grand Prince Judgment*, see note 52 at para. 79.   [58] Ibid., at para. 93.

[59] Ibid., Joint Dissenting Opinion of Judges Caminos, Marotta Rangel, Yankov, Yamamoto, Aki, Vukas, Marsit, Elriksson, and Jesus.

[60] Ibid., at para. 67–74.   [61] *M/V Saiga*, No. 2. Judgment, see note 52 at para. 44.

[62] *Juno Trader (Saint Vincent and the Grenadines v. Guinea-Bissau)*, Prompt Release, Judgment, (18 December 2004) ITLOS Reports 2004, p. 17, para. 62. ("The Tribunal also notes that, by suspending the execution of the fine imposed on the vessel, the decision of the Regional Court of Bissau has therefore rendered inapplicable any sanction for non-payment, including its confiscation.")

declarations filed under the LOS Convention that assigned compulsory jurisdiction to the Tribunal. On the basis of these declarations and the agreement of the parties, the Tribunal initially concluded that it had jurisdiction to delimit the territorial sea, the exclusive economic zone, and the continental shelf within 200 nautical miles of the respective countries on the basis of the parties' agreement.[63]

How the Tribunal proceeded to handle the dispute over jurisdiction for potential continental shelf boundaries beyond 200 nautical miles was important both in terms of maintaining the Tribunal's legitimacy for Myanmar as a party disputant as well as for other state parties who might be considering submitting maritime delimitation issues to the Tribunal. Understanding the sensitivity of weighing in on a subject without clear state consent, the Tribunal emphasized that Myanmar had conceded that delimitation of the continental shelf beyond 200 nautical miles "could fall within the jurisdiction of the Tribunal," even though Myanmar had advised against the Tribunal exercising its jurisdiction.[64] The Tribunal then provided seventeen paragraphs describing the numerous arguments and counterarguments presented by both parties including several large blocks of texts from the parties' memorials.[65] This practice of describing in detail each jurisdictional argument was significant because it was common practice with other well-regarded courts such as the ICJ and provided a signal to each of the parties that their positions had been fully considered by the Tribunal. While the Tribunal ultimately decided that it had the authority to exercise jurisdiction to delimit the continental shelf beyond 200 nautical miles,[66] there was no subsequent protest from Myanmar when the judgment was rendered.[67] In fact, the state-run newspaper in Myanmar indicated that in light of the decision "the countries will maintain a good relationship as neighbors and will continue cooperating in maritime affairs."[68]

Likewise, when ITLOS exercised for the first time its advisory jurisdiction powers, its approach to evaluating jurisdiction was predictable. Relying on specific text from the Convention authorizing advisory opinions, the Tribunal evaluated three preconditions for its jurisdiction and

---

[63] Ibid., at para. 49.   [64] Ibid., at para. 341   [65] Ibid., at para. 342–59

[66] Ibid., at para. 363,

[67] ITLOS Maritime Ruling "Fair Decision" for Burma, *Mizzima*, (19 March 2012) http://archive-1.mizzima.com/business/investment/6782-itlos-maritime-ruling-fair-decision-for-burma (describing the state-run newspaper *New Light of Myanmar's assessment of the ITLOS decision).

[68] Ibid.

then proceeded to test whether each precondition had been met.[69] This practice is at the center of ITLOS establishing itself as an institution with both source and process legitimacy. As a result, there have been few surprises when ITLOS exercises its jurisdiction under the ITLOS Statute except for the recent Request for an Advisory Opinion by the Subregional Fisheries Commission described in Part 3 and the Southern Blue Fin Tuna case.[70] Arguably, the predictability of its jurisdictional decisions supported by the Tribunal's systematic justification of its jurisdiction in each judgment and order enhances ITLOS's legitimacy as perceived by external stakeholders because this practice contributes to a degree of "coherence" within ITLOS jurisprudence.[71]

In practice, ITLOS's exercise of its jurisdiction has supported specific state interests by furthering the interests of participating states in either advancing or defending against a claim. Significantly, ITLOS has demonstrated that it will decline jurisdiction to protect state parties against unsubstantiated cases or overexpansive cases. For example, in the 2013 *M/V Louisa* Case, when the Tribunal was unable to find any connection between specific Law of the Sea obligations and the facts alleged by St. Vincent and the Grenadines, the Tribunal refused jurisdiction to protect Spain's priority interest in pursuing criminal matters associated with underwater cultural heritage.[72] Careful exercise of jurisdictional powers as a form of gatekeeping for various disputes may continue to enhance the perceived legitimacy of the Tribunal as a body that is constrained by the already negotiated jurisdictional limits provided for in the Law of the Sea.

2 Stating Legal Objective of Decision: The Tribunal Clarifies in Its Decisions the Specific Legal Questions It Will Answer Starting with Interpretation and Application of UNCLOS

In some instances, courts and tribunals exercise general jurisdictional powers that permit the bodies to broadly decide cases and controversies. ITLOS has been self-conscious after identifying whether it has jurisdiction

---

[69] *Responsibilities and obligations of States with respect to activities in the Area*, see note 27.

[70] B. Kwiatkowska, "Southern Bluefin Tuna (*New Zealand v. Japan*; *Australia v. Japan*), Order on Provisional Measures (ITLOS Cases Nos. 3 and 4)," *The American Journal of International Law*, 94(1) (2000), 154 (Questioning the practice by ITLOS in provisional measure cases of giving the applicants "the benefit of a great many doubts.").

[71] Grossman, see note 3 at 149–50. (Describing how Franck's concept of "coherence" can be fruitfully applied to assessing legitimacy associated with international court opinions.)

[72] *M/V Louisa*, see note 51.

THE INTERNATIONAL TRIBUNAL FOR THE LAW OF THE SEA 193

or not to articulate the specific legal questions that it believes it is charged with answering to resolve the dispute. This practice is important for building perceptions of legitimacy because it signals to the state parties involved that the Tribunal will only be exercising its powers to decide certain legal issues. Because Tribunal decisions bind the two parties to a dispute, this self-limiting practice ensures that the Tribunal is not certain expansive discretion to decide matters that theoretically could be decided as legal issues related to a given case but are unnecessary for resolving the core dispute.

In its first prompt release case, the Tribunal announced that it "is called upon to determine whether the detention consequent to the arrest is in violation of a provision of the Convention 'for the prompt release of the vessel or its crew upon the posting of a reasonable bond or other financial security.'"[73] In answering these prompt release questions, ITLOS, as a creation of UNCLOS, understands that it is largely limited to interpreting or applying UNCLOS to resolve disputes. In a later prompt release case, the Tribunal indicates that "When under article 292 of the Convention the Tribunal is called upon to determine what constitutes a reasonable bond, its determination must be based on the Convention and other rules of international law not incompatible with the Convention."[74] What this means in practice is that the Tribunal must start its legal analysis with UNCLOS and to the extent that it will apply other law must be able to justify that the laws are not "incompatible" with UNCLOS obligations. This interpretation of ITLOS as a body limited by the type of questions it can answer and the sources of law that it can use is reinforced by language in one of ITLOS most recent prompt release cases.[75]

This practice of clarifying its legal task is not limited to prompt release cases. In *Bangladesh v. Myanmar* which is perhaps ITLOS's most substantively significant resolution of a dispute, ITLOS indicated that it would be providing expert analysis on a number of specific UNCLOS

---

[73] *M/V Saiga No. 1. (Saint Vincent and the Grenadines v. Guinea)*, Prompt Release, Judgment (4 December 1997) ITLOS Reports 1997, p. 16, para. 62.
[74] *Monte Confurco (Seychelles v. France)*, Prompt Release, Judgment (18 December 2000), ITLOS Reports 2000, p. 86, para. 75.
[75] *M/V Virginia G (Panama/Guinea-Bissau)*, Judgment (14 April 2014), ITLOS Reports 2014 para. 227 (The Tribunal justified its purpose by indicating that it had been "called upon to determine whether, in enacting or implementing its law, a State Party has acted in conformity with the Convention.")

articles.[76] From the perspective of building a perception of legitimacy, the Tribunal's self-identification of the legal question that it is answering demonstrates a genuine effort to restrain the Tribunal and the types of substantive conclusions that it might reach in a judgment. Instead of issuing wide-ranging decisions on a variety of generic legal issues with some relation to law of the sea governance, ITLOS's legal opinions have been restricted to interpreting or applying specific Convention text. This effort on the part of the Tribunal eventually could pay "legitimacy" dividends for the Tribunal by increasing the relevancy of the Tribunal's work for states who need to understand the specific nature of the general rights and obligations embodied in UNCLOS and other related conventions.

3 Incremental Jurisprudence: The Tribunal Relies upon Its Preexisting Case Law as the Basis for Its Deliberation

A third means by which the Tribunal creates external legitimacy is by incrementally building a jurisprudence across almost two decades of cases. This bolsters legitimacy by providing both "determinacy" and "coherence" in the body of ITLOS jurisprudence so that the rules are clear to would-be disputants.[77] This same strategy of extending authority over a legal area very gradually has proven effective for the European Court of Human Rights.[78] Instead of reevaluating the same UNCLOS text anew in each case, the Tribunal instead reinforces its findings in former decisions and thereby provides some predictability for state parties in terms of what standards will applied to existing and future disputes. This practice is particularly apparent in the legal arena of prompt release required under Article 73 and Article 292 of the LOS Convention where the court has strived over nine decisions to craft a jurisprudence that both clarifies obligations and creates consistency between decisions.[79]

---

[76] *Delimitation of the maritime boundary in the Bay of Bengal (Bangladesh v. Myanmar)*, see note 39 at para. 48. (Indicating that ITLOS would be reviewing "relevant provisions of the Convention, in particular articles 15, 74, 76, and 83 thereof.")

[77] Grossman, see note 3 at 149. (Describing how Franck's concept of "determinacy" as a clarification of rules can be applied to international court decisions.)

[78] M. W. Janis, "The European Court of Human Rights" in M. Janis (ed.), *International Courts for the Twenty-First Century* (Dordrecht: Martinus Nijhoff, 1992), p. 105.

[79] UNCLOS, see note 5 at Article 73 (Providing that "(1) The coastal State may, in the exercise of its sovereign rights to explore, exploit, conserve and manage the living resources in the exclusive economic zone, take such measures, including boarding,

Beginning in 2000, the Tribunal referenced its former prompt release cases to establish legal findings on whether a given release bond demanded by the detaining state is "reasonable." In the *Camouco* case involving the prompt release of a Panamanian long-line fishing vessel accused of illegal fishing in the French Antarctic EEZ for Patagonian toothfish,[80] the Tribunal references the *Saiga* No. 1 case for a listing of reasonableness criteria to be reviewed by the Tribunal as part of its deliberation on a specific release bond.[81] The Tribunal also referred back to its reasoning in *Saiga* No. 1 for the premise that a bond does need to be posted for a party to pursue an application for prompt release under Article 292 of UNCLOS.[82] In a subsequent prompt release case in 2000, the Tribunal also referenced the *Saiga* No. 1 factor and then appended a number of additional factors that had been introduced by the *Camouco* case to determine the reasonableness of a release bond.[83]

The Court continues to reaffirm its jurisprudence in the prompt release area. In a Separate Opinion submitted during the *Juno Trader* case, Judge Park observed that the Tribunal's jurisprudence should be regarded as having external legitimacy. He writes "[w]hile in its entirety, the jurisprudence of the young Tribunal should be said to be still at a formative stage, that part of it which relates to the prompt release of vessels and crews has begun to assume a status of its own, and this is by virtue of the experience which it has acquired cumulatively since 1997, when it was first seized with a prompt-release case."[84]

---

inspection, arrest and judicial proceedings, as may be necessary to ensure compliance with the laws and regulations adopted by it in conformity with this Convention." and "(2) Arrested vessels and their crews shall be promptly released upon the posting of reasonable bond or other security"); Ibid., at Article 292 ("Where the authorities of a State Party have detained a vessel flying the flag of another State Party and it is alleged that the detaining State has not complied with the provisions of this Convention for the prompt release of the vessel or its crew upon the posting of a reasonable bond or other financial security, the question of release from detention may be submitted to any court or tribunal agreed upon by the parties or, failing such agreement within 10 days from the time of detention, to a court or tribunal accepted by the detaining State under article 287 or to the International Tribunal for the Law of the Sea, unless the parties otherwise agree.")

[80] *Camouco (Panama v. France)*, Prompt Release, Judgment, (7 February 2000), ITLOS Reports 2000, p. 10.

[81] Ibid., at para. 66. (Referencing "the amount, the nature and the form of the bond or financial security.")

[82] Ibid., at para. 62.   [83] *Monte Confurco*, see note 74 at para. 76.

[84] *Juno Trader* case, see note 62, Separate Opinion of Judge Park, Introduction.

196 ANASTASIA TELESETSKY

This strategy of building on previously adjudicated standards reinforces the legitimacy of the Tribunal's deliberations.[85] This is particularly true in the *M/V Virginia G* case where the court relied on some of its earliest cases to reaffirm a number of previously decided doctrines, including that UNCLOS does not allow a state who has concerns over the jurisdiction and control by a flag state to refuse to recognize the right of the ship to fly the flag of the flag State and that states cannot establish criteria to measure the validity of another state's vessel registration.[86] In weighing the reasonableness of detention standards and the "use of force," the Tribunal also chose to rely on standards that had been articulated and analyzed in earlier cases.[87]

There is no easily verifiable way of ascertaining why ITLOS relies on its former decisions. There is no requirement in UNCLOS or the ITLOS rules to cite former decisions. Perhaps it does so because it is analytically easy to build on a legal framework from an earlier decision and plug in new facts to determine whether a given bond is reasonable. This chapter suggests, however, that ITLOS's reason for creating a line of jurisprudence more likely has to do with concerns about creating legitimacy for the Tribunal than for saving time for the judges. Arguably, ITLOS relies on its former decisions because it provides a credible analytical history for the institution and ensures that ITLOS's decision making is not perceived as arbitrary. If every Tribunal approached prompt release cases *de novo*, then there is the risk that the Tribunal would not be exercising its powers uniformly across cases. Each decision would depend on the analytical preferences of the judges rather than on a consensus-built institutional approach reflected in the practice of incremental jurisprudence.

---

[85] Grossman, see note 3 at pp. 149–50.

[86] *M/V Virginia G*, see note 75 at para. 111–12 (relying on M/V Saiga to interpret UNCLOS Article 94).

[87] Ibid., at para. 270 (reinforcing its former interpretation of Article 73(2) in the *Hoshinmaru* case) and para. 359–60 (Relying heavily on its previous interpretation of the issue of "use of force" in the *Saiga* case to arrive at a conclusion involving the *M/V Virginia G*, which uses verbatim language from the *Saiga* case that the "use of force must be avoided as far as possible and, where force is unavoidable, it must not go beyond what is reasonable and necessary for the circumstances.")

4 Prioritize the Settlement of Disputes: In Instances Where a Dispute Touches on Matters Not Explicitly Contemplated in UNCLOS, the Tribunal Has Endeavored to Provide a Resolution Based on UNCLOS

In terms of building its reputation for predictable dispute resolution with states as the primary external stakeholder, the three strategies of articulating jurisdiction, adhering to an UNCLOS-based legal objective, and creating an incremental jurisprudence are all conservative strategies that might be characterized glibly as efforts by the Tribunal to "not rock the boat." In contrast to these legitimizing strategies, ITLOS has also on a couple of rare occasions taken decisive action to decide a dispute, even though this has meant deciding new matters not specifically contemplated during the UNCLOS negotiations. Such decisive action can cut both in favor of ITLOS's legitimacy and against it.

In favor of furthering legitimacy, ITLOS's decisions that fill in gaps within the UNCLOS framework can provide conclusive resolution and guidance in difficult circumstances. For example, in the case of the "Virginia G," where a Panamanian oil tanker and its cargo were confiscated by Guinea-Bissau government officials due to suspicions of the vessel aiding IUU fishing activities, the majority of the Tribunal decided that the provision of supplies ("bunkering") to foreign fishing vessels in the EEZ of a coastal state is an activity over which a coastal state can exercise jurisdiction even though there is no explicit right by coastal states under the UNCLOS.[88] This decision to include bunkering as an activity that could be regulated under coastal state jurisdiction was a significant decision for states that wanted to regulate the IUU chain of fishing, which includes not just standard fishing vessels but also bunkering vessels and transshipment vessels.[89] Although the majority of the Tribunal eventually found that Guinea-Bissau owed compensation to Panama due to the nature of the confiscation actions, the Tribunal in advancing in its judgment the idea that bunkering actions could be controlled by the coastal state also made a number of findings that validated Guinea-Bissau's general regulatory position in the case and confirmed for other states that it is acceptable under UNCLOS to control

---

[88] *M/V Virginia G*, see note 75 at paras. 217 and 222 (defining the legal authority for this obligation to Article 56 and 58).

[89] The Tribunal had formerly declined to decide the rights of Coastal state and others in relation to bunkering within an EEZ. *M/V Saiga No. 2*, see note 52, paras. 137–38.

domestically bunkering activities.[90] The *M/V Virginia G* decision is important because it reflects the Tribunal's commitment to resolving state-to-state disputes to further the goals of peaceful relations and conservation in marine law.

As a problem solver, ITLOS has the potential to assist states in achieving the broad objectives of marine treaties by logically developing the trajectory of marine law to apply to a growing number of legal problems that were not specifically contemplated when UNCLOS and other marine treaties were negotiated, such as rights to genetic material beyond national jurisdiction. Doing so, however, has the potential to open up the tribunal to accusations of activism. Although the *M/V Virginia G* decision has not generated any specific backlash from states, the decision by the Tribunal to engage in progressive development of the law might alienate the future engagement of states who have not yet assigned any specific jurisdictional powers to ITLOS. They may regard ITLOS as deliberating on matters of first impression that should be negotiated by the states. Politically conservative groups in the United States, for example, have argued that the United States should refuse to ratify UNCLOS because ITLOS might take on matters outside its scope.[91] Even as experts in the Law of the Sea, should ITLOS be responding to contemporary maritime conflicts that may not have been contemplated when UNCLOS was being negotiated? This issue of potential overreaching will be described further in Part III.

5 Cite and Rely on Other International Court and Tribunal Decisions

In addition to positioning itself as an expert qualified to clarify UNCLOS and other related agreements, ITLOS has adopted a strategy of "adherence" where it positions its decisions on the merits and its advisory opinions within preexisting jurisprudence.[92] ITLOS judges do not only cite ITLOS decisions but also rely on other sources of jurisprudence, particularly international decisions of the International Court of Justice

---

[90] *M/V Virginia G*, see note 75. (The Tribunal ultimately found that Guinea-Bissau had complied with most of its obligations under UNCLOS except for Article 73(1), where Guinea-Bissau had the right to board, inspect, and arrest the *M/V Virginia G* but not to confiscate the vessel and its cargo.)

[91] S. Grove, *Accession to UN Convention on the Law of the Sea Would Expose US to Baseless Climate Change Lawsuits* (Washington, DC: Heritage Foundation, 2012).

[92] Grossman, see note 3 at p. 151 (citing Franck's concept of "adherence" and applying it to decisions by international tribunals).

to support ITLOS findings.[93] For example, in the *Saiga* case, the court was called on to make a determination on a "necessity" defense. Instead of choosing to adjudicate in a vacuum, ITLOS referred to the ICJ's jurisprudence under the *Gabcikovo-Nagymaros* case and adopted the conditions articulated by the ICJ as the standards for ITLOS.[94] In a more recent case, ITLOS cited a number of ICJ cases and arbitral panels to explain the evolution of jurisprudence to determine equitable maritime boundaries.[95] The court then with specific reference to "taking into account the jurisprudence of international courts and tribunals" distilled the various international tests into a three-step process.[96] For stakeholders such as states, these citations to ICJ jurisprudence may be perceived as enhancing the legitimacy of ITLOS as a court relies on not only its own process but also the wisdom of the ICJ.

B Bolstering Legitimacy Inside the Tribunal

When the Tribunal issues its judgments, the members of the Tribunal do not address only external stakeholders but also the Tribunal itself. In addition to addressing issues that may be of relevance to external stakeholders such as the merits of a particular case, the Tribunal members' declarations, separate opinions and dissenting opinions consciously and explicitly reflect on how the Tribunal might improve its internal deliberation practices. Since ITLOS's formation, the Judges have provided a number of specific observations that seem addressed primarily to the other judges regarding the need to improve procedure and proceed cautiously in issuing judgments. In some respects, some of the most trenchant criticism of the Tribunal as an institution has come from Tribunal members. One possibility for this drive toward "internal legitimacy" is an effort to demonstrate the self-conscious nature of ITLOS as a body that is willing to learn iteratively to bolster its external approval

---

[93] *M/V Saiga* (No. 2), see note 52, paras. 133–35, *Bangladesh v. Myanmar*, see note 39 at paras 226–34; *M/V Louisa Case (Saint Vincent and the Grenadines v. Kingdom of Spain)*, see note 51 at paras. 81, 95, 99, 142, 146, 148; *Advisory Opinion, Responsibilities and obligations of States sponsoring persons and entities with respect to activities in the Area*, see note 27 at paras. 39, 57; *Request for an Advisory Opinion by the Sub-regional Fisheries Commission*, see note 38 at paras. 68, 71, 72, and 77.

[94] *M/V Saiga* (No. 2), see note 52, paras. 133–35.

[95] *Bangladesh v. Myanmar*, see note 39 at paras. 226–34.

[96] Ibid., at para. 240 (describing how ITLOS would proceed on the basis of tests developed by the ICJ and other tribunals).

by both states who have already assigned ITLOS primary adjudicatory authority and states who have yet to interact with ITLOS. This section will examine a variety of judicial responses drafted in response to "internal legitimacy" concerns raised by various Judges in their separate and dissenting opinions including applying a general Rule of Law, introducing new standards, ensuring respect for states' interests, restraining the necessary scope of the Tribunal's work, and creating respect for the Tribunal.

1 Rule of Law: As an Institution Embodying the Rule of Law on Marine Matters, the Tribunal Needs to Be Governed by a Rule of Law

A number of judges recognize that the Tribunal is still a young international judicial body in need of establishing its legitimacy as an active tribunal. One means to build legitimacy for the Tribunal is for ITLOS to be perceived as operating within the parameters of a broader and well-accepted Rule of Law. What becomes apparent in reading the separate and dissenting opinions is that many Tribunal members are concerned that the Tribunal exercises its powers under a transparent Rule of Law rather than based on discretion. To link the Tribunal to a broader Rule of Law, it is the opinion of some judges that the Tribunal needs more operational rules and explanations of how it operates.

Vice-President Wolfrum's separate opinion in *"Saiga" No. 2* is instructive on his views about the proper functioning of an international court. Because the Tribunal in the opinion of Judge Wolfrum applied an evidentiary standard that was not clearly identified in its majority opinion, Judge Wolfrum expressed deep concern. From his perspective, the Tribunal "is not totally free in deciding on the mode of appreciation of evidence."[97] Rather the Tribunal must be "guided" in deciding how to assign evidentiary responsibilities "by the principles of impartiality and fair trial." He calls for the Tribunal to be clear about which party will carry the burden of proof and what standard of proof will be used in assessing the evidence that is produced.

These adjudicatory decisions are important because they can implicate substantive issues for the party by determining "which party bears the negative consequences if the alleged facts have not been proven satisfactorily."[98] Even though "international tribunals are not tied by such firm

---

[97] *M/V Saiga No 2* supra note 52 Separate Opinion of Vice Present Wolfrum, para. 5.
[98] Ibid., at para. 6.

rules as developed in all national legal systems," there is a long history of international bodies deciding that the party who asserts a claim has the burden to initially prove the claim.[99]

In addition to who carries the burden of proof, Judge Wolfrum is especially concerned with what will be expected from the party carrying the burden. He warns against the tribunal simply exercising its discretion in each case about the probative value of the evidence. Rather, he calls for "a criterion against which the value of each piece of evidence as well as the overall value of evidence in a given case is to be weighed and determined." The reason for taking these extra formalistic steps is to ensure that any "criterion or standard is spelled out clearly, applied equally and that deviations therefrom are justified." Judge Wolfrum's eloquently drafted separate opinion is ultimately a call for transparency on the part of the Tribunal as part of creating an institutional Rule of Law culture within ITLOS. For Judge Wolfrum, the sustainability of the Tribunal as a judicial body depends on its ability to convince states and other potential users of the Tribunal's services that ITLOS operates within an articulated Rule of Law that is objective and fair.

2 Legal Standards and Terms: To Create a Predictable and Fair Institution, the Tribunal Must Introduce and Justify New Legal Standards for Itself

Because much of what the Tribunal is charged with doing as a specialized judicial entity is interpreting UNCLOS terms and applying these interpretations to resolve disputes, the ITLOS judges emphasize that the Tribunal majority must be circumspect in how it proceeds when it introduces a new legal test, standards, or definitions of a legal concept. In *Saiga No 1*, Judge Wolfrum and Yamamoto published a joint dissenting opinion expressing their concerns about the introduction by the majority in ITLOS's first case of an unjustified "standard of appreciation" for evaluating evidence that did not reflect how the standard was used by other courts.[100] As they indicated in their opinion, "[t]he

---

[99] Ibid., at para. 7. (Reviewing practice before the ICJ, PCIJ, conciliation commissions, mixed claims commission, Iran–U.S. Claims Tribunal.)

[100] *M/V Saiga No. 1*, see note 54 Dissenting Opinion of Judge Yamamoto and Wolfrum, para 5. (Indicating that even if the standard of appreciation approach adopted by the ITLOS majority might have been used by the ICJ, it was only applied to the admissibility phase and not the merits.)

202 ANASTASIA TELESETSKY

justification for the approach ... is not convincing, nor is the implementation of this approach."[101]

ITLOS judges repeatedly caution the Tribunal to be clear about how it applies potentially complex concepts in its judgment. In *Saiga No. 2*, Judge Wolfrum suggests that the Tribunal needs to clarify how it is using the concepts of nationality and registration within its opinion.[102] Because both of these terms appear in the same articles of UNCLOS, the terms can create confusion unless used with greater precision. Even though the terms are related, Judge Wolfrum argues that they should not be used interchangeably, and the opinion should distinguish between the two concepts.

Despite the sizable number of separate opinions and dissenting opinions that accompany most of the Tribunal's decisions, the members of ITLOS emphasize the need for the Tribunal in its majority opinions to proceed with some degree of uniformity. In the area of prompt releases where the Court has issued the most judgments, Judge Laing calls for "an international standard" because "[i]t is important that the Tribunal should carefully develop its jurisprudence on the issue of reasonableness."[103] In the vein of Judge Wolfrum's earlier opinion in the *Saiga* case, Judge Laing calls for the Tribunal to base its preferably uniform standard on "the values of consistency and proportionality."[104]

3   Respect for Sovereign States

As already noted, the sustainability of ITLOS depends largely on state consent to refer disputes to the Tribunal and comply with the Tribunal's decisions. Although the Tribunal has taken affirmative steps to enhance its external reputation as a predictable and fair judicial body, there are still pronounced concerns on the part of at least some judges that the interests of states are not sufficiently protected by the Tribunal when the Tribunal issues its judgments. These judges urge their colleagues to protect the institutional integrity of the Tribunal as a neutral decision maker by exercising caution when opining on the content of domestic law.

---

[101]   Ibid., at para. 6.

[102]   *M/V Saiga No. 2*, see note 52 Separate Opinion of Judge Wolfrum, para. 21.

[103]   *Camouco (Panama v. France)*, Prompt Release, Judgment, ITLOS Reports 2000, p. 10, Declaration of Judge Laing.

[104]   *M/V Saiga No. 1*, see note 54.

For example, in ITLOS's first decision, five judges cautioned the other Tribunal members about becoming too involved in analyzing a state party's domestic actions. They wrote:"[I]t is neither necessary nor appropriate for the Tribunal to comment on the validity or otherwise of Guinean actions under international law or advice Guinea on how it might defend its actions under international law. We cannot appear to be better custodians of Guinean interests than Guinea itself, apart from the fact that this is not role which properly belongs to the Tribunal."[105] Similar sentiments were expressed by Judge Laing when he commented on prompt release procedures in the January 2000 Camouco case that "[I]n determining reasonableness, the Tribunal must not ... normally imply criticism of the domestic law or institutions of either litigant State."[106]

Later in the *Monte Confurco* prompt release case decided in December 2000, Judge Laing repeated the same concerns when he wrote "[A]s in all of our prompt release cases to date, the Tribunal must continue to avoid the appearance of undergirding national goals and preoccupations, especially since both parties before it are sovereigns."[107] In the same case, Judge Mensah further contextualized Judge Laing's concerns when he expressed his concerns that ITLOS's approach to its judgment might disrupt domestic affairs. Judge Mensah observed "I am troubled by some statements in the Judgment which, in my view are neither necessary for the decisions nor, indeed, warranted in the context of proceedings for prompt release under article 292 of the Convention. I am particularly concerned because some of the statements come perilously close to an attempt by the Tribunal to enter into the merits of the case pending before the domestic forum in France."[108] He further commented that "[T]he Tribunal should exercise utmost restraint in making statements that might plausibly imply criticism of the procedures and decisions of the domestic courts."[109] Judge Bouguetaia issued an equally trenchant criticism in 2013 when he cautioned the Tribunal from judging "the way in which the Spanish authorities exercised their criminal jurisdiction."[110] He tersely indicated "this is not what it [the Tribunal] has been called upon to do."

---

[105] Ibid., Dissenting Opinion Park, Nelson, Chandrasekhara Rao, Vukas, and Ndiaye, para. 20.
[106] *Camouco*, see note 103, Declaration of Judge Laing.
[107] *Monte Confurco*, see note 1, Dissenting Opinion of Judge Laing, para. 7.
[108] Ibid., Declaration of Judge Mensah, p. 1.   [109] Ibid., at p. 3.
[110] *M/V Louisa*, see note 51 Separate Opinion of Judge Bouguetaia, para 13(a).

These comments suggest that protecting a sovereign state's rights entails two key lessons for the ITLOS judges if ITLOS is to maintain credibility with state parties so that states will refer matters to the Tribunal. First, ITLOS in its proceedings must not offer resolutions or advice that interfere in domestic matters that have no implications for compliance with international law. Both the group of dissenting judges in *Saiga No. 1* and Judge Mensah expressed fears that ITLOS might be perceived as intervening in domestic practices that belong to the states. Second, ITLOS must not be perceived as favoring or disfavoring one set of sovereign interests over another. As Judge Laing indicated in his comments, the Tribunal should focus its attention on matters of international law and not on validating or invalidating domestic concerns.

This set of internal critiques of the Tribunal asserted in various declarations and dissenting opinions illustrate how delicate the relationship is between the Tribunal and the states that bring matters to it. Even when the Tribunal disagrees with the states about certain practices that may have implications for effective marine conservation and management, the Tribunal cannot address those practices as long as they are outside the scope of the Tribunal's judgment authority.

4 Scope of Work: The Tribunal Should Not Seek to Act When It Does Not Need to Act

Even though the Tribunal has been eager to receive cases, the Tribunal also internally expresses its reservations about deciding any unnecessary issues on those matters that have been submitted to the Tribunal. In its first case, when there was a potential opportunity for the Tribunal to decide matters beyond the core dispute, Judge Wolfrum and Yamamoto argued that the Tribunal really should restrain itself from issuing dictum on the issues of "services to fishing vessels" until there is a case where it would "be appropriate to deal with such a question, taking into consideration all the aspects involved and, in particular after full argument by the parties before the Tribunal."[111]

5 Respect for the Tribunal: The Tribunal Should Be an Ethical Space for Fairness and Impartiality

Although most of the Tribunal's self-critiques focus on specific recommendations regarding either greater deference to the state parties or more

---

[111] *M/V Saiga No. 1*, see note 54, Dissenting Opinion Judge Wolfrum and Yamamoto, para. 25.

care in how to evaluate evidence before the Tribunal, a separate opinion by Judge Cot raised a significant question of the role of the Tribunal as an international adjudicatory body. In his comments on the *M/V Louisa* decision, Judge Cot expressed concern about the appearance of fraud associated with a contract that was "uncovered by the Tribunal," which suggested an intent on the part of one of the state agent's to "knowingly ... mislead the Tribunal."[112] He observed that there is no proper code of conduct for legal representatives to international judicial bodies perhaps because "States parties fear a possible abridgment of their sovereign right to present their cases as they wish."[113] Acknowledging the limitations on ITLOS's powers to create a binding code of conduct, Judge Cot made a proposal for improving the level of respect that parties accord the Tribunal. He suggested that "[i]nternational judicial bodies should at least warn those appearing before them that there is a body of fundamental principles and that the court or tribunal is responsible for ensuring compliance with them."[114] Judge Cot's opinion requesting the insertion of ethical principles into the practice directions of the Tribunal was ultimately a plea for individual respect of the Tribunal as a judicial institution concerned with ethical conduct.

A review of the body of ITLOS judgments reveals an intent on the part of the institution through its judges to define cautiously the powers of ITLOS as not just an expert body on the law of the sea but a body that states can trust to make impartial, methodologically reasonable, and equitable decisions. As already noted, ITLOS is painfully aware that it faces continuing legitimacy challenges to obtain specific state consent to refer substantive disputes to it outside of prompt release cases. Despite these challenges, ITLOS continues to proactively establish its credibility as an institution judgment by judgment. The question remains though whether ITLOS's conscientious efforts will generate not just greater respect for the Tribunal but also more opportunities for the Tribunal to resolve some of the most pressing maritime disputes. Ultimately, ITLOS's legitimacy will be defined by whether states are willing to sustain ITLOS as a judicial institution that can be trusted to follow the rule of law and respect core state interests. The final section of this chapter examines three future legitimacy challenges for ITLOS as it continues to define itself as a justified adjudicative body.

---

[112] *M/V Louisa*, see note 55, Separate Opinion of Judge Cot, para. 70. and 72.
[113] Ibid., at 59.   [114] Ibid., at 66.

III ITLOS's Future Legitimacy

As the previous sections have suggested, ITLOS exists today at the pleasure of states. Although at some future date it may, based on the jurisdictional powers assigned to it under UNCLOS Part XI, resolve disputes involving intergovernmental organizations and private contractors over rights and obligations associated with the high seas seabed floor, its current docket continues to be dominated by prompt release cases, occasional requests for provisional measures, and a handful of substantive cases. The reality of what from a financial resource perspective might be considered an underutilized adjudication institution raises question about the future sustainability of ITLOS.[115] Starting with more narrow questions about the Tribunal's current practices and moving to broader questions about the possibilities for peaceful marine dispute settlement through third-party dispute resolution, this last part of the chapter asks whether there needs to be a reinfusion of the Rule of Law into maritime matters that might involve a radical reimagination of the powers of ITLOS.

A ITLOS's Contemporary Practice Challenges: Revising Current Practices to Address Perceptions of Preference and Overreaching of ITLOS Authority

With twenty-one judges representing an array of legal traditions and geographical perspectives, the Tribunal has the potential to face internal conflicts over how best to decide cases neutrally. As the Tribunal continues to issue judgments and orders, the Tribunal may need to become even more self-conscious of the specific interests that are involved in each of the cases presented to the Tribunal. The prompt release cases that have been the sustenance of the Tribunal reflect a recurring tension over whose interests need to be protected.

All prompt release cases involve a flag state and a detaining coastal state. The Court has sought to balance the often-conflicting interests of these two stakeholders and has ended up in some respects with a "chicken and egg" problem. Whose interests should be examined first? Should one

---

[115] ITLOS's 2015–2016 budget was approximately $20 million. ITLOS, Finances, SPLOS/275 www.itlos.org/index.php?id=149&L=0. The proposed ICJ budget for 2014–2015 was USD $53 million. UN General Assembly, Proposed Programme budget for the biennium 2014–2015, (23 April 2013), A/68/6 (Sect. 7): Table 7.3.

start with the interest of the flag state, which often reflects the interest of the private ship owner, or should one start with the interest of the coastal state, who generally asserts its rights on behalf of the public to protect public resources? In the *Monte Confurco* case, the majority of the Tribunal observed that the object of prompt release "is to reconcile the interest of the flag State to have its vessel and its crew released promptly with the interest of the detaining State to secure appearance in its court of the Master and the payment of penalties."[116] The Tribunal proceeded in its decision to then analyze the interest of the flag state followed by the interest of the detaining state.

Although theoretically it might make no difference whether one starts with the flag state or the coastal state in analyzing the reasonableness of a bond, at least one judge has expressed concerns that the interest of the detaining coastal state are not properly weighed when the Tribunal starts its analysis with the applicant flag state's interests. Judge Treves observed, "In order to determine a bond which is reasonable from the point of view of the Tribunal, the starting point should be, in my opinion, to examine, first the function the bond performs for the State that has detained the ship and, second, the function the bond performs for the flag State and the private interests acting on its behalf before the Tribunal."[117] He later suggested that preference seems to be given to the flag state's interest when he observed "For the Tribunal, the task to be undertaken is to determine an amount for the bond which can reconcile the need of the State which has detained the ship to have a guarantee with the need of the flag State to obtain the release of the ship and its Master. The Tribunal should not give preference to one or the other of these two points of view."[118]

To ensure that ITLOS is perceived as fair and impartial, ITLOS may need to reconsider its approach to prompt release cases. Although it must start with one party or the other, it may be best to start with the coastal state's interests as the state acting on behalf of the public at large rather than the flag state, who is presumably acting in the context of a prompt release case on behalf of the concerns of a limited group of individuals. Although both public and individual crew interests need to be equally protected by ITLOS, starting with the detaining states, interest may reflect a more overt understanding on the part of ITLOS that sovereigns

---

[116] *Monte Confurco*, see note 74 para. 71.
[117] *Camuoco*, see note 80, Dissenting Opinion Judge Treves, para. 4.
[118] Ibid., at para. 6.

have the right to detain vessels to protect public interests. Even if coastal states must defend their detainment decision in light of countervailing interests for freedom of navigation and other law of the sea rights, it may be advisable to follow Judge Treves's advice to start with coastal state interests in a prompt release analysis. Starting with the coastal state's reasons for detainment, which may include public concerns such as the enforcement of conservation and management measures might signal a stronger acknowledgment by ITLOS that coastal states have legitimate reasons for exercising their rights to detain.

In addition to the concern of foregrounding public concerns, there has been a recurring concern that ITLOS may be intentionally or unintentionally interfering with domestic matters. As suggested in Part 2 earlier, ITLOS judges are aware of this recurring challenge and have repeatedly reminded their counterparts in their separate and dissenting opinions to exercise restraint. It may be advisable for ITLOS to approach its review in perhaps what can be best characterized as a "customer service" position where the court understands that it is delivering a dispute resolution service to states who have chosen to refer matters to it. Adjudication does not require the court to announce explicitly its authority. For example, relying on both a 1926 P.C.I.J. case and text from UNCLOS, the Tribunal observed in the *Saiga No. 2* prompt release case that "there is nothing to prevent it from considering the question whether or not, in applying its laws to the *Saiga* in the present case Guinea was acting in conformity with its obligations towards Saint Vincent and the Grenadines under the Convention and general international law."[119] Perhaps the Tribunal could select a different tone when deliberating on sovereign rights that involve applications of domestic law.

For Guinea, ITLOS's posture in the *Saiga No. 2* case was perceived as threatening Guinea's internal sovereign autonomy. During the case, Guinea suggested that ITLOS may be acting *ultra vires* by interfering with Guinea's domestic matters. In supporting their decision to detain the vessel, the government of Guinea indicated that the Guinean Court of Appeal had authoritatively decided that the *Saiga* violated the laws of Guinea and "that decision cannot be questioned in this case because the Tribunal is not competent to consider the question whether the internal legislation of Guinea has been properly applied by the Guinean authorities or its courts."[120] More geopolitically powerful countries may read

---

[119] *M/V Saiga No. 2*, see note 52 para. 120.   [120] Ibid., at para. 116.

cases like the *Saiga No 2* as cautionary cases that raise issues for government leaders of whether ITLOS can be trusted not to extend its decision-making reach beyond international law.

States watched carefully Case No. 21 involving a request from the Sub-regional Fisheries Commission (SRFC) in West Africa for an advisory opinion on a number of questions involving flag state rights and responsibilities and the liability for flag states and international organization. Although there were strong textual arguments in favor of ITLOS exercising jurisdiction to issue an advisory opinion, there were countervailing concerns vocalized by states that ITLOS would be overreaching its jurisdictional powers and acting *ultra vires* if it issued an advisory opinion on a matter involving existing factual disputes over state actions and omissions. For states that rejected ITLOS jurisdiction, the request for an advisory opinion was a thinly disguised strategy to seek resolution of matters between specific flag states accused of fishing illegally in SFRC waters and the SFRC. The United Kingdom in its written submission suggested that even if ITLOS has jurisdiction, it should exercise discretion and opt not to issue an opinion.[121] Given the challenges that ITLOS has faced in relation to gaining the trust of states to give their general consent to ITLOS's exercise of its dispute powers, the UK's submission presented a somewhat stark warning to ITLOS. The UK observed that declining discretion would be "consistent with the caution which it is appropriate for international courts and tribunals to exercise in approaching their advisory jurisdiction" in order "to maintain judicial integrity, to avoid blurring the boundary between contentious and advisory matters, and to avoid undermining the principle of consent which remains a key requirement for the jurisdiction of international courts and tribunals."[122]

ITLOS ultimately chose to exercise its advisory jurisdiction despite arguments by some states that it would be acting *ultra vires* because there is no express indication in UNCLOS that ITLOS has general advisory jurisdiction.[123] ITLOS concluded that Article 21 of the ITLOS statute governs so that ITLOS may decide "all matters specifically provided for in any other agreement which confers jurisdiction on the Tribunal" including requests for advisory opinion.[124] Because the Sub-regional

---

[121] *Request for Advisory Opinion Submitted by the Sub-Regional Fisheries Commission,* Written Statement of the United Kingdom (2013), para. 36. www.itlos.org/fileadmin/itlos/documents/cases/case_no.21/written_statements_round1/21_uk.pdf.
[122] Ibid.   [123] *SFRC Advisory Opinion*, see note 38 at paras. 40–7.   [124] Ibid., at 56.

Fisheries Commission's treaty conferred jurisdiction on the Tribunal, ITLOS could issue an advisory opinion in this case.[125] The explicit consent of states that were not members of SRFC would not impact ITLOS's authority.[126] It is unclear what the long-term ramifications of issuing the advisory opinion have been for ITLOS in light of written statements such as the government of UK. At least one of the judges expressed concern that ITLOS needs a procedural framework to bolster its procedural legitimacy to ensure that the Tribunal does not become subject to "the dangers of abuse and manipulation" if states "through bilateral or multilateral agreement, seek to gain an advantage over third States."[127]

Subsequent to the issuance of the advisory opinion in April 2015 in Case 21, ITLOS received an application in July 2015 for provisional measures from Italy requesting India to release two Italian nationals allegedly involved in shooting at an Indian vessel that appeared to be launching a pirate attack and for India to desist in national prosecutions.[128] The issuance of a provisional order preceded the hearing of the merits by an Annex VII tribunal and falls within ITLOS's default jurisdiction. Once again ITLOS appeared to be the bridesmaid and not the bride because the parties could not agree on ITLOS as the venue to deliberate the merits of the case.

B Lack of Enforcement Options for ITLOS

Although UNCLOS calls on states to comply with ITLOS decisions,[129] UNCLOS does not provide explicitly that national courts must enforce UNCLOS-related decisions except in the case of disputes between the

---

[125] Convention on the Determination of the Minimal Conditions for Access and Exploitation of Marine Resources within the Maritime Areas under Jurisdiction of the Member States of the Sub-Regional Fisheries Commission: Article 33 ("[t]he Conference of Ministers of the SRFC may authorize the Permanent Secretary of the SRFC to bring a given legal matter before the International Tribunal of the Law of the Sea for advisory opinion.").

[126] *SFRC Advisory Opinion*, see note 38 at para. 76.

[127] Ibid., Separate Opinion of Judge Cot (2 April 2015), para. 9.

[128] Dispute Concerning the Enrica Lexie Incident, see note 28.

[129] UNCLOS, see note 5 at Article 290 ("The parties to the dispute shall comply promptly with any provisional measures prescribed under this article."); Annex VI Article 33 ("The decision of the Tribunal is final and shall be complied with by all the parties to the dispute").

THE INTERNATIONAL TRIBUNAL FOR THE LAW OF THE SEA 211

International Seabed Authority and contractors.[130] What this means is that ITLOS has no certain mechanism for enforcement beyond the good faith of parties who may or may not have national laws providing for the domestic enforcement of international judgments and orders. This lack of adequate enforcement options for international decisions raises issues about outcome-based legitimacy.

As illustrated with the *Arctic Sunrise* case described in Part 1, enforcement can be a problem for a Tribunal attempting to enhance its external legitimacy. When a state refuses to comply with the terms of an order or a judgment, it becomes an issue not just for the parties involved in the particular dispute but also for ITLOS's reputation as an institution capable of furthering dispute resolution. When the lack of compliance is publicized, as it was in the *Arctic Sunrise* case by various news agencies, the value of ITLOS as a dispute settlement body is called into question not just by states but also by citizens who may urge their states not to refer future matters to ITLOS.

The Tribunal is acutely aware of its limitation and has remedied this issue in part by seeking information from parties as a soft-mechanism to encourage self-enforcement. Even though the Tribunal cannot directly enforce its orders, it is possible that indirectly it might have some sway over state behavior through its requests for compliance information. The Tribunal has attempted at least for provisional measures to exercise some continuing oversight over the implementation of its orders by requesting information from the parties involved regarding their compliance with an order.[131] Although the Tribunal has this power at its disposal, it is unclear from the materials that are publicly available on the ITLOS website whether the states have indeed complied with provisional measure orders. For example, only one copy of a compliance report has been posted by the Netherlands in the *Arctic Sunrise* case discussed earlier.[132]

---

[130] Ibid., at Annex III, Art. 31.2.

[131] Article 95(1) of the ITLOS rules provides that each party is required to submit to the Tribunal a report and information on compliance with any provisional measures prescribed ITLOS Rules (2009 www.itlos.org/fileadmin/itlos/documents/basic_texts/Itlos_8_E_17_03_09.pdf. In the Southern Bluefin Tuna cases, the MOX plant case, the ARA Libertad case, and the Malaysia/Singapore case, the Tribunal requested reports.

[132] The Netherlands Report on Compliance with the Provisional Measures Prescribed by the Tribunal on November 22, 2013 in the Case Concerning the *Arctic Sunrise*, December 2, 2013 www.itlos.org/fileadmin/itlos/documents/cases/case_no.22/C22_ini tial_report_orig.pdf.; states may have submitted compliance reports in other cases such as Case No. 12 on land reclamation issues between Malaysia and Singapore, but these are

Unfortunately, based on the lack of reports posted on the public websites, there is some question as to the usefulness of this procedure. Lack of easily available public information about compliance with either the Tribunal's orders or judgments poses a general legitimacy challenge. It may enhance the Tribunal's perception of legitimacy among states if it were to publicly post ITLOS-compiled compliance reports summarizing each party's compliance with provisional measures. Where there is insufficient compliance, the Tribunal could, where appropriate, offer additional legal guidance to assist a Party in complying. Favorable reports on the compliance of parties with prompt release judgments would highlight the value of the Tribunal's role in dispute resolution for both states and interested stakeholders such as shipowners.

C Legitimate but Irrelevant?

Although ITLOS may easily be able to offer additional deference to coastal states and post compliance reports, the greatest legitimacy challenge for ITLOS in terms of obtaining state consent for future referrals is the nature of the subject matter disputes that states have referred to ITLOS for resolution. Early in ITLOS's history, there were questions about whether the Tribunal would provide needed dispute resolution services. Although ITLOS has proven its value in the delivery of prompt release judgments, provisional measure orders, and its maritime delimitation judgment in the Bangladesh/Myanmar case, these are simply a subset of the ocean governance challenges for which the Tribunal might be able to offer its legal analysis.

Some of the most sensitive marine conflicts are not subject to automatic compulsory proceedings before ITLOS. Specifically, Articles 297 and 298 provide that parties need not submit issues involving military activities, law enforcement activities related to fisheries and marine scientific research matters, historic bays and titles, maritime boundary delimitations, or any situation in which the U.N. Security Council is exercising its U.N. Charter powers. A number of major maritime countries have declared in writing that they will not accept any dispute resolution mechanism regarding one or more of these topics.[133] As a result, crises such as the South China Sea disputes over sovereignty that

---

not posted. I. Karaman, *Dispute Resolution in the Law of the Sea* (Leiden, Netherlands: Martinus Nijhoff Publishers, 2012), p. 112.

[133] See, e.g., Declarations by Canada, China, Russia, Chile, Korea.

occasionally explode into violent maritime conflicts between sovereigns remain outside the subject matter reach of ITLOS. The public at large who do not understand how jurisdiction works under UNCLOS may be under the misperception that ITLOS should be proactively working to peacefully resolve these matters.

The Tribunal has judiciously not expressed any opinion about the South China Sea but may be relieved that the Philippines did not seek review by ITLOS. In the arbitration before an UNCLOS Annex VII arbitration panel, China did not make an appearance or give its consent to the process. Although the panel delivered a decision on the merits, the value of the judgment by the Tribunal has been called into question by China.[134] In some ways, the current experience of the arbitration panel parallels ITLOS's efforts in the *Arctic Sunrise* case. Even if the panel conscientiously protects the rights of all parties to the case, the lack of Chinese participation threatens the Rule of International Law, including the legitimacy of international dispute-resolution bodies, if states refuse to recognize a decision.

On other equally important maritime disputes, there is no indication that ITLOS's services will be requested. Despite the rise in piracy prosecutions, states have chosen to prosecute these nationally instead of providing any supporting role for ITLOS. When the UN began discussing the possibility of special piracy courts to combat Somali-based piracy, they did not, despite the Law of the Sea guidance on prosecuting piracy, appear to contemplate the contribution of ITLOS services or personnel in helping to set up and administer these courts.[135]

There are few opportunities for the Tribunal to be proactive. As a creation of states, it must wait for states to request the resolution of disputes before it can deliberate. States understandably do not want ITLOS to become like Mary Shelly's monster in Frankenstein, an entity

---

[134] Blanchard and M. Perry, "China vows to protect South China Sea sovereignty, Manila upbeat" (July 12, 2016) B. www.reuters.com/article/us-southchinasea-ruling-stakes/china-vows-to-protect-south-china-sea-sovereignty-manila-upbeat-idUSKCN0ZS02U. (Noting that China would take "all necessary measures to protect its territorial sovereignty and maritime rights and interests" in the region and observing that Philippine judicial advisers understood the difficulties of enforcing the Tribunal decision.)

[135] U.N. Security Council Resolution 1976 (2011): Para. 26 (Contemplating establishment of specialized Somali courts to try suspected pirates both in Somalia and in the region, including an extraterritorial Somali specialized antipiracy court that could include the participation of international personnel and support), http://www.un.org/en/ga/search/view_doc.asp?symbol=S/RES/1976(2011)

capable of complete autonomy from its creator.[136] Yet there are many pressing topics that twenty-one of the most-respected experts in Law of the Sea could weigh in on if states would empower them to offer legal viewpoints, such as existing tensions in the Arctic over energy development versus biodiversity preservation, geo-engineering experiments in oceanic waters, and harvesting of living marine genetic resources in areas beyond national jurisdiction. To a large degree, the potential of the Tribunal to resolve existing and emerging marine disputes has not yet been realized.

Despite its carefully constructed opinion in Bangladesh/Myanmar that was positively received by both parties, only one additional maritime boundary dispute has been referred to ITLOS for resolution. Other maritime boundary dispute issues have been referred instead to the ICJ. The future for ITLOS as an institution remains somewhat uncertain. Will it carry a caseload of yet more prompt release cases and more provisional measures? Or could ITLOS be empowered by states or nonstate actors to make other types of contributions?

Concluding Remarks

In large part due to the commitment of its judges, ITLOS has succeeded in silencing some of its earliest naysayers, particularly by delivering decisions in urgent matters and issuing provisional measures. Yet, all is not well with the oceans of the world. In the decades to come, it may be time for states to revisit the potential of ITLOS as not just a specialized tribunal but also a potential legal protector of the ocean. Although states have been somewhat wary of giving their consent for dispute resolution on matters involving boundaries and certain aspects of law enforcement, perhaps they would be willing in the decades to come to re-envision the Tribunal as a prosecution court like the International Criminal Court for transnational marine crimes like overfishing, habitat destruction and pollution? Perhaps this Tribunal would have the powers to prosecute individual vessels and companies involved in transnational crimes? Expanding the reach of the Tribunal to assert jurisdiction over perpetrators of marine crimes and perhaps even creating an office of marine prosecution focused on investigating individual cases would be a radically different role for ITLOS.

[136] A. Guzman, "International organizations and the Frankenstein problem," *European Journal of International Law*, 24(4) (2013), 999–1025.

Even if there is insufficient political will to reimagine the Tribunal in a prosecutorial role, perhaps there are still other opportunities for the Tribunal to engage in broader decision making. At a minimum, perhaps it is time for ITLOS to seek additional declarations under Article 287 on discrete maritime issues such as unresolved boundaries that are only partially contested. Or perhaps, the future for ITLOS lies in Article 20 of the ITLOS statute whereby the Tribunal is "open to entities other than State Parties ... in any case submitted to it pursuant to any other agreement conferring jurisdiction on the Tribunal"? Perhaps, ITLOS should seek to resolve private commercial disputes among parties to multinational seabed mining or fishing ventures.

ITLOS holds great promise even if it has not yet realized its potential. It remains committed to contributing to the mission of UNCLOS to "promote the peaceful uses of the seas and oceans, the equitable and efficient utilization of their resources, the conservation of their living resources, and the study, protection and preservation of the marine environment."[137] Now, the sustainability challenge may be whether states will remain committed to achieving these objectives of UNCLOS and what role, if any, ITLOS will play in supporting states in their efforts.

[137] UNCLOS, see note 5 Preamble.

8

Who Decides Matters

The Legitimacy Capital of WTO Adjudicators versus ICSID Arbitrators

JOOST PAUWELYN

Litigants devote an inordinate amount of time and resources to research and select the individuals who decide their disputes, both before the World Trade Organization (WTO) and in investor–state dispute settlement (ISDS). On that basis alone, we might think that who decides matters. It may, for example, matter in terms of the outcome or ruling in the particular dispute.[1] This contribution seeks to demonstrate that appointment patterns play a role also more broadly as evidence of the sources and limits of the legitimacy of the tribunal and the broader legal system within which the tribunal operates. Based on earlier work,[2] the

---

[1] See M. L. Busch and K. J. Pelc, "Does the WTO need a permanent body of panelists," *Journal of International Economic Law*, 12(3) (2009), 589–90 (finding that a WTO panel ruling is far more likely to be overturned by the WTO Appellate Body when the panel is relatively inexperienced but adding that "all of the effect of judicial experience identified ... is attributable to the chair of the panel ... the impact of the experience of the other two panelists is statistically insignificant"); M. Waibel and Y. Wu, "Are arbitrators political?" (2012) https://www.researchgate.net/publication/256023521_Are_Arbitrators_Political (last accessed on February 17, 2017) at 39 and 33–4 ("arbitrators with a track record of past appointments by investors are more likely to affirm jurisdiction than the average arbitrator, and arbitrators with track record of appointments by the host country are less likely to uphold jurisdiction than the average arbitrator"); E. Posner and M. Figueiredo, "Is the International Court of Justice biased?," *Journal of Legal Studies*, 34(2) (2005), 599 (finding that ICJ judges favor the appointing state and states at similar levels of development with a related political system); and E. Voeten, "The politics of international judicial appointments: Evidence from the European Court of Human Rights," *International Organization*, 61 (2007), 669 (finding that former diplomats tend to be more supportive of national governments).

[2] J. H. B. Pauwelyn, "The rule of law without the rule of lawyers? Why investment arbitrators are from Mars, trade panelists are from Venus," *The American Journal of International Law*, 109(4), 761, http://graduateinstitute.ch/files/live/sites/iheid/files/sites/ctei/shared/CTEI/working_papers/CTEI-2015-05_Pauwelyn-Mars%20and%20Venus.pdf (last accessed on February 17, 2017).

chapter summarizes striking differences between the pool of individuals deciding WTO as compared to ISDS disputes including their nationality, professional background, diversity, status, and ideology. This chapter, in turn, uses these differences to learn lessons about where WTO and ISDS, in particular, ISDS before the International Centre for Settlement of Investment Disputes (ICSID), source their legitimacy. Understanding the degree and composition of the legitimacy capital of WTO and ICSID tribunals is important both to assess their current functioning and limits, and to inform reform efforts.

I The Legitimacy Capital of International Tribunals

International tribunals wield public authority. If this authority is justified, these tribunals are said to be legitimate.[3] Legitimacy, in this context, has been defined as "a quality that leads people (or states) to accept authority – independent of coercion, self-interest, or rational persuasion – because of a general sense that the authority is justified."[4] For international tribunals, legitimacy can be particularly important: Lacking a police force or other methods of coercive power, real or perceived legitimacy of the tribunal may tip the balance between compliance and noncompliance. In Thomas Franck's words, at the level of international law, legitimacy – combined or not with coercion, self-interest, or rational persuasion – may explain "why ... powerful nations obey powerless rules."[5]

The "legitimacy capital"[6] of international tribunals – be it defined normatively (does it meet certain objective standards?) or sociologically (as perceived by regime insiders or the broader world) – is influenced by a number of factors. This chapter focuses on one particular factor, influencing especially sociological legitimacy: the pool and background of individuals serving on the tribunal.

For present purposes, the legitimacy capital of an international tribunal can be composed of normative legitimacy and sociological

---

[3] N. Grossman, "Legitimacy and international adjudicative bodies," *The George Washington International Law Review*, 41 (2009), 107 and 115.

[4] D. Bodansky, "The legitimacy of international governance: A coming challenge for international environmental law?" *The American Journal of International Law*, 93(3) (1999), 596 and 600.

[5] Thomas Franck, *The Power of Legitimacy among Nations* (New York: Oxford University Press, 1990), p. 3.

[6] See Yuval Shany, *Assessing the Effectiveness of International Courts* (Oxford University Press, 2014), p. 145 (Legitimacy as "Capital").

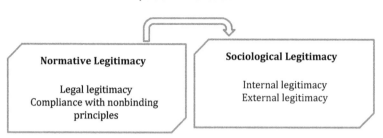

Figure 8-1: The Legitimacy Capital of International Tribunals

legitimacy (Figure 8-1). International tribunals may have normative legitimacy, that is, "*have* the right to rule," based on presumably objective criteria such as valid consent to jurisdiction and to the rules the tribunal applies, compliance with rules on adjudicator appointments and tribunal decision-making, or operation in conformity with normative principles such as impartiality, representativeness, transparency, accountability, and participation. To the extent these criteria are set out in legally binding rules and principles, they are also referred to as "legal legitimacy."[7] Yet, normative legitimacy – and the compliance pull it can generate – goes beyond strict legal legitimacy and may result also from respect for principles not explicitly binding on the tribunal. Grossman, for example, writes that international tribunals are legitimate when they "(1) are fair and unbiased, (2) interpret and apply norms consistent with what states believe the law is or should be, and (3) are transparent and infused with democratic norms."[8]

A sociologically legitimate tribunal is "*believed* to have the right to rule." Whereas normative legitimacy is about presumably objective criteria such as legality, sociological legitimacy implies a subjective determination: It asks empirically whether a particular constituency accepts the authority of a tribunal or believes this authority to be justified. In this chapter, I focus on sociological legitimacy (as evidenced by patterns of appointment) and will distinguish between the constituency of "insiders," or people operating within the WTO/ICSID expert community (for WTO purposes: WTO delegates, trade officials, WTO secretariat staff, WTO panel and Appellate Body members, the WTO law bar, other trade experts; for ICSID purposes: ICSID state parties, the

---

[7] Bodansky, "Legitimacy of international governance," 605.
[8] N. Grossman, "Sex on the bench: Do women judges matter to the legitimacy of international courts?" *Chicago Journal of International Law*, 12(2) (2012), 651.

ICSID Secretariat, arbitrators, law firms, and other ISDS experts), and the constituency of "outsiders," or the broader world beyond the WTO/ICSID expert community, described by Weiler as "the 'Real World' of States and their constitutional organs such as Parliaments, Governments and Courts as well as the world of multinational corporations, of NGOs, of the media and of citizens."[9] Sociological legitimacy with insiders has been referred to as "internal legitimacy"; sociological legitimacy with outsiders, as "external legitimacy."[10]

Constituencies may (sociologically) *believe* that a tribunal has the right to rule not only because the tribunal was validly established or complies with the law (i.e., because it is normatively legitimate), but also because the tribunal, for example, achieves desired outcomes or results, operates in a broader regime that the constituency supports, or is composed of adjudicators that the constituency particularly appreciates.

Normative and sociological legitimacy are obviously not sealed-off compartments. Normative legitimacy can be an important source of sociological legitimacy. That said, a normatively legitimate tribunal may lack sociological legitimacy (e.g., a WTO panel may comply with all relevant rules and principles, but still be labeled in certain press or by certain NGOs as a "kangaroo court"). Conversely, a sociologically legitimate tribunal may be deficient in normative terms (e.g., the European Court of Justice may have high levels of acceptance among the people of Europe, even if the Court, according to some, exceeded its legal mandate or wrongly decided certain cases).

What matters for present purposes is to realize that the legitimacy capital of a tribunal can vary both in overall legitimacy levels (degree) and in types or sources of legitimacy (composition). Normative legitimacy may be low but overall legitimacy capital may still be sufficient thanks to a high degree of sociological legitimacy (or vice versa). Strong sociological legitimacy with one group may compensate lack of legitimacy with another group. In combination, the overall legitimacy of a tribunal may be above or below the bar of minimum legitimacy required for a tribunal to survive or for legitimacy to exert compliance pull.

---

[9] J. Weiler, "The rule of lawyers and the ethos of diplomats: Reflections on the internal and external legitimacy of WTO dispute settlement," *Journal of World Trade*, 35(2) (2001), 193. (He describes "insiders," or what he calls "internal sources of legitimacy," as "the world of the WTO itself and its principal institutional actors: the Delegates and delegations, the Secretariat, the Panels, and even the Appellate Body among others").

[10] Ibid.

II Different Pools: Appointment Patterns in ICSID versus the WTO

Although increasingly addressing similar disputes, the pool of individuals deciding on WTO panels and ICSID arbitration tribunals remains remarkably different. WTO dispute settlement is purely state-to-state and has a two-tiered system of ad hoc panels and a standing Appellate Body. Panels are composed of three members, appointed by agreement of the parties or, if no agreement can be reached, as in 64% of panels, by the WTO Director-General. The Appellate Body is composed of seven members who are appointed by consensus of all WTO members for a (once renewable term) of four years. Three of the seven, selected at random, decide a particular appeal. Investor–state arbitration – for which ICSID is only one among several fora besides, in particular, arbitration under United Nations Commission on International Trade Law (UNCITRAL) rules – offers private standing to companies and individual investors, but lacks appellate review. ICSID tribunals are generally composed of three individuals: Generally, each party appoints one, the parties then agree on a president. If no agreement can be reached, the World Bank president nominates. Though not subject to appeal, ICSID tribunals are subject to review by ad hoc annulment committees but on limited procedural grounds.[11] Ad hoc annulment committees are composed of three members and appointed by the World Bank president from a roster of arbitrators nominated by ICSID state parties.

At the WTO's twentieth anniversary, I collected data on WTO panelists appointed between 1995, date of entry into force of the WTO, and the end of 2014.[12] I compared this data to information on ICSID appointments from 1972, when the first ICSID dispute was registered, to 2014.[13] The results can be summarized as follows.[14]

---

[11] See International Centre for Settlement of Investment Disputes (2003) *ICSID Convention, Regulations and Rules*, Washington DC (1818 H. St., N.W., Washington 20433), Article 52.

[12] See Pauwelyn, "The rule of law without the rule of lawyers," (201 disputes, 251 individuals, 603 appointments. In WTO's first twenty years of operation, 488 requests for consultation were filed. However, by the end of 2014, this led to (only) 201 distinct disputes for which a panel was established and composed. Moreover, in some cases there are multiple complainants leading to multiple, distinct requests for consultations but which are then collectively addressed by one and the same panel; 201 disputes counts compliance panels as separate disputes.).

[13] 502 cases; 94 percent of which were registered in the last twenty years; 396 individuals; 1666 appointments.

[14] See Pauwelyn, "The rule of law without the rule of lawyers," Section II (for a more detailed discussion).

On average, WTO panelists tend to be relatively low-key technocrats from developing countries (very few US/EU nationals), with a governmental/diplomatic background, an important minority of whom have no law degree or legal expertise. ICSID arbitrators, by contrast, are likely high-powered, elite private lawyers or legal academics from Western Europe or the United States. The pool of ICSID arbitrators is a closed network with a very small number of individuals attracting most nominations and is ideologically polarized (either inclined in favor of investors or of host states). WTO panelists face a relatively low reappointment, and nominations are more evenly distributed while being ideologically more homogeneous (neither outspokenly in favor or against trade but with government sensitivities).

Tellingly, of the 396 individuals who were ICSID arbitrators (1972–2014) and 251 appointed as WTO panelists (1995–2014), only 9 overlap. Another 5 individuals served on the WTO Appellate Body (but not WTO panels) as well as ICSID. Table 8-1 summarizes the six major differences between WTO and ICSID adjudicators, the data presenting not the number of individuals but the number of appointment slots (one individual can have more than one appointment slot).

The numbers on ICSID arbitrators include appointments on ICSID annulment committees. The background of individuals appointed on the WTO Appellate Body is addressed separately in Figure 8-2.

Overall, the profile of WTO Appellate Body Members (ABMs) is relatively similar to that of WTO panelists. Elsig and Pollack found that if the first wave of Appellate Body appointments "demonstrates a concern for the eminence and expertise of the candidates,"[15] the third wave (2006 to 2011) "favored candidates with non-controversial positions and those who had been careful in the past not to make enemies in Geneva," with WTO member representatives limiting their support to "candidates whose views were not too distant from their own."[16] Most ABMs have a governmental background. A drop in governmental background can be seen as of 2000 (dropping from 6 to 5), with a low point in 2007 (2 only). However, since 2007, the number of Appellate Body members with a former government affiliation has gone back up to 6 (out of 7). Even on the WTO Appellate Body (which only considers issues of law), 3 of the

---

[15] M. Elsig and M. Pollack, "Agents, trustees, and international courts: The Politics of judicial appointment at the World Trade Organization," *European Journal of International Relations*, 20(2) (2014), 404.

[16] Ibid at 407.

222   JOOST PAUWELYN

Table 8-1: *Comparing WTO Panelists and ICSID Arbitrators*

Criteria	WTO Panelists	ICSID Arbitrators
1. Nationality	52% Developing Countries Only 14% EU–28/US	69% Western Europe/ North America Less than 30% Developing Countries
2. Background	88% Governmental Service 57% Geneva-Based Diplomats 18% Academia 15% Private Law	76% Private Law, Followed by Academia and Governmental Background
3. Expertise	44% Nonlawyers	99.6% Lawyers
4. Diversity	"Relatively High" 2.1 Repetition Rate[17] 54% Single Shooters Top 10 = 14.4% of appointments Winner: 10 or 1.7% Women = 15.6%	"Low" 4.2 Repetition Rate 56% Single Shooters Top 10 = 20% of Appointments Winner: 57 or 3.4% Women = 7%
5. Status	"Faceless Bureaucrats"	"Star Arbitrators"
6. Ideology	Homogeneous	Polarized

25 members appointed to date (12%) have no law degree. Only 4 of the 25 had any prior court experience as a judge. Elsig and Pollack point at data showing that "WTO Members increasingly select candidates with extensive trade policy experience and who have a familiarity with the WTO system and its particularities, gained through negotiation and panel activities, to the disadvantage of other key characteristics (e.g. public international law background, court experience)."[18] Updated statistics on AB membership show, indeed (see Figure 8-2), that even though there was a dip in the early 2000s in ABMs with governmental background and trade law/negotiator experience and an increase in academics, more recently (as of 2007), this trend has been reversed: more members with governmental background, trade law/negotiator experience, fewer academics or individuals with court experience.

---

[17] Excluding compliance proceedings.   [18] Ibid at 402.

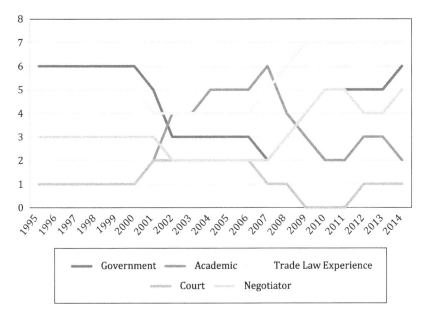

Figure 8-2: Professional Experience of the Seven AB members by Year (20 years since the WTO's formation)

Perhaps the most striking piece of evidence in support of the "higher status" of ICSID arbitrators compared to WTO panelists is the fact that of the fifteen individuals who served as adjudicators in both ICSID and the WTO (be it as panelist or ABM), no less than eight served on the WTO Appellate Body.[19] If we include also UNCITRAL appointments, ten of the to-date twenty-five AB members have served in investor–state arbitration. Most tellingly, for present purposes, eight of these ten AB members served on the AB first and were appointed as arbitrators only *after* their AB appointment. As Costa put it, "the exercise of a prestigious international function backed by the approval of states [being an ABM] is an important asset to enter arbitration, while previous links to commercial and investment arbitration does not seem to be important to step into [the] WTO's courtroom ... Reputation flows ... from the WTO to arbitration and not in the other direction."[20]

---

[19] Of these eight, five never served on a WTO panel.
[20] J. A. F. Costa, "Comparing WTO panelists and ICSID arbitrators: The creation of international legal fields," *Oñati Socio-Legal Series*, 1(4) (2011), 14.

These differences between WTO adjudicators and ICSID arbitrators can be rationally explained. They are not the result of some dark conspiracy, hidden from the public. Formal qualification requirements play some role, but far more important determinants of the adjudicator pool are:[21] (i) who appoints the adjudicators (unilateral party appointments in ICSID versus neutral appointments by agreement of the parties or the Director-General (DG) in the WTO); (ii) whether the parties are exclusively states (WTO) or also private actors (ICSID); (iii) whether the system is a stand-alone dispute settlement institution (ICSID) or embedded in a broader community (WTO); (iv) how adjudicators are remunerated (fairly poorly in the WTO; a multiple of that at ICSID); (v) whether there is an appeal procedure (only in the WTO); (vi) whether the system is supported by a strong secretariat (only in the WTO); (vii) whether there are nationality limitations (as in both the WTO and ICSID), how membership is defined (only in the WTO is the EU a member in its own right) and who is most commonly involved in disputes; and (viii) must adjudicators come from a roster (every time the World Bank president appoints) or can they be more freely appointed (as in the case of WTO panelists)?

III The Legitimacy Capital of WTO Adjudicators

If legitimacy is acceptance of authority, the sources of legitimacy of WTO versus ICSID dispute settlement – the *reasons why* WTO/ICSID tribunal rulings are generally accepted and largely implemented – vary remarkably.

As indicated earlier, this chapter focuses on sociological legitimacy as evidenced by patterns of adjudicator appointments. In the WTO, sociological legitimacy is mainly "internal"; it flows from *within* its diplomatic, governmental surroundings.[22] The main audience conferring legitimacy to WTO dispute settlement is that of insiders, especially WTO member governments. It is WTO members who appoint WTO adjudicators, by agreement of the parties (or, in the absence thereof, neutral appointment by the DG) or, for ABMs, consensus of all WTO members. Eighty-eight

---

[21] See Pauwelyn, "The rule of law without the rule of lawyers," Section III (for a more detailed discussion).

[22] See also Weiler, "Rule of lawyers and the ethos of diplomats," 193. (He defines "internal" sources of legitimacy, coming from "The World of the WTO itself and its Principal Institutional Actors: The Delegates and delegations, the Secretariat, the Panels, and even the Appellate Body among others.")

percent of WTO panelists have a governmental background and also most ABMs previously worked for a government. The pool of WTO adjudicators is broadly representative and relatively diverse; 52 percent of appointments are from developing countries, reappointment rates are low, and panelists are not ideologically polarized. If anything, in the WTO, representativeness and impartiality of WTO adjudicators comes at the expense of expertise and (legal) experience. However, WTO dispute settlement is successful not *despite* it being run by relatively inexperienced trade diplomats but *because* it is so run.

Lest it be forgotten, the WTO does more than dispute settlement. It is also a broader negotiation and monitoring forum where trade diplomats meet on a daily basis (on average 10 meetings per day) in the guise of the WTO General Council, specialized committees or subcommittees as well as informal sessions. The WTO both makes and enforces the substantive rules. Panels and the AB meet in the same building in Geneva where trade negotiations and monitoring (trade policy review) meetings are held. Many of the panelists are trade diplomats walking the same halls before and after their panelist appointment with a different (country negotiator) hat on. Many ABMs have been trade diplomats or were stationed in Geneva in prior careers. WTO panel and AB reports have no legal value unless they are adopted by the WTO's Dispute Settlement Body (DSB), a diplomatic body on which all 164 WTO members have a seat. Although DSB adoption is virtually automatic (one single vote in favor suffices), DSB meetings are religiously attended, members provide formal feedback on reports, and the DSB plays a prominent role in monitoring implementation.

In short, WTO panels and the AB are embedded in a thicker normative, bureaucratic regime part and parcel of the same organization, with two-way communication mechanisms (such as the DSB) between WTO members and the dispute settlement branch. In WTO dispute settlement, the legitimating process depends less on the quality of the decision makers (e.g., their individual expertise and experience) and more on the quality of the broader system (its representativeness and diversity), including the system's diplomatic context and the WTO Secretariat.[23]

---

[23] Costa, "Comparing the WTO panelists and ICSID arbitrators," at 22 and 24. (The WTO system stays close to bureaucratic and formalized rational legitimacy, while investment arbitration seeks more support from charisma (maybe through the special attributes of arbitrators) and tradition (maybe from the strong links to commercial arbitration)).

The relative inexperience or lack of status of WTO panelists is compensated by the existence of an Appellate Body, a skilled Secretariat and the overall control of, and continuous interaction of adjudicators with, WTO members through WTO diplomatic channels. That explains and makes palatable – at least to WTO insiders and member countries – the type of WTO panelists we now see. Joseph Weiler's prediction, in 2001, that WTO dispute settlement was destined to legalize further and to move away from its "diplomatic ethos" in order to gain more "external legitimation" – since "the rule of law requires the rule of lawyers"[24] – has *not*, or at best only partly, materialized. Over time, more (not fewer) panelist appointments have a substantial governmental background, more than half continue to be serving or former Geneva-based diplomats, and around a third are serving or former ambassadors or government ministers. Over time, more WTO panelists have had a law degree and more have professional experience with a law firm, but fewer are academics, and only a tiny fraction has any judicial experience in their home country. Equally, if not more, important, when it comes to appointments on the WTO Appellate Body, the trend is in favor of "trade insiders" (former negotiators, with trade law experience and a governmental background) and against academics, former judges or individuals with a public international law background.

At the same time, this relative status quo in the diplomatic/insider ethos of WTO dispute settlement also points at its current limits and fragility. With the types of WTO adjudicators now prevailing (relatively inexperienced, serving or former diplomats), we can, indeed, detect limits to what the WTO legal system itself can achieve, or was set up to achieve: It is not an adjudicator-driven, carefully designed "constitutional" legal system with sophisticated, long-term, economics-based, but easy to read, rulings that compel rule compliance following a logic of appropriateness (the kind of system many WTO commentators, including Joseph Weiler,[25] John Jackson,[26] Ernst-Ulrich Petersmann,[27] Petros Mavroidis,[28]

---

[24] Weiler, "Rule of lawyers and the ethos of diplomats," at 197. (It would be nice if one could take the rule of law without the rule of lawyers. But that is not possible.)

[25] Weiler, "Rule of lawyers and the ethos of diplomats," at 197.

[26] John H. Jackson, *The World Trading System: Law and Policy of International Economic Relations* (Cambridge, MA: The MIT Press, 1997), p. 110.

[27] Ernst-Ulrich Petersmann, *Constitutional Functions and Constitutional Problems of International Economic Law* (Beijing: Higher Education Press, 2004).

[28] P. Mavroidis and D. Neven, "Land rich and cash poor? The reluctance of the WTO dispute settlement system to entertain economics expertise: An institutional analysis" in

and David Unterhalter,[29] hoped for or continue calling for[30]). Instead, it is a relatively ad hoc, party-driven mechanism to settle disputes under the cautious control of government members, based on lengthy, often impenetrable rulings that only insiders can understand and where politically sensitive cases against big players result in diplomatic, give-and-take settlements with trade or cash compensations rather than rule compliance.[31] That may be the secret of the WTO dispute settlement system's success so far. It also gives an idea of its limits. The core audience and source of (sociological) legitimacy of WTO dispute settlement is and remains WTO insiders and member countries, what Shany refers to as "mandate providers."[32] Internal legitimacy weighs heavier than external legitimacy. This, in turn, may explain, for example, the careful, textual approach to treaty interpretation and limited openness to other, non-WTO rules in WTO dispute settlement.[33] WTO adjudicators, sourcing the core of their legitimacy from their "mandate providers," are careful not to exceed the explicit mandate given to them.

And today, even this relatively limited normative regime stands at risk. With a larger and more diverse membership, keeping the diplomatic engine and communication channels running between negotiators/members and adjudicators has proven increasingly difficult. Without

---

J. H. B. Pauwelyn, M. Jansen, and T. Carpenter (eds.), *The Use of Economics in International Trade and Investment Disputes* (Cambridge University Press, 2016).

[29] See Unterhalter's Farewell Speech, 2014, www.wto.org/english/tratop_e/dispu_e/unterhalterspeech_e.htm (last accessed on February 17, 2017).

[30] See J. H. B. Pauwelyn, "The transformation of world trade," *Michigan Law Review*, 104(1) (2005). (For a different narrative of the world trade system, based on a bidirectional interaction between law and politics (not a unidirectional process of ever more legalization.))

[31] See the recent U.S. settlements in *US – Cotton* and *US – Clove Cigarettes* pursuant to which the U.S. kept the nonconforming cotton subsidies and tobacco control measures in place and paid Brazil US$ 300 million in cash and granted unrelated trade concessions to Indonesia. See also the US–EU settlement in *EC – Hormones*. See S. Evenett and A. Jara, "Settling WTO disputes without solving the problem: Abusing compensation," *VOX* (December 4, 2014), www.voxeu.org/article/settling-wto-disputes-without-solving-problem-abusing-compensation (last accessed on February 17, 2017).

[32] Y. Shany, "Assessing the effectiveness of international courts: A goal-based approach," *The American Journal of International Law*, 106(2) (2012), 240. (The international organizations and member states that jointly create, fund, and monitor international courts, and that exercise certain powers of control over their operations.)

[33] See J. H. B. Pauwelyn and M. Elsig, "The politics of treaty interpretation: Variations and explanations across international tribunals" in J. L. Dunoff and M. Pollack (eds.) *International Law and International Relations: Taking Stock* (New York: Cambridge University Press, 2013), pp. 445–73.

broader diplomatic activity and some successful negotiations coming out of the WTO, WTO dispute settlement is unlikely to survive in its current guise. WTO adjudicators need the interaction with and feedback from WTO member countries to maintain what remains to this day the core source of their legitimacy (internal legitimacy). Informal steering by members of the WTO dispute settlement branch through, for example, DSB comments and feedback, has also stalled: There is too much diversity and disagreement among WTO members for the judiciary to detect guidance. That WTO political negotiations have stalled may also explain why governmental panelists or Geneva insiders continue to be appointed on WTO panels and the Appellate Body: They have more time available and, crucially, maintain the umbilical cord between the WTO legislative branch and its dispute settlement arm.

If the system's internal/diplomatic sources of legitimacy were to seriously decline – e.g., because of less interaction between WTO adjudicators and WTO member countries – the long-term survival of WTO dispute settlement would be at risk unless a way is found to tap into new, complementary sources of legitimacy, such as the expertise and prestige of adjudicators individually (as in ICSID) or external legitimacy (as in support by the private sector or civil society[34]). The former would require major change in WTO appointment patterns; the latter, a major effort in opening up to the broader public (e.g., through a vibrant amicus curiae and open hearings culture where people actually attend and express their views and where adjudicators actually take these views into account in their decisions). Even then, it remains doubtful whether these other sources of legitimacy would be sufficient to keep WTO members on board.

IV   The Legitimacy Capital of ICSID Arbitrators

Like the WTO's main source of (sociological) legitimacy, ICSID's is also *internal*. But it is of an individual/adjudicator, not a collective/diplomatic, nature. ICSID, in contrast to the WTO, is simply a set of arbitration rules serviced by a small number of World Bank officials based in Washington, DC. The substantive rules applied by ICSID tribunals were made outside

---

[34] Weiler, "Rule of lawyers and the ethos of diplomats," at 193. (He defines "external" sources of legitimacy, coming from "the 'Real World' of States and their constitutional organs such as Parliaments, Governments and Courts as well as the world of multinational corporations, of NGOs, of the media and of citizens.")

ICSID, in state contracts, bilateral investment treaties, NAFTA, or the Energy Charter Treaty, negotiated and monitored all over the world. ICSID state parties meet only once a year, on purely institutional or procedural matters. No substantive investment treaty negotiations are held at ICSID. ICSID tribunals may meet in Washington but also often meet in Paris or elsewhere. Arbitration awards have self-standing value; no diplomatic meeting at ICSID or elsewhere needs to adopt them, and no formal feedback on awards is provided. In short, there is a genuine "WTO diplomatic community." In ICSID, this is missing.

ICSID tribunals operate on a thin institutional platform with no substantive foundations and no diplomatic community surrounding or interacting with it on a regular basis. In the WTO, there is by definition a contract between the disputing parties, namely, the WTO treaty. In ICSID, most claimant–investors do not even have a prior contractual relationship with the host state (so-called arbitration without privity) as only in 19 percent of ICSID cases the basis of consent is an investment contract between the investor and the host state (in most other cases, the basis of consent is a treaty).[35]

This lack of embeddedness or institutionalization of ICSID means that legitimacy must, at least in part, come from other sources, in particular, the expertise, standing, exceptional character, and social cohesiveness (a small group of arbitrators getting repeat appointments) of the individuals appointed on ICSID tribunals.[36] Without it (for example, in case a major conflict of interest crisis were to explode), the system risks collapse. This explains why, in ICSID, arbitrator selection and identity has attracted major attention; in the WTO (with the possible exception of ABMs), it is a topic hardly discussed.

Apart from arbitrators and a small, largely administrative secretariat in Washington, ICSID is not much else. As Costa put it, "in a less regulated

---

[35] The World Bank, "The ICSID caseload – statistics," 2014(2) at 10, http://documents .worldbank.org/curated/en/646011468142790944/The-ICSID-caseload-statistics-issue-2014-2 (last accessed on February 17, 2017).

[36] See I. E. Shihata, "The settlement of disputes regarding foreign investment: The role of the World Bank, with particular reference to ICSID and MIGA," *American University International Law Review*, 1(1) (1986), 116. (Describing ICSID's value as "an effective and truly neutral forum where disputes are to be settled according to objective non-political criteria.") S. Puig, "Recasting ICSID's legitimacy debate: Towards a goal-based empirical agenda," *Fordham International Law Journal*, 36 (2013), 465. (Arguing that ICSID's legitimacy is based on its claim to offer expert, specialized and neutral settlement of investment disputes.)

and institutionally weaker system ... a strong non-formal leadership is more necessary, since legitimacy must be asserted case by case."[37] This "demands a professional profile of arbitrators who can provide technically correct decisions and the special aura given by sanctified arbitrators."[38] Elite, frequently reappointed arbitrators must "be able to become a hard core, reinforced by high rates of social direct interactions and networks of diffusion of behavioural standards." Hence, the high prestige/status level of ICSID arbitrators (who also cumulate a broader variety of backgrounds than WTO panelists) and the closed, less evenly distributed network of frequently appointed, star arbitrators. In contrast, the more embedded and institutionalized WTO dispute settlement system "does not need such an underlying social structure."[39] It "does not need to be operated by arbitration stars."[40]

The repeat appointment of a very closed group of experienced, star arbitrators, as objectionable as it may seem at first sight, can further be explained by the fact that parties get to unilaterally appoint "their arbitrator" (in the WTO, adjudicators are never unilaterally appointed, but only by agreement of both parties or neutrally by the DG). This naturally leads a party to appoint an arbitrator with a proven track record and prior disclosed preferences (rather than a novice with no reputation among her peers) to maximize a party's chances of success. Arbitrators, in turn, accept repeat ICSID appointments because the financial rewards are much higher than in the WTO. The closed network of ICSID arbitrators also compensates for the absence of an Appellate Body or strong Secretariat: Through arbitrator selection, a certain level of centralization (consistency and authority) is thereby achieved organically. If anything, in ICSID, the high level of expertise and (legal) experience of ICSID arbitrators comes at the expense of their representativeness and impartiality.

If ICSID's legitimacy, indeed, depends on the individual quality and impartiality of its arbitrators – after all, one of the core, original reasons to set up ISDS was to offer specialized, neutral arbitration to fill deficiencies and gaps in the relatively weak domestic legal institutions of poor developing countries[41] – the current ideological divide and predisposition of

---

[37] Costa, "Comparing the WTO panelists and ICSID arbitrators," at 13.
[38] Costa, "Comparing the WTO panelists and ICSID arbitrators," at 17.
[39] Costa, "Comparing the WTO panelists and ICSID arbitrators," at 13.
[40] Costa, "Comparing the WTO panelists and ICSID arbitrators," at 17.
[41] See I. E. Shihata, "Towards a greater depoliticization of investment disputes: The role of ICSID and MIGA," *ICSID Review: Foreign Investment Law Journal*, 1(1) (1986), 12.

WHO DECIDES MATTERS

arbitrators represents a serious risk, both to sociological and normative legitimacy (the latter including, as defined earlier, conformity with normative principles such as impartiality, representativeness, and transparency). In response, many recent investment agreements have strengthened conflict of interest rules for arbitrators and enhanced transparency.[42] More broadly, fifty years ago, when ICSID was created mainly with contract disputes in mind, the model of private (commercial) arbitration, where each party gets to appoint "its arbitrator" may have been appropriate. Today, investor–state tribunals are performing a predominantly public function (more than 70 percent of ICSID cases are based on a treaty). Where fulfilling a public function, the model of private adjudication needs rethinking both in terms of transparency and openness to the public (on which both UNCITRAL and ICSID are making major advances) and in terms of adjudicator appointments (where doing away with party-appointed arbitrators remains, however, a taboo[43]). Instead of relying on a closed group of repeat arbitrators to achieve a modicum of consistency and predictability, a more structured appellate system is now seriously considered.[44]

A reduction in the individual quality, neutrality, or closed network of ICSID arbitrators may be compensated by other sources of legitimacy: more control and substantive oversight by ICSID state parties (that is, the type of diplomatic culture that has been the foundation of WTO dispute settlement), the creation of an appellate system,[45] a stronger ICSID secretariat or broader, external legitimacy (as in support by the private sector or civil society). A recent trend in ISDS is, indeed, that of state parties to investment treaties seeking more control and substantive oversight of investor–state arbitration by means of more carefully worded treaty provisions, ex post interpretation mechanisms or treaty-based joint commissions that allow the parties to clarify their intentions,

---

[42] E.g., Comprehensive Economic and Trade Agreement (CETA) between Canada and the European Union, http://ec.europa.eu/trade/policy/in-focus/ceta/ (last accessed on February 17, 2017).

[43] See J. Paulsson, "Moral hazard in international dispute resolution," *ICSID Review*, 25(2) (2010), 352. (Provides an influential argument against unilaterally appointed arbitrators, concluding that "the only decent solution – heed this voice in the desert! – is thus that any arbitrator, no matter the size of the tribunal, should be chosen jointly or selected by a neutral body.")

[44] See A. J. Bret, "Why we need a global appellate mechanism for international investment law," *Columbia FDI Perspectives*, 146 (2015), https://academiccommons.columbia.edu/catalog/ac:186806/ (last accessed on February 18, 2017).

[45] Ibid.

or gatekeeping or denial of benefits provisions that give some control or input back to states before or during investor–state proceedings.[46] This "return of the state" will add sociological legitimacy sourced from ICSID member countries and build important bridges and communication channels between treaty parties and adjudicators. It is likely to thicken the institutional platform on which ICSID tribunals operate and may create the type of diplomatic culture or community that has been the foundation and major success of WTO dispute settlement. At the same time, given that private investors represent the other side of the ICSID system's legitimacy "audience" (unlike in the WTO, which is a purely state-to-state system), care should be taken to also represent investor interests (e.g., by making it more accessible to smaller investors or offering more predictable rules and outcomes). If the pendulum were to shift too much in favor of state interests only, there is a risk of alienating the other half of ICSID's constituency. That, in turn, would reduce part of the regime's legitimacy capital.

External legitimacy, finally, is currently sought by injecting more transparency in ICSID (as well as UNCITRAL) proceedings. Whether this will suffice to compensate for deficits in, or questions around, ICSID's internal legitimacy remains to be seen.

Conclusion

Given their diverse history, goals, and design features, it should be no surprise that the universe of WTO adjudicators is different from that of ICSID arbitrators. However, with the increasing convergence of, and forum shopping between, the two systems, these differences have become striking. On average, and obviously with many individual exceptions to this general rule, WTO panelists tend to be relatively low-key technocrats from developing countries (very few US/EU nationals), with a governmental background, often without a law degree or legal expertise. ICSID arbitrators, in contrast, tend to be high-powered, elite private lawyers or legal academics from Western Europe or the United States. The pool of ICSID arbitrators is an ideologically polarized, closed network with a very small number of individuals attracting most nominations.

---

[46] See W. Alschner, "The return of the home state and the rise of 'embedded' investor–state arbitration" in S. Lalani and R. Polanco (eds.), *The Role of the State in Investor–State Arbitration* (Leiden: Martinus Nijhoff/BRILL, 2014), pp. 192–218.

The universe of WTO panelists, in contrast, is ideologically more homogeneous, with a relatively low reappointment or experience rate and nominations more evenly distributed.

The point is not that WTO panelists are "better" than ICSID arbitrators, or vice versa. The two groups are simply different, and the crucial thing is to understand why. Some may be troubled by the lack of experience or status of WTO panelists or their closeness to governments. Others may be outraged when finding the closed network of ICSID arbitrators, appointed over and over again by either investors or host states. What this chapter tries to show is that differences between WTO panelists and ICSID arbitrators (i) can be rationally explained and (ii) are key determinants of the legitimacy capital of the respective dispute settlement regimes.

In the WTO, sociological legitimacy flows from *within* its diplomatic, governmental surroundings. The relative inexperience or lack of status of WTO panelists is compensated by the existence of an Appellate Body, a skilled Secretariat, and the overall control of, and continuous interaction of, adjudicators with WTO members through WTO diplomatic channels. That explains and makes palatable – at least to WTO insiders and member countries – the type of WTO adjudicators we now see. From this perspective, WTO dispute settlement is successful not *despite* it being run by relatively inexperienced trade diplomats but *because* it is so run.

Like the WTO's main source of sociological legitimacy, ICSID's is also *internal*. But it is of an individual/adjudicator, not a collective/diplomatic, nature. ICSID tribunals operate on a thin institutional platform with no substantive foundations and no diplomatic community surrounding or interacting with it on a regular basis. Legitimacy at ICSID comes from a different source: the individual neutrality, expertise, and status of adjudicators.

As the examples of the WTO and ICSID illustrate, the legitimacy capital of an international tribunal can vary both in overall legitimacy levels (degree) and in types or sources of legitimacy (composition). Strong sociological legitimacy with one group may compensate lack of legitimacy with another group. In combination the overall legitimacy of a tribunal may be above or below the bar of minimum legitimacy required for a tribunal to survive or for legitimacy to exert compliance pull.

9

The Legitimacy of the International Centre for Settlement of Investment Disputes

ANDREA K. BJORKLUND[*]

Introduction

ICSID – the International Centre for Settlement of Investment Disputes – is the premiere venue for the settlement of disputes between foreign investors and the sovereign states that host their investments. As such it is a lightning rod for the criticism that is currently levelled at investor-state dispute settlement (ISDS) and at investment law generally. Yet ICSID is a relatively modest institution, with limited powers. Many of the criticisms expect more from ICSID than it can possibly deliver and seem not to understand ICSID's role in the settlement of investment disputes, or its even more limited role in investment law itself.

To explore ICSID's legitimacy – the extent to which its decisions are honoured because 'the rule or institution has come into being and operates in accordance with generally accepted principles of right process'[1] – I will briefly explore two approaches to legitimacy: first, factors related to normative legitimacy, including reference to Yuval Shany's insights about the contributions that effectiveness makes to legitimacy; and second, factors related to sociological legitimacy set out by Thomas Franck to assess international law generally, and then modified and expanded on by Nienke Grossman to assess international tribunals. With those ideas as background, Section II then turns to the legitimacy critiques that have

---

[*] Full Professor; L Yves Fortier Chair in International Arbitration and International Commercial Law, McGill University Faculty of Law. I am grateful to Nienke Grossman, Andreas Follesdal, Harlan Cohen, and other participants in the Legitimacy and International Courts symposium hosted by the University of Baltimore and the PluriCourts initiative at the University of Oslo for suggestions; any errors are of course my own. I thank Lukas Vanhonnaeker for indefatigable research assistance.

[1] Thomas M. Franck, *The Power of Legitimacy among Nations* (Oxford University Press, 1990), p. 24.

234

been levelled at investment arbitration to isolate both their normative and sociological elements. Section III then focuses on ICSID itself to assess several key decisions in its design on which its internal operations are based. Finally Section IV revisits the legitimacy critiques of Section II in light of ICSID's features and limitations. Were the decisions made in the founding of ICSID reasonable? Has it worked as intended? Finally, a short conclusion assesses whether and how ICSID, which in many instances bears the brunt of blame for problems it did not cause and that it cannot solve, can be delinked from the criticisms levelled at investment law more generally.

I   Legitimacy and Investment Treaty Arbitration

Definitions of legitimacy tend to be slippery, circular, and highly subjective: institutions are viewed as legitimate if the relevant public regards them as justified. Investment arbitration – and investment treaty arbitration in particular – is difficult to assess because the substantive rules are usually found in a different instrument from the procedural rules, and different entities created and are responsible for the honouring and implementation of those rules. ICSID is a case in point. It provides a framework for the resolution of disputes and was set up by states. It provides only a framework, however: the content of an investment arbitration is supplied by an investment treaty, investment contract, or investment statute. In the case of the most common form of investment arbitration – investment treaty arbitration – two or more states will have signed the treaty permitting the submission of claims brought under the treaty to arbitration, yet only one of those states will be active in a case, as the other party will be an investor from the other state party to the treaty.[2]

Critics of investment arbitration will not, however, necessarily make distinctions between the sources from which their concerns stem. Defenders of investment arbitration are not always more careful in their rhetoric either because often they take for granted the structure of investment arbitration and assume everyone hearing them does, too. Indeed, sometimes it seems that critics and proponents of investment arbitration are simply talking past each other. They do so because each is primarily addressing a different facet of legitimacy and assessing investment

---

[2] It is possible that a state entity can be a claimant in an investment arbitration, which might mean the other state party to the treaty is closer to the dispute than would otherwise be the case.

arbitration vis-à-vis their particular concerns. Even when their legitimacy critiques intersect, however, one sees differences in assessment depending on whether the perspective is 'internal' – given by one who is an active incumbent in the investment law 'system' – or external – given by one who is situated outside the system.[3] This does not mean that incumbents cannot be critical, or that external actors cannot be complimentary; my suggestion is that their perspective affects the type of legitimacy concerns they tend to view as most problematic, and the ones that their defences or suggested amendments are designed to address.

The legitimacy concerns levelled against investment arbitration are primarily normative and sociological.[4] The normative critique focuses on whether arbitral tribunals are justified in exercising the authority they do. The sociological critique focuses on *perceptions* about the exercise of that authority. As Nienke Grossman rightly observes, normative legitimacy can and does influence sociological legitimacy, yet considering them separately helps to pinpoint the 'talking past each other' phenomenon that currently afflicts critics and proponents of investment arbitration. It also helps to highlight the ways in which defences of an institution's normative legitimacy will not necessarily allay concerns linked to sociological legitimacy.

A   Normative Legitimacy

Traditional assessments of the normative legitimacy of international adjudicative bodies have hinged on state consent and procedural fairness

---

[3] Of course, people can move from 'inside' to 'outside' and back again.

[4] I exclude 'legal' legitimacy in this chapter because the ICSID Convention and bilateral investment treaties are unquestionably in place. Even though some have questioned the knowledge with which developing countries signed investment treaties, especially in the 1980s and 1990s prior to the increase in the number of investment arbitrations, no credible allegations of duress to invalidate treaties have been raised. See Vienna Convention on the Law of Treaties, Vienna, 23 May 1969, in force 27 January 1980, 1155 UNTS 331; (1969), art 52 (Coercion of a State by the threat of use of force):

'A treaty is void if its conclusion has been procured by the threat or use of force in violation of the principles of international law embodied in the Charter of the United Nations'.

Individual cases can raise legal legitimacy concerns, such as whether the provisional application of the Energy Charter treaty should be viewed as binding Russia to arbitrate disputes under the treaty. See *Yukos Universal Ltd.* v. *Russian Federation*, PCA Case No. AA 227, Interim Award on Jurisdiction and Admissibility, 30 November 2009, pp. 88–147; *Russian Federation* v. *Yukos Universal Ltd.*, C/09/477162/ HA ZA 15-2, Hague District Court, 20 April 2016, paras. 5.6–5.96.

THE LEGITIMACY OF THE ICSID 237

to litigants.[5] Focusing on state consent emphasizes the formal trappings of authority – if a tribunal is formed by the consent of states, its legitimacy is presumed under the Westphalian model of international law. A focus on procedural fairness to the litigants themselves is similarly formalistic; so long as the two parties to the dispute are adequately represented and are treated equally, the process will be considered legitimate.[6] Professor Nienke Grossman has suggested that these criteria are outmoded because the effects of international court decisions extend far beyond the parties to the case and because international tribunals 'promote specific normative regimes like human rights or free trade'.[7]

Both of Professor Grossman's insights are especially important for investment arbitration and explain some of the failures of engagement by its critics and proponents. Formalists will point to investment treaties and the ICSID Convention, highlight the state consent to those instruments, and suggest that they are ipso facto legitimate. Similarly, proponents will point to the procedural safeguards inherent in arbitration – indeed, arbitration is rife with procedural safeguards, and the applicable control mechanisms police heavily abuses of procedure[8] – to demonstrate its fairness and hence its legitimacy. On the other hand, critics will focus on the broader public interest inherent in every arbitration; on the potential spillover effects, including 'regulatory chill', the potential for a decision in one case to discourage desirable social regulation in other cases; the identity of the decision makers; and concerns about substantive correctness in the decisions rendered by tribunals.[9]

---

[5] See N. Grossman, 'The normative legitimacy of international courts', *Temple Law Review*, 86 (2013), 61, 65–8.

[6] Professor Grossman has noted that an alternative approach is to look at the fairness of the outcomes to ensure they are neither immoral nor unjust, yet she notes that this has not been a traditional normative legitimacy criterion. Ibid., 68.

[7] Ibid.

[8] See, e.g., Gary B. Born, *International Commercial Arbitration*, 2nd ed., (Alphen aan den Rijn: Kluwer Law International, 2014), Chapter 15 (Procedures in International Arbitration). See especially ibid. p. 2123:

> The international arbitral process seeks to achieve a number of related objectives. The most significant of these are procedural neutrality, procedural fairness, efficiency, expertise and tailoring procedures to specific disputes and parties.

See also generally W.W. Park, 'Challenging arbitral jurisdiction: The role of institutional rules', *Boston University School of Law Public Law & Legal Theory Paper*, (2015) No. 15–40.

[9] See generally D. Behn, 'Legitimacy, evolution, and growth in investment treaty arbitration: Empirically evaluating the state-of-the-art', *Georgetown Journal of International Law*, 46 (2015), 363, 365–70.

This dichotomy also explains the different expectations brought by different actors; procedural safeguards are paradigmatic in international commercial arbitration, and those familiar with that system are likely to be comfortable with the safeguards offered, whereas those focused on the public law aspects of investment treaty arbitration are likely to be uncomfortable with the commercial arbitration paradigm.[10] Traditionalists might also be more comfortable with pointing to the consent by the state as the ultimate guarantor of legitimacy, whereas others might point to the increasing role that nonstate actors play in the development of international law and the unrepresentativeness of states.[11]

A slightly different view of normative legitimacy has been presented by Yuval Shany, who has suggested that a goal-based approach is the appropriate way to assess whether international tribunals are effective (and presumptively legitimate).[12] This approach requires identifying the organizational goals the evaluated organization, or court, seeks to achieve, as well as the operative goals the organization might develop in the course of its regular activities.[13] The goals-based approach does not (except in an implicit way) assess the normative value of the goal itself; rather, the focus is on whether the goals are achieved.[14] Professor Shany in fact presents legitimacy as one of the factors by which to assess effectiveness. His observations also identify one of the central challenges in assessing the effectiveness of ICSID – he describes one of the goals of international courts as conferring legitimacy 'on the

---

[10] See A. Roberts, 'Clash of paradigms: Actors and analogies shaping the investment treaty system', *American Journal of International Law*, 107 (2013), 45.

[11] See Jutta Brunnée and Stephen J. Toope, *Legitimacy and Legality in International Law: An International Account* (Cambridge University Press, 2010) and E. M. Leonhardsen, 'Looking for legitimacy: Exploring proportionality analysis in investment treaty arbitration', *Journal of International Dispute Settlement*, 3(1) (2012), 95, 102–3 (noting three spheres – government, civil society [comprising NGOs and individuals] and investors – who might view legitimacy differently).

[12] Y. Shany, 'Assessing the effectiveness of international courts: A goal-based approach', *American Journal of International Law*, 106 (2012), 225. Shany is skeptical of traditional compliance factors, including (1) compliance with court judgements, (2) usage rates, and (3) impact on state conduct. Ibid., 227.

[13] Ibid., 230–1.

[14] Ibid., 230. On the implicit assessment of normative value, Shany notes '[e]ven so, as discussed below, normative considerations relating to courts cannot be completely divorced from a goal-based analysis of international court effectiveness; among other things, the goals set for international courts (like other public organizations) are likely to derive from a plausible conception of the public good'. Ibid., 230–1.

THE LEGITIMACY OF THE ICSID 239

norms and institutions that constitute the regimes in which the courts operate'.[15] Yet given that ICSID does not operate within a single regime and is, in some respects, divorced from those regimes in that it has no ability to affect the formation or content of investment treaties, its ability to confer legitimacy on investment arbitration writ large – on investment treaties themselves – is limited. The converse, however, is not necessarily true. Indeed, criticisms of investment treaties both reflect on and extend to ICSID itself.[16]

Professor Shany also notes that a court's ability to attain its goals of norm compliance, dispute resolution, and support for the goals of the overarching regime might depend 'on the court's perceived legitimacy in the eyes of key constituencies' – what he describes as 'internal legitimization'.[17] Yet he also notes that 'external' legitimization is 'one of the ultimate ends of international courts', and that courts are chosen as dispute resolution bodies precisely because they have the capacity to generate acceptance of the mandate promoted by the court among a larger audience.[18]

This latter point leads to the discussion of sociological legitimacy presented later. Effectiveness and legitimacy might be part of a mutually reinforcing feedback loop, yet if the legitimacy of the court's mandate is perceived as illegitimate from the point of view of outsiders, no amount of 'effectiveness' will suffice to counter the concerns levelled at the tribunal or its underlying mandate: in fact, effectiveness might serve to further delegitimize the court in the eyes of observers. This phenomenon has been described by José Alvarez as 'penance envy' – proponents of strengthening the power of human rights tribunals criticize investment arbitration precisely because it is powerful and effective.[19] Again, too, one sees the disparity between ICSID and the underlying normative regime. ICSID administers the resolution of disputes but is not a norm-enforcing body with power to affect the interpretation of investment treaties or to change their content.

---

[15] Ibid., 265.

[16] J. Pauwelyn, 'The rule of law without the rule of lawyers? Why investment arbitrators are from Mars, trade adjudicators from Venus', *The American Journal of International Law*, 109(4) (2015), 761, 766–8; 804.

[17] Shany, (above note 12), 265.   [18] Ibid., 265.

[19] J. E. Alvarez, 'The new treaty makers', *Boston College International and Comparative Law Review*, 25 (2002), 213, 226.

B Sociological Legitimacy

Sociological legitimacy is grounded in questions about why states or individuals comply with the law. Tom Franck proposed four factors that influence legitimacy in international law generally: determinacy (a rule's clarity of meaning); symbolic validation (honoring the authenticity of a rule); coherence (consistently applying rules to similar situations); and adherence (the implementation of primary rules of obligation through secondary rules that make, interpret, and apply them).[20] In the investment landscape these criteria are most salient when directed at investment treaties themselves and at the substantive obligations contained therein. By assessing each of his criteria the reason for discontent about investment law is evident. The first criterion, determinacy, is arguably absent from obligations such as the duty to accord 'fair and equitable' treatment.[21] Symbolic validation, too, can be seen in criticisms levied at the elevation of investment law and its property-based norms over other goals, such as the protection of human rights and environmental concerns.[22] Coherence is a problem with respect to the multiple obligations that have spawned divergent jurisprudence – most-favoured-nation treatment, umbrella clauses, definitions of investment, etc.[23] Whilst explicable on some bases – the ad-hoc nature of investment law and the dispersed nature of the substantive obligations in more than 3,000 treaties mean that there is not one investment law, but that there are multiple investment laws[24] – inconsistency and incoherence are unquestionably viewed as problematic. Though there is some tendency to seek consistency through the doctrine of 'quasi-precedent' or *jurisprudence constante*,[25] investment law has no overarching system in which to achieve harmony, assuming states even desire that harmony, a not

---

[20] Franck, (above note 1), p. 24. The author defines and examines these 'indicators of rule-legitimacy' in the different chapters of his book to prove his hypothesis that 'to the extent a rule, or rule process, exhibits these four properties it will exert a strong pull on states to comply'. Ibid., p. 49.

[21] See discussion in section II.B, below.   [22] See discussion in section II.A, below.

[23] See discussion in section II.B, below.

[24] But *cf.* Stephan W. Schill, *The Multilateralization of International Investment Law* (Cambridge University Press, 2009).

[25] G. Kaufmann-Kohler, 'The 2006 Freshfields Lecture – Arbitral precedent: Dream, necessity, or excuse?', *Arbitration International*, 23 (2007), 357, 368–73; A. K. Bjorklund, 'Investment treaty arbitral awards as *jurisprudence constante*' in D. Arner, I. Bunn, and C. Picker (eds.), *International Economic Law: The State and Future of the Discipline* (Oxford: Hart Publishing, 2008) pp. 265 *et seq.*

THE LEGITIMACY OF THE ICSID

entirely self-evident proposition.[26] Adherence – his final criterion – is shared between the procedural rules implementing substantive obligations and the obligations themselves, as well as by the administering institutions. The latter place is where ICSID itself is most strongly evident.

I include these criteria despite the imperfect fit with an analysis of international courts because the critics of ICSID do not necessarily distinguish between the legitimacy of investment law generally, the legitimacy of deciding investment disputes by means of international arbitration, and the legitimacy of ICSID itself. Moreover, it is a reasonable question whether ICSID's legitimacy can be separated from the underlying treaties that it helps to enforce.

Because Professor Franck's criteria do not altogether fit the functioning of courts and tribunals,[27] Nienke Grossman has suggested three criteria by which to judge the sociological legitimacy of international tribunals: first is the perception that a tribunal is fair and unbiased; second is the commitment to the underlying normative regime, which will be affected by the quality of the decisions made about the norms in addition to the norms themselves; and third is the question of transparency and other democratic institutional norms.[28] Whilst the first and third of these criteria go to process, and the second is arguably assessed by reference to outcomes (which could be affected by deliberative processes), it is not altogether clear that all three are entirely appropriate for assessing ICSID either, due to the ad hoc nature of tribunals convened under it and due to elements of its design, though they help to explain some of the dissatisfaction with it. In other words, to the extent ICSID is assessed as a juridical institution it is bound to fall short because it is not, nor was it designed to be, a juridical institution. A question for the not-too-distant future is whether ICSID can or should change to become more court-like; this question might be answered sooner rather than later if the European Union's proposal for

---

[26] A. K. Bjorklund, 'Practical and legal avenues to make the substantive rules and disciplines of international investment agreements converge' in P. Sauvé and R. Echandi (eds.), *New Directions and Emerging Challenges in International Investment Law and Policy* (Cambridge University Press, 2013) pp. 176–80; J. Pauwelyn, 'At the edge of chaos? Foreign investment law as a complex adaptive system, how it emerged and how it can be reformed', *ICSID Review – Foreign Investment Law Journal*, 29 (2014), 37.

[27] N. Grossman, 'Legitimacy and international adjudicative bodies', *The George Washington International Law Review*, 41 (2009), 107, 121.

[28] Ibid., 121–2.

a multilateral investment court gains traction and as other EU investment agreements are negotiated and implemented.[29]

II 'Legitimacy Critiques'

Three states – Bolivia, Ecuador, and Venezuela – have withdrawn from the ICSID Convention.[30] This public display of disaffection drew extensive coverage, yet the complaints of those three governments might more properly be levied against their bilateral investment treaties, rather than against ICSID. By withdrawing from ICSID, however, they made a strong statement that did not remove them from the investment treaty regime – most of their investment treaties remained in place. More recently these states and others have commenced actually withdrawing from at least some of their treaties.[31]

---

[29] See *Transatlantic Trade and Investment Partnership – European Union's proposal for Investment Protection and Resolution of Investment Disputes*, 12 November 2015, http://trade.ec.europa.eu/doclib/docs/2015/november/tradoc_153955.pdf, Section 3 (Resolution of Investment Disputes and Investment Court System), Sub-Section 4: Investment Court System (T-TIP proposal); *Comprehensive Economic and Trade Agreement (CETA) Between Canada, of the one part and the European Union, of the other part* http://trade.ec.europa.eu/doclib/docs/2014/september/tradoc_152806.pdf, Chapter 8, Section F – Resolution of investment disputes between investors and states (CETA); *Free Trade Agreement between the European Union and the Socialist Republic of Vietnam* (in negotiation), http://investmentpolicyhub.unctad.org/Download/TreatyFile/3563, Section 3 (Resolution of Investment Disputes), Sub-Section 4: Investment Tribunal System (EU-Vietnam FTA).

[30] The Plurinational State of Bolivia notified its intention to withdraw from the ICSID Convention (pursuant to article 71 of the ICSID Convention) on 2 May 2007; the withdrawal took effect on 3 November 2007. Ecuador's withdrawal from the ICSID Convention became effective on 7 January 2010. Venezuela became the third state to withdraw from the ICSID Convention after it submitted its written notice of denunciation of the ICSID Convention on 24 January 2012; the withdrawal took effect on 25 July 2012. See UNCTAD, *Denunciation of the ICSID Convention and BITs: Impact on investor-state claims*, IIA Issues Note No 2 (December 2010).

[31] Ecuador started the process of withdrawing from its treaties in 2008 but only completed the withdrawal in 2017. Venezuela is of a similar mind. Bolivia had withdrawn from its treaties as of March 2015. South Africa (which is not a party to the ICSID Convention) has terminated some of its investment treaties with European countries (for instance, it terminated its BITs with the Belgian-Luxembourg Economic Union, Germany, the Netherlands or Spain. See http://unctad.org/en/PublicationsLibrary/webdiaepcb2015d1_en.pdf and IISD, 'News in Brief', *Investment treaty news*, 30 October 2012 www.iisd.org/itn/2012/10/30/news-in-brief-9/). Indonesia and India have also started withdrawing from their treaties (see, e.g., B. Bland and S. Donnan, 'Indonesia to terminate more than 60 bilateral investment treaties', *The Financial Times*, 26 March 2014, www.ft.com/cms/s/0/3755c1b2-b4e2-11e3-af92-00144feabdc0.html#axzz3PPXqDH1r, and P. Ranjan, 'India and bilateral investment treaties – A changing landscape', *ICSID Review*, 29(2) (2014), 419.

Legitimacy critiques of investment arbitration started in earnest after the decisions in two cases – *CME v. Czech Republic* and *Ronald Lauder v. Czech Republic*.[32] These initial concerns focused on the apparently inconsistent decisions of two tribunals, as well as the impression that the aggrieved investor had brought duplicative claims under two investment treaties, thereby demonstrating a potential for abusing the process. Since that time, the interest of the general public in investment arbitration has ebbed and flowed, but is now at an all-time high. There is anti-ISDS graffiti in Germany, and when the European Commission called for public comment on the proposed inclusion of investor–state dispute settlement in the nascent Transatlantic Trade and Investment Partnership between the United States and the European Union it received some 150,000 comments. By far the majority of those were 'form' comments generated by opponents of investor–state arbitration, but some 3,500 were individualized.[33]

The legitimacy concerns levied against investment arbitration can be – and have been – parsed in many different ways.[34] I divide them below into four areas that represent the most frequent concerns: sovereignty, consistency, transparency, and process. These areas overlap, and indeed each has several subparts that could be broken out as independent sections.

---

[32] On the legitimacy of investment arbitration see, e.g., S. D. Franck, 'The legitimacy crisis in investment treaty arbitration: Privatizing public international law through inconsistent decisions', *Fordham Law Review*, 73(4) (2005), 1521; M. Wu, 'The scope and limits of trade's influence in shaping the evolving international investment regime' in Z. Douglas, J. Pauwelyn, and J. E. Viñuales (eds.), *The Foundations of International Investment Law: Bringing Theory into Practice* (Oxford University Press, 2014), pp. 169, 178 *et seq*; M. Sornarajah, 'A coming crisis: Expansionary trends in investment treaty arbitration' in K. P. Sauvant (ed.), *Appeals Mechanisms in International Investment Disputes* (Oxford University Press, 2008) p. 39 *et seq.*; Michael Waibel et al. (eds.), *The Backlash against Investment Arbitration: Perceptions and Reality* (Alphen aan den Rijn: Kluwer Law International, 2010).

[33] European Commission, *Report – Online public consultation on investment protection and investor-to-state dispute settlement (ISDS) in the Transatlantic Trade and Investment Partnership Agreement (TTIP)* (Commission Staff Working Document, SWD (2015) 3 final) 13 January 2015, 3, http://trade.ec.europa.eu/doclib/docs/2015/january/tradoc_153044.pdf.

[34] See, e.g., J. E. Alvarez and G. Topalian, 'The paradoxical Argentina cases', *World Arbitration and Mediation Review*, 6(3) (2012), 491, 491–2 (the authors identify six major legitimacy issues in investment treaty law and conclude that 'the investment regime is the enemy of the state'); Behn, (above note 9), 363; Franck, (above note 32), 1521.

A Sovereignty

Investment treaties impinge on state sovereignty. They are also unquestionably exercises of sovereignty – entering into a treaty is one of the quintessential acts of a state and is indeed one of the indicia of statehood.[35] But it is true that in investment treaties states take on obligations that constrain their ability to act freely, and with the addition of investor-state arbitration they waive their jurisdictional immunity and agree to justify their conduct before a neutral tribunal and to make reparation if those justifications are unavailing.

Particular concerns are that private individuals (ad hoc arbitrators) make decisions that affect matters of public law.[36] Some of the measures challenged in investment arbitration have related to environmental or human health protection, and it is these issues which seem to incite the most disenchantment with investment arbitration.[37] A different facet of that concern is the regulatory 'chill' argument, which posits that states will be reluctant to undertake otherwise beneficial regulations for fear of facing liability in an investor–state arbitration.[38] Other concerns are that the treaties are asymmetric and impose obligations on states without imposing any obligations on investor, thereby limiting a state's ability to discipline the investor by means of international arbitration.[39]

---

[35] See the *Montevideo Convention on the Rights and Duties of States*, Montevideo, 26 December 1933, in force 26 December 1934, (1933) 165 LNTS 19, 49 Stat 3097 and for a comment on the Convention, T. D. Grant, 'Defining statehood: The Montevideo Convention and its discontents', *Columbia Journal of Transnational Law*, 37 (1999), 403. See also on the question of sovereignty the *Case of the S.S. Wimbledon*, PCIJ Ser A. 1, 1923, p. 25, in which the Court decline[d] to see in the conclusion of any Treaty by which a state undertakes to perform or refrain from performing a particular act an abandonment of its sovereignty. No doubt any convention creating an obligation of this kind places a restriction on the exercise of the sovereign rights of the state, in the sense that it requires them to be exercised in a certain way. But the right of entering into international engagements is an attribute of state sovereignty.

[36] Pauwelyn, (above note 16), 772–83.

[37] See, e.g., C. Rogers, 'The politics of international investment arbitrators', *Santa Clara Journal of International Law*, 12 (2013), 223; C. Henckels, 'Balancing investment protection and the public interest: The role of the standard of review and the importance of deference in investor-state arbitration', *Journal of International Dispute Settlement*, 4 (2013), 197.

[38] K. Tienhaara, 'Regulatory chill and the threat of arbitration: A view from political science' in C. Brown and K. Miles (eds.), *Evolution in Investment Treaty Law and Arbitration* (Cambridge University Press, 2011) p. 606.

[39] This issue is, of course, a process concern as well. See generally G. Foster, 'Striking a balance between investor protections and national sovereignty: The relevance of local remedies in investment treaty arbitration', *Columbia Journal of Transnational Law*,

A slightly perplexing issue is not that so much attention is paid to those cases with clear public law implications but that relatively little attention is given to 'private' law issues – generally, breach-of-contract cases. The quintessential investment dispute involves a contract between a foreign investor and the host state for the exploitation of natural resources. The contract is governed by private law (typically the law of the host state, though perhaps with international law serving as a backstop) and often calls for arbitration, whether under the ICSID Convention or under another dispute resolution regime. When these disputes unfold under a contractual mechanism they have drawn less concern than when they have been brought under an investment treaty. Yet a state's decisions about how to exploit its natural resources is a question of state power and public interest, and when it seeks to change that decision the same concerns about state authority would seem to apply, whether or not the governing law is private or public.[40]

In short, investment treaties purport to constrain state behaviour. They permit foreign investors to challenge state acts before an international tribunal and thus displace the national courts that would otherwise hear the claims.

B   Consistency, Predictability, and Correctness

Substantial concerns centre on inconsistency and unpredictability in tribunal decision making, as well as on the indeterminacy of substantive standards such as 'fair and equitable treatment'. Moreover, current control mechanisms do not permit revision of arbitral awards if they are incorrect either as to their appreciation of the law or of the facts.

Insofar as consistency is concerned, several doctrines are unsettled and have been decided in different ways by different tribunals. They include (but are not limited to): whether the definition of investment found in a

---

49 (2011), 201; A. K. Bjorklund, 'The role of counterclaims in rebalancing investment law', *Lewis & Clark Law Review*, 17 (2013), 461.

[40] That is not to say that there is no attention paid to these contracts; quite the contrary. See, e.g., L. J. Danielson and M. D. Phillips, 'The International Bar Association Model Mining Development Agreement Project: A step toward better practice and better development results' in K. P. Sauvant (ed.), *Yearbook on International Investment Law and Policy 2011–2012* (Oxford University Press, 2013), p. 185 *et seq.*; The Extractive Industries Transparency Initiative, available at: https://eiti.org/ (last visited 10 February 2017). But the dispute resolution aspect of these cases has not given rise to similar levels of attention or criticism.

246 ANDREA K. BJORKLUND

bilateral investment treaty can suffice to satisfy the requirement that there be an investment under the ICSID Convention;[41] whether most-favoured-nation clauses apply to import dispute settlement provisions and the substantive provisions from other investment treaties;[42] what purpose 'umbrella clauses' serve;[43] whether there is a doctrine of fair and equitable treatment separate from the 'international minimum standard of treatment';[44] whether and when moral damages are available in investment arbitration;[45] and what the appropriate relationship is between the customary international law defense of necessity and a treaty-based emergency-measures clause.[46]

Some of these inconsistencies can be explained by differences in the provisions of the applicable investment treaties. Others, however, simply result from different interpretations of identical provisions or provisions whose differences are insignificant. The unsettled nature of the meaning of oft-seen provisions impedes predictability. Moreover, the outcome in any particular case, in addition to being fact-dependent, might vary depending on the language of the treaty in question the identity of the arbitrators, and the arguments made by counsel.

In a few celebrated cases ICSID ad hoc annulment committees have adverted to what they viewed as mistakes in the decisions they were reviewing but have pointed to their inability, given the standards against which they were reviewing the awards, to correct those errors.[47]

---

[41] See J. D. Mortenson, 'The meaning of "investment": ICSID's travaux and the domain of international investment law', *Harvard International Law Journal*, 51(1) (2010), 257.

[42] Y. Banifatemi, 'The emerging jurisprudence on most-favoured-nation treatment in investment arbitration' in A. K Bjorklund, I. A Laird, and S. Ripinsky (eds.), *Investment Treaty Law: Current Issues III* (London: British Institute of International and Comparative Law, 2009), pp. 241 *et seq.*

[43] K. Yannaca-Small, 'What about this "umbrella clause"?' in K. Yannaca-Small (ed.), *Arbitration under International Investment Agreements: A Guide to Key Issues* (Oxford University Press, 2010), pp. 479 *et seq.*

[44] Patrick Dumberry, *The Fair and Equitable Treatment Standard: A Guide to NAFTA Case Law on Article 1105* (Alphen aan den Rijn: Kluwer Law International, 2013), pp. 36–46.

[45] B. Sabahi, 'Moral damages in international investment law: Some preliminary thoughts in the aftermath of Desert Line v Yemen' in J. Werner and A. H. Ali (eds.), *A Liber Amicorum: Thomas Wälde – Law beyond Conventional Thought* (London: Cameron May, 2009), pp. 253 *et seq.*

[46] A. K. Bjorklund, 'Emergency exceptions: State of necessity and force majeure' in P. Muchlinski, F. Ortino, and C. Schreuer (eds.), *The Oxford Handbook of International Investment Law* (Oxford University Press, 2008), pp. 459 *et seq.*

[47] See generally F. Ortino, 'Legal reasoning of international investment tribunals: A typology of egregious failures', *Journal of International Dispute Settlement*, 3 (2012), 31.

THE LEGITIMACY OF THE ICSID

C Transparency

Transparency plays many roles in the investment arbitration arena. Transparency is arguably a substantive standard of international law – although this position is not without controversy – that requires states to make their laws and regulations, and general business practices, readily available to the public and capable of being understood by any aspiring investor. More commonly of concern is transparency of the arbitral process itself. This procedural transparency can encompass access to the awards, to the submissions of the parties that underlie those awards, access to hearings, and participation in the arbitration by nondisputing parties.

Complaints about lack of transparency have bedevilled investment arbitration since 2001, when Anthony DePalma wrote his *New York Times* article that started: 'Their meeting are secret. Their members are generally unknown. The decisions they reach need not be fully disclosed'.[48] Some of these concerns are exaggerated, but some are real. In fact, very soon after Mr. DePalma's article appeared, the United States, Canada, and Mexico issued a Note of Interpretation in 2001 that nothing in NAFTA Chapter 11 imposes a duty of transparency.[49] All three NAFTA parties maintain websites about the investment disputes in which they are engaged.[50] The United States and Canada post awards, procedural orders, and memorials of the disputing parties for all of their investment cases. Mexico does the same for NAFTA cases; for cases under other Mexican investment treaties the practice of transparency is less uniform. Several other websites and web services (some available only with a subscription, others available to the public) offer access to awards.[51]

Other states have not embraced transparency as readily as the United States and Canada (and to a lesser extent Mexico), either in their treaties or in their practice, but have left questions about transparency to the

---

[48] A. DePalma, 'NAFTA's powerful little secret; obscure tribunals settle disputes, but go too far, critics say', *New York Times* (11 March 2001).

[49] NAFTA Free Trade Commission, *North American Free Trade Agreement – Notes of Interpretation of Certain Chapter 11 Provisions*, July 31, 2001, para A.

[50] United States: www.state.gov/s/l/c3433.htm; Canada: www.international.gc.ca/trade-agreements-accords-commerciaux/topics-domaines/disp-diff/gov.aspx?lang=eng; Mexico: www.gob.mx/se/acciones-y-programas/comercio-exterior-solucion-de-controversias?state=published.

[51] These include, in no particular order, *Investment Treaty Arbitration*, www.italaw.com; *InvestmentClaims.com*, http://oxia.ouplaw.com/home/ic; *Investor-State Law Guide*, www.investorstatelawguide.com; *UNCTAD Investment Policy Hub*, http://investmentpolicyhub.unctad.org; *ICSID*, https://icsid.worldbank.org/en/Pages/cases/searchcases.aspx

248 ANDREA K. BJORKLUND

applicable arbitration rules (subject to revision by agreement of the parties to the dispute), though that is slowly changing. After many years of negotiation, UNCITRAL has promulgated new rules for transparency in investor–state disputes.[52] These rules apply only prospectively (in the absence of party agreement), so they apply to arbitrations conducted under treaties that came into effect on or after 1 April 2014.[53] To make it possible for states to apply the new rules retroactively to existing treaties, a United Nations treaty (the Mauritius Convention) was opened for signature on 17 March 2015[54] and entered into force on 18 October 2017. The UNCITRAL transparency rules will apply retroactively to existing investment treaties for those states that sign the treaty. UNCITRAL will also maintain a registry of awards and of supporting documents that will be freely available to the public.

The notion of transparency has stretched to include the possibility of amicus curiae participation by nondisputing parties.[55] It is now widely accepted that investment treaty tribunals have the authority to permit

---

[52] *UNCITRAL Rules on Transparency in Treaty-based Investor-State Arbitration*, effective 1 April 2014, www.uncitral.org/pdf/english/texts/arbitration/rules-on-transparency/Rules-on-Transparency-E.pdf.

[53] Ibid. art 1(1):

1. The UNCITRAL Rules on Transparency in Treaty-based Investor–State Arbitration ('Rules on Transparency') shall apply to investor–State arbitration initiated under the UNCITRAL Arbitration Rules pursuant to a treaty providing for the protection of investments or investors ('treaty') concluded on or after 1 April 2014 unless the Parties to the treaty have agreed otherwise.

2. In investor–State arbitrations initiated under the UNCITRAL Arbitration Rules pursuant to a treaty concluded before 1 April 2014, these Rules shall apply only when:

    (*a*) The parties to an arbitration (the 'disputing parties') agree to their application in respect of that arbitration or

    (*b*) The Parties to the treaty or, in the case of a multilateral treaty, the State of the claimant and the respondent State, have agreed after 1 April 2014 to their application.

[footnotes omitted].

[54] Belgium, Canada, Congo, Finland, France, Gabon, Germany, Italy, Luxembourg, Madagascar, Mauritius, The Netherlands, Sweden, Switzerland, Syria, the United Kingdom, and the United States have already signed the Mauritius Convention (United Nations Convention on Transparency in Treaty-based Investor–State Arbitration, adopted 10 December 2014, opened for signature 17 March 2015). It recently entered into force when Switzerland joined Canada and Mauritius in ratifying it. www.uncitral.org/uncitral/en/uncitral_texts/arbitration/2014Transparency_Convention_status.html (last visited 16 November 2017).

[55] See A. K. Bjorklund, 'The emerging civilization of investment arbitration', *Penn State Law Review 1269*, 113(4) (2009), 1290–4.

THE LEGITIMACY OF THE ICSID   249

the participation of amici curiae.[56] Amici have generally been non-governmental organisations, but recently industry groups and private individuals have sought to participate as amici.[57] Aspiring amici do not have the ability to participate as of right. This limitation has drawn less criticism than access to information more generally, perhaps because it reflects practice in national courts.

For some time ICSID was a pioneer with respect to transparency.[58] Its embrace of transparency predated UNCITRAL's by some eight years. Now, however, assuming the Mauritius Convention becomes more widely applicable and makes the new UNCTRAL rules applicable to all, or nearly all, investment arbitrations, ICSID's transparency innovations will be eclipsed by those new rules.

In short, some investment arbitrations are quite transparent (more so than domestic court practice in many countries). But others are not, or the information that is available is piecemeal. Some cases are not

[56] See generally C. Knahr, 'Transparency, third party participation and access to documents in international investment arbitration', *Arbitration International*, 23 (2007), 327. In particular, the author notes that under the ICSID Arbitration Rules and the NAFTA regime, it is 'clear that Tribunals have the power to accept and consider written submissions from non-disputing parties'. Ibid., 354.

[57] For example, in *Apotex I* (*Apotex Inc* v. *The Government of the United States of America*, UNCITRAL, Award on Jurisdiction and Admissibility, 2013), the Study Center for Sustainable Finance of Business Neatness Magnanimity BNM srl requested permission to submit an amicus petition. Similarly, in *Apotex II* (*Apotex Holdings Inc and Apotex Inc* v. *United States of America*, ICSID Case No ARB(AF)/12/1, Award, 2014), both BNM and Mr. Barry Appleton requested leave to submit amicus petitions. BNM and Mr. Barry Appleton's requests were rejected in both *Apotex I* (*Apotex Inc* v. *The Government of the United States of America*, UNCITRAL, Procedural Order No 2 on the Participation of a Non-Disputing Party, 2011) and *Apotex II* (*Apotex Holdings Inc and Apotex Inc* v. *United States of America*, ICSID Case No ARB(AF)/12/1, Procedural Order on the Participation of the Applicant, BNM, as a Non-Disputing Party, 2013); *Apotex Holdings Inc and Apotex Inc* v. *United States of America*, ICSID Case No ARB (AF)/12/1, Procedural Order on the Participation of the Applicant, Mr Barry Appleton, as a Non-Disputing Party, 2013). More recently, in the Eli Lilly proceedings (*Eli Lilly and Company* v. *The Government of Canada*, UNCITRAL, ICSID Case No UNCT/14/2), nine industry groups and private individuals requested leave to submit amicus submissions. The Tribunal denied four of these applications (*Eli Lilly and Company* v. *The Government of Canada*, UNCITRAL, ICSID Case No UNCT/14/2, Procedural Order No 4, 2016).

[58] See C.-S. Zoellner, 'Third-party participation (NGO's and private persons) and transparency in ICSID proceedings' in R. Hofmann and C. J. Tams (eds.), *The International Convention on the Settlement of Investment Disputes (ICSID): Taking Stock after 40 Years* (Baden-Baden: Nomos 2007), pp. 179–208.

250 ANDREA K. BJORKLUND

public, and while the number is unlikely to be large, no one knows with absolutely certainty how many nonpublic cases there are.[59]

D Process

Other concerns involve the investment arbitration process, and in particular allegations of abuse of process. The *Lauder* and *CME* cases – in which a multinational corporation took apparent multiple 'bites at the cherry' of investor–state dispute resolution thanks to the intricacies of corporate ownership – give rise to concerns about the integrity of investor–state dispute settlement writ large. The ability to pursue relief in multiple fora can create a perception of systemic dysfunction. Given the current network of over 3,000 investment agreements, the potential for parallel proceedings is very real.

A related concept is the idea of 'treaty-shopping' (a.k.a. 'nationality-planning'). This occurs when a company deliberately employs a structure to ensure that its investment is covered by the protections of an investment treaty. For example, a Brazilian company might route its investment in Argentina via a Dutch subsidiary, thereby causing its investment to be a Dutch investment covered by the Argentina – The Netherlands BIT. When this tactic is employed in advance of any dispute's having risen, it is viewed as a fair tactic akin to minimizing tax obligations; when done when a dispute has arisen or is clearly on the horizon it is viewed as an abuse of process.[60]

---

[59] The University of Oslo's PluriCourt's Centre of Excellence has a comprehensive database in which it has identified 760 registered investment disputes. D. Behn, 'The worst option but for all the others: The performance of investment treaty arbitration in historical context' in T. Squatrito et al. (eds.), *The Performance of International Courts and Tribunals* (Cambridge University Press, 2017). By comparison, as of 7 April 2016, UNCTAD's *Investment Policy Hub* website indicated a total of 696 known treaty-based investor–state arbitrations (amongst which 243 were pending; 442 were concluded; and 11 were of unknown status). See http://investmentpolicyhub.unctad.org/ISDS?status=0.

[60] See R. Happ, 'The "foreign nationality" – requirement and the "exhaustion of local remedies" in recent ICSID jurisprudence' in Hofmann and Tams (eds.), *The International Convention on the Settlement of Investment Disputes (ICSID): Taking Stock after 40 Years* (Baden-Baden: Nomos 2007), pp. 103, 112–114. For a recent discussion of the issue, see the decision in *Philip Morris* v. *Australia*, in which Philip Morris's claim was dismissed for abuse of process. Philip Morris had restructured its investments through Hong Kong in 2011, just before Australia enacted the plain packaging legislation that was the subject of the claim but after the legislation was on the horizon *Philip Morris Asia Ltd.* v. *Australia*, PCA Case No. 2012–12, Award on Jurisdiction and Admissibility, 17 December 2015, paras. 557–66.

THE LEGITIMACY OF THE ICSID 251

A constellation of concerns surrounds the identity of the decision makers themselves and the method by which they are chosen. The advent of greater public attention to investor–state dispute arbitration in the popular press has brought with it public skepticism about the wisdom of ad hoc arbitral bodies deciding matters of potential public import.[61] These criticisms have addressed, inter alia, the public nature of the disputes and the expertise of at least some arbitrators in commercial law and arbitration, rather than in public law and policy;[62] and the distance of the arbitrators (at least two of whom will not be drawn from the state whose measure has been called into question) from knowledge about local concerns.[63]

In addition, the process of party appointment, whereby each disputing party selects a 'wing' arbitrator, and either the parties together or the party-selected arbitrators choose a chairman, has caused some concern, particularly because some arbitrators are known for being 'state-oriented' arbitrators and some are known as being 'claimant-oriented' arbitrators.[64] Some arbitrators have also recently been subject to challenge for so-called issue conflicts. Issue conflicts involve arbitrators who also act as counsel in other cases or even those who sit repeatedly as

---

[61] A spate of articles in the early 2000s claimed to identify a general threat to democracy posed by investor–state dispute settlement. See, e.g., Editorial, 'The secret trade courts', *New York Times* (27 September 2004); A. Liptak, 'Review of U.S. rulings by NAFTA tribunals stirs worries', *New York Times* (18 April 2004). Similar discussions are now occurring around the world, notably in Canada regarding the Canada–EU Comprehensive Economic and Trade Agreement (CETA) and the Canada–China Foreign Investment Protection and Promotion Agreement (see, e.g., P. Eberhardt, B. Redlin, and C. Toubeau, *Trading Away Democracy – How CETA's Investor Protection Rules Threaten the Public Good in Canada and the EU*, November 2014 http://canadians.org/sites/default/files/publications/trading-away-1114.pdf), in Europe regarding CETA and the T-TIP agreement with the United States (see generally PublicCitizen, 'Tens of thousands of U.S. firms would obtain new powers to launch investor-state attacks against European policies via CETA and TTIP', https://www.citizen.org/sites/default/files/eu-isds-liability.pdf). in the United States regarding T-TIP and the TPP (see, e.g., J. Kilcourse, 'TTIP faces political hurdles on both sides of the Atlantic', Institute of International and European Affairs, 3 February 2014, www.iiea.com/blogosphere/ttip-faces-political-hurdles-on-both-sides-of-the-atlantic), and in Australia regarding the TPP and the value of investment arbitration more generally (see, e.g., Australian Government, Department of Foreign Affairs and Trade, *Gillard Government Trade Policy Statement: Trading Our Way to More Jobs and Prosperity*, April 2011 http://blogs.usyd.edu.au/japaneselaw/2011_Gillard%20Govt%20Trade%20Policy%20Statement.pdf.).

[62] Pauwelyn, (above note 16), 772–4.   [63] Henckels, (above note 37), 197.

[64] Ibid., 786–7.

arbitrators in cases that raise similar issues.[65] In the repeat-appointment context, the concern is that the arbitrator might have a firm position on an issue such that she is not open-minded to arguments that new counsel in the subsequent case would put to her. This criticism has more resonance in the investment arbitration context than in the domestic court context because of the unsettled nature of investment law and the fact that prior decisions are not precedential; parties expect each case to be decided anew on its own terms.

In the arbitrator/counsel context, the concern is that the arbitrator might have some incentive to decide a case in a way that would be beneficial to her client in the second case. The existence of an issue conflict also is affected by the publication of awards. Although arbitral decisions are in no way precedential, they are often referred to as persuasive authority, and thus an arbitral decision might have influence in a later case. These concerns have given rise to challenges against arbitrators.[66] In one such case, Ghana argued that the arbitrator in question had an issue conflict because he would be espousing a pro-investor position on the interpretation of an issue of expropriation law that would be before him in his capacity as arbitrator in the case against Ghana.[67] The Dutch court charged with hearing the challenge determined that the arbitrator in question could not fill both the role of arbitrator and maintain his position as counsel in the other case.[68] The arbitrator resigned as counsel and retained his arbitral appointment.[69]

---

[65] See J. Levine, 'Dealing with arbitrator "issue conflicts" in international arbitration', *Dispute Resolution Journal*, 61(1) (2006), 60, 61–5 (describing various cases involving issue conflicts); P. Sands, 'Conflict and conflicts in investment treaty arbitration: Ethical standards for counsel' in C. Brown and K. Miles (eds.), *Evolution in Investment Treaty Law and Arbitration* (Cambridge University Press, 2011), pp. 19, 22–3.

[66] See, e.g., C. Harris, 'Arbitrator bias in investment and commercial arbitration', *Transnational Dispute Management*, 5(4) (2008), 1; Levine, (above note 65), 61–5; L. E. Peterson, 'Belgian appeals court rejects Poland's challenge to arbitrator in Eureko case', *Investment Treaty News* (15 November 2007); L. E. Peterson, 'Decrying past "contradictory" rulings, Argentina challenges arbitrator', *Investment Treaty News* (10 July 2008); L. E. Peterson, 'Argentina and UK firm send arbitrator-challenge to venue where reasons are provided', *Investment Treaty News* (30 October 2007); B. Legum, 'Investor-state arbitrator disqualified for pre-appointment statements on challenged measures', *Arbitration International*, 21 (2005), 241; *cf.* T. Carbonneau, 'At the crossroads of legitimacy and arbitral autonomy', *American Review of International Arbitration*, 16 (2005), 213, 233 (noting that in the domestic US context, calls for broader disclosures by arbitrators were prompted by potential, rather than actual, abuse).

[67] *Republic of Ghana* v. *Telekom Malaysia Berhad*, HA/RK 2004.667, 18 October 2004, para. 3.

[68] Ibid. paras. 4–5.   [69] Harris, (above note 66), 1.

More general concerns hover around the general financial interest that arbitrators and counsel have in ensuring that investment arbitration is a successful enterprise.[70]

****

The preceding section surveys some of the criticisms levied against investment law and investment arbitration. It does not purport to be exhaustive, but to give a basis from which to assess ICSID's performance. The divisions between areas are somewhat arbitrary, and certainly concerns can and do overlap with each other. For example, sovereignty considerations are exacerbated by process concerns, process concerns are exacerbated by incoherence and unpredictability, and so on.

III ICSID's Normative Legitimacy

The preceding paragraphs look at investment law and arbitration generally. But the precise focus of this chapter is ICSID itself – one of the institutions that provides a framework for arbitration. Before assessing the relationship of ICSID to the legitimacy concerns expressed earlier, it is necessary to understand how ICSID functions and some of its key features and limitations.

It is not enough to establish that an organization works well for it to be legitimate, though that is one consideration.[71] The purpose the organization serves must in the first instance also be acceptable.[72] Thus, before turning to the question of whether ICSID is normatively legitimate insofar as its operations are concerned – whether it works effectively, in Yuval Shany's formulation – one must establish ICSID's legitimacy of purpose.

A   The Goals of ICSID

ICSID's goal is providing a neutral forum for dispute settlement. It is available to resolve investment disputes between states who are party to

---

[70] Pia Eberhardt and Cecilia Olivet, *Profiting from Injustice: How Law Firms, Arbitrators, and Financiers Are Fueling an Investment Arbitration Boom* (Brussels/Amsterdam: Corporate Europe Observatory 2012).

[71] *Cf.* Shany, (above note 12), 225.

[72] I accept Professor Shany's point that ordinarily that assessment will be implicit in the analysis of effectiveness. Given the strength of the criticisms levied against ICSID and the investment arbitration regime generally, however, I think it worth addressing the point directly here.

254 ANDREA K. BJORKLUND

its constituting Convention and investors in those 'host' states whose 'home' states are also party to the Convention.[73]

Encouraging the peaceful settlement of disputes is uncontroversial in itself.[74] The extent to which that dispute settlement infringes on state sovereignty in any given case is a slightly different matter that causes concern and is addressed in Section II.A. Whether ICSID's current design adequately furthers that goal while taking into account other factors is something I will address in Section IV.A. I note, however, that even vociferous critics of international investment law and arbitration propose that it be replaced or enhanced by some other form of quasi-judicial international dispute settlement, even if that were to be available only after the exhaustion of local remedies.[75] The most ambitious proposal suggests the establishment of an international investment court.[76]

---

[73] See Christoph Schreuer et al., *The ICSID Convention: A Commentary*, 2nd ed., (Cambridge University Press, 2009) p. 144 *et seq.*, paras. 211 *et seq.*

[74] Indeed, one can trace the goal of ending the violent settlement of international disputes to the Peace conferences at the end of the nineteenth century and beginning of the twentieth century, if not earlier (the Peace conferences generally refer to the Hague Conference of 1899, which led to the adoption of several conventions and declarations and the Hague Conference of 1907, which also led to the adoption of several international instruments. See http://avalon.law.yale.edu/subject_menus/lawwar.asp). In the context of disputes relating to foreign investment, it is easy to forget how prevalent and frequent 'gunboat' diplomacy was in the not-too-distant past. Starting in 1805, the United States used its military forces eighty-eight times to protect the private commercial interests of US citizens. S. Miller and G. N. Hicks, 'Investor-state dispute settlement: A reality check, Center for Strategic & International Studies' (January 2015), http://csis.org/files/publica tion/150116_Miller_InvestorStateDispute_Web.pdf. See also Hege Elisabeth Kjos, *Applicable Law in Investor-State Arbitration: The Interplay between National and International Law* (Oxford University Press, 2013) p. 53 ('In 1965, the World Bank promulgated the ICSID Convention in an attempt to remove legal and political obstacles to the flow of foreign investment, particularly to developing states. For this purpose, the Convention provides for an International Centre for the Settlement of Investment Disputes (ICSID), facilitating the *peaceful settlement* of investment disputes between foreign investors and host states through arbitration'. [footnotes omitted; emphasis added]).

[75] Recently (in Spring 2015) criticism of investment arbitration in particular reached new heights, and one set of eminent academics expressed their scepticism that international arbitration involving the United States is compatible with the US Constitution. The letter, dated 30 April 2015, is available online at www.washingtonpost.com/r/2010-2019/ WashingtonPost/2015/04/30/Editorial-Opinion/Graphics/oppose_ISDS_Letter.pdf. The US Supreme Court decided to the contrary in *Dames & Moore* v. *Regan*, though that case involved state–state, rather than investor–state, dispute settlement, and the tribunal in question – the Iran – US Claims Tribunal – was established after a period of strife. *Dames & Moore* v. *Regan*, 453 U.S. 654 (1981).

[76] See in this regard the European Union's T-TIP Proposal (above note 29); Gus Van Harten, *Investment Treaty Arbitration and Public Law* (Oxford University Press, 2008), pp. 175 *et seq*, especially 180–5; H. King Jr., T. Smith, V. Bradbrooke, and H. Rojas,

THE LEGITIMACY OF THE ICSID

Other proposals include the establishment of an appellate body,[77] changing the system of party-appointed arbitrators,[78] reintroducing the requirement that local remedies be exhausted before an investor can switch to investor–state dispute settlement[79] and establishing a reference

'Dispute settlement under a North American free trade agreement', *Int'l Lawyer*, 26 (1992), 855 ('The Group, therefore, recommends that the Agreement specifically authorize the Parties, if and when they determine it will be of assistance, to establish a permanent mechanism to assist with the resolution of disputes, although not necessarily to have some independent role in their management. It could be international. It could be joint, with three sections. It would be permanent, although it ought to be called upon only when certain tasks are required'); J. Patton, 'A case for investor–state arbitration under the proposed Transatlantic Trade and Investment Partnership', *The Arbitration Brief*, 4(1) (2014), 75, 88 (in order to respond to challenges regarding ISDS, 'options include . . . the creation of an international investment court'). See also, in the context of the WTO, A. Porges, 'Step by step to an international trade court' in D. L. M. Kennedy and J. D. Southwick (eds.), *The Political Economy of International Trade Law* (Cambridge University Press, 2002), pp. 535–6 ('There was no appetite then for creating an institution that, like the European Court of Justice (ECJ), would claim for itself an independent role in constructing a new legal order under the treaty. . . . If a professional panel body is created, it will look like a court and at least potentially be a court. The make or break issue for its success will be whether it succeeds in creating a string institutional culture for itself, as the Appellate Body has').

[77] Patton (above note 76), 88–91 ('Although the U.S. and EU have taken significant steps to create a more transparent, fair, and effective ISDS system, challenges and concerns remain regarding arbitrators' impartiality and independence, forum shopping, consistency of arbitral decisions, and a lack of a review system. These challenges have prompted further debate regarding a number of alternatives the U.S. and EU have addressed and may consider when negotiating the TTIP agreement. These options include . . . the creation of an appellate mechanism . . . . An investment appellate body at the international level could . . . enhance the consistency, predictability, and perceived impartiality of decisions rendered by arbitral tribunals' at 88–89 [footnote omitted]); C. J. Tams, 'Is there a need for an ICSID appellate structure?' in Hofmann and Tams (above note 58) pp. 223, 231–246; S. Singh and S. Sharma, 'Investor-state dispute settlement mechanism: The quest for a workable roadmap', *Utrecht Journal of International and European Law*, 29(76) (2013), 88, 99–101. See also D. McRae, 'The WTO Appellate Body: A model for an ICSID appeals facility?', *Journal of International Dispute Settlement*, 1(2) (2010), 371.

[78] See generally J. Paulsson, 'Moral hazard in international dispute resolution', *ICSID Review – Foreign Investment Law Journal*, 25 (2010), 339.

[79] See UNCTAD, *Investor–State Dispute Settlement*, UNCTAD Series on Issues in International Investment Agreements II (Geneva: United Nations 2014) 82–6 ('Customary international law requires an injured foreign person to exhaust all effective domestic legal remedies before his claim becomes admissible at the international level. Most investment treaties waive the exhaustion of local remedies rule, and permit the investor to have direct recourse to international arbitration. However, a number of IIAs require investors to pursue local remedies (judicial or administrative) in the host State for a certain period of time, or – in rare circumstances – even to exhaust local remedies'. Ibid., p. 82 [footnote omitted]). See also UNCTAD, *Recent Developments in Investor–State Dispute Settlement (ISDS)*, IIA Issues Note No 1 (April 2014) 13 (analysing the decision in *Apotex*) and *Apotex Inc* v. *The Government of*

mechanism akin to referral on matters of EU law to the Court of Justice of European Communities.[80] These proposals are not mutually exclusive. Thus, it seems that there is nothing inherently illegitimate about establishing an international body to facilitate the legalistic settlement of disputes – even those involving public law issues. There is, however, concern about how that body conducts its business and about the substantive content of the law it applies.

B Key Features of ICSID's Functioning

ICSID's purpose – providing a framework for the settlement of disputes without establishing substantive obligations – directed many of the decisions made by states in its drafting. Commencing in late 1961, the Convention on the Settlement of International Investment Disputes (the 'ICSID Convention') was negotiated under the auspices of Aron Broches, then General Counsel of the World Bank.[81] The goal was to provide a neutral venue for the resolution of disputes between foreign investors and host states. This decision was prompted by the fact that the World Bank General Counsel was with increasing frequency asked to mediate or broker disputes between foreign investors and host states.[82] He thought that the demand for this service was high enough to warrant establishing a permanent mechanism. In addition, private investment was seen as an essential piece of the broader development puzzle, so to the extent that foreign investment could be encouraged by providing a neutral venue for dispute settlement the ICSID Convention fulfilled that goal, too.[83]

---

the United States of America, UNCITRAL, Award on Jurisdiction and Admissibility, 2013, para. 282 ('a claimant cannot raise a claim that a judicial act constitutes a breach of international law, without first proceeding through the judicial system that it purports to challenge, and thereby allowing the system an opportunity to correct itself') discussing doctrine of finality as applicable in the judicial context.

[80] See C. Schreuer, 'Preliminary rulings in investment arbitration' in K. P. Sauvant (ed.), Appeals Mechanism in International Investment Disputes (Oxford University Press, 2008), pp. 207–12.

[81] Antonio Parra, The History of ICSID (Oxford University Press, 2012), p. 25.

[82] Ibid., pp. 21–4.

[83] See the Preamble to the ICSID Convention (Convention on the Settlement of Investment Disputes between States and Nationals of other States, 17 UST 1270, 575 UNTS 159 (1966) (ICSID Convention)) at 3:

> **Recognizing** that while such disputes would usually be subject to national legal processes, international methods of settlement may be appropriate in certain cases.

In the course of their negotiations, the drafters of the Convention made several decisions about the design of the system. Next I examine several of those key decisions with respect to their justification and their actual functioning.

1 External Consent

The idea of external consent is a foundational element. Arbitration is a creature of consent, and an ICSID arbitral tribunal only has power when parties have agreed to refer disputes to it. Consent to arbitration can be found in a contract, in investment legislation, or in an investment treaty. At the time of the Convention's drafting by far the most likely source of consent was a concession agreement between an investor and a host state.[84] Consent found in a bilateral investment treaty (BIT) was a theoretical possibility – Aron Broches anticipated that BITs would develop in that way[85] – but it is unlikely that even he, let alone anyone

---

See also Aron Broches, *Selected Essays: World Bank, ICSID, and Other Subjects of Public and Private International Law* (Dordrecht: Martinus Nijhoff, 1995), p. 163 ('it would seem desirable to provide that, once an investor and a host government have agreed to submit a dispute to arbitration, the investor should be deemed to have waived the right to seek the protection of his national government and his government would not be entitled to take up his case. This development of existing international law would have the great merit of helping to remove investment disputes from the intergovernmental political sphere'); I. F. I. Shihata, 'Toward a greater depoliticization of investment disputes: The roles of ICSID and MIGA' in K. W. Ly, G. Verheyen and S. M. Perera (eds.), *Investing with Confidence: Understanding Political Risk Management in the 21st Century* (Washington, DC: World Bank, 2009), pp. 2–35.

[84] Indeed, the first BIT to have investor-state arbitration was the Indonesia–Netherlands BIT in 1968 (the treaty entered into force in 1971 and was later terminated in 1995 and replaced by the *Agreement between the Government of the Kingdom of the Netherlands and the Government of the Republic of Indonesia on Promotion and Protection of Investment*, signed 6 April 1994, entered into force 1st July 1995). The arbitration provision in the 1968 Indonesia-Netherlands BIT (art. 11) provided that

The Contracting Party in the territory of which a national of the other Contracting Party makes or intends to make an investment, shall assent to any demand on the part of such national and any such national shall comply with any request of the former Contracting Party, to submit, for conciliation or arbitration, to the Centre established by the Convention of Washington of 18 March 1965, any dispute that may arise in connection with the investment.

For an analysis of this provision and its ambiguities, see Andrew P. Newcombe and Lluís Paradell, *Law and Practice of Investment Treaties: Standards of Treatment* (Alphen aan Rijn: Kluwer Law International, 2009), p. 44.

[85] Parra (above note 77), pp. 134–6.

else in the negotiating party, envisioned the conclusion of 3,200 investment agreements, with 2,700 of them in force.[86]

Once an investor submits a claim that prima facie satisfies the Convention's requirements, the arbitral tribunal will be constituted. Even then, however, one should not overestimate the power of the Centre, which administers cases but does not decide them – that is left to the arbitrators. The question of consent is brought to bear in particular when there are questions about jurisdiction *ratione materiae* (regarding whether there is an investment entitled to invoke the jurisdiction of the Centre) or *ratione personae* (regarding whether there is an investor entitled to invoke the jurisdiction of the Centre).

2 Ad Hoc Arbitral Tribunals and the Arbitral Roster

Dispute settlement under the ICSID Convention operates in an ad hoc fashion; arbitrators are selected for each case. Neutrality (as regards nationality) was key for the drafters of the Convention. Although each side can appoint its arbitrator, that arbitrator cannot share the nationality of the appointing party unless both parties agree, and a majority of the arbitrators cannot have the nationality of the state party to the dispute and the home state of the investor, again unless the parties agree.[87] If the chairman of ICSID's Administrative Council is acting as appointing authority, he or she cannot appoint an arbitrator of the nationality of either party.[88]

The ICSID Convention calls for the Secretary–General to maintain a roster of arbitrators. Those arbitrators are to be appointed by the states party to the Convention; each state can appoint four arbitrators to the roster.[89] The Chairman of the Administrative Council of the World Bank also can name ten people to the roster.[90] People designated to serve on the rosters must be 'persons of high moral character and recognized competence in the fields of law, commerce, industry or finance, who may be relied on to exercise independent judgment'.[91] Arbitrators must not have a 'manifest lack of the qualities' identified in the preceding sentence.[92]

---

[86] http://investmentpolicyhub.unctad.org/IIA. These 2,700 hundred are the BITs and international investment agreements that have entered into force. Others are pending. At the end of 2014, UNCTAD identified a total of 3,271 international investment agreements. See UNCTAD, *World Investment Report 2015 – Reforming International Investment Governance* (Geneva: United Nations 2015), p. 106.

[87] ICSID Convention (above note 83) art. 39; ICSID Rules of Procedure for Arbitration Proceedings (ICSID Arbitration Rules), Rule 1(3).

[88] ICSID Convention (above note 83) art. 38.   [89] Ibid., arts. 12 and 13(1).

[90] Ibid., art. 13(2).   [91] Ibid., art. 14.   [92] Ibid., art. 57.

Notwithstanding the existence of this roster, there is no standing body of arbitrators who serve solely as ICSID arbitrators, nor need arbitrators in ICSID disputes be drawn from it. Disputing parties were and are free to select arbitrators who have characteristics suitable for the particular case in question. In most cases the parties to the dispute agree on the arbitrators. Ordinarily each party appoints its own arbitrator, and either the parties or their arbitrators agree on a presiding arbitrator. In the event the parties cannot agree on a presiding arbitrator, the Chairman of the Administrative Council (the President of the World Bank) acts as appointing authority to name an arbitrator from the panel of arbitrators established under the ICSID Convention (the chairman will also appoint a party-nominated arbitrator in the event that the party does not name its arbitrator within the requisite time frame).[93] Members of ad hoc committees in annulment cases must be drawn from the roster.[94]

The appointing authority had been called on for only 529 nominations out of the 1,849 nominations (including the nomination of arbitrators, conciliators and ad hoc Committee Members) in cases registered or administered by ICSID as of December 31, 2015.[95]

The roster has not been an unmitigated success. Many countries have not named arbitrators to the roster or have not updated their appointments, while several have named only a few. As of April 2016 there were approximately 400 people on the arbitral roster.[96] Given that as of 9 April 2016, ICSID had 152 contracting states,[97] there could be as many as 608 arbitrators on the roster. ICSID encourages states to complete their nominations but cannot fill them itself.

A generally applauded innovation by the Secretary–General is that before the chairman of the Administrative Council makes appointments

---

[93] Ibid., art. 38.

[94] Ibid., art. 52(3). Annulment committee members must not share the same nationality as the parties, nor can they have been appointed by either the respondent party or by the claimant's home state.

[95] ICSID, 'The ICSID caseload – statistics', Issue 2016–1, 19 https://icsid.worldbank.org/en/Documents/resources/ICSID%20Web%20Stats%202016-1%20(English)%20final.pdf. In 2015, there were 51 appointments by ICSID (including arbitrators, conciliators and ad hoc Committee members) as compared to 134 appointments by the parties. Ibid., p. 31.

[96] ICSID, 'Members of the Panels of Conciliators and of Arbitrators', ICSID/10 (April 2016) (some people have been named to the roster by more than one state).

[97] See Database of ICSID Member States, https://icsid.worldbank.org/en/Pages/about/Database-of-Member-States.aspx.

of presiding arbitrators in those cases where it is necessary, the Secretary–General encourages the parties to agree on their president by sending to each a roster of at least five names. The parties return the roster indicating whether they accept any of the names (without explanations as to why or why not). If there is agreement, that person will then be selected to preside over the tribunal, but if not the choice will be given to the chairman, who will appoint from the roster.

The ICSID Convention requires that arbitrators be independent and impartial. Though there has been some disquiet that ICSID's rules require that arbitrators 'manifestly' lack the requisite criteria in order to be subject to challenge, that apparent qualification to independence and impartiality has not played an enormous role in challenges decided under the ICSID Convention, and it seems that the Convention has been interpreted in a manner consistent with the interpretation of independence and impartiality required by the rules of other arbitral venues.[98]

3 Definition of Investment

The drafters of the ICSID Convention did not include a definition of 'investment' because they could not agree on one.[99] Mr. Broches explained this omission as insignificant given another key decision – consent to ICSID arbitration is external to the ICSID Convention itself. Thus a state could determine for itself whether its relationship with a particular investor contained an investment about which it was willing to arbitrate should a dispute arise in future.

The determination about the kinds of disputes that could be submitted to ICSID was thus placed in the hands of the state that was party to the agreement to submit the dispute to ICSID arbitration. That state is the one directly implicated by a determination that the dispute falls within the jurisdiction of the Centre because it is in fact an investment dispute. For ICSID cases that arise pursuant to concession contracts that refer those disputes to arbitration this delegation of authority has not been

---

[98] See Catherine A. Rogers, *Ethics in international arbitration* (Oxford University Press, 2014) and M. Kinnear and F. Nitschke, 'Disqualification of arbitrators under the ICSID Convention and rules, in C. Giorgetti (ed.), *Challenges and Recusals of Judges and Arbitrators in International Court and Tribunals* (Leiden: Brill 2015), pp. 34–79.

[99] See Mortenson (above note 41) 280 *et seq.* (the formula finally adopted after numerous discussions 'was a broad and open-ended reference to "investment" without limitation, combined with specific procedural mechanisms that allowed each state to create an individualized definition of "investment" after the Convention was ratified'. Ibid., 290).

THE LEGITIMACY OF THE ICSID   261

an issue. Concession contracts facilitating foreign investment in the development of a state's resources fall squarely within the types of investment the World Bank encourages and that the ICSID Convention was meant to encourage.

When the definition is found in an investment law or, more frequently, in an investment treaty, more difficult questions are raised. Definitions of investment under investment treaties, and how those definitions relate to the existence of an 'investment' for purposes of Article 25 of the ICSID Convention, have been the source of contention and confusion. Most investment treaties contain quite broad 'definitions' of investment; I put the word 'definition' in quotation marks because most of the definitions are in fact lists of examples of types of investment.[100] Specific examples often include stocks and bonds. Some of those lists are open, and some of them are closed. Even the latter, however, often contain potentially far-reaching examples:

> interests arising from the commitment of capital or other resources in the territory of a Party to economic activity in such territory, such as under
>
> (i) contracts involving the presence of an investor's property in the territory of the Party, including turnkey or construction contracts, or concessions or
> (ii) contracts where remuneration depends substantially on the production, revenues or profits of an enterprise.[101]

'Interests arising from the commitment of capital' is very broad indeed. To the extent there is a 'definition', it is often circular, e.g.: '"investment" means every asset that an investor owns or controls, directly or indirectly, that has the characteristics of an investment'.[102]

The decision to place the decision about what constitutes an investment in the hands of the state party to the arbitration has proved problematic. Notwithstanding this apparent delegation of authority, it is accepted that the Centre's jurisdiction is at least theoretically independent of jurisdiction under the investment treaty. In other words, there is some outer limit on what can be defined as an investment to

---

[100] See UNCTAD, *Investor–State Dispute Settlement* (above note 76), pp. 50–1 and UNCTAD, *Scope and Definition*, UNCTAD Series on Issues in International Investment Agreements II (Geneva: United Nations 2011), pp. 7–13 and 21–72.

[101] *North American Free Trade Agreement between the Government of the United States of America, the Government of Canada, and the Government of the United Mexican States,* 32 ILM 289, 605 (1993) (NAFTA) art. 1139.

[102] *US Model Bilateral Investment Treaty* (2012) art. 1.

support the jurisdiction of the Centre. Thus, for an ICSID tribunal to decide an investment treaty dispute it must have jurisdiction under the investment agreement (or other consent instrument) *and* under the Convention itself.[103]

Tribunals have approached the existence of an investment in two general ways. One is to defer to the definition in the consent instrument. If the respondent party has designated a dispute as an investment dispute, there is no need to go further (except perhaps in extreme cases).[104] A second approach is to ensure that the investment satisfies certain criteria, such as a commitment of capital, an assumption of risk, a commitment to a certain duration, an expectation of profit, and a contribution to the economic development of the host state, first outlined in *Fedax v Venezuela*[105] and then elaborated on in *Salini v Morocco*.[106] Whether or not there must be a contribution to the development of the host state (and what precisely is meant by that) has been the most contentious criterion. At present (early 2017) there is no general agreement on this issue. In many cases the approach does not matter – the investment in question clearly satisfies any potentially relevant criteria. In close cases the approach does matter.

ICSID is, of course, a multilateral Convention. Other states party are affected indirectly by the decision to refer a matter to arbitration under the Convention because they have an obligation to enforce any award as

---

[103] See Schreuer et al. (above note 73), pp. 117–9, paras 122–8; E. Cabrol, 'Pren Nreka v. Czech Republic and the notion of investment under bilateral investment treaties – does "investment" really mean "every kind of asset"?' in K. Savant (ed.), *Yearbook on International Investment Law & Policy 2009–2010* (Oxford University Press 2010), pp. 230–1.

[104] Mortenson (above note 41), 315:

> 'Given the drafting history of the ICSID Convention and the practical advantages of restraint, tribunals should exercise near-total deference to state definitions of 'investment'. So long as an activity or asset is colorably economic in nature, it should constitute an investment under Article 25. On this approach, every single enterprise that has been rejected by the restrictive approach would pass muster. In fact, none of them would be particularly close calls.
>
> This does not strip the investment requirement of meaning. It simply places primary control over that meaning back in the hands of the states parties to the Convention. Nor, it should be noted, does it totally eliminate the tribunal's role of gatekeeper. In the apt formulation of one tribunal, 'something absurd' can still be excluded from ICSID jurisdiction.'

[105] *Fedax v. Republic of Venezuela*, ICSID Case No ARB/96/3, Decision of the Tribunal on Objections to Jurisdiction, 1997.

[106] *Salini Costruttori, SpA v. Kingdom of Morocco*, ICSID Case No ARB/00/4, Decision on Jurisdiction, 2001.

THE LEGITIMACY OF THE ICSID   263

if it is a final judgement of a domestic court. This obligation requires some amount of effort on the part of the enforcing state whose courts will oversee the enforcement motion in the event that a state does not pay the award voluntarily. In one sense the enforcing state's court performs a ministerial act only because the judgement debtor cannot challenge the award in the domestic court. But in the event that enforcement is sought against the state, and not against the investor, the ability to execute the award against the state's assets will depend on the forum's laws on sovereign immunity. Arguments about which assets are commercial and thus eligible to be seized might require more than a minimal expenditure of judicial resources, as might overseeing any discovery sought by the judgement creditor to ascertain the existence and status of the assets.[107] Thus, one cannot say that the decision about what constitutes an investment dispute has no effects external to the respondent party, but those effects would ordinarily be quite limited.

4 Identity of the Investor

Under the customary international law principle of nonresponsibility, only a nonnational has standing to bring a claim against a state.[108] The ICSID Convention precludes claims by dual nationals.[109] Thus, if

---

[107] See *Republic of Argentina v. NML Capital, Ltd*, 573 US ___ (2014) in which NML, one of Argentina's bondholders prevailed in eleven debt-collection actions filed against Argentina in New York after the country defaulted on its external debt. In order to execute its judgements, NML sought extraterritorial discovery of Argentina's property and served subpoenas on nonparty banks for records relating to global financial transactions. See also generally A. K. Bjorklund, 'State immunity and the enforcement of investor–state arbitral awards' in C. Binder et al. (eds.), *International Investment Law for the 21st Century – Essays in Honour of Christoph Schreuer* (Oxford University Press, 2009), pp. 302–21 and S. A. Alexandrov, 'Enforcement of ICSID awards: Articles 53 and 54 of the ICSID Convention' in C. Binder and others (eds.), *International Investment Law for the 21st Century – Essays in Honour of Christoph Schreuer* (Oxford University Press, 2009), pp. 322–37.

[108] See, e.g., Ian Brownlie, *Principles of Public International Law*, 6th edn. (Oxford University Press, 2003), pp. 459–61 and James Crawford, *The International Law Commission's Articles on State Responsibility – Introduction, Text and Commentaries* (Cambridge University Press, 2002), pp. 264–5.

[109] Article 25(1)-(2)(a) of the ICSID Convention (above note 79) provides that

(1) The jurisdiction of the Centre shall extend to any legal dispute arising directly out of an investment, between a Contracting State (or any constituent subdivision or agency of a Contracting State designated to the Centre by that State) and a national of another Contracting State, which the parties to the dispute consent in writing to submit to the Centre. When the parties have given their consent, no party may withdraw its consent unilaterally.

the claimant has the nationality of the respondent state, he or she is not eligible to submit a claim under the ICSID Convention. There is no room for the customary international law principle of dominant and effective nationality.[110] The ICSID Convention does, however, derogate from the customary international law principle of nonresponsibility in a different way. If a juridical person of one contracting state is under the control of a national of another contracting state, the juridical person is deemed to have the nationality of the other contracting state providing that state agrees.[111]

The dual nationality rule has not been as contentious as the definition of investment. A few cases have raised questions about whether individuals had satisfactorily renounced their citizenship, thereby eliminating dual nationality problems, but those questions involve fact-specific applications of national law.[112]

5 Annulment (Rather Than Appeal) of Arbitral Awards

A strong goal of the ICSID Convention's drafters was 'finality' – that once a dispute was arbitrated the decision would not be subject to challenge. In general, because the parties to an arbitration have selected private dispute settlement to escape the complex, and often prolonged, protections that often accompany court proceedings, the control mechanisms established for arbitrations provide for only limited review of the arbitral awards.[113] Even when the parties have selected arbitration,

> (2) 'National of another Contracting State' means:
> (a) any natural person who had the nationality of a Contracting State other than the State party to the dispute on the date on which the parties consented to submit such dispute to conciliation or arbitration as well as on the date on which the request was registered pursuant to paragraph (3) of Article 28 or paragraph (3) of Article 36, but does not include any person who on either date also had the nationality of the Contracting State party to the dispute;

[110] See Schreuer et al. (above note 73), p. 271, para. 662 ('If the investor has the nationality of the host State, Art. 25(2)(a) presents an absolute bar to jurisdiction') and generally paras 664–78.

[111] ICSID Convention (above note 83) art. 25(2)(b).

[112] See generally R. A. Luzi and B. Love, 'Individual nationality in investment treaty arbitration: The tension between customary international law and lex specialis' in A. K. Bjorklund, I. A. Laird, and S. Ripinsky (eds.), *Investment Treaty Law: Current Issues III – Remedies in International Investment Law Emerging Jurisprudence of International Law* (London: British Institute of International and Comparative Law, 2009), pp. 183–208.

[113] See generally W. M. Reisman, 'The breakdown of the control mechanism in ICSID arbitration', *Duke Law Journal*, 1989(4) (1989), 739.

THE LEGITIMACY OF THE ICSID   265

however, there is a place for a control mechanism to ensure the legitimacy of the process and to provide some kind of quality control. To give effect to the intent of the parties, then, ICSID Convention awards are subject to annulment rather than appeal.

Annulment has been described as 'at the same time a drastic and limited remedy'.[114] The choices an Article 52 ad hoc Committee can make are fairly stark: it can either annul the award (or a part thereof) or leave it intact. It cannot substitute its judgement for that of the original tribunal.[115] Its function is not to correct errors of fact or of law, but to police the integrity of the award and of the process leading to the award. Incidentally, the idea of annulment is not limited to the ICSID Convention; most review of arbitral awards by national courts is similarly limited.[116]

The results of the two processes – annulment and appeal – are potentially very different. 'Annulment can void, while appeal can modify'; annulment permits review of the legitimacy of the process, while appeal concerns itself with both 'legitimacy of the process of decision and the substantive correctness of the decision'.[117] In plain terms, by selecting annulment over appeal, the drafters of the ICSID Convention may be said to have sacrificed correctness in favour of finality.[118] This is not to say that arbitral tribunals are in the habit of making unjust decisions; on the contrary, many are of the highest quality. But the authority of ad hoc committees is limited, and they have only very limited ability to alter first-instance decisions. Indeed, they have drawn the most criticism from scholars when they have apparently exceeded their authority by very broadly interpreting the grounds on which they could annul awards[119] and when they have roundly criticized the reasoning in the

---

[114] H. V. Houtte, 'Article 52 of the Washington Convention – a brief introduction' in E. Gaillard and Y. Banifatemi (eds.), *Annulment of ICSID Awards*, IAI Series on International Arbitration No 1 (Huntington: Juris Publishing 2004), pp. 11–12.

[115] D. D. Caron, 'Reputation and reality in the ICSID annulment process: Understanding the distinction between annulment and appeal', *ICSID Review – Foreign Investment Law Journal*, 7(1) (1992), 21, 23 ('In appeal, the decision under review not only may be confirmed, it more generally may be modified').

[116] See generally Hamid G. Gharavi, *The International Effectiveness of the Annulment of an Arbitral Award* (Alphen aan Rijn: Kluwer Law International, 2002).

[117] Caron (above note 115), 23–5.

[118] Schreuer et al. (above note 72), p. 903, para. 15 ('Annulment (. . .) is designed to provide emergency relief for egregious violations of a few basic principles while preserving the finality of the decision in most respects').

[119] Reisman (above note 113), 763–4.

case below but declined to annul the award as beyond their powers.[120] They have also been criticized for issuing decisions that are inconsistent with each other. Like panels, annulment committees are ad hoc; nothing in the ICSID Convention suggests that they are in a superior hierarchical role in terms of establishing norms or principles that subsequent committees (or panels) must follow. The mere fact that a decision comes first does not mean that it must be accorded precedence; whatever quasi-precedential role it might fulfil must come from the quality of its reasoning.

6 Enforcement of Awards in State–Party Courts Subject to the Doctrine of Execution Immunity

Enforcement of awards was designed to be as smooth as possible. Awards can be rendered against either an investor or a host state – disputes based on contracts can very easily be bilateral, and the jurisdiction of the Centre can be invoked by a host state as well as by an investor. Awards under an investment treaty are most likely to be against the host state, as most investment treaties permit investors to submit claims against states but do not provide for counterclaims.[121] Yet states might well seek recourse against investors for unpaid costs awards, even in treaty cases.

---

[120] For a critical review of decisions of ad hoc Committees, see, e.g., L. F. Reed and G. F. Mandelli, 'Ad hoc or ad arbitrium? An audit of recent ICSID annulment decisions' in A. W. Rovine (ed.), *Contemporary Issues in International Arbitration and Mediation: The Fordham Papers (2011)* (Leiden: Martinus Nijhoff, 2012), pp. 70–90 ('In the *CMS v. Argentina* annulment decision, although the *ad hoc* committee (in the authors' view, inappropriately) found that the original tribunal had incorrectly interpreted certain issues of international law (the first decision on the interplay between ASR Article 25 and Article XI of the US–Argentina BIT) and proceeded to explain the "correct" international law, the committee respected its circumscribed competence-competence under Article 52(1) and declined to annul the award. The committee was clear that it wanted to annul the award, but the award was, under Article 52(1), not annullable'. Ibid. p. 82); Mariel Dimsey, *The Resolution of International Investment Disputes: Challenges and Solutions* (Utrecht: Eleven International Publishing, 2008), pp. 162 *et seq*; C. Schreuer, 'Three generations of ICSID annulment proceedings' in Gaillard and Banifatemi (above note 114), p. 17 *et seq*.

[121] See generally Bjorklund (above note 39); A. K. Hoffmann, 'Counterclaims in investment arbitration', *ICSID Review – Foreign Investment Law Journal*, 28(2) (2013), 438; A. K. Hoffmann, 'Counterclaims by the respondent state in investment arbitrations – The decision on jurisdiction over respondent's counterclaim in Saluka Investments B.V. v Czech Republic', *Transnational Dispute Management*, 3(5) (2006), 1; Y. Kryvoi, 'Counterclaims in investor–state arbitration', *Minnesota Journal of International Law*, 21(2) (2012), 216.

THE LEGITIMACY OF THE ICSID

Awards under the ICSID Convention are to be treated as final awards of courts of the states party to the convention.[122] They are not subject to further review in those states. They are, however, subject to the local laws on execution immunity – the ICSID Convention itself explicitly preserves execution immunity.[123] The drafters of the ICSID Convention were certain that states would honour their obligations under the Convention, and thought that formal provisions regarding execution of judgements would be necessary to ensure that recalcitrant investors paid awards rendered against them. Although most judgement debtors (who are usually states in investment treaty cases) have paid awards rendered against them, difficulties with recalcitrant respondents have shown that ICSID itself cannot compel compliance. If a state refuses to honour an award against it, enforcement must be sought in places where that state has (or is likely to have) assets that are not protected by state immunity.[124]

7 Transparency

Transparency is a multipurpose word that is applied to many areas of investment law. As far as dispute settlement is concerned, it generally refers to access to information about cases; the potential for third parties – often but not exclusively nongovernmental organizations – to participate in cases, usually by means of filing amicus curiae briefs; and public access to hearings, often through closed-circuit television or increasingly by means of webcasting.

ICSID, in common with many institutions, has become more transparent over the years. The fact that a case has been registered with ICSID is public, so the existence of a dispute is ascertainable. When

---

[122] ICSID Convention (above note 83), art. 53 ('The award shall be binding on the parties and shall not be subject to any appeal or to any other remedy except those provided for in this Convention'); art. 54 ('Each Contracting State shall recognize an award rendered pursuant to this Convention as binding and enforce the pecuniary obligations imposed by that award within its territories as if it were a final judgment of a court in that State').

[123] Ibid. art. 55 ('Nothing in Article 54 shall be construed as derogating from the law in force in any Contracting State relating to immunity of that State or any foreign State from execution').

[124] See A. K. Bjorklund, 'Sovereign immunity as a barrier to the enforcement of investor-state arbitral awards: The re-politicization of international investment disputes', *American Review of International Arbitration*, 21 (2010), 211; Bjorklund (above note 107); L. A. Markert and C. Titi, 'States strike back – old and new ways for host states to defend against investment arbitrations' in A. K. Bjorklund (ed.), *Yearbook on International Investment Law & Policy 2013–2014* (Oxford University Press, 2015), pp. 401–35; Tams (above note 77), pp. 242–3.

ICSID amended its arbitration rules in 2006, it changed the provision on confidentiality to give the Secretariat the authority to publish the *ratio* of decisions, notwithstanding the decision of the disputing parties about publication of the entirety of the awards.[125] Prior to that change, the rules had vested decisions about publication solely in the parties to the dispute. The 2006 rule changes also added provisions to expressly permit tribunals to consider and accept the application by interested parties to participate as amici curiae;[126] ICSID tribunals had been divided on whether the rules permitted the acceptance of amici.[127] ICSID has also facilitated public access to hearings. They are frequently webcast, and ICSID hosted the first investor–state hearings that were open to the public via closed-circuit television – in the *UPS v. Canada* case – in 2002.[128] Decisions about public access to hearings is, however, governed by party consent in individual cases.

***

[125] ICSID Arbitration Rules (above note 87) Rule 48(4):

> The Centre shall not publish the award without the consent of the parties. The Centre shall, however, promptly include in its publications excerpts of the legal reasoning of the Tribunal.

See also ICSID Convention (above note 83), art. 48(4):

> Any member of the Tribunal may attach his individual opinion to the award, whether he dissents from the majority or not, or a statement of his dissent.

[126] ICSID Arbitration Rules (above note 87), Rule 37(2).

[127] A. Antonietti, 'The 2006 amendments to the ICSID Rules and Regulations and the Additional Facility Rules', *ICSID Review–Foreign Investment Law Journal*, 21(2) (2006), 427, 433–7.

[128] J. Delaney and D. B. Magraw, 'Procedural transparency' in Muchlinski, Ortino, and Schreuer (above note 43), p. 746:

> By the end of 2004, three NAFTA tribunals had allowed open hearings: *UPS, Methanex,* and *Canfor v. United States*. In *UPS*, the disputing parties set a precedent by becoming the first Chapter 11 parties to allow public access to a hearing. The parties agreed to allow access to a hearing on jurisdiction that took place from 29 to 31 July 2002 through a live closed-circuit broadcast. The *Methanex* case was also ground-breaking in allowing increased transparency and nondisputing party participation in Chapter 11 arbitration. Public hearings through live closed-circuit broadcast were held at the World Bank from 7 to 17 June 2004 after consent by the *Methanex* parties. Afterwards, public hearings were broadcast live through closed-circuit television in the *Canfor* case from 7 to 9 December 2004. [footnotes omitted].

THE LEGITIMACY OF THE ICSID   269

The preceding *tour d'horizon* of certain features of the ICSID Convention shows the limited power held by ICSID as an institution. The decisions made by the drafters of the Convention were to establish a framework for the settlement of disputes; the interstices of the framework are filled by states who choose to make ICSID Convention arbitration a possibility for disputes brought under it.

IV   The Intersection of Legitimacy Critiques and ICSID

Section II addressed the four main criticisms of investment treaty law and arbitration, while Section III outlined key decisions taken in the establishment of ICSID, which now, some fifty years later, limit the ability of the institution to respond. Some of those concerns go to process, while some go to substance. Some of the criticisms levied at ICSID are simply misdirected. Others are more salient and illustrate that decisions taken years ago may no longer be appropriate given current expectations about international arbitration.

A   Legitimacy vis-à-vis Sovereignty

Judged against the criteria listed earlier, sovereignty is both a normative and sociological legitimacy concern. The classic normative defense of international treaty obligations is the *S.S. Wimbledon* case: that the quintessential exercise of a state's sovereignty is an agreement to limit it.[129] This grounding in the traditional Westphalian conception of international law is viewed as unsatisfactory by many observers today; the monopoly on legitimacy in international law matters hitherto enjoyed by states has been eroded.[130] Thus the natural response in defense of investment law and arbitration – that states have consented to it and indeed that they continue to support it even against multiplying criticism- rings hollow for those sceptical about the democratic representativeness of states and their capture by corporate and other monied interests.

[129] *S.S. Wimbledon* (above note 35); Leonhardsen (above note 11), 100.
[130] See A. von Bogdandy, M. Goldmann, and I. Venzke, 'From public international to international public law: Translating world public opinion into international public authority' (2005), 3, 5–6, http://papers.ssrn.com/sol3/papers.cfm?abstract_id=2662391 (describing shift from a purely horizontal order to one that includes vertical structures and 'from consent to multifaceted accounts of legitimacy [to] respond to developments in many fields of international law').

There is widespread concern about whether the investment regime and ICSID itself are valid expressions of democratic will or whether they are impermissible infringements of state sovereignty. Some sovereignty-based concerns can not be resolved by any change to investment arbitration. Decision making by adjudicative bodies raises concerns even domestically; in the international context those concerns are an 'intensified version'[131] of the countermajoritarian difficulty raised when courts review and possibly overturn or amend laws made by democratic bodies.[132]

Disaggregating consent to ICSID arbitration and consent to an investment treaty is important to isolate and respond to these concerns. Consent to ICSID Convention arbitration is external to the ICSID Convention. Signing the ICSID Convention brings with it no obligation to refer any dispute whatsoever to ICSID. States themselves choose which particular disputes to refer to ICSID. Thus, the fact that an ICSID tribunal hears a case involving public functions is a result of a decision made either in a concession contract or in an investment treaty (or in rarer cases in investment legislation). ICSID cannot force any case to come to it, and the mere fact that a state is party to the ICSID Convention does not mean that any case involving that state will be heard by an ICSID Convention tribunal.

Thus, ICSID can do nothing unless its authority is externally activated. If one believes that investment treaty disputes should not be heard in arbitration, the mechanism to target is the treaty, rather than ICSID (or another arbitral body).

Parsing this concern also involves treating separately Grossman's first two criteria: ICSID might be assessed with respect to the first and the third, i.e., whether the tribunal hearing the claim infringing state sovereignty is fair and unbiased and whether it meets democratic institutional norms, but ICSID is neither the architect nor the builder of the underlying normative regime, though it is involved in facilitating the resolution of disputes under it.

Perhaps this is not altogether different from other courts and tribunals, but there are two significant features of ICSID Convention tribunals worth emphasizing. Many international courts have one of these features,

---

[131] Leonhardsen (above note 11), 96.

[132] See Alexander Bickel, *The Least Dangerous Branch: The Supreme Court at the Bar of Politics* (Indianapolis: The Bobbs-Merrill Company Inc., 1962), p. 16 *et seq.*; G. Ulfstein, 'International courts and judges: Independence, interaction, and legitimacy', *N.Y.U. Journal of International Law and Policy*, 46 (2013–2014), 849.

but few have both. First, there is no standing or even quasi-standing tribunal of individuals who will sit on arbitral tribunals. Second, no single treaty is being interpreted. The International Court of Justice hears disputes brought under all kinds of international instruments, but there is a standing body of decision makers. Panelists in WTO disputes are drawn from an extensive roster that could be likened to the arbitrators who serve in investment cases,[133] but they are applying a single family of instruments in which the substantive and procedural elements are integrated, and their decisions are subject to the control of a single appellate body.

The source of consent to ICSID Convention arbitration is of under-standable concern to those worried about sovereignty, and it likely explains much of the concern about ICSID Convention arbitration. Consent found in an investment treaty is an open offer to arbitrate an undefined class of claims – those brought by investors for damage to their investments – when a state has allegedly breached an investment agreement. Thus the identity of the claimant, the nature of the claim, and the underlying facts might all be unknown to the host state until the investor files its documents initiating the claim to arbitration. Those claims that involve state contracts are less problematic from the point of view of unknown and unexpected claims. Even if the subject matter of the case is about the national patrimony, the state in that instance has a much better idea of what any dispute is likely to be about.

These sovereignty concerns illustrate perfectly the gap between normative and sociological legitimacy. Adherence to investment treaties is a textbook exercise of state sovereignty. If those treaties select (or offer to the investor the choice of) ICSID Convention arbitration, the sovereign choice is squared – the ICSID Convention is yet another treaty to which states must adhere for the process to be applicable. The process was designed by states for use particularly in investment arbitration cases. And, indeed, there is no obligation of a state ever to choose ICSID Convention arbitration, so the consent to arbitration in a particular case will always be found in an external document. There still might be some concerns about the process, which are dealt with later, but

---

[133] I say this in a general sense, in that they are a category of persons who sometimes serve in that role. Joost Pauwelyn has identified various ways in which WTO panellists and investment arbitrators differ. See Pauwelyn (above note 16). For a criticism of Pauwelyn's view, see C. Rogers, 'Apparent dichotomies, covert similarities: A response to Joost Pauwelyn', *AJIL Unbound* (13 April 2016).

as an exercise in sovereign choice ICSID Convention arbitration is not problematic.

From a sociological legitimacy perspective, however, the story changes. The sovereignty concern appears to implicate directly Grossman's second criterion. If there are doubts about the underlying normative regime – the investment treaty itself – it is not surprising that there are doubts about the forum in which disputes arising under that regime are going to be heard. Indeed, doubts about the underlying normative regime are linked to Franck's adherence factor; ICSID Convention arbitration effectively implements the primary rules of obligation found in investment treaties. If one is concerned that those investment treaties restrict regulatory authority in the domestic sphere to the detriment of the local populace and at the expense of environmental and human rights protection, and that they give too many rights to foreign investors as compared to local investors, and that they were signed, at least in part, by countries who were unaware of the authority they were delegated to an international tribunal, the straightforward exercise of sovereignty argument rings hollow.

Similarly, Shany's emphasis on the effectiveness of the process is unlikely to assuage those critics who are concerned precisely because the process gives effect to what they regard as a problematic underlying normative regime. To follow up on Shany's observations about internal and external perceptions, from an internal perspective the fact that the system functions reasonably well – most states honour their awards; there is a robust enforcement mechanism in the event that awards are not paid voluntarily; states continue to include ICSID Convention arbitration as an option in investment treaties; and ICSID enjoyed a record-breaking year in 2015 when 52 cases were filed under the Convention and the additional facility rules[134] – are the very qualities that serve to heighten the external sense of dissatisfaction with and sense of illegitimacy of the investment regime overall and of ICSID in particular.

B   Legitimacy vis-à-vis Coherence

One of the longest standing concerns levied at investment arbitration is that decisions are inconsistent – there are divergent lines of reasoning

---

[134] ICSID, 'The ICSID caseload – statistics' (2016:1), p. 7.

in key areas, and there is no appellate tribunal to resolve splits among tribunals. Again, to address questions of legitimacy it is essential to distinguish between the decision-making process and the underlying rules. This is where Thomas Franck's legitimacy criteria are most cogent and most difficult to satisfy. There is at least some incoherence in the underlying rules, and a 'regime' that is not designed to bring any coherence to them or, one might say, no 'regime' at all.

Most inconsistency involves the substantive obligations contained in different treaties. Many inconsistent decisions thus stem from different treaties with different language in them. Moreover, some rules are inherently discretionary, such as the fair and equitable treatment standard found in the *Lauder* and *CME* cases. Some rules are simply hard to capture because they defy, as Jan Paulsson puts it, 'resolution by abstraction'.[135] Some concerns cannot be so readily dismissed because treaty provisions are often similar or even identical. Nonetheless, one might well say that the fact that tribunal decisions are not always coherent is not surprising given the differences in treaty language, difference in arbitrators, and the deliberate lack of a control mechanism that would prioritize accuracy and consistency over finality.

As far as the decision-making process is concerned, decisions in investment cases are made by ad hoc tribunals, not by a standing court. Thus, there is no single tribunal – no 'it' – because arbitral tribunals are established on an ad hoc basis. ICSID itself does not decide investment cases, so to say that 'ICSID' renders inconsistent decisions is inaccurate and misleading. Individual ICSID tribunals might render inconsistent decisions, but those tribunals have no obligation under the ICSID Convention or under international law to be consistent with each other.

There is not even any way for ICSID itself to reconcile the competing approaches to the requirements of Article 25.[136] State parties could at

---

[135] J. Paulsson, 'Avoiding unintended consequences" in K. P. Sauvant (ed.), *Appeals Mechanism in International Investment Disputes* (Oxford University Press, 2008), pp. 241, 244. Paulsson lists the identity of compensable regulatory measures, abuse of power, minimum standards of fairness, denials of justice, and discrimination as areas that elude resolution by abstraction.

[136] In an interesting twist, this question has arisen in arbitrations brought under the UNCITRAL Rules as well. Article 25 of the ICSID Convention of course does not apply, so one might expect the question of whether or not there has been an investment to be answered exclusively by reference to the investment agreement itself. A few tribunals have, however, sought to import the '*Salini*' test, or a version of it, even into non-ICSID cases. See, e.g., Cabrol (above note 100).

274 ANDREA K. BJORKLUND

least theoretically amend the ICSID Convention to include a definition (although as one can see from the definitions in investment treaties themselves, it could be challenging to provide a definition that did not give rise to ambiguity in a given set of circumstances). This inconsistency in approach is problematic both because it does not give much certainty either to states or to investors about which investments will satisfy the jurisdiction ratione materiae requirements of the ICSID Convention and also because it gives an appearance of arbitrariness.

In the absence of a procedural mechanism to ensure consistency, some, like Gabrielle Kaufmann-Kohler, have suggested that arbitrators, as decision makers, have an obligation to follow precedent 'so as to foster a normative environment that is predictable', and that this obligation is heightened when a nascent legal system is struggling to develop rules.[137] Others have suggested a more limited duty – to explain why they are departing from previously decided cases.[138] If there is such a duty, it would extend beyond the realm of ICSID tribunals to encompass all investment treaty tribunals.

In 2004 the ICSID Secretariat suggested adding an appellate body option to ICSID cases.[139] At that time most ICSID states were not at all interested in the idea. The possibility of an appellate body is once again alive, with the European Commission notably advocating the establishment of an appellate body and including provision for one in the EU – Vietnam FTA and in the Comprehensive Economic and Trade

---

[137] Kaufmann-Kohler (above note 25), 374.   [138] Bjorklund (above note 25), pp. 275–9.
[139] ICSID, 'Possible improvements of the framework for ICSID arbitration' (2004) ICSID Secretariat Discussion Paper, 14 *et seq.*, paras. 20–3 and Annex (Possible features of an ICSID Appeals Facility) https://icsid.worldbank.org/en/Documents/resources/Possible%20Improvements%20of%20the%20Framework%20of%20ICSID%20Arbitration.pdf:

> A further, potentially most important, issue that has been raised is whether an appellate mechanism is desirable to ensure coherence and consistency in case law generated in ICSID and other investor-to-State arbitrations initiated under investment treaties. (Ibid., para. 6).
>
> . . .
>
> As indicated in the introduction of this paper, interest has been shown in awards in investor-to-State cases under investment treaties being made subject to a mechanism for the appeal of the awards. (Ibid., para. 20).
>
> This proposal was likely in response to recent US investment agreements that had put into place a 'socket' for an appellate body. B. Legum, 'The introduction of an appellate mechanism: The U.S. Trade Act of 2002' in Gaillard and Banifatemi (above note 114), 289.

THE LEGITIMACY OF THE ICSID 275

Agreement with Canada.[140] The European Union has also proposed the inclusion of an investment court, including as appellate body, in the Transatlantic Trade and Investment Partnership negotiations in which it is currently engaged with the United States; whether or not the United States will be receptive to the idea, and whether or not it constitutes a sea change remains to be seen. The notion is that these individual appellate bodies could be joined together to provide a locus for coherence.

In short, the decision to prioritize finality over correctness in the ICSID Convention meant that annulment rather than appeal was selected as the control mechanism in ICSID Convention arbitration. Thus, ICSID was not designed to achieve coherence. That is a decision that might need to change, now that the bulk of its caseload involves investment treaty cases, and there are greater expectations for consistency. But that change involves a fundamental decision about the nature of dispute resolution for investment treaties. We may indeed be at a watershed moment where that discussion is occurring.

When speaking about coherence, one can again identify divergent views about normative versus sociological legitimacy. From a normative view, one can say that ICSID works, for the most part, precisely as it was designed to work. It was not created to construct a coherent, integrated regime of investment law characterized by the consistent application of rules. It was designed to be a neutral means of dispute resolution that emphasized finality over correctness. Ad hoc arbitrators were not intended to create a body of jurisprudence. Although it was created with an eye towards contractual disputes, it is flexible enough to encompass treaty disputes. And, indeed, if states do not regard the regime as satisfactory for the resolution of treaty-based disputes, they are free not to refer to ICSID as a venue for the settlement of disputes. Yet no other existing mechanism would offer a control mechanism any more capable of achieving consistency. Arbitrations taking place under the auspices of the New York Convention would be subject to set aside in the place of arbitration, but the place of arbitration would not necessarily be the same, and most arbitration laws do not provide for substantive review of the merits of cases. When enforcement was sought in a New York Convention country, the state resisting enforcement could raise objections, but again only on limited grounds.

---

[140] EU–Vietnam FTA (above note 29) especially arts. 13 and 28 and Annex IV of the Investment Chapter; CETA (above note 29) arts 8.28 and 8.29.

The preceding paragraphs offer a normative defence of ICSID vis-à-vis the coherence critique, but it cannot help the fact that if one looks at the underlying regime, coherence will be viewed as a problem. Moreover, to the extent that external perception views ICSID as a 'court', its inability to ensure consistence will look like a failure to ensure the quality of decision making that one expects of a juridical institution. This is where the underlying normative regime, and its deficiencies, has the strongest influence on ICSID and perceptions of ICSID. If one measures investment law against Franck's criteria, investment arbitration (and ICSID) falls short. First, international investment law is characterized by indeterminate rules. Their symbolic validation is questionable, given doubts about whether those rules seem to have precedence over other obligations a state has or ought to have. Coherence is almost by definition unachievable given the ad hoc nature of investment arbitration and the lack of an appellate body. And finally, adherence to the underlying regime is questionable, for the reasons adverted to earlier.

C   Legitimacy vis-à-vis Transparency

Investment arbitration is becoming slowly more transparent, though not quickly enough to satisfy its critics. The public interest is unquestionably served by permitting open access to investment proceedings. It is useful to explore briefly what is meant by the public interest – this language is often used when the investment arbitration involves hot-button issues such as environmental regulation, human or animal health and safety regulation, or the regulation of land use in areas of cultural sensitivity, such as ancient Native-American spiritual lands. But the public interest is also served by simply having access to the proceedings, whether or not any particular interest cares too much about the given case or not. It permits 'the people' to assure themselves that their civil servants are representing them adequately and might serve to dissipate concerns about secret proceedings in which unidentified arbitrators strip US citizens of their rights and strip the US government of its sovereign authority.

Parties can, if they wish, increase the transparency of any dispute; the provisions in the ICSID Convention and the applicable arbitration rules are default provisions subject to modification. ICSID made initial changes to its rules in 2006. At the time it was a pioneer in transparency, and its decision to publish at least the *ratio* of awards was quite bold. ICSID makes a great deal of information available about its cases. All cases registered by the Centre are listed on its website, as are the identities of the parties and of the arbitrators. If the parties agree, documents related to the case are made freely available.

ICSID's 2006 rules change also provided explicitly for the potential participation of amicus curiae. This change brought ICSID's rules into line with what was the generally accepted practice in UNCITRAL cases (and in some ICSID Convention cases). In addition, ICSID has hosted numerous proceedings in which the proceedings were open to the public via webcast, or closed-circuit television, or both.

Thus, one could say that ICSID helps to facilitate transparency, though it does not require that all details of all disputes under it be transparent. Yet one still reads, frequently, complaints that investment arbitration involves secret proceedings held behind closed doors in which decisions of public moment are made.

Again, one notices a disparity between reality and perception, and perhaps a disparity in views about how much accessibility to documents, to decisions about the procedure, and to the oral proceedings themselves is required for a procedure to be viewed as legitimate. On a normative level, one might say that the state is representing the public interest in the arbitration. Amici curiae can petition to participate, and the rules governing their participation are very similar to those governing participation in the US Supreme Court. Although the accessibility of documents might vary by case, their availability is governed primarily by the state parties to the treaty, and to a lesser extent by the disputing parties in a particular case and by the applicable, i.e., ICSID Convention arbitration rules. ICSID lists every case it registers on its website, so that it is arguably more transparent than any other arbitral institution and is a good deal more transparent than many state courts, whose dockets are only available at the courthouse itself.

The perception of accessibility is, however, very different. The fact that some proceedings are secret, and some awards are not published, arouses suspicion and discontent. Even though an enormous amount of information is available, there are concerns about the information that is *not* available. Although it seems unlikely that very many awards are unpublished, and unlikelier still that cases about which no one knows exist, cursory knowledge of cases is far different from the ability to scrutinize awards rendered in those cases. And, in fact, to assess adequately those decisions access to the materials underlying them is essential. In addition, one realizes that even access to documents might not be enough. Investment law is sufficiently cumbersome and complex that nonexperts cannot be expected either to read dozens of 100-plus page cases and thereby gain proficiency in its intricacies. The same holds true for the complexities of the arbitral process itself.

Transparency is one of the key criteria that Professor Grossman points to with respect to ensuring sociological legitimacy. It raises concerns in and of itself insofar as a lack of transparency violates democratic norms related to dispute settlement, but one can see also the link to other concerns, such as whether the tribunal is fair and unbiased, and how the underlying normative regime affects the quality of decision making. Because the underlying standards are often indeterminate, and tribunals have come to different conclusions about them, it is difficult to prove that a tribunal is fair and unbiased. In other words, all of the transparency in the world cannot demonstrate that decision making is fair and unbiased if there are significant doubts about the identity of the decision makers or the underlying normative regime, or both.

D   Legitimacy vis-à-vis Process

Legitimacy concerns directed at process issues include concerns of abuse of process, such as the initiation of parallel proceedings by claimants and the structuring of investments to take advantage of investment treaties, the identity of the arbitrators who decide disputes, and the fact that disputes are decided by ad hoc tribunals rather than by a permanent court.

As far as parallel proceedings and treaty shopping are concerned, these practices are permitted by the instruments in which consent to arbitration is found – the investment treaties themselves. The ICSID Convention does in fact prevent the simultaneous prosecution of a state–state claim and an investor–state claim.[141] But neither the Convention nor the rules address parallel proceedings of the kind found in the *CME* and *Lauder* cases. Insofar as nationality planning is concerned, the ICSID Convention is in fact less generous than some investment treaties, which permit claims by dual nationals. This is applicable for individuals; with respect to the nationality of artificial persons, their eligibility is governed by the applicable treaty, rather than by the ICSID Convention. The one exception is Article 25(2)(b) of the ICSID Convention, which permits a state to agree to designate a locally owned corporation as a "foreign"

---

[141] ICSID Convention (above note 83), art. 27(1).

person for ICSID Convention purposes. This provision, too, is more protective than investment treaties, which do not have a similar state-consent hurdle.

The other significant procedural concern addressed earlier has to do with the identity of the decision makers, and the array of issues surrounding party appointment and ethical conflicts. Disputing parties are increasingly challenging arbitral appointments under the Convention, demonstrating some dissatisfaction with the status quo. Yet this is the system that states created in their investment treaties. No matter what set of rules governs an investment arbitration, the tribunal deciding the matter will be created for that specific dispute. Unless states decide to establish a standing body of arbitrators, or a court, ICSID's operation of the system is no different than any other. Indeed, states name arbitrators to the panel, and they can and do appoint people who act as counsel in addition to sitting as arbitrator, thereby constraining the freedom of the Chairman of the Administrative Council when he acts as appointing authority.

The PluriCourts Centre of Excellence at the University of Oslo has data showing that approximately 38.3 per cent of the 760 registered investment cases have *not* been administered by ICSID.[142] This means that ICSID has administered 61.7 per cent of investment cases. Of those, ICSID has appointed approximately 29 per cent of the possible arbitrators.[143] When ICSID appoints an arbitrator in an ICSID Convention arbitration, it does so either through a roster process, which permits the disputing parties, including the disputing state, to agree on an arbitrator, or it appoints from the ICSID roster, which is filled by the states party. States themselves exert a great deal of control over who the arbitrators are – a great deal more control than ICSID exerts.

Two other facets of ICSID can be regarded as raising process concerns. The first is the decision to permit only annulment of awards, rather than appeal. This decision was made in the middle of the 1960s and would perhaps change today. In fact, ICSID proposed in 2004 the possibility of establishing an appellate body.[144] That proposal was not at the time well received by the states party to ICSID, but the climate now is different, and a different result might ensue should another proposal be made. Indeed, ICSID has already prepared itself to host CETA's investment

---

[142] Behn (above note 59).   [143] See supra note 95 and accompanying text.
[144] ICSID Secretariat, 'Possible improvements of the framework for ICSID arbitration' (above note 138).

court system, but it is uncertain how broadly the idea of a multilateral appellate court will gain adherence. One can expect ICSID to respond to the demands of the investment law community to propose innovations and reforms for approval by the states party to it, but ICSID will not be able to go beyond what its member states want it to do. The second is the enhanced enforcement procedure – the requirement that states party to the ICSID Convention treat ICSID Convention arbitral awards as if they were final judgements of their own courts. This requirement forecloses the possibility of challenge to an ICSID award in domestic courts. Even there, however, the ICSID Convention does not waive execution immunity, that 'last bastion' of state immunity. This means that in most countries only a state's commercial assets can be seized to pay an award, a functional reservation of sovereign power. ICSID itself has no ability to force states to pay awards rendered under its auspices.

This section is perhaps the most surprising. The focus on process would seem to implicate ICSID quite directly, yet even here one sees the control of the states party to the ICSID Convention over the ability of the Secretariat or of ICSID tribunals to address matters such as treaty shopping or parallel proceedings. The fact that decisions themselves emanate from an ICSID tribunal, and are available on the ICSID website, suggests that ICSID has a greater amount of control over these matters than it actually does.

This control by the states highlights one of Grossman's key insights on why traditional normative legitimacy justifications are unsatisfactory. If members of civil society or individuals view the states as inadequate guardians of the public interest, pointing to a state's decision to enter into investment treaties, adhere to the ICSID Convention, and to engage in investor–state dispute settlement does not suffice to allay concerns about the arbitration process. The possibility of parallel proceedings smacks of 'forum shopping,' a practice generally (though not always justifiably) reviled in domestic courts as well. When forum shopping starts to look not just like choosing the most favourable forum but also like permitting multiple bites of the cherry, the arbitral regime looks unfair. In a similar vein, when one looks at matters such as 'issue conflicts' concerns about fairness and lack of bias are not surprising. Although these practices can be defended (especially by lawyers to other lawyers), to the public the system looks suspect. This practice, too, highlights Shany's distinction between internal and external legitimacy, in which those inside the regime tend to have different reactions than those outside it.

V   Conclusion

As investment treaty arbitration is maturing, both normative and socio-logical legitimacy concerns are increasing. In some ways investment arbitration can be viewed as a microcosm of international law generally as traditional views are challenged by practical changes. States see themselves as the proper creators and controllers of international law. Yet they have created a mechanism in which ad hoc tribunals have the authority to make decisions that bind those states, and that in practice help to develop the substance of the law. The power of those tribunals has led to both criticism and a desire to co-opt that power for other purposes, such as the furtherance of human rights and environmental norms.

One could reasonably regard ICSID as a victim of its own success. The dispersed nature of investment treaties as compared to the localized nature of ICSID could explain why it is a focus for criticism.

The decisions made in the establishment of ICSID in 1965 were reasonable then and help to bolster ICSID's normative legitimacy. Yet, as Grossman points out, notions of legitimacy change over time.[145] Indeed, one might say that ideas about normative legitimacy have not kept pace with sociological legitimacy. Thus, ironically the efficacy of ICSID and of investment arbitration, while bolstering its normative legitimacy, tends to undermine its sociological legitimacy given concern about the treaties underlying investment arbitration.

As far as sociological legitimacy is concerned, concerns about sovereignty in particular are raised in each of the criteria to which Professor Grossman points. Whether a tribunal is fair and unbiased might not be viewed as an advantage from this standpoint; the distance between a tribunal and the national polity whose acts are being challenged is viewed as problematic because they are too divorced from the community to understand its concerns. Questions about the underlying governance regime – the obligations found in investment treaties – are often exacerbated by dissatisfaction with the quality of decisions, particularly given the concerns with consistency and predictability, discussed later. Finally, the lack of transparency in investment arbitration exacerbates concerns about unfairness and bias and about the underlying normative regime.

Many of the rules ICSID tribunals are applying are inherently indeterminate, but this is a problem that is separate from ICSID, and ICSID tribunals lack the authority to make them clear. The drafters of the ICSID

---

[145] Grossman (above note 27), 111.

Convention were not designing a 'system' of investment arbitration. They were establishing a neutral mechanism to settle discrete disputes in an (ideally) expeditious manner. The ICSID Convention contains no substantive rules. As an arbitration institution, it is an 'opt-in' mechanism that is divorced from the substantive rules it applies – indeed, those can change depending on the referring document.

One of the most effective responses to the sociological legitimacy concerns identified earlier, and especially concerns about coherence, would be the establishment of a multilateral instrument, yet states have resisted that option. The failure of the multilateral agreement on investment is legendary, as is the failure of the Doha round of WTO negotiations, which would have potentially added investment to the WTO's competence. Whether this resistance is diminishing is an open question. Some posit convergence along the lines of the 'North American' model because the European Commission's investment agreements negotiated after it gained competence over foreign investment with the ratification of the Lisbon Treaty seem to adopt the complex, lengthy US and Canadian models, even though internal details differ.[146] The European Union is now negotiating the Trans-Atlantic Trade and Investment Partnership (T-TIP) with the United States, and the United States concluded negotiation of the Trans-Pacific Partnership (TPP) with eleven other nations, although the TPP has not yet been ratified by its member states. President Trump has withdrawn the United States from the TPP, and it is unclear whether the treaty will survive or, if it does, who its adherents will be. If these two 'mega-regional' treaties come to fruition, they could form the nuclei for a multilateral agreement, or at least for fewer treaties.

The other potential 'game changer' is the European Union's proposal to establish an investment 'court' and accompanying appellate body. I put the word 'court' in quotes because at least as presented in the T-TIP proposal the court is not comprised of permanent judges whose sole job would be to

---

[146] See, e.g., CETA (above note 29) Chapter 8; EU – Singapore Free Trade Agreement (in negotiation). See generally A. Reinisch, 'The EU on the investment path – Quo vadis Europe?: The future of EU BITs and other investment agreements', *Santa Clara Journal of International Law*, 12 (2013), 111; J. A. Maupin, 'Where should Europe's investment path lead? Reflections on August Reinisch, "*Quo Vadis* Europe?"', *Santa Clara Journal of International Law*, 12 (2014), 183; Marc Bungenberg, Jörn Griebel, and Steffen Hindelang (eds.), *European Yearbook of International Economic Law – Special Issue: International Investment Law and EU Law* (Berlin: Springer, 2011).

THE LEGITIMACY OF THE ICSID   283

decide investment disputes under the T-TIP.[147] Yet what is less than clear is whether and how the investment court could be modified to be available for the resolution of disputes under all investment treaties, an essential feature for the facilitation of coherence in investment law more generally. UNCITRAL'S working group III is now considering this question. One of the venues proposed for hosting the investment court is ICSID (the other is the Permanent Court of Arbitration in The Hague). The European Union and Canada have selected ICSID as the venue for the investment court proposed for CETA.[148]

ICSID showed its adaptability in 2006 when it amended its rules to permit more transparency; its proposal in 2004 to establish an appellate body was in many ways prescient. ICSID can host the CETA investment court, assuming it is in fact established (investor–state dispute settlement is among the parts of CETA that has not been provisionally applied).[149] That alone will not be enough to introduce coherence to international investment law, although it might increase predictability and uniformity in the interpretation of CETA. If a multilateral investment court encompassing an appellate body comes to fruition, which is far from clear, it will be interesting to see how ICSID will accommodate those proposals. The ICSID Convention stipulates that the only recourse against an ICSID Convention arbitral award is annulment under the ICSID Convention itself[150] and that only states (which would not include the European Union as such) can be adherents.[151] Should ICSID be able to surmount these incompatibilities, perhaps by amendment, perhaps by the addition of a protocol to the ICSID Convention that establishes a parallel mechanism for investment court arbitrations and which would permit the European Union to become a party, it would bolster both its normative and sociological legitimacy.

---

[147] T-TIP proposal (above note 29), art. 9.   [148] CETA (above note 29), art. 8.27(16).

[149] Council Decision on the provisional application of the Comprehensive Economic and Trade Agreement (CETA) between Canada, of the one part, and the European Union and its Member States, of the other part, Interinstitutional File: 21016/0220 (NLE) (5 October 2016), available at: http://data.consilium.europa.eu/doc/document/ST-10974-2016-INIT/en/pdf.

[150] ICSID Convention (above note 83), art. 52.   [151] Ibid. art. 67.

10

The Human Rights Treaty Bodies and Legitimacy Challenges

GEIR ULFSTEIN[1]

I Introduction

The United Nations human rights treaty bodies, such as the Human Rights Committee, the Committee against Torture, and the Committee on the Elimination of Discrimination against Women, oversee national implementation of international human rights obligations. In this chapter I discuss the legitimacy of the human rights treaty bodies' court-like function of deciding cases on individual complaints.

These international organs have been a success in the sense that they have increasingly extended their functions and importance. As stated by UN Secretary-General Ban Ki-moon: they are 'one of the greatest achievements in the history of the global struggle for human rights.'[2] Since the end of the Cold War the treaty bodies have asserted their powers to adopt Concluding Observations noting both positive and negative aspects of the relevant states' implementation of treaty obligations in connection with examination of state reports. They adopt General Comments specifying the rather general obligations of the treaties. More and more states have ratified additional protocols empowering the treaty bodies to adopt Views in cases of individual complaints. They adopt interim measures in urgent cases, as well as follow-up measures to ensure implementation of their findings.[3]

---

[1] Department of Public and International Law, University of Oslo. This chapter was written under the auspices of ERC Advanced Grant 269841 MultiRights–on the Legitimacy of Multi-Level Human Rights Judiciary; and partly supported by the Research Council of Norway through its Centres of Excellence Funding Scheme, project number 223274 PluriCourts – The Legitimacy of the International Judiciary.

[2] OHCHR, *Strengthening the United Nations Human Rights Treaty Body System. A Report by the United Nations High Commissioner for Human Rights*, (2012), 7.

[3] H. Keller and G. Ulfstein, 'Conclusions' in H. Keller and G. Ulfstein (eds.), *UN Human Rights Treaty Bodies: Law and Legitimacy* (Cambridge University Press, 2012), pp. 414–26, 415.

But the treaty bodies are also facing challenges and political backlash. They are criticized for not being sufficiently effective in ensuring protection of human rights. On the other hand, it is claimed that they unjustifiably interfere with the freedom of states parties in applying excessively expansive interpretations of the substantive treaty obligations and of their procedural mandate. The system is also overloaded, resulting in increasing backlogs. This gave rise to the treaty body strengthening process by the UN High Commissioner for Human Rights, which culminated in adoption of General Assembly resolution 68/268, 'Strengthening and Enhancing the Effective Functioning of the Treaty Body System', in 2014.[4]

The criticism can be taken as claims that the treaty bodies suffer from distinct legitimacy deficits. They exercise political authority in the sense of interfering with state sovereignty. Therefore, to be legitimate, this authority should be justifiable.[5] We can start with the legitimacy standards known from national constitutional law, especially the '[t]rinitarian mantra of the constitutionalist faith'[6]: democracy, the rule of law and human rights. But the legitimacy standards applicable to the treaty bodies should take into account that they have international court-like functions, as well as the special features of such treaty bodies compared to international courts.

I will discuss legitimacy standards proposed for international courts[7] as adapted to the human rights treaty bodies in their function of resolving claims from individuals. First, members of the treaty bodies should be independent and impartial and highly competent in international law. But the members should also be competent to undertake the non-court-like functions of the treaty bodies. The treaty bodies must furthermore apply procedures that allow both parties to be heard and ensure that relevant facts are taken into account.

---

[4] General Assembly Resolution A/68/L.37 Strengthening and Enhancing the Effective Functioning of the Human Rights Treaty Body System (2014). www.ohchr.org/EN/HRBodies/HRTD/Pages/TBStrengthening.aspx.

[5] D. Bodansky, 'Legitimacy in international law and international relations' in J. L. Dunoff and M. A. Pollack (eds.), *Interdisciplinary Perspectives on International Law and International Relations: The State of the Art* (Cambridge University Press, 2013), pp. 321–45, 324.

[6] M. Kumm et al., 'How large is the world of global constitutionalism?', *Global Constitutionalism*, 3 (2014), 1–8, 3.

[7] See N. Grossman, 'The normative legitimacy of international courts', *Temple Law Review*, 61 (2012), 61–106; Andreas Follesdal et al., *The Legitimacy of International Human Rights Regimes: Legal, Political and Philosophical Perspectives* (Cambridge University Press, 2014); and Armin von Bogdandy and Ingo Venzke, *In Whose Name? A Public Law Theory of International Adjudication* (Oxford University Press, 2014).

Moreover, an essential basis for the legitimacy of the treaty bodies is that they respect their legal mandate as set out in the respective conventions. The vagueness of the human rights treaty obligations leaves, however, wide discretion to the treaty bodies in their interpretation. What is more, the legal status and powers of treaty bodies are not clearly defined in international law.[8]

In addition to these requirements, it is essential that the treaty bodies protect human rights as set out in the relevant conventions, i.e. a requirement of effectiveness.[9] This means in our context that the complaints procedure should actively be used by individuals; that the complaints are dealt with efficiently; that conventions are interpreted so that the rights are relevant in changing circumstances; and that the findings are implemented by states.

Unlike von Bogdandy and Venzke, I will use the term *accountability* rather than *democracy* as a legitimacy requirement.[10] The reason is that although a normative requirement to a legal system should include democracy, this does not mean that courts – or court-like structures such as the human rights treaty bodies – should be democratic. Their most prominent legitimacy feature is their independence and their power to control national organs in accordance with their legal mandate. Accountability will be discussed both in an international and a national context, i.e. that the treaty bodies may be accountable both to international and national organs. Transparency is one of the conditions for fulfilling requirements of accountability.

A feature that the treaty bodies have in common with human rights courts is that human rights review interferes with what has traditionally been seen as a prerogative of state sovereignty, i.e. the relationship between the state and its population.[11] This may require a balancing of effective human rights protection and respecting national decision making, i.e. the principle of subsidiarity.

Next, account must be taken of the fact that the treaty bodies' findings, unlike international courts, are nonbinding. This means that the treaty

---

[8] G. Ulfstein, 'Treaty bodies and regimes' in D. B. Hollis (ed.), *The Oxford Guide to Treaties* (Oxford University Press, 2012) pp. 428–48.

[9] See Yuval Shany, *Assessing the Effectiveness of International Courts* (Oxford University Press, 2014), Chapter 7.

[10] Bogdandy and Venzke, *In Whose Name? A Public Law Theory of International Adjudication*, 139. See also Chapter 11 in this volume by Andreas Follesdal.

[11] See A. Follesdal, 'The legitimacy deficits of the human rights judiciary: Elements and implications of a normative theory', *Theoretical Inquiries in Law*, 14 (2013), 339–60.

THE HUMAN RIGHTS TREATY BODIES AND CHALLENGES 287

bodies interfere less with national sovereignty – but at the possible expense of their effectiveness. Finally, I will discuss how the individual complaints procedure fits with the other functions of the human rights treaty bodies, i.e. a question of separation of powers in exercising these functions.

My discussion is primarily related to normative legitimacy, i.e. how the treaty bodies fulfil the aforementioned standards. I will generally not focus on sociological legitimacy, i.e. how relevant actors perceive the legitimacy. But I will include some express or anticipated views of states, scholarly debates, and opinions by civil society on particular legitimacy issues, as available.

I will first examine the legitimacy of the human rights treaty bodies in relation to their composition (Section 2); then I discuss their procedures (Section 3); before I move to their substantive decision making (Section 4); the effectiveness (Section 5); and accountability (Section 6); and I finally draw some conclusions (Section 7).

II Composition

The independence and professional qualifications of the members of the treaty bodies are essential for their legitimacy. Because their findings are nonbinding, these features may be even more important than in international courts for states' willingness to implement such findings. Representation of different regions and cultures of the world may also be of special importance because the treaty bodies deal with culturally and politically sensitive matters, such as the status of religious freedom and the freedom of expression.[12]

The human rights conventions have stipulated the required qualifications of the treaty bodies' members and the procedure for their nomination and election. The meeting of the states' parties of the relevant convention is the election body. The members are generally elected in the same manner as in other UN bodies and international courts, and the same issues of political considerations and horse-trading apply.[13] The High Commissioner for Human Rights has earlier concluded that the composition of the human rights treaty bodies has been 'uneven in

---

[12] See, generally, G. Ulfstein, 'Individual complaints' in H. Keller and G. Ulfstein (eds.), *UN Human Rights Treaty Bodies: Law and Legitimacy* (Cambridge University Press, 2012), pp. 73–116, 76–86.

[13] Ibid., 85.

288 GEIR ULFSTEIN

terms of expertise and independence, as well as geographical distribution, representation of the principal legal systems and gender balance'.[14] General Assembly resolution 68/268 on the strengthening of the treaty bodies acknowledges, however, in its preamble that 'the independence and impartiality of members of the human rights treaty bodies is essential for the performance of their duties and responsibilities'.[15]

One aspect particular for the human rights treaty bodies compared to international courts and tribunals is the part-time character of the members' work. This may have implications for the availability of persons, but may also result in a membership comprising more professors, and even government officials, at the expense of national judges. The representation of government officials may compromise the independence of the treaty bodies. It seems that such representation has been limited so that the independence is not severely affected,[16] but it should be avoided completely.

The part-time character of these positions has two other negative effects. The first is that it represents clear limitations on the treaty bodies' capacity to deal with the cases and therefore contributes to the backlog discussed later. Next, the possible unavailability of national judges as members of the treaty bodies may also have the negative effect of insulating these organs from the special skills of judges, such as the expertise to assess evidence when the dealing with individual complaints.

Another special aspect of the treaty bodies is the fact that the members should be competent to exercise all the functions of the treaty bodies, including examination of state reports and the adoption of General Comments on the interpretation of the treaty obligations – which may require both abilities in fact-finding and law-making. The usefulness of including members with different professional backgrounds has been noted.[17] But this should not present insurmountable difficulties in composing a membership that is well suited also for dispute settlement. It would suffice to have enough competent lawyers to ensure the treaty

---

[14] OHCHR, *Concept Paper on the High Commissioner's Proposal for a Unified Standing Treaty Body* (2006), para. 22.

[15] See also *Guidelines on the independence and impartiality of members of the human rights treaty bodies ("the Addis Ababa guidelines")* adopted by the Chairs of the Human Rights Treaty Bodies (2012) http://tbinternet.ohchr.org/_layouts/treatybodyexternal/Download .aspx?symbolno=A/67/222_&Lang=en.

[16] Ulfstein, 'Individual complaints', pp. 80–1.

[17] C. Flinterman, 'The United Nations Human Rights Committee: Some reflections of a former member', *Netherlands Quarterly of Human Rights*, 33 (2015), 4–8, 4.

THE HUMAN RIGHTS TREATY BODIES AND CHALLENGES 289

bodies' credibility in terms of sound legal reasoning. Although the Human Rights Committee has been completely dominated by lawyers, the Convention to Eliminate All Forms of Discrimination against Women (CEDAW) Committee is an example of a treaty body in which the traditionally low proportion of lawyers may have threatened its judicial credibility.[18]

III Procedures

The treaty bodies' handling of individual complaints is generally based on a written procedure, and neither the individual nor the respondent state meet before the treaty body – implying that there is no room for oral interventions. Two exceptions are, however, the Committee for the Elimination of Racial Discrimination and the Committee against Torture, which may invite the complainant as well as the respondent state to appear before the Committees to provide additional information or answer questions.[19] But they are not invited to plead their cases.

Neither do nongovernmental organizations (NGOs) have the right to submit amicus curiae or to be present during the proceedings. This limits both the treaty bodies' ability to fact-finding, their possibilities to insight in relevant domestic law, as well as the transparency of the process.

It may be difficult to change these characteristics of the procedure while preserving the 'equality of arms' because the individual may have more difficulties in traveling to Geneva with a good lawyer than the respondent state – and may also experience obstructions from the state in ensuring necessary travel permissions and obtaining visa from the host state. It has, however, been pointed out that modern technology allows interaction with the parties without their presence, and that complainants are often represented by pro bono lawyers or by NGOs.[20]

Nontransparency is a consequence of the fact that there are no oral proceedings: the treaty bodies go directly to their deliberations about the

---

[18] Ulfstein, 'Individual complaints', pp. 78–7.
[19] ICERD, Rules of Procedure art. 94 para. 5 and CAT, Rules of Procedure, rule 117 para. 4. See G. Kletzel et al., 'Strengthening of the UN treaty bodies, complaint procedures: Elements for a reform agenda from a NGO perspective' in W. A. Schabas and M. C. Bassiouni (eds.), *New Challenges for the UN Human Rights Machinery* (Cambridge: Intersentia, 2011), pp. 193–239, 205.
[20] Ibid., 205–9.

outcome of the case. Although these aspects of the procedure may be acceptable as long as the treaty bodies only adopt nonbinding decisions, they may be seen as arguments against allocating more powers to the treaty bodies, in the form of adopting binding decisions.

The different functions of the treaty bodies have advantages in their quest for effective protection of human rights treaty obligations. The treaty bodies may use their findings in individual cases both in developing their General Comments and as a basis for examination of state reports by the respective states. But the different functions may also present challenges in their possible tension with the ideal of separation of powers. But to the extent that General Comments are not sufficiently based on the treaty bodies' case-law, they may be seen as unjustified legislative acts. They may also unduly prejudice their case by case approach in dealing with individual complaints. The examination of state reports can lead to assessments of the implementation of treaty obligations in concrete situations – which again can prejudge the judicial function of dealing with individual complaints.

IV Substantive Decisions

The treaty bodies' legitimacy depends on the extent to which their activities conform to accepted methods of treaty interpretation. However, they have been criticized for too expansive and dynamic interpretations of the substantive obligations. It may also be discussed whether they should allow states a margin of appreciation in their implementation of treaty obligations. Finally, there has been disagreement about the legal status of the treaty bodies' findings.

If we start with the treaty bodies' style of interpretation, authors have pointed to examples where the treaty bodies allegedly may have gone too far in their interpretation. Kerstin Mechlem refers to General Comments adopted by the Committee on Economic, Social and Cultural Rights (CESCR) on the obligations of international organisations, states' extra-territorial obligations and the concept of 'core obligations'.[21] Urfan Khaliq and Robin Churchill speak of the CESCR's 'quasi-legislative approach to certain issues, notably the rights to adequate housing and water' and that the Human Rights Committee (HRC) with regard to the

---

[21] K. Mechlem, 'Treaty bodies and the interpretation of human rights', *Vanderbilt Journal of Transnational Law*, 42 (2009), 905–47, 931.

right to life has adopted 'an extremely expansive approach, one that encompasses, inter alia, housing, health and nutrition'.[22]

It is difficult to see that the treaty bodies generally apply interpretation methods deviating from the methods used in other parts of international law. The expansion of treaty obligations through effective or dynamic (evolutive) interpretation is at the outset perfectly legal and well advised.[23] But it is a double-edged sword to the extent that states may argue that the treaty bodies do not respect accepted principles for treaty interpretation, and thus that they engage in law-making beyond their mandates.

Such opinions may prevent implementation of treaty bodies' findings in national law. But they may also prevent necessary political and financial support by states. It is therefore of importance for their sociological legitimacy, i.e. how the legitimacy is perceived by states parties, that the treaty bodies in their protection of human rights do not stretch their interpretation of the human rights treaty obligations beyond what is acceptable on the basis of the canons of treaty interpretation. This has also been reflected in General Assembly resolution 68/268 on strengthening of the treaty bodies, stating that the treaty bodies should not create 'new obligations for States parties'.[24]

The treaty bodies – unlike the European Court of Human Rights (ECtHR) – do not seem to allow a margin of appreciation in states' implementation of their treaty obligations.[25] The wide diversity in cultural, religious and political conditions between states at the global level may be an argument both pro and contra the application of a margin of appreciation. It might be difficult to understand why such a margin should only be accepted at the European level, where the diversity is lesser than at the global level. On the other hand, respect for global diversity may have the negative effect of diluted human rights obligations.

It can be argued that a margin of appreciation should be accepted in a community of democratic states, such as in the European context –

---

[22] U. Khaliq and R. Churchill, 'The protection of economic and social rights: A particular challenge?' in H. Keller and G. Ulfstein (eds), *UN Human Rights Treaty Bodies. Law and Legitimacy* (Cambridge University Press, 2012), 199–260, 260.

[23] See, generally, Eirik Bjørge, *The Evolutionary Interpretation of Treaties* (Oxford University Press, 2014).

[24] General Assembly Resolution 68/268, para. 9.

[25] B. Schlütter, 'Aspects of human rights interpretation by the UN treaty bodies', above note 22 at 261–320, 304.

and not at the global level with a number of nondemocratic states. In democratic states the diversity in implementation of human rights presumably are under control of collective decision making by the individuals concerned – admittedly with imperfections. This is not necessarily the case in a global context. Although there are good reasons, based on the principle of subsidiarity, to allow a certain margin of appreciation at the global level with its wide cultural, religious and political diversity, such margin should therefore be tempered by the presence of several undemocratic states in the world.

Practicing a margin of appreciation might also be good policy if the treaty bodies' findings shall be domestically implemented and the supervisory system shall enjoy continued support, rather than fostering antagonism. This is an argument based on the sociological legitimacy of the treaty bodies. But the treaty bodies should not try to establish a global common denominator of what all states might accept, at the expense of effective human rights protection.

Unlike the regional human rights courts, the treaty bodies cannot adopt binding judgements. The legal status of their findings ('Views') has been the subject of debate.[26] The Human Rights Committee stated in its General Comment No. 33 (2008) that the Committee's function is not 'as such, that of a judicial body'. But the reasoning and conclusion of this Comment give an impression of the Views as tantamount to being legally binding.

The International Court of Justice expressed its opinion about the legal status of the HRC's findings in the *Diallo* case (2010). The Court held that it was 'in no way obliged, in the exercise of its judicial functions, to model its own interpretation of the Covenant on that of the Committee'. Furthermore, the ICJ only applied the HRC's practice as support

---

[26] See Raija Hanski and Martin Scheinin, *Leading Cases of the Human Rights Committee* (Turku: Institute for Human Rights, Åbo Akademi University, 2007), p. 23; Manfred Nowak, *U.N. Covenant on Civil and Political Rights: CCPR Commentary* (Kehl: N.P. Engel, 2005), n. 5, XXVII; Henry J. Steiner et al., *International Human Rights in Context: Law, Politics and Morals* (Oxford University Press, 2008), p. 915; Manfred Nowak, et al., *The United Nations Convention against Torture* (Oxford University Press, 2008), p. 777; Sarah Joseph et al., *The International Covenant on Civil and Political Rights: Cases, Materials, and Commentary* (Oxford University Press, 2004), p. 24; Christian Tomuschat, *Human Rights: Between Idealism and Realism* (Oxford University Press, 2008), p. 225; Ulfstein, 'Individual complaints', pp. 92–100 and W. A. Schabas, 'On the binding nature of the findings of the treaty bodies', in W. A. Schabas and M. C. Bassiouni (eds.), *New Challenges for the UN Human Rights Machinery* (Cambridge: Intersentia, 2011), pp. 97–107.

for its own interpretation: '[t]he interpretation above is fully corroborated by the jurisprudence of the Human Rights Committee'. But the Court stated that the HRC's practice should be given 'great weight' because the HRC 'was established specifically to supervise the application of that treaty'. The ICJ also referred to the need for promoting 'the necessary clarity', the 'essential consistency' and 'legal security' for both individuals and states.[27] Thus, although not legally binding, states have an obligation to take the treaty bodies' findings seriously by ascribing them 'great weight'.

The ICJ did not only strike a good balance between acknowledging the nonbinding legal status of the treaty bodies' findings and the need for taking their findings into account. The obligation to attach 'great weight' to the findings has also the benefit of engaging national courts in a dialogue with the treaty bodies, in the sense that they must give reasons for not applying the interpretation authorized by the treaty bodies.[28] Such a 'dialogue' between national courts and the treaty bodies may potentially lead to better informed outcomes, as well as increasing the willingness to implement the findings in ways acceptable to national courts. This can also be seen as an aspect of subsidiarity, by leaving the final say to the national – rather than the international – level. But the nonbinding status of the findings may also lead to less-effective human rights protection, an aspect we now turn to.

V   Effectiveness

The legitimacy of the treaty bodies depends also on their ability to fulfil their mandates, i.e. their effectiveness. The effectiveness of an organisation – or a court or a treaty body – may be defined by its ability to reach its objectives.[29] The effectiveness of human rights treaty bodies should accordingly be assessed on the basis of their ability to ensure human rights protection. But the legitimacy of the treaty bodies depends also, as already explained, on respect for their legal mandate.

The effectiveness of the treaty bodies has to do with how widely they are used, their efficiency in taking decisions, to what extent their decisions are final or may be contradicted by other international decisions,

---

[27] Ahmadou Sadio Diallo (*Republic of Guinea v. Democratic Republic of Congo*), Merits, Judgment [2010] ICJ Rep 639, para. 66.

[28] Ulfstein, 'Individual complaints', 100.

[29] See Shany, *Assessing the Effectiveness of International Courts*, Chapter 1, 13–30.

and the effects of such decisions. The effectiveness of decisions by the treaty bodies may be examined from a legal point of view: to what extent do states comply with their legal obligations to respect such decisions? But it may also be examined in terms of the political effectiveness: do the decisions result in behavioral change beyond the legal obligations, including among actors that are not legal addressees, such as individuals and multinational corporations?[30] I will limit the discussion to the legal aspects, i.e. the question of the treaty bodies' ability to command compliance with their findings.

The individual complaints procedure is not widely used despite its global reach among the ratifying states. The High Commissioner for Human Rights has argued that 'the system is little known outside academic circles, government departments and officials directly interacting with the system, and specialized lawyers and NGOs. The treaty body system is rarely perceived as an accessible and effective mechanism to bring about change.'[31] But the dilemma is that the system is already severely overloaded and that it would collapse if it became widely used by the millions of individuals in states that have accepted the complaints procedure.[32]

The present overload means that there are delays in handling state reports as well as deciding individual complaints.[33] The outcome of the

---

[30] There is an extensive literature on the effectiveness of human rights obligations, but it does not always distinguish between the effects of the conventions and of the activities of the supervising organs. See O. Hathaway, 'Do human rights treaties make a difference?', *The Yale Law Journal*, 111 (2002), 1935–2042, R. Goodman and D. Jinks, 'Measuring the effects of human rights', *European Journal of International Law*, 14 (2003), 171–83; O. Hathaway, 'Testing conventional wisdom', *European Journal of International Law*, 14 (2003), 185–200; E. Neumayer, 'Do international human rights treaties improve respect for human rights?', *Journal of Conflict Resolution*, 49 (2005), 925; E. M. Hafner-Burton and K. Tsutsui, 'Human rights in a globalizing world: The paradox of empty promises', *American Journal of Sociology*, 110 (2005), 1373–1411; Beth A. Simmons, *Mobilizing for Human Rights: International Law in Domestic Politics* (Cambridge University Press, 2009); Ryan Goodman and Derek Jinks, *Socializing States: Promoting Human Rights through International Law* (Oxford University Press, 2013); Emilie M. Hafner-Burton, *Making Human Rights a Reality* (Princeton University Press, 2013); and Thomas Risse et al., *The Persistent Power of Human Rights: From Commitment to Compliance* (Cambridge University Press, 2013).

[31] OHCHR, *Concept Paper on the High Commissioner's Proposal for a Unified Standing Treaty Body*, para. 21.

[32] The High Commissioner has stated that the treaty bodies system 'stands on the verge of drowning in its growing workload' (OHCHR, *Strengthening the United Nations Human Rights Treaty Body System* (2012), 94).

[33] Ibid., 9.

treaty body strengthening process means more resources to the treaty body system. But it will not solve the problems in the long term.[34] What can be done?

The secretariat of the human rights treaty bodies, i.e. the Office of the High Commissioner for Human Rights, has difficulties in serving the increasing number of treaty bodies, which each are expansive in their ambition to protect human rights through examination of state reports, deciding individual complaints and adopting General Comments. Although more meeting time can be allocated to the treaty bodies, there are inherent limitations represented by the part-time character of the members' commitment. And the more meeting time, the more difficult it may become to find the most competent and independent persons.

This means that efficiency is not only a matter of allocating resources, but also of deciding the ambitions and prioritization of the tasks. There has in recent years been an extensive debate about how the European Court of Human Rights (ECtHR) should cope with its immense overload of cases, and it seems that the treaty bodies could have elements to learn from this reform process.

First, the ECtHR has a diversified procedure allowing single judges to declare cases inadmissible if such decision 'can be taken without further examination'.[35] Furthermore, a Committee of three members – instead of a Chamber of seven judges – may by unanimous vote render judgements if the case can be decided on the basis of 'well established caselaw' of the Court.[36] The treaty bodies should also consider a diversity of procedures depending on the characteristics of the cases. It is, however, essential that fundamental procedural guarantees are fulfilled. It is worth mentioning that the Human Rights Committee seems to have questioned the lack of reasoning in the *Achabal* case, which was declared inadmissible by the ECtHR by a committee of three judges.[37]

Second, it has been discussed whether the ECtHR should become more like national constitutional courts in the sense that it should be able to

---

[34] C. Broecker and M. O'Flaherty, 'The outcome of the General Assembly's treaty body strengthening process: An important milestone on a longer journey', *Policy Brief. Universal Rights Group,* June (2014), p. 27.

[35] ECHR, art. 27 (1).   [36] ECHR, art. 28 (1) (b).

[37] *María Cruz Achabal Puertas v. Spain* (1945/2010), CCPR/C/107/D/1945/2010 (2013); 20 IHRR 1013(2013), para. 7.3. See also J. Gerards, 'Inadmissibility decisions of the European Court of Human Rights: A critique of the lack of reasoning', *Human Rights Law Review*, 14 (2014), 148–58, 149.

select its cases.[38] It would, however, seem that the Court comes a long way by its competence to prioritize its cases.[39] A similar system applied to the treaty bodies would mean that they should primarily focus on cases suitable to have precedence effect – in addition to cases on serious breaches of human rights. A focus on cases giving precedence would also conform to the comparable advantages of the treaty bodies. In the absence of oral proceedings their procedure is better suited to interpret the treaty obligations than to give justice based on the facts of individual cases. As argued by Martin Scheinin: the most important function of the treaty bodies may be 'to contribute towards the concretization and evolution of international human rights law.'[40]

An additional challenge is represented by legal fragmentation. It has for long been a concern that international law is increasingly becoming fragmented. This may in the context of the human rights treaty bodies result in three sets of difficulties.[41] One is of a procedural character in the sense that applicants may apply forum shopping, resulting in parallel proceedings in different treaty bodies. Or bring a case before another tribunal although it has already been decided by a tribunal. The increasing number of treaty bodies represents also capacity strains on the OHCHR secretariat, which shall serve all these bodies. The third challenge – which will be addressed now – is the potential for inconsistent and conflicting substantive outcomes. The practice of the different treaty bodies may result in fragmentation within the field of human rights, at the expense of effective human rights protection, and ultimately represent a threat to the international rule of law.

So far, it seems, however, that the practice of the treaty bodies supports each other rather than creating conflicts between different legal rights and obligations. It would therefore seem that at this stage, the multiplicity of human rights treaty bodies from the perspective of protection of human rights and developing a nuanced jurisprudence is generally

---

[38] S. Greer and L. Wildhaber, 'Revisiting the debate about "constitutionalising" the European Court of Human Rights', *Human Rights Law Review*, 12 (2012), 655–87.

[39] Rules of Procedure, Rule 41. See also The Court's Priority Policy: www.echr.coe.int/Documents/Priority_policy_ENG.pdf.

[40] M. Scheinin, 'International mechanisms and procedures for monitoring' in C. Krause and M. Scheinin (eds.), *International Protection of Human Rights: A Textbook* (Åbo Akademi University, Institute for Human Rights, 2009), pp. 601–21, 619.

[41] See L. McGregor, 'The relationship of the UN treaty bodies and regional systems' in S. Sheeran and N. S. Rodley (eds.), *Routledge Handbook of International Human Rights Law* (London: Routledge, 2013), pp. 505–21.

beneficial.[42] Nothing has come out of the High Commissioner's proposal to establish a 'unified standing treaty body'.[43] This means that we will continue to live with the existing number of treaty bodies and may even have further added. The main negative impact is the strain on the capacity and resources of the system. It calls even more for prioritization of the work of the treaty bodies, including in their function of deciding individual complaints.

Finally, the legal effectiveness of decisions by the human rights treaty bodies depends ultimately on their implementation in the domestic legal systems. But available data show that too many states do not respect findings by the treaty bodies.[44] This applies both to findings directed to the respondent state and to the general practice of the treaty bodies. The reason for nonimplementation is partly lack of measures at the disposal for the treaty bodies, but also the difficulties in implementing findings in national law.[45] The response to this failure may either be to provide incentives to relevant states; or to apply enforcement measures; or to grant the treaty bodies powers to adopt binding decisions, perhaps even to establish a World Court of Human Rights. I will address each of these three approaches.

First, an important outcome of the treaty body strengthening process was to increase assistance to states to improve their capacity to fulfil their human rights treaty obligations.[46] But, of course, the outcome of this approach depends on the resources the member states are willing to make available at any given time. And incentives are not useful if domestic authorities – whether they are law-making, executive or judicial – are reluctant to implement the treaty bodies' findings.

Second, the human rights treaty bodies do not have an executive institution like the European Council of Ministers, which shall ensure that judgements of the European Court of Human Rights are implemented in domestic law. There is only the limited pressure represented by the regular examination of state reports by the treaty bodies, and the Universal

---

[42] Ulfstein, 'Individual complaints', p. 111.

[43] OHCHR, *Concept Paper on the High Commissioner's Proposal for a Unified Standing Treaty Body*.

[44] Ulfstein, 'Individual complaints', pp. 104–5.

[45] R. van Alebeek and A. Nollkaemper, 'The legal status of decisions by human rights treaty bodies in national law', in H. Keller and G. Ulfstein (eds.), *UN Human Rights Treaty Bodies. Law and Legitimacy* (Cambridge University Press, 2012), pp. 356–414.

[46] Broecker and O'Flaherty, 'The outcome of the General Assembly's treaty body strengthening process: An important milestone on a longer journey', 20.

Periodic Review (UPR) by the Human Rights Council. This has led the treaty bodies themselves to adopt follow-up measures to put pressure on the states parties to implement the findings.[47]

But the legal power of the treaty bodies to address noncompliance by states parties has been an issue of controversy. A consensus has gradually developed that follow-up procedures could be based on the treaty bodies' implied powers.[48] This is plausible, given the need for effective implementation of the treaty obligations. But in their submissions to the treaty body strengthening process, China stated, for example, that '[f]ollow-up procedures should not burden the States parties with extraneous obligations', while Russia said that '[f]ollow-up procedures have been developed by treaty bodies and are not covered by international treaties. Thus, States parties are under no obligation to work with committees on follow-up procedures'.[49] It is also appropriate here to remind of the outcome General Assembly resolution 68/268 stating that the treaty bodies should not create 'new obligations for states parties'.[50] The Optional Protocol to the CEDAW is, however, an example of a more recent treaty explicitly providing for an obligation for states parties to report on their follow-up on findings by the CEDAW Committee.[51]

Another legitimacy issue related to follow-up measures concerns the separation of powers. The treaty bodies have already three important functions: the examination of state reports, resolving individual complaints, and adoption of General Comments. If the treaty bodies in addition embark on active follow-up measures, this could easily undermine their credibility in the other functions, including their role as organs for dispute settlement. Comparable issues have been discussed in relation to so-called pilot judgements by the European Court of

---

[47] See, e.g., the Human Rights Committee's procedure as reflected in CCPR/113/3, adopted on 29 June 2015.

[48] A. de Zayas, 'Petitions before the United Nations Treaty Bodies: Focus on the Human Right Committee's Optional Protocol Procedure' in G. Alfredsson et al. (eds.), *International Human Rights Monitoring Mechanisms: Essays in Honour of Jacob Th. Möller* (Leiden: Martinus Nijhioff Publishers, 2009), 35–77, 75 and M. Schmidt, 'Follow-up activities by UN human rights treaty bodies and special procedures mechanisms of the Human Rights Council - Recent developments' in G. Alfredsson et al. (eds.), *International Human Rights Monitoring Mechanisms: Essays in Honour of Jacob Th. Möller*, pp. 25–35, 26.

[49] See 'The treaty body strengthening process: Individual submissions by states parties', www.ohchr.org/EN/HRBodies/HRTD/Pages/StatesPartiesSubmissions.aspx.

[50] General Assembly resolution 68/268, para. 9.   [51] CEDAW, article 7(4).

THE HUMAN RIGHTS TREATY BODIES AND CHALLENGES 299

Human Rights, where the Court arguably has entered into aspects of enforcement.[52] Finally, it is a question of prioritization of available resources, and how much can realistically be achieved via follow-up measures. As the High Commissioner states: follow-up procedures are 'resource intensive'.[53]

Should the treaty bodies be empowered to make binding decisions? This would presumably increase the weight of their decisions in domestic legal systems, including in national courts. But this would require that the procedure of dealing with individual complaints – and possibly also the composition of the treaty bodies – became more like an international court. It is also of importance that several states would not be prepared to continue to be parties to the individual complaints procedure if the treaty bodies' findings became binding.[54] This leads to the proposal of establishing a World Court of Human Rights.

A World Court of Human Rights has been proposed by Manfred Nowak and Martin Scheinin.[55] The authors argue that such a World Court is not only feasible. It is also high time to discuss this idea instead of pursuing the discussion on treaty body reform. This would bring human rights on a par with international criminal law, with its International Criminal Court. Philip Alston, on the other hand, argues strongly against this proposal, including its feasibility, the emphasis it places on judicial mechanisms, and distracting attention from more pressing issues.[56]

The focus of this chapter is the treaty bodies, and not the prospects of establishing a World Court of Human Rights. But the discussion about a World Court raises the issue of whether there are limits to the

[52] Nino Tsereteli, *Legal Validity and Legitimacy of the Pilot Judgment Procedure of the European Court of Human Rights* (Oslo: Det juridiske fakultet, Universitetet i Oslo, 2015), 179–98.

[53] OHCHR, *Strengthening the United Nations Human Rights Treaty Body System*, 81.

[54] N. Bernaz, 'Continuing evolution of the United Nations treaty bodies system' in S. Sheeran and N. S. Rodley (eds.), *Routledge Handbook of International Human Rights Law* (London: Routledge, 2013), pp. 707–25.

[55] M. Nowak, 'The need for a World Court of Human Rights', *Human Rights Law Review*, 7 (2007), pp. 251–9; and M. Scheinin, 'The proposed optional protocol to the covenant on economic, social and cultural rights: A blueprint for UN human rights treaty body reform without amending the existing treaties', *Human Rights Law Review*, 6 (2006), 131–42. See also the most recent version: Julia Kozma, Manfred Nowak, and Martin Scheinin, *A World Court of Human Rights - Consolidated Statute and Commentary* (Vienna/Graz: Neuer Wissenschaftlicher Verlag, Studienreihe des Ludwig Boltzmann Instituts fur Menschenrechte, 2010).

[56] P. Alston, 'Against a world court of human rights', *Ethics & International Affairs*, 28 (2014), 197–212.

international judicialization, or even constitutionalization of the international human rights judiciary. Should a few persons be given global powers to determine with binding effect the relationship between a government and its citizens, or would this be too much delegation of power? Or does it depend on the modalities in designing the court and its functions? For example, is there a trade-off between subsidiarity in form (nonbinding decisions) and substance (margin of appreciation), in the sense that binding judgements by a World Court would need to apply such a wide margin of appreciation that we are better served with the existing nonbinding findings of the human rights treaty bodies? Is there a need to strike a balance between the benefits of binding regional judgements at the potential expense of universally consistent practice? Of no less importance is the realism of such as World Court, i.e. its feasibility.

VI Accountability

A general dilemma with international courts and tribunals is how to balance their independence and their accountability. I have already discussed the need for independent and competent membership of the treaty bodies and procedural guarantees to control the decision making. Furthermore, the treaty bodies should be guided by accepted principles of treaty interpretation, both in their substantive and procedural decisions. The question now is whether more accountability control is needed – taking into account the treaty bodies' need for independence in dealing with individual complaints.

Such control may be exercised either at the international or at the national level, or in a combination between the two levels. International control is to some extent exercised by the UN General Assembly, as exemplified by the recent treaty body strengthening process. This is consistent with the fact that the General Assembly is allocated some functions in the human rights conventions. The conventions have been adopted by the Assembly, and it receives annual reports and approves amendments to the conventions. The United Nations also provides the Secretariat for the treaty bodies through the Office of the High Commissioner for Human Rights. It may be argued that the role of the General Assembly is unsatisfactory because it includes states that are nonparties to the conventions. But this is a consequence of seeing these treaties as a matter for the United Nations, not only for the states parties to the respective conventions. It is, however, important to note that the General Assembly cannot instruct the treaty bodies either in procedural or in substantive matters.

The meeting of states parties of the different conventions has presently no other function than to elect members of the treaty bodies. Nothing is explicitly said about the meeting of the states parties' competence to adopt rules for nomination and election of their members, It would, however, seem that the power to elect members should also imply competence to develop rules for the qualifications of members of the treaty bodies and procedures for their nomination and election, as done by the Human Rights Council in their election of experts as special rapporteurs.[57]

The meeting of the parties is the representative organ of states parties to the relevant convention. It could be argued that this would be a suitable organ for the parties to express their opinion about procedural as well as substantive issues raised by the treaty bodies' activities. This seems also to be supported by the Dublin statement during the treaty body strengthening process: 'It is recommended that States, acting multilaterally, consider such reform issues as the enhancement of the role and the potential of Meetings of States parties to the various treaties.'[58] General Assembly resolution 68/268 on strengthening of the treaty bodies system also supports a stronger role for the meeting of states parties in recommending 'the more efficient and effective use of the meetings of States parties, inter alia, by proposing and organizing discussions on matters related to the implementation of each treaty'.[59] But opinions from the meeting of the parties on the substantive interpretation of treaty obligations would easily interfere with the independence of the treaty bodies. Therefore, the meeting of states parties should not express any assessment on such matters. It is also established in the respective conventions that the treaty bodies adopt their own rules of procedures. The meeting of states parties cannot interfere with this prerogative.[60]

---

[57] Human Rights Council Resolution 16/21 Review of the work and functioning of the Human Rights Council (2011), para. 22 http://www.refworld.org/docid/4dc0ff632.html

[58] The Dublin Statement on the Process of Strengthening of the United Nations Human Rights Treaty Body System, para. 19, www2.ohchr.org/english/bodies/HRTD/docs/DublinStatement.pdf.

[59] General Assembly resolution 68/268, para. 7.

[60] See, for example, ICCPR, Article 39 (2).

Let us now turn to national control of the treaty parties. States parties may express their opinion about the treaty bodies' work in connection with the treaty bodies' adoption of General Comments on the proper interpretation and application of the human rights conventions as well as when they are subject to examination of their reports to the respective treaty bodies. They may, of course, also criticize the treaty bodies' decisions in individual cases.

But the fact that treaty bodies' findings on individual complaints, although nonbinding, should be given 'great weight' gives an opportunity for the authorities of states parties – including their courts – to enter into a form of dialogue with the treaty bodies on the content of the treaty obligations. This can be seen as an expression of the principle of subsidiarity in form, i.e. the nonbinding status of the treaty bodies' decisions. I have in addition proposed that the treaty bodies should apply a substantive aspect of subsidiarity through the margin of appreciation.

The nonbinding status of the findings means ultimately that the control rests with the individual states parties. Therefore, the findings of the treaty bodies in cases of individual complaints do not represent an illegitimate interference in state sovereignty or democratic freedom. Instead, the legitimacy problem lies primarily in the fact that the nonbinding character of the findings means less effective protection of human rights treaty obligations.

VII Conclusions

The human rights treaty bodies serve the same functions as formal international courts and tribunals in interpreting and applying international law in complaints against states parties. But four particular features of the treaty bodies stand out in a legitimacy context. First, the substantive scope of their function is the protection of human rights, an essential constitutional value. Second, the treaty bodies face an increasing overload of cases. Third, the findings of the treaty bodies are nonbinding. Finally, the treaty bodies have functions beyond dealing with individual complaints in the form of examining state reports and adopting General Comments. Let us examine these four aspects of the treaty bodies based on the earlier discussion.

First, there is general agreement about the need for protection of human rights. But a difficulty the treaty bodies share with regional human rights courts is that human rights review interferes with what has traditionally been seen as a prerogative of state sovereignty, i.e. the relationship between the state and its population.

I see no difficulty in itself of the treaty bodies applying an effective and a dynamic interpretation of the treaty obligations. This may result in outcomes that could hardly have been foreseen at the time a state ratified the relevant convention. But such interpretation should be seen as an integral part of the treaty bodies' function. I have, however, advocated – on the basis of the principle of subsidiarity – that they should allow states a margin of appreciation in their implementation of the human rights obligations. This is of especial significance given their global ambit. But they must ensure effective protection of human rights and not opt for a common global denominator. Furthermore, the existence of several nondemocratic states parties to the human rights conventions means that the margin of appreciation should be adapted to a global environment different from the context of the European Court of Human Rights. Consequently, the margin should be narrower than in a community consisting of democratic states, which generally respect the rule of law.

Second, the overload of cases is a serious problem for the treaty bodies. This problem may be alleviated by administrative improvements and increased resources. But it is unrealistic that states are willing to provide necessary resources to accommodate a widespread use of the complaints procedure by individuals covered by this procedure. The part-time character of the treaty body members' assignment represents also inherent limitations on the capacity. I have argued that the treaty bodies should consider implementing simplified procedures for cases that do raise difficult legal issues. Furthermore, the treaty bodies should prioritize cases that could serve as important precedent and cases that involve serious breaches of human rights obligations. Lessons could be learnt from the reform process of the European Court of Human Rights.

Third, the nonbinding character of the treaty bodies' findings has admittedly negative effects on the possibility to obtain compliance and is thereby threatening effectiveness as an aspect of legitimacy. On the other hand, the nonbinding status of the findings leaves enough room for national, democratic decision making, while forcing states parties to engage with the practice of the treaty bodies. It is therefore difficult to see that there is an accountability gap, either at the international or the national level.

The nonbinding status means that the quality of the reasoning and decisions becomes even more important than in regular international courts in convincing national authorities on the proper interpretation of the treaty obligations. Furthermore, the legitimacy of the treaty bodies as judicial organs will increase with features that are commonly associated with courts, such as ensuring that members do not have a government function, that a sufficient proportion of the members are lawyers at a high professional level, and that an adequate number of members have background as judges. Both the substantive and procedural quality of the treaty bodies' activities may serve to enhance national willingness to implement the findings, and thereby their effectiveness in protecting human rights. Although a World Court of Human Rights would be more effective in terms of binding dispute settlement, such a Court raises distinct issues of legitimacy and feasibility.

Finally, the combination of the dispute settlement function of the treaty bodies with their other functions may raise additional legitimacy issues. The different functions may have the positive potential of supplementing each other. But there are legal limits to how far the treaty bodies could go in their follow-up measures to ensure national implementation of their findings. Such measures may also stretch the treaty bodies' capacity in a situation where they face an overload of work. But as important as that is, pushing the enforcement function of follow-up measures and the quasi-legislative function of adopting General Comments too far may undermine the separation of powers of the court-like function of the treaty bodies in deciding individual complaints.

PART II

Legitimacy – Cross-Cutting Issues

11

Constitutionalization, Not Democratization

How to Assess the Legitimacy of International Courts

ANDREAS FOLLESDAL

Introduction: The Call for More Democratic International Courts

International courts and tribunals (ICs) are often said to suffer from various legitimacy deficits.[1] Several authors argue that part of the solution is to make them more democratic, by increasing their transparency, accountability, or participation by various audiences. The following discussion focusses on some of these recent insightful contributions, by von Bogdandy and Venzke, Buchanan and Keohane, Gráinne de Búrca, and Nienke Grossman. This chapter considers only the claims concerning democratization made within each of these rich accounts.

We should welcome reasoned use of normative standards to improve flawed institutions. A central methodological concern when bringing normative political theory to bear on ICs is how to best extrapolate established standards of justification. This chapter seeks to assess and improve on some such suggestions that seek to apply normative standards concerning *democracy,* standards originally developed to assess domestic institutions. A benefit of such borrowing is that these standards may be sufficiently independent of the existing international institutions

---

[1] This article was written under the auspices of ERC Advanced Grant 269841 MultiRights – on the Legitimacy of Multi-Level Human Rights Judiciary; and partly supported by the Research Council of Norway through its Centres of Excellence Funding Scheme, project number 223274 – PluriCourts The Legitimacy of the International Judiciary. An earlier version was presented at a Symposium on Legitimacy and International Courts at the Center for International & Comparative Law, University of Baltimore 19 September 2014, at a workshop at the EUI 15 January 2015, and at the Center for Deliberative Democracy, Canberra, 19 October 2016. I am grateful for comments received there and for further detailed comments by Nienke Grossman and Geir Ulfstein.

to allow critical assessment.[2] Yet such innovative use of domestic standards must be appropriate for the peculiar functions and capacities of various ICs, and how each is embedded – in different ways – in complex interdependence with other institutions within a multilevel political and legal order. Several attempts to extend standards of *democracy* to ICs are helpful but fall short in this regard.

The calls for infusion of more democratic values into ICs are mistaken, but understandable. Pleas for more legitimate ICs are especially likely given their increase in numbers, domain and impact on states and individuals. A wide range of ICs such as those of the WTO panels and human rights courts can bolster domestic democratic processes and rule of law.[3] On the other hand, ICs also strike down or challenge domestic decisions that stem from bona fide democratic processes. Such charges have fueled protests against the European Court of Human Rights' criticism of the United Kingdom's denial of prisoners' voting rights,[4] against the Inter-American Court of Human Rights' overruling of Uruguay's amnesty of former autocrats,[5] and protests against investment arbitration rulings in Bolivia and Argentina.[6]

Historically, direct democratic control has seldom been an ideal for any court, domestic or international. With few exceptions, domestic judges are not directly democratically elected. A central rule of law standard is typically that the judiciary should enjoy independence from the legislative and executive branches. As for ICs, states often establish them precisely to obtain some degree of independence from domestic control – including majoritarian democratic influence. WTO panels are set up to ensure that states will do their share in securing common objectives such as freer trade, even contrary to domestic democratic pressure. ICSID investment tribunals and human rights courts help

---

[2] N. Grossman, 'The normative legitimacy of international courts', *Temple Law Review*, 86 (2013), 61–105, 29; L. Meyer and P. Sanklecha (eds.), *Legitimacy, Justice and Public International Law* (Cambridge: Cambridge University Press, 2009), 19.

[3] A. Buchanan and R. O. Keohane, 'The legitimacy of global governance institutions', *Ethics and International Affairs*, 20 (2006), 405–37; A. Moravcsik, 'Is there a "democratic deficit" in world politics? A framework for analysis', *Government and Opposition*, 39 (2004), 336–63.

[4] *Hirst v. The United Kingdom* (No. 2), Reports of Judgments and Decisions 74025/01 (European Court of Human Rights, Grand Chamber).

[5] R. Gargarella, 'In search of democratic justice: What courts should not do: Argentina, 1983–2002', *Democratization*, 10 (2004), 181–97.

[6] Michael Waibel, *The Backlash against Investment Arbitration: Perceptions and Reality*, (Alphen aan den Rijn: Kluwer, 2010).

CONSTITUTIONALIZATION, NOT DEMOCRATIZATION 309

ensure other bodies that the state will stand by its commitments, domestic democratic political pressure notwithstanding.[7] Critics may argue that the concern of the founders to avoid democratic control over ICs is insufficient for the ICs' legitimacy today. Among the grounds for concern are the IC's dynamic interpretation of treaties and the cumbersome revision procedures.[8] Hence several scholars arrive at a diagnosis that flaws of ICs stem from their low democratic quality, and the solution is their 'democratization.'

I shall argue that several insightful contributions that argue for the democratization of ICs often blur important distinctions relevant for institutional assessment and reform. Some conceptual distinctions will enhance the analysis, the standards and the prescriptions and avoid misplaced criticism. Several of the proposed changes may be valuable, though they will not advance democratic institutions of the kind worth having: institutionalized levers in the form of elections based on prior public deliberation, whereby individuals can influence the rules they live by.

Three related issues should be kept distinct to foster constructive discussions and sound extrapolation of normative premises for legitimacy familiar from domestic constitutional thought and political theory. We should distinguish between democratic *institutions* of decision making, the normative *principles* that justify such institutions, and important *features* of such institutions that contribute to their justification, such accountability, participation, or transparency. It is only calls for the first of these – institutions of decision making - that is broadly consistent with scholarship on democracy, and which should be considered *democratication* proper.

The authors considered do not call for democratic legitimation of ICs according to the first sense of democracy – increasing direct or indirect electoral majoritarian control on the basis of prior deliberation. Their recommendations are rather about multipurpose 'building blocks' that are of great value but for several reasons that have little to do with such democratic electoral accountability.

These sound suggestions for institutional reform should not be based on a normative principle of democracy, but instead be justified from a global cosmopolitan constitutionalist perspective. The proposals should

---

[7] Moravcsik, 'Is there a "democratic deficit" in world politics?'
[8] Grossman, 'The normative legitimacy of international courts'.

appeal not to democratic norms or values, but instead to the normative justification that *also* gives us reason to value domestic democratic institutions: The set of institutions we are forced to uphold must treat us all with the respect owed political equals.

To justify these claims, Section I lays out some aspects of a normative theory of *global constitutionalism*. It does not assume democracy as a normative premise, but allows us to develop a theory of democracy, sketched in Section II. It brings normative theory to bear on ICs and other parts of international law by first identifying the reasons we have to value democratic rule, the rule of law and other standards often applied to domestic political and legal orders. Then these reasons are extended to develop standards that primarily apply to the 'global basic structure' as a whole, while other standards may apply to ICs as important components within that structure.

Sections III–V contrast several prominent contributions that seek to bring to bear democratic ideas – mainly normative standards or features – to regional and international institutions, and to ICs in particular. One upshot of these discussions is that to call these standards 'democratic' or aspects of 'democratization' fosters misunderstanding. The use of these terms by several of the authors canvassed is at odds with how these terms are ordinarily used. This is not to deny that several of the calls for institutional changes may be sensible and normatively well supported. The reform proposals may well enhance the legitimacy of ICs, but they seldom recommend standards or institutions that are unique to democratic modes of governance. The normative values justifying their proposals are not helpfully labelled 'democratic'; nor are the institutional arrangements they propose recognizably 'democratic' in the common sense of including both arenas for deliberation and participation and widely dispersed *institutional levers for collective decision making* in the form of political voting rights. This is not to deny that 'democracy' or 'democratic values' is used in other ways by other authors; I shall argue that some such uses are misleading and hinder the formulation and arguments about normative standards of legitimacy.

Finally, the proposals might well enhance the legitimacy of ICs, but for reasons unrelated to democracy: Transparency, accountability and participation may be of value even if they do not lead to more democratic governance of the ICs. Instead, I shall suggest that the reforms are better interpreted as calling for certain kinds of constitutionalization of the combination of international and domestic law, which constitute our 'Global Basic Structure', and of ICs in particular.

The conclusion returns to consider the importance of distinguishing normative standards from institutions and of separating democratic institutions from those that have value for other reasons as well – from a constitutionalist perspective.

I Global Constitutionalism

The main functions of constitutions are to constitute institutions of governance: to establish and limit government power.[9] Written and de facto constitutions typically do so by performing four tasks. They create institutions and curb them, channel their use by laying out their objectives, and specify rules for constitutional change.[10] When authors speak of the 'constitutionalization' of international law, and of international courts in particular, their claims often relate to one or more of these tasks.

A global constitutionalist perspective as understood here includes three distinct elements that pertain to these four functions. I shall suggest that we get a better perspective on the legitimacy deficits of ICs and their resolution by taking global constitutionalism rather than democracy as the overarching framework of interpretation and assessment.

First, this constitutionalist perspective is *global,* not *international.* The object of concern is the 'Global Basic Structure' (GBS) as a whole, which includes much international law and central features of the various domestic constitutional and legal orders.[11] Thus the primary unit of analysis is this multilevel legal order as a whole, rather than international or regional law and institutions in isolation from domestic legal systems.[12]

---

[9] See, e.g., Zachary Elkins et al. (eds.), *The Endurance of National Constitutions* (Cambridge: Cambridge University Press, 2009).

[10] J. Elster, 'Constitution-making in Eastern Europe: Rebuilding the boat in the sea', *Public Administration*, 71 (1993), 167–217; A. Follesdal, *Drafting a European Constitution Challenges and Opportunities*, ConWEB Online – Constitutionalism Web Papers, University of Manchester School of Law. No 4(2002) http://follesdal.net/ms/Follesdal-2002-EU-constit-ecpr-2001.doc, visited on 28 March 2017.

[11] A. Follesdal, 'The distributive justice of a global basic structure: A category mistake?', *Politics, Philosophy and Economics*, 10 (2011), 46–65.

[12] M. Kumm, 'The legitimacy of international law: A constitutionalist framework of analysis', *European Journal of International Law*, 15 (2004), 907–31; M. Kumm, 'The cosmopolitan turn in constitutionalism: On the relationship between constitutionalism in and beyond the state', in J. L. Dunoff and J. P. Trachtman (eds.), *Ruling the World? Constitutionalism, International Law, and Global Governance* (Cambridge: Cambridge University Press, 2009), pp. 257–324.

Second, the global constitutionalist perspective has a particular set of concerns, namely how the institutions of the GBS do and can maintain the four constitutional functions given the complex interdependence among the institutions – which themselves have varying normative legitimacy. Their interdependence raises important challenges on how they are best assessed and changed. To illustrate: consider discussions concerning the role of state consent to jurisdiction for international courts.[13] From this constitutionalist perspective, this is a question about what reasons we have for holding such consent as a standard necessary condition for holding states to international legal obligations, or whether there are other criteria and sources for international law that states should be held to.[14] Such reflection enhances our assessment of other supplementary or alternative candidates for sources of international law, including 'dynamic treaty interpretation', state practice and customary rules – or a future global democratic legislature or general assembly. Another example concerns the role of many ICs as dispute resolution bodies: they may often have important roles in this regard even though some of the states they adjudicate for lack democratic credentials. How to design and assess such ICs are important and very challenging tasks.

The third premise is normative: *normative cosmopolitanism*, which provides standards for assessing such proposed creation of institutions and allocation of authority among them within the global basic structure. For our purposes here, mention of some central features suffices. The normative premise is broadly Kantian: The set of institutions must be justifiable to all subject to them, as political equals. What are the material requirements of institutions that are thus justifiable to all subjects? Leaving details aside, we may think of these as the requirements of normative cosmopolitanism of the GBS. I submit that the GBS as a whole must respect and promote important interests of each, including

A) human rights that protect basic human interests against standard threats.[15]
B) influence over institutions that shape their lives, and
C) protection against domination – i.e. protection against being subject to the arbitrary discretion of others.

---

[13] Grossman, 'The normative legitimacy of international courts'.
[14] Buchanan and Keohane, 'The legitimacy of global governance institutions', 414.
[15] Ibid., 419; Joseph Raz, *The Morality of Freedom* (Oxford: Clarendon Press, 1986).

CONSTITUTIONALIZATION, NOT DEMOCRATIZATION   313

Note that this is *normative*, rather than *institutional* cosmopolitanism.[16] Versions of institutional cosmopolitanism maintain that there should be more global institutions – such as a world parliament, or world courts in more sectors. For normative cosmopolitanism this remains an open but highly contested empirical question: it is not at all obvious that global institutions such as a global parliament, executive or court better satisfies this normative standard than more decentralized institutional structures. Kant famously denied this, due to the high risk of domination by a world government.[17]

A third feature is that the normative standards of normative cosmopolitanism apply to the GBS as a whole, rather than to every institution within it. Thus courts are usually required to interpret and adjudicate existing laws, rather than in every case make judgments that benefit the interests of all parties. It remains an open question whether and how judges – of ICs or at domestic courts – should appeal to normative cosmopolitanism when they interpret existing laws. Such distinctions about the subject of various normative standards are due to the complex division of labour among the institutions, specified by the domestic constitutions and the GBS.

I submit that many authors share several aspects of global constitutionalism as laid out here. For instance, a typical feature of constitutionalisation is to curb or constrain the power of institutions relative to each other. This is central to two topics often described as the 'constitutionalization' of international courts. First, that they have taken on functions that de facto curb the competence of national constitutional organs – i.e. performing the second of the four tasks typically specified by a constitution.[18] Thus judicial review is a mechanism typical of constitutionalism, offering a case of 'non-electoral accountability'.[19] Second, the impact of these ICs be it as mechanisms for dispute resolution or as

---

[16] Or 'moral' rather than 'political', Thomas W. Pogge, *World Poverty and Human Rights* (Cambridge: Polity, 2002).

[17] I. Kant, 'Perpetual peace: A philosophical sketch' in H. Reiss (ed.), *Kant's Political Writings* (Cambridge: Cambridge University Press, 1796), pp. 93–130, 102; ibid.

[18] G. Ulfstein, 'Institutions and competence', in J. Klabbers, et al. (eds.), *The Constitutionalization of International Law* (Oxford: Oxford University Press, 2009), pp. 45–80, 50.

[19] T. Macdonald and K. Macdonald, 'Non-electoral accountability in global politics: Strengthening democratic control within the global garment industry', *European Journal of International Law*, 17(1) (2006), 89–119; *cf.* N. Krisch and B. Kingsbury, 'Introduction: Global governance and global administrative law in the international legal order', *European Journal of International Law*, 17(1) (2006), 1–13.

314   ANDREAS FOLLESDAL

review bodies, raises issues of the extent to which and how these ICs themselves should be curbed and channeled by constitution-like checks or procedural arrangements such as closer scrutiny and control.[20] Three remarks help distinguish this perspective from other uses of 'constitution' and 'constitutionalization.' First, note that this description of global constitutionalism does not include claims that particular normative standards – such as democratic accountability - must be in place for there to be a constitution at all. To the contrary, it seems most conducive for clear normative arguments to grant that authoritarian or nondemocratic states, and arguably the global basic structure, may have a constitution, albeit with grave normative flaws. Note that other authors choose to use these terms differently, to include some (minimal) level of legitimacy in any constitution:

> Our interest, however, as far as it concerns legitimacy to begin with, resides predominantly with the legitimacy of the rules and institutions that make up international law. In other words: *we will presume that the global constitutional order is legitimate, otherwise we would not refer to it as constitutional.* But that does not mean that all its institutions and rules are therefore legitimate.[21]

Second, as this quote shows, some authors appear to hold that only legitimate constitutional orders merit the label 'constitutional.' This may be because they include in the definition of a constitution that it respects and promotes certain procedural or material values or standards – e.g. the rule of law, democratic self-governance, human rights protection or social security.[22] In contrast, the global constitutionalist perspective laid out here holds that a constitution, and the GBS, may serve the four functions, yet the legal order may be normatively deeply illegitimate.

A third implication of this account is that not all forms of constitutionalization are normative improvements. There is not a monotonic

---

[20] Jan Klabbers, et al., *The Constitutionalization of International Law* (Oxford: Oxford University Press, 2009), p. 25.

[21] J. Klabbers, 'Setting the scene' in J. Klabbers et al. (eds.), *The Constitutionalization of International Law* (Oxford: Oxford University Press, 2009), pp. 37–8, my emphasis *cf.* A. von Bogdandy and I. Venzke, '"In whose name?" An investigation of international courts' public authority and its democratic justification', *The European Journal of International Law* (2012), 7–41; J. Weiler, 'The Geology of International Law - Governance, Democracy and Legitimacy', *Zeitschrift für ausländisches öffentliches Recht und Völkerrecht*, 64 (2006), 547–62.

[22] Klabbers, et al., *The Constitutionalization of International Law*, p. 347.

relationship between any institutional changes and particular normative standards. One reason is that the impact of changes in some institutions may have untoward effects on the GBS as a whole; another reason is that some improvements require multiple institutional changes. Consider claims that the WTO system is becoming constitutionalized – whereby GATT norms are given priority over other international and national law. Some observers rightly point out that such 'partial constitutionalisation' may leave large segments of the population worse off.[23]

From the perspective of global constitutionalism many calls to democratize ICs may be interpreted in one of two ways. Some may not want a multilevel system of checks and balances, but rather ensure that *every* influential international institution – such as ICs – has an internal composition, procedures and structure that ensures its long-term pursuit of its objectives. Others may be read as recommending that ICs are *constitutionalized*, guided by normative cosmopolitan standards when determining how their objectives should be specified and how they should be checked. Few of the proposals call for democratization proper, in the central sense of increasing democratic decision making into the ICs.

Some may object to this use of 'democracy' as too narrow: that widespread institutional levers of control are not a necessary condition for calling an institution 'democratic.' We turn to this issue now.

II A Brief Sketch of Democratic Theory

A Three Concepts of Democracy

Many scholars and proponents of democratic rule use the term *democracy* to refer to certain kinds of *institutions for decision making*. These institutions typically include majoritarian electoral control over the decision makers, as well as arenas for deliberation, opportunities for real party competition – and more. A central normative issue of the *legitimacy* of democratic institutions is why those who find themselves outvoted under such democratic rule have a moral obligation to defer to these decisions that they oppose. This understanding of democracy as centrally concerned with institutions that allow and foster majoritarian decision

---

[23] E.-U. Petersmann, 'Welthandelsrecht Als Freiheits – Und Verfassungsordnung', *Zeitschrift für Ausländisches Öffentlicher Recht und Völkerrecht*, (2005), 543.

316   ANDREAS FOLLESDAL

making on the basis of prior public deliberation is standard among political scientists and theorists.[24] Thus Brian Barry held that

> By a democratic procedure I mean a method of determining the content of laws (and other legally binding decisions) such that the preferences of the citizens have some formal connection with the outcome in which each counts equally.[25]

A democratic theorist more known for insistence on the need for public deliberation, Jürgen Habermas's account similarly includes elections in his understanding of democracy:

> It is the formal vote and the actual opinion and will formation of individual voters that together connect the peripheral flows of political communication in civil society and the public sphere with the deliberative decision making of political institutions at the center, thus filtering them into the wider circuitry of deliberative politics.[26]

A similar understanding is also prevalent among many legal scholars. Thus Weiler plausibly claims that

> any functioning notion of democracy ... is based on the ... premise, ... that a majority within a collectivity, a demos, has the authority to bind its individual members, even against their will.[27]

This common use of the term *democracy* should be distinguished from two further, different uses in the literature concerning the legitimacy of ICs.

The second usage occurs when authors blur the distinction between such institutions and the *normative standards* of legitimacy or justice used to assess them – such as normative cosmopolitanism mentioned earlier. Thus they write of 'democratic principles for ... justification',[28]

---

[24] However, it is not shared by all democratic theorists. For instance, John Dryzek in some publications appears to downplay the legal and institutional aspects of electoral control (John Dryzek, *Deliberative Global Politics* [Oxford: Polity Press, 2006]), *cf.* T. Christiano, 'Democratic legitimacy and international institutions' in S. Besson and J. Tasioulas (eds.), *The Philosophy of International Law* (Oxford: Oxford University Press, 2010), pp. 119–38.

[25] B. Barry, 'Is democracy special?', in B. Barry (ed.), *Democracy and Power* (Oxford: Oxford University Press, 1991) pp. 24–60, 25.

[26] J. Habermas, 'Political communication in media society: Does democracy still enjoy an epistemic dimension? The impact of normative theory on empirical research', *Communication Theory*, 16 (2006), 411–26, 418.

[27] Weiler, 'The Geology of International Law - Governance, Democracy and Legitimacy', 548.

[28] von Bogdandy and Venzke, '"In whose name?" An investigation of international courts' public authority and its democratic justification'.

'basic premises of democratic theory',[29] or 'the key values that underlie demands for democracy'.[30]

Defensible normative standards may well justify democratic decision procedures over the alternatives. But these premises should not be labelled 'democratic' lest we conflate the premises and conclusions of important arguments.

A third phenomenon that is sometimes referred to as 'democratic' concerns certain *features* of democratic decision-making institutions, such as accountability, participation and transparency. The relationship is complex. Such features indeed appear crucial if democratic decision making is to be a process based on deliberation, and which yields outcomes that are normatively justifiable. But these components are also valuable for reasons quite unrelated to democratic rule. A wide range of nondemocratic institutional mechanisms provide accountability through checks or review procedures. Their effective functioning require *transparency* about the procedures and outcomes they hold accountable.

It is misleading to label such features as transparency and accountability 'democratic.' That adjective obscures the issues of why and when such features are normatively desired. Neither transparency of decision procedures nor the practice of judicial review become 'democratic' simply because judicial review requires *transparency* concerning how the executive has made a decision. This is not to deny that such review may enable *other* bodies, such as the legislature, to subject the executive to democratic account. Judicial review can thus facilitate the sorts of democratic decision making we have reason to value. But transparency should not be labelled a 'democratic' value.

We now consider several calls to 'democratize' ICs made by some of the convincing and thoughtful theories or perspectives of legitimacy of international law. This chapter considers only claims concerning democratization made within each of these rich accounts, to consider what appear to be their sound conclusions and further challenges. The focus is on how each perspective seeks to extrapolate, translate or transpose 'democratic' norms and standards from similar discussions as regards the legitimacy of domestic law and courts to their international counterparts. Several contributors are clear that they provide *incomplete* accounts of standards of legitimacy. For instance, rule of law standards,

---

[29] Ibid.
[30] Buchanan and Keohane, 'The legitimacy of global governance institutions', 417.

318 ANDREAS FOLLESDAL

human rights or consistency are further necessary conditions. Few if any of the authors claim that these strands are mutually exclusive.[31]

B What Is Democracy, and Why Value It?

What is democratic rule, and what reasons are there to value such modes of collective decision making? Several democratic theorists hold that a central value of democratic majoritarian rule is that it more reliably than alternatives serves to identify or create normatively acceptable decisions.

Consider a fairly standard description of democracy, agreeable to a broad range of democratic theorists.[32] Virtually all modern political systems that are called 'democratic' have a set of *institutionally established procedures*. They

- regulate competition for control over political authority
- on the basis of deliberation
- where nearly all adult citizens are permitted to participate in
- an electoral mechanism where their expressed preferences over alternative candidates determine the outcome,
- in such ways that the government is responsive to the majority or to as many as possible.

There are several normative reasons offered for favouring democratic decision making of alternatives.[33] A distinction between 'effective power' and 'procedural control' elaborated by Amartya Sen helps distinguish and relate the normative standards to democratic and other institutions.

We should differentiate between which effective power individuals have, from the sort of institutional control they enjoy. A person has effective power in this sense insofar as a certain outcome is brought about *because* it is in the person's interest:

---

[31] *cf.* J. E. Nijman and A. Nollkaemper, 'Beyond the Divide' in A. Nollkaemper and J. E. Nijman (eds.), *New Perspectives on the Divide between National and International Law* (Oxford, Oxford University Press, 2007), pp. 341–60; C. Harlow, 'Global administrative law: The quest for principles and values', *European Journal of International Law*, 17 (2006), 187–214, 194.

[32] *cf.* Robert A. Dahl, *Polyarchy: Participation and Opposition* (New Haven, CT: Yale University Press, 1971); Barry, 'Is democracy special?'; T. Christiano, 'An instrumental argument for a human right to democracy', *Philosophy and Public Affairs*, 39 (2011), 142–76, A. Follesdal and S. Hix, 'Why there is a democratic deficit in the EU: A response to Majone and Moravcsik', *Journal of Common Market Studies*, 44 (2006), 533–62.

[33] For an overview, *cf.* T. Christiano, 'Democracy' *Stanford Encyclopedia of Philosophy* (2006), accessed 29 December 2016.

CONSTITUTIONALIZATION, NOT DEMOCRATIZATION 319

> Precisely who exercises the control may be less important than the ability to achieve what we would have chosen. If the streets are cleared of the muggers because we would choose not to be mugged, our freedom is being well served, even though we have not been given control over the choice of whether to be mugged or not.[34]

An individual may enjoy such effective power by means of a trustee, or by legal regulations. In contrast to enjoying such effective power, the person has *procedural control* when she actually has institutional levers to bring about what she prefers, 'actively doing the choosing in the procedure of decision and execution.'[35] What characterises a democracy is that almost all adult individuals have such procedural controls in the form of freedom of expression and association, voting rights, etc.

The normative standards of normative cosmopolitanism outlined earlier helps rank mechanisms that ensure all individuals' effective power over the outcomes. In the domestic setting, such mechanisms are the stuff of a constitution. They may include legal human rights and various constitutional checks and balances such as judicial review – and democratic decision making. Note that a set of institutions as specified by a constitution that satisfies people's interests reasonably well will not necessarily suffice for such forms of effective power to be 'rule by the people'.[36] Democratic rule requires some *procedural controls*, which ensure that individuals are agents. When we claim that the normative case for democratic procedural control is comparative, this means that among sets of institutions, those that include democratic mechanisms provide individuals with more effective power of the kind worth having than alternative sets of institutions.

One argument for majoritarian democracy is that under certain conditions, such democratic accountability mechanisms ensure that the decisions can be trusted to be *more* reliably responsive to the interests of every citizen than are other collective decision-making arrangements.[37]

---

[34] A. K. Sen, 'Well-being, agency and freedom', *Journal of Philosophy*, 82 (1985), 169–221, 210.
[35] Ibid.
[36] E. Erman and A. Follesdal, 'Multiple citizenship: Normative ideals and institutional challenges', *Critical Review of International Social and Political Philosophy*, 15(3) (2012), 279–302; Christian Rostboll, *Deliberative Freedom* (Albany, NY: SUNY Press, 2008), pp. 45–77.
[37] Brian Barry, *Theories of Justice* (Berkeley: University of California Press, 1989); Jürgen Habermas, *Between Facts and Norms* (Cambridge MA: MIT Press, 1996); Thomas M. Scanlon, *What We Owe to Each Other* (Cambridge, MA: Harvard University Press, 1998); John Rawls, *A Theory of Justice* (Cambridge, MA: Harvard University Press, 1971); Christiano, 'An instrumental argument for a human right to democracy';

Disagreements exist concerning which interests of individuals should be protected and promoted to a certain extent. There appear to be at least three distinct reasons to value democratic decision-making institutions.[38]

First, these procedural controls are *intrinsically* justified insofar as they distribute equal shares of political influence among individuals.

Second, democratic levers are instrumentally justified to the extent that they secure several other interests, including the interest in nondomination: to not be subject to the arbitrary will of others;[39] and the interest in protection of basic human interests by means of human rights.[40]

Third, democracy is instrumentally justified insofar as it secures a more just distribution of *other* goods under certain conditions than do nondemocratic procedures:[41] Majority rule ensures an equitable distribution of benefits if the benefits and burdens of the various decisions are roughly equal in weight, and where the chances of being in the majority are roughly equal.[42]

Note that other institutions than democratic rule may secure nondomination and distributive justice – in particular, human rights constraints may safeguard against domination and constrain the distribution of benefits.

Which institutions and features are properly regarded as part of democratic institutions? Several institutional features and conditions must be in place at least to a minimum degree if democratic institutions are to be better than alternative decision procedures. We can identify some such features and conditions by considering why and when democratic institutions provide normatively desirable outcomes. Only under some conditions can we expect democratic institutions to provide a more equal distribution of influence over the shaping of common institutions,

---

Philip Pettit, *Republicanism: A Theory of Freedom and Government* (Oxford: Clarendon Press, 1997), P. Pettit, 'Democracy: Electoral and contestatory' in I. Shapiro and S. Macedo (eds.), *Designing Democratic Institutions* (New York: New York University Press, 2000), pp. 104–44.

[38] E. Erman and A. Follesdal, 'Multiple citizenship: Normative ideals and institutional challenges', *Critical Review of International Social and Political Philosophy*, 15 (2012), 279–302.

[39] Quentin Skinner, *Liberty before Liberalism* (Cambridge: Cambridge University Press, 1998); Pettit, *Republicanism: A Theory of Freedom and Government*; Ian Shapiro, *The State of Democratic Theory*, (Princeton, NJ: Princeton University Press, 2003).

[40] Christiano, 'An instrumental argument for a human right to democracy'.

[41] Amartya Sen and Jean Dréze, *Hunger and Public Action* (Oxford: Oxford University Press, 1990).

[42] Barry, 'Is democracy special?'

CONSTITUTIONALIZATION, NOT DEMOCRATIZATION   321

and of the political decision making within them. In effect, democratic rule secures this by real *competitive elections on the basis of public deliberation*. This includes 'genuine competition by decision-makers for the votes of those who are actually affected by their decisions.'[43] On this view competitive elections are a necessary and crucial condition to make policies and elected officials responsive to the preferences of citizens.[44]

This view must not be confused with the claim that competitive elections are a *sufficient* condition to call the system democratic, and to value it. That would be a 'fallacy of electoralism'.[45] In particular, *arenas for public deliberation* are necessary to shape these preferences. It must also be possible for an opposition to form against the current leadership elites and policy status quo.[46] Constitutionally protected *active opposition parties* and *free media* that can scrutinize their claims are crucial for fact finding, agenda setting and assessments of the effectiveness of alternative policies. Several scholars will include further civil and political rights and require a minimum of rule of law as conditions for when democratic procedural control will promote decisions in accordance with the requirements of normative cosmopolitanism. This account thus agrees with Buchanan and Keohane, that

> Democracy worth aspiring to is more than elections; it includes a complex web of institutions, including a free press and media, an active civil society, and institutions to check abuses of power by administrative agencies and elected officials.[47]

Consider, in particular, the important functions that domestic, independent courts serve on this account.

A judiciary serves several valuable roles on this account, roles that require that the judiciary is not under direct majoritarian democratic control. The following arguments are familiar within a constitutional perspective. An independent judiciary is justified within a complex system of governance with a separation of powers and various checks

---

[43] Shapiro, *The State of Democratic Theory*, 7; cf. Dahl, *Polyarchy: Participation and Opposition*.

[44] G. B. Powell, *Elections as Instruments of Democracy: Majoritarian and Proportional Visions* (New Haven, CT: Yale University Press, 2000).

[45] T. Karl, 'Imposing consent? Electoralism versus democratization in El Salvador' in P. Brake and E. Silva (eds.), *Elections and Democratization in Latin America, 1980–1985* (San Diego: Centre for Iberian and Latin American Studies, University of California at San Diego, 1986) pp. 9–36.

[46] Dahl, *Polyarchy: Participation and Opposition*.

[47] Buchanan and Keohane, 'The legitimacy of global governance institutions', 417.

and balances – where other bodies such as the democratically elected legislature in turn is justified as part of such a larger complex basic structure. A court helps adjudicate according to the democratically decided legislation and is crucial to ensure several of the scope conditions that give us reason to value majoritarian decision procedures. A court also monitors the executive to ensure that the democratically decided decisions are actually carried out. An independent court is also important to uphold a wide range of procedures to ensure the rule of law. Likewise, a court can protect freedom of association and expression, especially for those who oppose the current majority in power. Independent courts are also important to ensure that the majoritarian decisions do not violate the human rights of anyone. This is a perennial risk of majority rule, either due to oversight by the majority or ill will. A further important role of independent courts is to provide public assurance of these requirements, so that the public are assured that the executive, administration and legislature do in fact govern consistent with rule of law standards and human rights.

These comments indicate that the sort of democratic decision making worthy of respect requires more than electoral competition. However, this does not detract from the fact that there is broad overlapping agreement among a wide range of democratic theories that electoral competition is a *necessary* condition for democracy.[48]

Against this background, two ways to bring democratic theory to bear on the GBS in general, and to ICs in particular, appear flawed. Recall that we must consider how the system *as a whole* secures conditions for democratic decision making, and secure checks and balances to reduce the risk of domination and abuse of power. So several institutions must clearly be transparent, and allow participation by affected parties – such as courts, administrative bodies, etc. – may have to secure transparency and participation, and provide arenas for deliberation. However, not every institution within the GBS needs to be democratically accountable or otherwise express 'democratic values.' In particular, such standards do not easily apply to ICs, given that domestic courts by design are not held to democratic standards. Such a case would have to be made, otherwise proponents may commit a 'fallacy of composition', the belief that what holds for some element of the GBS must also hold for it as a whole.

---

[48] Joseph A. Schumpeter, *Capitalism, Socialism and Democracy* (London: Allen and Unwin, 1976); P. Schmitter and T. L. Karl, 'What democracy is . . . and what it is not', *Journal of Democracy*, 2 (1991), 75–88.

For instance, a theory may value democratic forms of governance for both intrinsic and instrumental reasons, yet deny that *every* institution should make decisions by unconstrained majority rule after suitable deliberation. To the contrary, we should heed Philip Pettit's warning against theories of democracy that associate democracy exclusively with the rule of the collective people:

> If the role of democracy is to empower all and only the common, recognizable interests of people, then a very bad way of pursuing that role will be to give over control of government to anything like unconstrained, majority rule.[49]

'Undemocratic' ICs may thus be a valuable part of a legitimate GBS, if that structure as a whole is sufficiently controlled by democratic mechanisms to be legitimate, i.e. it is justifiable toward all affected parties as equals. In particular, ICs may well be legitimate bodies for resolving international disputes even though they are not closely controlled by international or national democratic bodies.

Those who seek to apply democratic theory directly to ICs may still argue that given the lack of a well-functioning GBS with well-developed checks and balances, and in the absence of a global legislature, standards drawn from democratic theory – such as majoritarian accountability – should inform each of the institutions more directly – and in particular, ICs. Such a move still seems unjustified from the point of view of the democratic theory sketched earlier on at least two counts. There is, first, no fundamental presumption for democratic decision-making standards – these institutions are instead justified by empirical claims about the benefits wrought by democratic rule, as measured by the normative standards of normative cosmopolitanism. Second, even that case for democratic rule is constrained: it only holds within a system of checks and balances, constrained by institutions that protect human rights, etc. A quite different and slightly more plausible claim may be to hold that the standards of normative cosmopolitanism may be brought more directly to bear on the design and procedures of ICs, absent a stable and well-developed division of powers within the present GBS. However, this is also a strategy wrought with problems, including the following.

The second mistake is a 'fallacy of accumulation.' A constitutionalist perspective does not assume that any increase in democratic accountability, transparency or other standard of legitimacy, in any part of

---

[49] Pettit, 'Democracy: Electoral and contestatory'.

the GBS, also increases the overall normative legitimacy of the global basic structure. Such a *fallacy of accumulation* ignores the complex interplay among institutions. Accountability, authorization and human rights are important aspects of any theory of legitimate democratic global governance, but they are component parts of a conceptual and normative package.[50] For instance, the quality of *democratic* decisions is not automatically enhanced as soon as one or more of these standards are more satisfied. There are two kinds of problems. First, there is no monotonic relationship between an increase in any of these features and an increase in normative justifiability of the institution they are part of. Increased participation, say, may make the institutions neither more justifiable nor more democratic. Indeed, an increase in one such feature may render the decision procedures *less* legitimate. To move from a dictatorship to include some of those affected in the decision making – but not all – may render the situation worse for those excluded. Thus corporatist arrangements may have untoward effect insofar as only some parties will enjoy actual participation and influence, ignoring or intentionally imposing externalities on the others.[51]

Second, we must distinguish between enhancing legitimacy and enhancing *democratic* legitimacy. To illustrate: there are numerous valuable ways for authorities and agents to be held accountable in politics, by various agents and by various standards.[52] Such checks may be very important to grant individuals *effective power*. Yet increased accountability of a legislature toward an IC, valuable and legitimacy-enhancing as it may be, need not increase *democratic* accountability or legitimacy.[53]

The upshot of this presentation of democratic theory is that there is broad – but not universal – agreement among democratic theorists that something reminiscent of competitive elections or majority rule seem central and possibly necessary (but of course not jointly sufficient) conditions for labelling a decision making procedure 'democratic', and that features such as accountability and transparency need not be tied to

---

[50] Erman and Follesdal, 'Multiple citizenship: Normative ideals and institutional challenges'.
[51] P. C. Schmitter, 'Still the century of corporatism?', *Review of Political Studies*, 36 (1974), 85–131.
[52] Mark Bovens, *The Quest for Responsibility: Accountability and Citizenship in Complex Organizations* (Cambridge: Cambridge University Press, 1998).
[53] R. W. Grant and R. O. Keohane, 'Accountability and abuses of power in world politics', *American Political Science Review*, 99 (2005), 29–43; Buchanan and Keohane, 'The legitimacy of global governance institutions'.

CONSTITUTIONALIZATION, NOT DEMOCRATIZATION · 325

democratic rule for them to have great value. We now turn to consider the claims for democratization of ICs by several important contributions.

III Democracy: Decision-Making Institutions, Not Normative Principles of Justification

We now turn to consider several valuable contributions about how to enhance the legitimacy of ICs. Several authors argue that discussions of the legitimacy of international law must draw on arguments concerning domestic public authorities, wherein democracy is a central requirement. Thus von Bogdandy and Venzke explicitly call for more democratic accountability of ICs. A central issue is 'in whose name' international authorities – such as ICs – govern:

> the central problem in the justification of international courts: in domestic contexts of functioning democracies judicial law-making is embedded in a responsive political system whereas the international level is marked by the absence of a functionally equivalent system.[54]

One of von Bogdandy and Venzke's contributions is to lay out several of the 'functions' of ICs, which underscore the need to consider their legitimacy anew and with great care:

> we identify three more functions beyond dispute settlement. International courts stabilize normative expectations, which include the reassertion of international law's validity and its enforcement; they develop normative expectations and thus make law; and they control and legitimate the authority exercised by others.[55]

The legitimacy of ICs is especially challenged when they – unavoidably – interpret international instruments and in effect make law. They take this task away from 'political-legislative bodies – the most important source of democratic legitimation.' A first response is to weaken this charge. States have knowingly agreed to treaties that the ICs will interpret according to the Vienna convention on the law of treaties.[56] Indeed, several of these treaties were intentionally agreed as 'incomplete contracts',

---

[54] von Bogdandy and Venzke, '"In whose name?" An investigation of international courts' public authority and its democratic justification', 19.

[55] A. von Bogdandy and I. Venzke, 'On the functions of international courts: An appraisal in light of their burgeoning public authority', *Leiden Journal of International Law*, 26 (2013), 49–72, 50.

[56] United Nations, Vienna Convention on the Law of Treaties, United Nations Treaty Series, vol. 1155, p. 331 (1969).

326 ANDREAS FOLLESDAL

charging the IC with the task of filling in gaps too demanding or cumbersome for states to negotiate.[57] Still, a legitimation challenge remains. Von Bogdandy and Venzke claim that it is insufficient for ICs to be embedded among other institutions that are legitimate:

> Nor can they draw sufficient legitimacy from the fact that they form part of the legitimation of public authority exercised by other institutions, be it states or international bureaucracies.

Their solution is that ICs should be related to a 'principle of democracy':

> how does the power of international courts relate to the principle of democracy? In other words, how can the rule of international courts be justified *in accordance with basic premises of democratic theory?*[58]
>
> A multi-dimensional view of international adjudication shows that international courts have overall become institutions that exercise public authority and demand a modus of justification *that lives up to basic premises of democratic legitimacy.*[59]

What is the 'democratic principle' and 'premises' they insist must be drawn upon to justify ICs?

> all aspects of judicial activity need a convincing justification in light of the principle of democracy. Democratic justification is ineluctable for the exercise of any public authority.[60]

This reference to democracy seems best understood as a normative standard of justification, and not democracy as procedural control over decision making. They seek to explore

> how this judicial lawmaking *can be linked* to the values, interests, and opinions of those whom it governs, i.e. its *democratic* credentials.[61]

---

[57] J. Pauwelyn and M. Elsig, 'The politics of treaty interpretation: Variations and explanations across international tribunals' in J. L. Dunoff and M. A. Pollack (eds.), *Interdisciplinary Perspectives on International Law and International Relations: The State of the Art* (Cambridge: Cambridge University Press, 2012), pp. 445–73.

[58] Armin von Bogdandy and Ingo Venzke, *In Whose Name? On the Functions, Authority, and Legitimacy of International Courts* (Oxford: Oxford University Press, 2014), my emphasis.

[59] Above note 49, p. 50, my emphasis.

[60] A. von Bogdandy and I. Venzke, 'On the Democratic Legitimation of International Judicial Lawmaking', *German Law Journal*, 12 (2011), 1341–70, 1343.

[61] A. von Bogdandy and I. Venzke, 'Beyond Dispute: International Judicial Institutions as Lawmakers', *German Law Journal*, 12 (2011), 979–1004, 980, my emphasis.

CONSTITUTIONALIZATION, NOT DEMOCRATIZATION 327

They assume one particular normative theory, reminiscent of normative cosmopolitanism:

> In the Kantian tradition, and this is the best one we have, there is philosophically only one answer to the question: the starting point of *democratic justifications* are the individuals whose freedom shape the judgments, *however indirect and mediated this may be*. In this vein, international adjudication in the postnational constellation should be guided by the idea of world citizenship.[62]

This normative principle of justification should not be labelled 'democratic'. In particular, their specific proposals for institutional reform are not geared toward institutional mechanisms of democratic decision making on the basis of public deliberation:

> it is not our intention to bring the noise and heat of quarrelling political parties into the dignified hearing chambers and shielded deliberation rooms of international courts, to transform them somehow into political assemblies.[63]

Instead, they point to ways that ICs may provide and strengthen democracy-promoting institutions, such as arenas that ensure transparency of reason-giving, and inclusion of affected parties. On occasion they do insist on what appears to be democratic decision making:

> the democratic politicization of a legal order is of such eminent importance for the concept of a constitution that we reject any conception that wholly dispenses with democratic politicization.[64]

Note that the case these authors make for the value of democratic institutions is incomplete. They claim without much evidence that democratic control is 'ineluctable' or inescapable:

> History cautions that not too much confidence should be placed even on the benevolent and enlightened ruler – democracy as a normative foundation is ineluctable.[65]

The bad track record of the alternatives is not sufficient, their claim notwithstanding. One reason to be wary is that the benefits of the authors' favoured democratic theory, that of Habermas, is difficult to assess. They note that Habermas

---

[62] von Bogdandy and Venzke, '"In whose name?" An investigation of international courts' public authority and its democratic justification'.

[63] Ibid.   [64] Ibid., 23.   [65] Ibid., 26.

328   ANDREAS FOLLESDAL

> underlines that domestic constitutional orders have built democratic
> processes of forming public opinion and political will that are hard to
> reproduce (if ever) at the supranational level.[66]

Unfortunately, the quality of deliberative processes required by Habermas's theory is extremely difficult to produce and secure also at the domestic level.

I submit that von Bogdandy and Venzke's case for democratic mechanisms of accountability *as applied to ICs* remain unconvincing. This is not to deny the need for checks against domination by rulers – but democratic accountability mechanisms of this kind are not the obviously best and only solution to enhance the legitimacy of ICs. It is not at all clear how the suggestions of von Bogdandy and Venzke will bring a standard of democratic accountability mechanisms to bear on such ICs. Indeed, the authors agree that there are reasons to be wary of such democratic accountability when it comes to certain ICs. I submit that the case for democratic accountability mechanisms may be weak for a wide range of ICs, for instance, human rights courts and investment tribunals, which are explicitly set up to tie the hands of politicians – including those that are democratically accountable. Thus many critics of investment tribunals do not complain that they lack democratic control, but that the tribunals tie the hands of democratically accountable politicians in ways that undermine rather than promote the general welfare.[67]

Von Bogdandy and Venzke elaborate in helpful ways how ICs are often asked to make, and make, contested decisions including dispute settlement and law development with direct and indirect distributive implications among individuals. Moreover, several ICs have multiple, sometimes competing, objectives, and the objectives of different ICs compete without a common arbiter.[68]

There are different ways of resolving such fragmentation. In all such cases, decisions could be otherwise, and often with repercussions beyond the immediate parties to the dispute. No doubt such contestable impact is

---

[66] Ibid.

[67] Steffen Hindelang and Markus Krajewski, *Shifting Paradigms in International Investment Law: More Balanced, Less Isolated, Increasingly Diversified* (Oxford: Oxford University Press, 2016); Stephan W. Schill, *The Multilateralization of International Investment Law* (Cambridge: Cambridge University Press, 2009).

[68] von Bogdandy and Venzke, '"In whose name?" An investigation of international courts' public authority and its democratic justification', 26.

CONSTITUTIONALIZATION, NOT DEMOCRATIZATION 329

one important reason why some powerful international organizations and their courts – such as the European Union – should be under better democratic control.[69] The authors are right in expressing concern that such authority is somewhat unchecked and to ask how this can be alleviated. However, I submit that the authors move too quickly from normative standards – their Kantian premises of justification among political equals – to the claim that the institutions that must be established should primarily be those that strengthen transparency, inclusion, etc. *because* these serve to enhance institutional democratic decision making over ICs.

Against this argument, I submit that the strengthening of such institutions need not make the overall structure neither more democratic nor more legitimate. Furthermore, it remains an open question whether these changes should be valued because they enable some more democratic control on the basis of public deliberation, or because transparency and other features are necessary for better checks, review and balances. The latter is not justified because they enhance the levers of democratic decision making, but because their overall impact on the GBS within a constitutional perspective best promotes the normative standard of normative cosmopolitanism. Rather than call for more democratization, the latter appears a more fruitful approach: to explore how the multilevel system of institutions can curb, check and guide ICs as part of a legitimate constitutionalization of the GBS.

IV The Subject of Normative Assessment: Every Institution, or the GBS?

Allan Buchanan and Robert Keohane have elaborated a sophisticated conception of legitimacy for international governance institutions, including ICs.[70] Three standards should apply to every institution, and guide their reform:

> First, global governance institutions should enjoy the ongoing consent of democratic states. That is, the democratic accountability channel must function reasonably well. Second, these institutions should satisfy the substantive criteria of minimal moral acceptability, comparative benefit,

---

[69] Follesdal and Hix, 'Why there is a democratic deficit in the EU: A response to Majone and Moravcsik'.

[70] Buchanan and Keohane, 'The legitimacy of global governance institutions', 406 and elsewhere.

330 ANDREAS FOLLESDAL

> and institutional integrity. Third, they should possess the epistemic virtues needed to make credible judgments about whether the three substantive criteria are satisfied and to achieve the ongoing contestation and critical revision of their goals, their terms of accountability, and ultimately their role in a division of labor for the pursuit of global justice, through their interaction with effective external epistemic agents.[71]

The 'minimal moral acceptability' criteria include respect for 'the least controversial human rights.' These three standards combined are a *global* standard in at least two senses. They should be brought to bear on *every* global governance institution: 'it might be hard at present to justify a more extensive set of rights that *all* such institutions are bound to respect.'[72] And the set of standards is crafted so as to reduce contestation based on *disagreements across the globe* on standards of justice and the role of each institution. Thus every institution must respect only 'the least controversial human rights.'

This approach draws together several plausible insights. Yet some comments and comparisons with global constitutionalism are appropriate.

Keohane and Buchanan claim that every IC – as every other global governance institution part of the GBS – should be held to the same three standards. However, there is some inconsistency about this even in the quote, which acknowledges the 'division of labour' among the institutions. From a global constitutionalist perspective, we observe that each institution has different legal competences and different impact in a multilevel, complex interdependent web of institutions. It would thus seem plausible that appropriate criteria of legitimacy for international human rights courts may require compliance with more demanding human rights norms, but more independence from democratically elected domestic authorities, than, say, standards for WTO bodies or investment tribunals, given the nature of the different problems they are set up to address. Indeed, human rights ICs may prevent many human rights violations even if they are only partially complied with and thus score low on 'institutional integrity', whilst the WTO regime may fail to resolve the collective action problems it was set up for if it is not generally complied with. Thus the standards need not be the same – not even among ICs.

Moving to the relationship between their theory and democracy, Buchanan and Keohane claim that this is

---

[71] Ibid., 432–3.   [72] Ibid., 420.

CONSTITUTIONALIZATION, NOT DEMOCRATIZATION   331

a middle ground *between* an increasingly discredited conception of legitimacy that conflates legitimacy with international legality understood as state consent, on the one hand, and the unrealistic view that legitimacy for these institutions requires *the same democratic standards* that are now applied to states, on the other.[73]

In what sense is this complex standard such a 'middle ground'? It is no doubt a third way to conceptualize and defend standards. But it is hardly 'in the middle' between the two others: the former appears to regard states as the ultimate units of normative concern whose consent bind; whilst the latter maintains that individuals' interests are better secured through democratic competitive, deliberative decision-making procedures than by other means. The authors hold that

> Although the standard should not make authorization by a global democracy a necessary condition of legitimacy, it should nonetheless promote the key *values* that underlie demands for democracy.[74]

What are these *values* of democracy? One interpretation is that they are the normative premises that justify democracy, e.g. those of normative cosmopolitanism. Such normative standards of mutual justifiability supports electoral democracy with majority rule in the domestic setting, – supported and constrained by a web of other institutions regulated by a constitution, as sketched in Section II. Yet this is hardly a 'middle ground.' I submit it is rather regarded as a 'common ground', which indicates why we have reason to value state consent – under some conditions – and democratic institutions for decision making – under some conditions. This interpretation fits Buchanan's and Keohane's plausible general strategy for nonideal circumstances:

> Although the standard should not make authorization by a global democracy a necessary condition of legitimacy, it should nonetheless *promote the key values* that underlie demands for democracy.[75]

The upshot is thus that their plausible proposals have little to do with strengthening democratic decision-making institutions directly, but are based on normative premises such as those of global constitutionalism which also support democratic rule.

A third point concerns a problematic assumption of incrementalism: they hold that

---

[73] Ibid., 405, my emphasis.   [74] Ibid., 417, my emphasis.   [75] Ibid., 417.

332   ANDREAS FOLLESDAL

> Our three substantive conditions are best thought of as what Rawls calls "counting principles": the more of them an institution satisfies, and the higher the degree to which it satisfies them, the stronger its claim to legitimacy.[76]

This particular claim suffers from two weaknesses. First, it commits the *fallacy of accumulation*. More opportunities for some parties to contest and critically revise the treaties or the procedures of an IC need not improve their normative quality – rather, this may skew the decisions unfairly. Second, not all increases in 'institutional integrity' will ensure an increase in the legitimacy of the institution, not to mention the set of institutions of the GBS as a whole. That depends crucially on the normative justifiability of the objectives of the treaty. If the objectives of the IC are normatively unsound, an increase in its 'effectiveness' does not ensure increased legitimacy. Consider controversies concerning the patent directive for important medicines. Unless those patent rights allow the poor access to medicines, an IC that ensures secures stricter compliance and hence 'institutional integrity' may well render the regime less legitimate.[77] From a global constitutionalist perspective the complex interdependence of ICs and other international organizations thus merit caution, as does the normative assessment of the system.

V   Democratic Institutions of Decision Making - or Features and Building Blocks Thereof

Gráinne de Búrca and Nienke Grossman share a presumption for democratic legitimacy as an important condition for legitimate modes of governance and government. De Búrca labels nondemocratic institutional arrangements for global governance as 'compensatory'.[78] A better strategy, she argues, is to extend democracy, to

> try to identify its conceptual 'building blocks' with a view to thinking about the possible design of legitimate democracy-oriented governance processes beyond and between states.[79]

---

[76] Ibid., 424.

[77] Médecins Sans Frontières, 'Will the lifeline of affordable medicines for poor countries be cut? Consequences of medicine patenting in India', External Briefing Document (2005), www.msf.fr/sites/www.msf.fr/files/2005-02-01-msf.pdf.

[78] G. de Búrca, 'Developing democracy beyond the state', *Columbia Journal of Transnational Law*, 46 (2008), 221–78.

[79] Ibid., 222.

CONSTITUTIONALIZATION, NOT DEMOCRATIZATION   333

She recommends a 'democracy-striving' approach:

> This approach is built on one particular building-block of democracy, which is the fullest possible participation and representation of those affected, with a view to ensuring the public-oriented nature of the norms and policies made.[80]

Nienke Grossman argues for a similar strategy to increase participation. Under conditions where individuals are subject to ICs engaged in law making, these bodies should satisfy what she regards as a requirement of democracy:

> ... one of the most fundamental 'building block[s] of democracy' – participation by those affected. Participation in the conduct of public affairs is an integral part of democracy.[81]

Note that this interpretation of democracy is difficult to categorize as requiring *majoritarian procedural control* on the basis of public deliberation. It rather seems to focus on one feature of such democratic rule, namely participation or influence. Grossman's interpretation of participation includes some forms of consultation by the IC, but not an institutional lever, which subjects may use to force a change in policies, e.g. by replacing office holders.

Under conditions where domestic democratic decision making is impossible, Grossman argues that several 'building blocks' of democracy should nevertheless be implemented. She agrees with de Búrca that among these building blocks is participation – which includes some form of procedural control:

> Participation not only allows those affected to influence judicial processes, but it also provides opportunities to monitor what is taking place and to utilize mechanisms of control and accountability outside the courthouse. But how does one justify the application of this democratic principle to international institutions and to international courts in particular?[82]

A standard objection to participation as an incremental ideal is the fallacy of accumulation: more participation may make the set of institutions normatively worse. Recall the risks of corporatist arrangements that include some powerful organizations in the decision procedures,

---

[80] Ibid., 221.   [81] Grossman, 'The normative legitimacy of international courts', 87.
[82] Ibid.

334 ANDREAS FOLLESDAL

which leave other affected parties even more disenfranchised and arguably worse off due to their exclusion. Grossman rebuts this concern concerning partial and skewed participation:

> International courts can institutionalize safeguards to address these concerns. They can adopt approaches to limit the type of stakeholder who gets to participate. For example, courts could mandate that nonlitigants apply for some kind of consultative status or preauthorization before a particular dispute resolution system.[83]

Two points of concern merit mention. First, if the point is to ensure that the IC is more impartial or inclusive to reduce biases, it may well be counterproductive to let the IC itself be the gatekeeper. The risk remains that the IC will dismiss arguments that challenge its rulings.

Second, whilst broad participation may have many arguments in its favour, it is misleading to regard its role here as a building block of *democracy*. General if not universal formal opportunities for participation in the decision-making process is clearly important for democratic decision-making institutions. But the focus of de Búrca and Grossman is not democratic decision-making institutions. Rather, they – plausibly – argue that more participation may render certain nondemocratic institutions such as ICs more legitimate. But that does not make the ICs more democratic in the sense of majoritarian decision making; nor is the only value of such increased participation due to its benefits for other democratic processes down the line.

The metaphor of building blocks is apt: there are many other reasons to urge participation that have little to do with democratic decision making. For instance, several constitutional mechanisms such as judicial review of the exercise of democratically accountable power only function insofar as those who may have suffered abuse can lodge complaints. Yet to label these features 'democratic' conveys a view that the contribution of participation in democratic decision making is the general normative standard of justification. The global constitutionalist perspective begs to differ from de Búrca's description of nondemocratic institutional arrangements as 'compensatory'. A constitutionalist approach rejects this: institutions for democratic decision making are but one component of a complex set of institutions that must be assessed in combination.

---

[83] Ibid., 93.

VI Conclusion: Three Concepts of Democracy

In conclusion, recall the three different uses of 'democracy' by various authors who all urge 'democratic' reforms of ICs. None of the contributions have argued for democratization in the standard sense of institutions for majoritarian decision making on the basis of public deliberation. Their many reforms largely appear plausible, but it is misleading to label them 'democratization'. The central use of 'democracy' is as a description of an institutionalized decision process whereby the preference of the majority of the electorate determines the result, on the bases of deliberation, and competition among candidates. Many laments about 'the democratic deficit' of the EU concern precisely this: the lack of institutionalized direct and indirect controls by Union citizens over the regulations and policies of the EU. None of the authors canvassed earlier defend or elaborate on such decision-making institutions that would somehow influence ICs.

A second use of 'democratic premises' is to label certain *institutional features* such as transparency, inclusive deliberative arenas, and accountability mechanisms. These are familiar *components* of well-functioning democratic governance structures. Separately, these components are insufficient for democracy as majoritarian control: For instance, transparency is not sufficient without the ability to replace legislators or executives by voting. Rather, these components must fit together in intricate ways if they are to contribute to the sort of democratic decision making we have reason to value. Second, enhancement of any such component does not reliably enhance the democratic quality or the legitimacy of the global basic structure. Again, this is a matter of how the various institutions with their legal powers and real opportunity spaces interact. Thus, a global constitutionalist perspective or something equivalent is needed, to consider and assess precisely these issues of complex interdependence among several institutions.

Several of these components or building blocks are of value also for quite other reasons than their contribution to democratic majoritarian control. For instance, transparency is important for valuable – albeit nondemocratic – checks and review mechanisms, and to provide public assurance about the authorities' goodwill. Thus there are several reasons to value participation by the broader public, dialogue among courts, and justification according to the standards of the profession including the VCLT rules of interpretation.[84] The recommendations for participation,

---

[84] von Bogdandy and Venzke, '"In whose name?" An investigation of international courts' public authority and its democratic justification', 14.

336   ANDREAS FOLLESDAL

transparency and so forth are plausible and suggest intriguing forms of checks and arenas for participation and contestation. But these components are not first and foremost 'democratic', even though they are used inter alia for democratic rule.

The third sense in which 'democracy' is used in some of these discussions is about the normative standard of *justifiability to all subjects*. This seems inter alia to be the concern when referring to 'democratic premises'[85] and 'the key values that underlie demands for democracy'.[86] On the global constitutionalist account the institutions of the global basic structure as a whole must be justifiable in this way: they must respect, protect and otherwise is *responsive to certain interests* of *all* individuals – at least as well as any institutional alternative. In this way individuals enjoy *effective power* in the sense defined by Sen: An institution may in principle be *justifiable* to a large extent to its subjects even if they exercise few and only indirect formal levers of influence – institutions need not be of democratic decision making in the *first* of these three senses. However, individuals' interest in affecting the institutions they are subject to seems to require some democratic institutions that exercise sufficient control over the complex, multilevel legal and political order.

Note that in the normative tradition developed by Kant and others, justify-*ability* is not enough: such a justification must at least also be publicly available. This requires some public account and justification of principles of legitimacy for the various institutions, and sufficient transparency about how these institutions work and their effects. Only then can the public determine whether the institutions are indeed justify-*able*. Whether all individuals as a matter accept such a justification is a separate matter. For this and other reasons increased transparency is of value *independent of whether there is effective democratic control*: transparency and public reason giving by authorities is necessary for a wide variety of checks and reviews.[87]

Global Constitutionalism of the kind sketched here agrees with the empirical claims that under certain conditions, mechanisms of deliberation combined with competitive elections may be more responsive to the interests of individuals than alternative decision procedures. But individuals may enjoy much effective power also without institutionalized procedural control in the form of democratic procedures.

---

[85] Ibid.
[86] Buchanan and Keohane, 'The legitimacy of global governance institutions', 417.
[87] Above note 78, 27.

International human rights courts are examples: they are partly designed by contracting authoritarian states, staffed by judges some of whom are nominated by autocratic rulers. The norms are reformed by law-making judges – and still they may be justifiable in this sense: such court may help secure some such best interests of individuals, e.g. by limiting the scope for majoritarian legislation and executive rule.

The upshot of these considerations is that the authors considered do not call for *democratic* legitimation of ICs according to the first sense of democracy – increasing direct or indirect electoral majoritarian control. Their recommendations are rather about multipurpose 'building blocks' that are of great value but for several reasons that have little to do with democratic electoral accountability.

The authors surveyed appear to defend their recommendations by appeal to 'democratic values', namely by appeal to normative principles, which give us reason to value democracy in domestic settings. I conclude that is not at all obvious that mechanisms of democratic accountability need to play stronger or more direct roles for ICs. Yet there appear to be good reasons to include such multipurpose 'building blocks' or features such as transparency, inclusion, public debate, etc. However, neither the 'building blocks' nor the normative premises that support democracy should be labelled 'democratic'. Such conflation of important distinctions hinder well-reasoned extrapolation of normative standards from the domestic setting to the global basic structure.

Rather than justify these many sound contributions for institutional reform from a normative principle of democracy, we should base the arguments on the alternative approach laid out earlier. A global constitutionalist perspective helps address several of the contested issues concerning the four functions typically served by constitutions: to create and curb institutions, channel their use by laying out their objectives, and specify rules for changing the de facto constitution. These discussions should not be guided by appeals to democracy, but rather be based on the normative justification that also gives us reason to value democracy: the institutions we must defer to, must treat us all with the respect owed political equals.

12

Democracy, Justice, and the Legitimacy of International Courts

MORTIMER N. S. SELLERS

I Introduction

This chapter will consider whether democracy plays or ever should play a role in measuring or advancing the legitimacy of international courts. "Legitimacy" here signifies the status of being correct according to some external standard or – more specifically – being correct in the light of the most *appropriate* standard for evaluating the practice in question.[1] International courts are legitimate when they meet the external standards that actually apply to them. "Legitimacy," understood in this way, gives rise to two related but not entirely congruent discourses focusing on *actual* or "real" legitimacy on the one hand and *sociological* or "apparent" legitimacy on the other. *Actual* legitimacy is achieved by actually fulfilling the appropriate external standards of legitimacy. *Sociological* legitimacy is achieved by persuading the subjects of an institution or practice to believe or act *as if* a rule or system is legitimate in fact.[2] Reviewing the nature of legitimacy and the purpose of international law will reveal that

[1] See, e.g., M. N. S. Sellers, "The actual validity of law," *American Journal of Jurisprudence*, 37 (1992), 283; Mortimer N. S. Sellers, *Republican Principles in International Law: The Fundamental Requirements of a Just World Order* (London: Palgrave Macmillan, 2006).

[2] For a good recent discussion of Legitimacy, see J. Tasioulas, "The legitimacy of international law" in S. Besson and J. Tasioulas (eds.), *The Philosophy of International Law* (Oxford University Press, 2010) at 97 ff. and A. Buchanan, "The legitimacy of international law" in ibid., at 79 ff. See also Jutta Brunnée and Stephen J. Toope, *Legitimacy and Legality in International Law: An Interactional Account* (Cambridge University Press, 2010); Hilary Charlesworth and Jean-Marc Coicaud (eds.), *Fault Lines of International Legitimacy* (Cambridge University Press, 2010); Lucas H. Meyer (ed.), *Legitimacy, Justice, and Public International Law* (Cambridge University Press, 2009); Jean-Marc Coicaud and Veijo Heiskanen (eds.), *The Legitimacy of International Organizations* (New York: United Nations, 2001); Jean-Marc Coicaud, *Légitimité et politique. Contributions a l'étude, du droit et de la responsabilité politique* (Presses Universitaires de France, 1997); Thomas M. Franck, *The Power of Legitimacy among Nations* (Oxford University Press, 1990).

338

although democracy in its broadest sense is of vital importance to any just world order, democracy plays a small, subsidiary, and almost entirely instrumental role in supporting the legitimacy of international courts.

The usual standard for assessing the actual legitimacy of law and legal institutions is their effectiveness in securing or advancing justice.[3] The *actual* legitimacy of international courts depends on the court's efficacy in advancing justice *in fact*. The *sociological* legitimacy of international courts, in contrast, depends on their subjects *believing* or accepting that the courts advance justice in fact. The second standard often depends on the first because people more readily act as if institutions are legitimate when the institutions in question actually are legitimate in fact. But the obverse is also often true: Institutions really do become more legitimate when they can secure the obedience of those whose actions they purport to coordinate, adjudicate, or rule. Sociological legitimacy is particularly significant whenever *effectiveness* plays a role in the actual legitimacy of international courts. Effective institutions may deserve our support, even when in some other respects they fail to meet the external standards against which we most properly evaluate them.

Democracy plays at best a subsidiary and contingent role in the legitimacy of international courts because democracy has almost no direct connection with justice. Given its majoritarian bias, democratic control over the judiciary may often present a threat to judicial independence and impartiality and therefore to the legitimacy of the judiciary. Democracy's value to judges in international courts arises less from any direct contribution that democracy makes to the *actual* legitimacy of courts, than from the support the illusion of "democracy" may sometimes give to judicial influence and effectiveness. Democracy or the impression of democracy contributes to the legitimacy of international courts when it does so at all, less through any effects that democracy itself may have on justice or judicial procedure than from the indirect support that apparent democracy may give to judicial independence and impartiality, by securing broader public support for judicial decisions that are legitimate on other grounds.

This discussion will make ten primary points: (1) *Legitimacy* signifies conformity to the appropriate external standard. (2) *Democracy* signifies decision making by majority rule. (3) International law strives for legitimacy by claiming to realize international *Justice*, (4) through the *Rule of Law*.

---

[3] See, e.g., Constitution of the United States of America (1787) Preamble. Cf. Declaration of Independence of the United States of America (1776).

340   MORTIMER N. S. SELLERS

(5) The nature of the judicial role therefore depends to a large extent on the structure and legitimacy of the *Legal System* in which the judges find themselves, (6) but above all on *Fidelity* to the basic principles of international law. (7) Democracy threatens both the *Impartiality* and (8) the *Independence* of international courts. (9) Therefore although *Diversity* may bring broader knowledge and experience to the bench, (10) the *Selection* of judges should concentrate primarily on securing just, learned, and independent magistrates. Democracy has many virtues, but maintaining an effective and impartial judiciary is not prominent among them – without some mechanism to secure the moderating virtues of learning, rationality, and fidelity to justice.

II Legitimacy

By "legitimacy" I mean the status of being correct according to the appropriate standard for evaluating the practice in question. "Legitimacy" must be distinguished from "legality," which signifies correctness according to the internal standards proposed by the legal system itself. For example, in discussing international relations, politicians and scholars sometimes argue that invasions, interventions, or other acts of state are "illegal, but legitimate" – signifying that although the acts in question fail to meet one standard (lawfulness), they satisfy some other standard that more properly governs international relations.[4] This is paradoxical because proponents of international law almost always assert that law itself is the standard that ought to govern international relations. But this assertion only applies to law and legal systems that are themselves legitimate, and therefore a source of authority. When legal systems fail this test, their subjects lose their duty and inclination to obey the law.[5]

Public acts can be legitimate, though illegal, if they meet the standards that justify acting illegally, or when the legal system fails to meet the standards that would justify its authority to rule. This has some relevance for international courts, whose primary purpose is usually understood to be deciding all cases "in accordance with international law."[6] Those courts and tribunals that most accurately decide cases in accordance with

---

[4] See, e.g., The Independent International Commission on Kosovo, *The Kosovo Report: Conflict, International Response, Lessons Learned* (Oxford University Press, 2000).
[5] See M. N. S. Sellers, "Law, reason, and emotion," *Archiv für Rechts-und Sozialphilosophie*, 101 (2015), p. 71.
[6] *Statute of the International Court of Justice* at Art. 38.

international law would then be legitimate, according to this standard. Those courts that are less successful in finding and applying international law would be less legitimate. But lawfulness may not always be the best standard by which to measure the legitimacy of international courts. Whether fidelity to law is in fact the most appropriate standard of judicial legitimacy will depend to a large extent on the underlying legitimacy of the legal systems that the judges and courts exist to serve. When the system itself is illegitimate, the duty of judges to apply the law's internal logic in good faith will be significantly reduced.

This necessary recourse to first principles means that courts can be or become legitimate in three ways. First, courts may be legitimate because they faithfully apply and interpret the valid (and therefore legitimate) laws of a legitimate legal system. Second, courts may be legitimate because they disregard or misinterpret the pernicious laws of an illegitimate legal system to make the laws more just and effective. Third, courts may be legitimate because, although the legal system they serve is not fully just or effective, they offer the best available resource for dispute resolution and social coordination, even though they remain flawed and imperfect institutions. Let us call these *systemic* legitimacy, *personal* legitimacy, and *opportunistic* legitimacy. All three of these variants or legitimacy are forms of *actual* legitimacy, but opportunistic legitimacy will often arise from *sociological* legitimacy, when circumstances give rise to de facto obedience that does not necessarily rest on an underlying systemic justification.

It is in the nature of law that it claims to be just.[7] All legal systems make the explicit or implicit claim to be just and are legitimate only to the extent that they actually do so. Given this universal standard of legitimacy for assessing all law and legal systems, evaluating the legitimacy of legal institutions is not particularly difficult. Does this proposed law, law court, or legal institution serve the law's general purpose of justice? If so, then it is legitimate. If not, the law or legal institution's status becomes much more problematic. Courts serve the useful purpose of providing authoritative judgments in disputed cases and decisive interpretations of disputed laws. They gain legitimacy by doing so well, which is to say, by playing their role in a way that ultimately advances substantive justice in the society and legal system that they exist to serve.

---

[7] See M. N. S. Sellers, "The value and purpose of law," *University of Baltimore Law Review*, 33 (2004), 145.

III Democracy

Democracy is a word that has come to have favorable connotations in many communities and therefore lost much of its meaning in ordinary discourse, as different factions alter and misapply the term to advance their own ends. In its central and original sense, "democracy" signifies rule by the majority of the members of a given community, usually through mass votes by large assemblies gathered in *fora* or *agorai* for the purpose of making decisions, as in ancient Greece or Rome. By extension, the use of the word *democracy* has expanded to embrace other values and activities that favor or are supposed to favor the people or popular control, as in the democratic pretensions of the "Deutsche Demokratische Republik" or the "democratic" self-criticism sessions of the Chinese Communist Party. But whichever conception of democracy is in play, democracy, like any other value or procedure, confers legitimacy only to the extent that it is or advances the appropriate standard for the practice in question.

"Democracy" in the broadest and most general sense may sometimes be extended beyond its central meaning as the direct plebiscitary decision making of large public assemblies to the more refined representative "democracy" of the Western republics, to the socialist "democracy" of the old Warsaw Pact, or to the redistributive "democracy" of the Bolivarian Revolution. All these and many other extended conceptions of democracy will only be legitimate to the extent that they meet the appropriate standard for the institutions that they purport to serve. In the case of international courts, both the obvious standard of fidelity to international law, and the deeper and more fundamental standard of fidelity to international justice, have very little direct association with democracy, in any sense of that word. Thus any contribution that democracy makes toward the legitimacy of international law will be oblique and instrumental. Democratic practices and procedures make international courts more legitimate only to the extent that they advance the purposes that justify international courts in the first place.[8]

The most obvious way in which courts could be made to be more democratic would be to subject the judges to popular election or reelection by popular vote. This method of selection is unusual, but does exist in several American states. For example, judges on the Supreme Court of

---

[8] *Cf.* N. Grossman, "The normative legitimacy of international courts," *Temple Law Review*, 86 (2013), 61.

DEMOCRACY, JUSTICE, AND LEGITIMACY 343

the State of Alabama are elected for six-year terms in partisan contested elections.[9] This has the effect of making the court highly responsive to popular opinion in all its decisions and therefore often capricious or unjust.[10] International courts and tribunals sometimes attempt a modified form of judicial elections, in which the States Parties to multilateral treaties vote on the choice of judges, acting in the name of their subjects. For example, the Statute of the International Court of Justice provides that "the members of the court shall be elected by the General Assembly and by the Security Council."[11] As judges are eligible for reelection this makes them responsive to the views of the governments that select them.[12] The doubtful legitimacy of the governments of many states extends to undermine the legitimacy of the judges that they help select.

International courts might also be seen as more "democratic" in a certain sense if their membership were seen to reflect the general composition of international society.[13] For example, the Statute of the International Court of Justice provides that "in the body as a whole the representation of the main forms of civilization and the principal legal systems of the world shall be assured."[14] The implication here is that although judges should be "independent" and "jurisconsults of recognized competence," who are "elected regardless of their nationality,"[15] they should also be collectively familiar with all aspects of the world and its various legal systems and as much as possible "look like" the subjects of their jurisdiction.[16] This representative aspect of the judicial role is almost never presented as primary or decisive, nor is it particularly democratic in the usual sense of that word, but it does reflect a general desire that courts seem to retain a connection with ordinary people – and has a very strong influence on the actual composition of most international courts and tribunals.

---

[9] *Constitution of Alabama*, (1901) Art. VI Section 152.

[10] See, e.g., Roy Moore and John Perry, *So Help Me God: The Ten Commandments, Judicial Tyranny, and the Battle for Religious Freedom* (Los Angeles, CA: WorldNetDaily, 2009) for an example of the reasoning of elected judges, in response to popular prejudice and religious enthusiasm.

[11] *Statute of the International Court of Justice*, Art. 4.1 cf. Art. 8.   [12] Ibid., Art. 13.

[13] For this very oblique form of democracy, see F. Michelman, "The Supreme Court, 1985 Term – Foreword: Traces of Self-Government," *Harvard Law Review*, 100 (1986), 4.

[14] *Statute of the International Court of Justice*, Art. 9.   [15] Ibid., Art. 2.

[16] Cf. Barack Obama, *Remarks by the President on Nominating Judge Sonia Sotomayor to the United States Supreme Court* (26 May 2009).

IV Justice

The two most obvious standards of judicial legitimacy are justice and the rule of law. Although closely connected, these two values are not synonymous, and neither has a very close relationship with democracy, in any usual sense of that word. By "justice" I mean the best disposition of rights and duties, benefits, and burdens in society to serve the collective and individual well-being of all its members.[17] Law is (or claims to be) the set of public rules that realizes justice in practice. Thus international law is, or claims to be, as Henry Wheaton explained it, following Hugo Grotius, Emer de Vattel, and James Madison: "those rules of conduct which reason deduces, as consonant to justice, from the nature of the society existing among independent nations."[18] Such claims may be false, but when they are false, the law loses its legitimacy. International law derives its legitimacy from its claim to realize international justice, and international courts derive their legitimacy from their claim to realize justice through international law.

Although the obvious and standard measure for the legitimacy of any legal system is justice, the same is not as clearly and directly true of judges. The systemic role that judges play within the broader legal system may often make their fidelity to law more important than direct appeals to justice. The great principle of judicial independence was first established in the modern world to constrain the discretion of princes.[19] When James I asserted that his reason and sense of justice were just as good or better than that of any learned judge, Sir Edward Coke responded that the "artificial reason" of judges and the law, acquired by "long study and experience" is more accurate and just than that of the most educated monarch.[20] This became the foundation of the principles of judicial independence and judicial authority that drive the modern rise of international courts and tribunals. Courts base their claims to authority on the supposed knowledge and impartiality of their judges and legal procedures.

---

[17] *Cf.* M. N. S. Sellers, "The justice of international law," *Transnational Legal Theory*, 3 (2012), 297.

[18] Henry Wheaton, *Elements of International Law*, edited by Richard Henry Dana Jr., 8th edition (Boston, 1866) at 20.

[19] *Act of Settlement* (1701). See *The Statutes of the Realm 1695–1701*, vol. 7 (1820) at pp. 636–8.

[20] Sir Edward Coke, *Reports*, XII 64–5.

Justice justifies judges when judges and courts make justice real through their decisions. The greatest problem for international law as for any legal system is how best to clarify the law in practice. The basic principles of international law were settled long ago when Grotius, Vattel, and Wheaton transferred the liberal principles of liberty, equality, and fraternity from individuals to the international community of states.[21] The problem arises in applying these fundamental principles of justice as they express themselves in more specific rules of law. In the absence of an international supreme court, Henry Wheaton found evidence of the law in text writers of authority, treaties, ordinances of particular states, adjudications of international tribunals, in history, and in the written opinions of public officials and jurists.[22] This widely shared method of interpretive specification reappears in the Statute of the International Court of Justice.

The "artificial justice" of the courts provides or should provide the best available approximation and practical application of abstract justice to concrete situations. In most legal systems courts have the support of legislation, codes, elections, and other instruments of practical deliberation that are absent in international society. This makes direct recourse to first principles more necessary, more frequent, and more difficult in international courts and tribunals than is the case in most other systems of law. Courts, whose function it is to decide cases in accordance with international law must look for "evidence" of practices accepted as law and work forward from "the general principles of law recognized by civilized nations."[23] This gives judges in international tribunals a more creative and philosophical role and more intimate relationship with justice than would be appropriate in municipal courts of law.

V The Rule of Law

The concept of the rule of law, or "*imperium legum*," is as often confused and even deliberately misstated in international affairs as it is in much

---

[21] See Emer de Vattel, *Le Droit des Gens ou principes de la loi naturelle appliqués à la conduite et aux affaires des Nations et des Souverains* (Neuchâtel and London, 1758).

[22] Henry Wheaton, *The Elements of International Law*, edited by Richard Henry Dana, Jr. 8th ed., (Boston, 1866).

[23] *Statute of the International Court of Justice,* Art. 38. Wheaton thought that "an almost perpetual succession of treaties" would "go very far toward proving what the law is on a disputed point," above at 21.

legal scholarship.[24] "The rule of law" signifies the effort to limit arbitrary government by law and therefore implies constitutionalism and limited government, constrained to serve justice and the common good.[25] This offers the avenue through which democracy first entered political respectability. A well-constructed polity should include and make use of the people that it rules and harness their knowledge and insights in discovering and developing its laws. Laws established without public consultation will overlook the welfare of those excluded. The "artificial reason" of a just legal system should incorporate the wisdom of the people as a whole to forestall the domination of any particular faction on individual.

The first necessary and inescapable desideratum of the rule of law is an independent judiciary. Judges must be secure and well paid, so that they can apply the law without fear or favor. Judges secure in their salaries and tenure in office, who believe the law to be just, will do their best to uphold law's authority, not least because their own status and prestige depends on the legal system's standing in society. The origins and method of selection of judges, although important, pale in significance next to the importance for judicial effectiveness of the judges' security in office, once chosen. Judges liberated from external control have the opportunity to serve justice and the legal system as duty requires. Subordinated judges, whatever their origins, will serve the interests of those who control their advancement, retention, and salary. Without independent judges, there can be no rule of law.

The effort to restrain arbitrary authority by subjecting power and government to the law requires independent judges. But it also requires the development of other effective deliberative procedures – the institutional checks and balances of enlightened constitutional government.[26] This connects the judiciary in most rule-of-law states with democracy (in its broadest sense) by encouraging deference to laws developed in consultation with the people, often through the participation of elected representative assemblies, or elected executive officers.[27]

---

[24] For a discussion and bibliography see James R. Silkenat, James E. Hickey, Jr., and Peter D. Barenboim (eds.), *The Legal Doctrines of the Rule of Law and Legal State (Rechtsstaat)* (New York: Springer, 2014).

[25] See M. N. S. Sellers, "What is the rule of law and why is it so important?" in ibid, p. 1.

[26] See Mortimer N. S. Sellers, *Republican Principles in International Law: The Fundamental Requirements of a Just World Order* (London: Palgrave Macmillan, 2006).

[27] See Mortimer N.S. Sellers and Tadeusz Tomaszewski (eds.), *The Rule of Law in Comparative Perspective* (New York: Springer, 2010).

DEMOCRACY, JUSTICE, AND LEGITIMACY

Judges interpreting the laws of substantially just legal systems will often implement the decisions of representative legislatures, which bring a useful element of democratic deliberation to the development and clarification of the laws.[28]

This raises the question of where to find deliberative controls in the disorganized and fragmented society of international relations. International actors seeking to regulate their behavior according to international law must look to the "general principles of law recognized by civilized nations."[29] This standard of "civilization" signifies those states and governments that attempt in good faith to implement the rule of law in their domestic and international relations. The conventions, practice, opinions, and judicial decisions of such states have a salience and legitimacy that is absent in the views and decisions of arbitrary and illiberal states and their courts. Thus the legitimacy of international institutions and courts may depend in large part on their association with or derivation from the better-organized institutions of the more legitimate governments of states. Judges selected or reselected by illegitimate state governments fail to achieve legitimacy themselves. Doctrines developed or advanced by arbitrary governments will lack authority in international law.

VI The Judicial Role

The proper role of judges in any legal system depends to a large extent on the nature of the legal system itself. Judges should decide cases "in accordance with international law," only if the international legal system itself is substantially just. To the extent that international law or the international legal system is substantially unjust, judges should strive to correct it. Thus justice remains the ultimate measure of judicial legitimacy, tempered by such rule-of-law virtues as fidelity, impartiality, and independence, all of which play a greater role than democracy both in the actual and in the sociological legitimacy of international courts. Judges should be faithful to the law if the legal system itself is substantially just. Judges should be impartial between the parties. And judges should be independent enough to preserve their capacity for fidelity, impartiality,

---

[28] James Bohman and William Rehg (eds.), *Deliberative Democracy: Essays on Reason and Politics* (Cambridge, MA: MIT Press, 1997). *Cf.* Gregory H. Fox and Brad R. Roth (eds.) *Democratic Governance and International Law* (Cambridge University Press, 2000).

[29] *Statute of the International Court of Justice*, Art. 39 (c).

and justice. The greatest function of democracy is to clarify what the majority of the people want, but the people do not always want justice, and democracy can also be capricious, partial, and deeply unjust.

Hugo Grotius believed the basis of society and therefore of international law to be good faith (*"bona fides"*). Applied to the judicial role, this means that judges should look to the necessary rules of any just society, as discovered by reference first to the considered views of the most civilized states (*"moratiores"*), then to consent, then to practice, as evidence of what the law requires. These standards, reflected and preserved in Article 38 of the Statute of the International Court of Justice, encourage the judicial virtue of fidelity to settled law. Judges owe a measure of deference to previous judicial decisions and the opinions of the most highly qualified publicists that may set them at odds with public opinion or even their own less-considered sense of justice. Legal certainty is itself an element of justice that may justify respect for even poor or mistaken precedents in the interest of stability and justified expectations. Democracy asks the people what they want. Legitimacy demands justice. The two standards do not always coincide.

The judicial virtue of impartiality requires judges to decide cases according to the appropriate legal standard, rather than their own interests or affinities or those of any other party. Democratic decision making (however defined) is not well suited to this purpose. Large groups of people are seldom as impartial or learned or well-trained as experienced judges, which is why the judiciary is necessary. Subjecting judges to elections would make them subordinate to the interests and opinions of the majority at the expense of all others. Defining or selecting judges as the representatives of particular parties or factions in society would encourage them to advance the interests of those groups, against justice and the welfare of society as a whole. Encouraging judges to follow public opinion would undermine their fidelity to law. Thus direct democracy, representative democracy, virtual democracy, and interest-group democracy all share the disadvantage of putting will above judgment. Only deliberative democracy sets out to advance justice, but does so most effectively indirectly, through legislation, rather than directly in the adjudication of particular cases.

The single greatest source of protection for judicial legitimacy is judicial independence. Not all independent judges live up to their duties of justice and impartiality, but without independence judges will never be impartial or legitimate, because subordination will corrupt their decisions. The democratic selection of judges, although often arbitrary

DEMOCRACY, JUSTICE, AND LEGITIMACY 349

and ill-considered, will not necessarily destroy judicial independence or legitimacy, so long as judges serve long terms and cannot be reselected or removed by popular vote. The tenure of judicial offices and personal safety and security of judges and their families are therefore more important to upholding judicial impartiality than their mode of selection. This applies as much to international courts as it does anywhere else. When judicial terms are too short or judges are subject to reselection or removal or are personally insecure, then judicial independence is compromised and with it the impartiality and therefore the legitimacy of the bench.

VII Diversity

The Statute of the International Court of Justice requires that no two of judges on the Court be nationals of the same state[30] and that "the body as a whole" represent "the main forms of civilization and the principle legal systems of the world."[31] This indicates a desire for diversity and representativeness among the judges of the court that does not necessarily advance the Statute's more fundamental commitment that judges have "high moral character" and "recognized competence in international law."[32] Although diversity is not democracy, this emphasis on representation indicates an underlying belief that courts should to some extent mirror those subject to their jurisdiction, even in traits that have no conceivable connection to the learning, temperament, or impartiality that characterize the best judges on any court, international or domestic.

Diversity and representation among judges contribute to the *sociological* legitimacy of international courts by giving as many of the court's subjects as possible the impression that their group and opinions are respected and taken into account by the court and the polity as a whole. This benefit may be entirely unrelated to the actual performance or impartiality of the court in executing its function. Those subject to the jurisdiction of courts may feel comforted and included to see judges that share their contingent (and legally irrelevant) characteristics such as physical appearance, nationality, language, or religion. This benefit of diversity is not necessarily or universally the case. Sometimes judges may gain sociological legitimacy by seeming to be entirely outside all ordinary social categories – dedicated members of a special priesthood or profession like the Roman college of *fetiales*. Yet although it is not particularly

---

[30] *Statute of the International Court of Justice*, Art 3 (1). [31] Ibid., at Art. 9.
[32] Ibid., at Art. 2.

democratic in the most accurate sense of the word, diversity on the bench may sometimes advance a court or tribunal's sociological legitimacy, by making it seem less alien to its subjects.

Diversity on the bench may also advance an international court or tribunal's *actual* legitimacy by bringing insights and sensitivity to judicial deliberation that would otherwise be absent from the decision-making process. Different "forms of civilization" and "legal systems of the world" arise in geographical and cultural settings whose needs and perceptions should be taken into account in realizing international justice. The same is true of differences within society. A court or any other forum of public deliberation on which no women serve will be more likely to overlook the needs and insights of women (for example) than a court on which women are present. A court made up entirely of city-dwellers will overlook the needs and insights of those who live in the countryside. A court of Europeans will overlook or not fully appreciate the circumstances beyond Europe – and so forth. This lack of understanding undermines the *actual* legitimacy of the court. International courts or tribunals whose duty it is to realize justice through international law will be less able to do so if their judges collectively have the same shared narrow background and experiences.

The primary duties of judges to justice and the rule of law precludes a conception of diversity through which judges would be thought to "represent" any particular constituency or group of people. Courts and tribunals with necessarily limited numbers of judges on them will never in any case be able to reflect the full diversity and variety of international society. But it does seem likely that diversity in gender, ethnicity, religion, and other notable markers of origin and geography will advance the sociological and even the actual legitimacy of international courts and tribunals. This seems likely, first, because courts in which judges "look like" the societies they serve may enjoy greater sympathy and compliance, and second, because the different experience and knowledge of judges from varied backgrounds may in fact contribute to the better understanding of the court as a whole, which might otherwise overlook or undervalue important aspects of the case. Diversity is not equivalent to democracy, but it shares with democracy the useful perception that broader participation and input often brings greater accuracy to decisions of any kind.

VIII Selection

The selection of judges plays a significant role in securing the actual legitimacy of courts and tribunals. The primary virtues of judges are impartiality, learning, and fidelity to the law and justice. When selection secures judges who exhibit these characteristics, then the legitimacy of courts in question will increase. Democratic selection is not well suited to this purpose – but apparent representation in the form of actual judicial diversity may bring real benefits to the bench. Monolithic courts will be less well informed than more diverse arrays of judges, making judicial diversity desirable, so long as those selected share a common commitment to impartiality, justice, and the law. This raises the question how to secure such judges, whose presence will do more than anything else to secure both the actual and the sociological legitimacy of international courts.

The most striking limitation of international society is the absence of effective procedures to interpret or enforce the law. "the great question therefore is" – for international society as for any other society – "What combination of powers ... or what form of government, will compel the formation of good and equal laws, an impartial execution, and faithful interpretation of them, so that citizens may constantly enjoy the benefit of them, and be sure of their continuance."[33] International society has well established the fundamental principles and rules of international law and justice in a series of treaties, declarations, and universally respected writings, such as the United Nations Charter, the Universal Declaration of Human Rights, the International Covenant on Civil and Political Rights, and the books of Henry Wheaton and Emer de Vattel. The law is settled, but its interpretation and enforcement remain haphazard and incomplete. The decisions of the International Court of Justice (for example) have no binding force except between the parties and in respect of that particular case.[34]

The current world of international adjudication contains a plethora of international courts and tribunals, asserting simultaneous and often overlapping jurisdiction over all aspects of international law.[35] This makes the selection of courts as much an issue as the selection of judges. International courts and tribunals will have varying degrees of actual and sociological legitimacy, depending on their composition, their prior

---

[33] See John Adams, *A Defence of the Constitutions of Government of the United States of America* (Dilly, 1787) at vol. I, p.128.

[34] *Statute of the International Court of Justice*, Art. 59.

[35] See, e.g., *Fragmentation of International Law: Difficulties arising from the Diversification and Expansion of International Law*. Report of the Study Group of the International Law Commission Finalized by Martti Koskenniemi. General Assembly A/CN.4/L.682 (13 April, 2006).

decisions, their provenance, and their stability, among other factors. Many decisions about international law are made by domestic or regional courts and tribunals, such as the U.S. Supreme Court or the European Court of Justice. These too are players in the competition for international legitimacy and may have better methods of judicial selection and greater legitimate authority than treaty-based international courts and tribunals.

Democracy may sometimes play an indirect role both in the selection of the most appropriate courts to govern international disputes and the legitimacy of the courts themselves, once chosen. Although the direct election of judges tends to undermine judicial independence and legitimacy, judges chosen through the quasi-democratic procedures of liberal representative republics have always enjoyed more actual and sociological legitimacy than those selected through other procedures of appointment.[36] This constitutionalist advantage depends primarily on the security that liberal constitutions guarantee to judges in their tenure in office,[37] but liberal constitutions also usually maintain the checks and balances between the different representatives of the people as they participate in judicial selection.[38] The legitimacy and therefore the authority and effectiveness of international courts and tribunals becomes severely compromised when their tenure of office is too short, or the process that selects judges depends too directly on the participation of the undemocratic and illiberal (and therefore illegitimate and unjust) governments of poorly constituted states.

IX Conclusion

Democracy plays at best an indirect and supporting role in measuring or advancing the legitimacy of international courts and tribunals. The more appropriate standard of legitimacy for international courts arises from their effective advancement of international law and justice. This does not mean that democracy in its broadest sense is not of vital importance to any just world order, but rather that the requisite virtues of judges transcend and sometimes supersede democracy. Judges should

---

[36] See Philip Pettit, *Republicanism: A Theory of Freedom and Government* (Oxford University Press, 1997).
[37] "Quamdiu se bene gesserint" or "during good behavior" according to the locution of the *Constitution of the United States* (1787), Art. III, sec. 1.
[38] E.g. Ibid., Art. II, sec. 2.

be learned, independent, impartial, and just – all attributes more or less unconnected with democracy. Democracy plays a role only inasmuch as the spirit of democracy reinforces an equal concern for all those subject to the law, which may have implications for the selection and diversity of judges to serve on international courts and tribunals. Justice is the standard against which the world measures the legitimacy of international law and the courts that support it. Justice depends on respecting the dignity, liberty, and interests of all persons and peoples – not just the majority or most powerful among them.

Judges should be the servants of the law and justice, and their legitimacy arises from their effectiveness in fulfilling this function. Democracy is not in any of its forms a direct or particularly useful source of judicial legitimacy, although it may in some cases be helpful identifying or developing the law. Although the claim or illusion of "democracy" may perhaps at times serve a useful purpose in encouraging support for judges and courts, helping to enhance their effectiveness and independence and therefore their legitimacy, this is at best an indirect benefit. The primary value of "democracy" to the legitimacy of international courts is the benefit that the word itself has in reminding judges that they serve all of society – not only the elites that train and select them. Democracy in international courts should be less a process than a principle – the belief that every state, society, and person should matter to judges, as they fight to maintain the just and impartial *imperium* of the international rule of law.

13

Stronger Together? Legitimacy and Effectiveness of International Courts as Mutually Reinforcing or Undermining Notions

YUVAL SHANY*

I Introduction

Legitimacy and effectiveness are two key conceptual frameworks for evaluating social institutions, including judicial institutions. At the international level, attaining either judicial legitimacy or judicial effectiveness is particularly challenging: International institutions typically lack both the kind of democratic legitimation possessed by domestic institutions in liberal democracies[1] and the strong law-enforcement facilities available at the domestic level in 'rule of law' states.[2] Given these structural deficiencies, international courts may need to resort to supplementary legitimacy-enhancing and effectiveness-bolstering factors to perform their functions in a satisfactory manner and to realize the expectations attendant to their operations. Arguably, such legitimacy-enhancing and effectiveness-bolstering factors tend to operate in a mutually reinforcing manner: A more legitimate international court may function more effectively, and a more effective international court may be deemed more legitimate. Still, at times, legitimacy-detracting and effectiveness-decreasing factors may operate in a mutually undermining manner, judicial illegitimacy producing judicial ineffectiveness and vice versa.

---

* Hersch Lauterpacht Chair in Public International Law, The Hebrew University of Jerusalem. I thank the editors of this volume and participants in the 2014 Baltimore Symposium on Legitimacy and International Courts for their excellent comments and suggestions.

[1] See, e.g., R. Wolfrum, 'Legitimacy of international law from a legal perspective: Some introductory considerations' in R. Wolfrum and V. Roben (eds.), *Legitimacy in International Law* (Berlin, 2008), 1, 3–4.

[2] See, e.g., A. Thompson, 'Coercive enforcement of international law' in J. L. Dunoff and M. A. Pollack (eds.), *Interdisciplinary Perspectives on International Law and International Relations: A State of the Art* (New York: Cambridge University Press, 2013), 502, 504.

STRONGER TOGETHER? 355

This chapter examines the relationship between judicial legitimacy and judicial effectiveness, as applied to international courts, and explores, in particular, their mutually reinforcing or mutually undermining attributes. Following these introductory remarks, Part II defines and discusses the concepts of judicial legitimacy and judicial effectiveness and examines their common and different constitutive elements. Part III then explores possible interactions between the said two notions, which may affect their interrelated implementation in concrete situations, using a number of examples from the case law of international courts. Part IV concludes.

II Defining Legitimacy and Effectiveness

A Aspects of Judicial Legitimacy

There is an abundance of philosophical, social science and legal literature that wrestles with alternative definitions of judicial legitimacy and effectiveness.[3] With respect to legitimacy, it is possible to identify two main approaches in the literature: sociological (or descriptive) and normative legitimacy.[4] A sociological approach to legitimacy investigates whether the relevant judicial institutions are in fact regarded as authoritative by their relevant constituencies, and a normative approach explores whether they should be regarded as authoritative (or whether their authority is justified). In both cases, the perspective adopted is an external one – that is, how relevant constituencies perceive or should perceive the authority of courts. Furthermore, both approaches have a certain normative component. Under normative legitimacy, one asks directly whether the

---

[3] See, e.g., E. Rasmusen, 'Judicial legitimacy as a repeated game', *Journal of Law, Economics, & Organization*, 10 (1994) 63; Aharon Barak, *The Judge in a Democracy* (Princeton University Press, 2006), pp. 272–3; G. C. Pingree, 'Where lies the emperor's robe – An inquiry into the problem of judicial legitimacy', *Oregon Law Review*, 87 (2007), 1095; N. Huls, M. Adams, and J. Bomhoff (eds.), *The Legitimacy of Highest Courts' Rulings: Judicial Deliberations and Beyond* (The Hague, 2009); N. Grossman, 'Legitimacy and international adjudicative bodies', *George Washington International Law Review*, 41 (2009), 107, 115 *et* seq; Gerald N. Rosenberg, *The Hollow Hope: Can Courts Bring about Social Change?* (Chicago: University of Chicago Press, 1991), pp. 21–30; Elaine Mak, *Judicial Decision-Making in a Globalized World* (Oxford University Press, 2013), pp. 232–3; Kenneth W. Dam, *The Law Growth Nexus: The Rule of Law and Economic Developments* (Washington DC: The Brookings Institution, 2006), pp. 93–103.

[4] See, e.g., C. Thornhill and S. Ashenden, 'Introduction: Legality and legitimacy – between political theory and theoretical sociology' in C. Thornhill and S. Ashenden (eds.), *Legality and Legitimacy: Normative and Sociological Approaches* (Baden-Baden, 2010), pp. 7–12.

authority of courts should be accepted, and under sociological legitimacy, one asks whether the authority of courts has in fact been accepted – a question that, in turn, revolves around subjective perceptions of normativity. Relevant constituencies are likely to support and accept an institution exercising public authority if they believe that its exercise of power is normatively justified. Hence, one would expect to find a correlation between obedience to international court decisions and the prevalence of justifications of their authority.[5] In any event, the discourse around judicial legitimacy under both approaches is intimately linked to the concept of authority – a notion that pertains to the social force or power that generates obedience or, where relevant, generates support and acceptance of public institutions. Significantly, the concept of legitimacy involves support or acceptance of authority that is independent of the relevant constituency's support for any specific decision or policy the relevant institutions adopt (this type of support of authority is sometimes referred to as 'diffuse support').[6] It has been further suggested in the theoretic literature on judicial legitimacy that the power to generate obedience on the basis of legitimate authority is a form of motivation to obey, situated on a spectrum of social forces that influence the conduct and views of members of social polities spanning between coercion and persuasion (although the distinction between the different motivations to obey or support decisions is hardly clear cut).[7]

When discussing the justifications underlying the legitimacy of international courts, a few factors stand out as particularly challenging when compared to the justifications of similar factors involving national courts. Applying Weber's legitimating criteria of rational, traditional

---

[5] *Cf.* A. J. Simmons, 'Political obligation and authority' in G. Adams and M. Berzonsky (eds.), *The Blackwell Guide to Social and Political Philosophy* (Malden MA: Blackwell, 2008), p. 17, 19 (discussing the relationship between the legitimacy of states and the duty of obedience to their authority). Or Bassok also claims that the existence of widespread support of a court bolsters the normative case for accepting its authority. Or Bassok, 'The Supreme Court's New Source of Legitimacy', *University of Pennsylvania Journal of Constitutional Law*, 16 (2013), 153, 155–6.

[6] See, e.g., T. S. Clark, in Bruce Peabody (ed.), *The Politics of Judicial Independence: Courts, Politics and the Public* (Baltimore: Johns Hopkins University Press, 2011), pp. 123, 125; David Easton, *A Systems Analysis of Political Life* (New York: Wiley, 1965), p. 278.

[7] I. Venzke, 'Between power and persuasion: On international institutions' authority in making law', *Transnational Legal Theory*, 4(3) (2013), 354. See also D. Bodansky, 'Legitimacy in international law and international relations' in J. L. Dunoff and M. A. Pollack (eds.), *Interdisciplinary Perspectives on International Law and International Relations: The State of the Art* (New York: Cambridge University Press, 2013), pp. 321, 326.

and charismatic authority[8] to international courts, one may find skepticism directed at the rational nature of certain norms of international law (e.g., opaque rules of customary international law) and at whether decisions issued by international courts pursuant to such norms or taken outside their precise scope of application fall under a neat pattern of legal rationality.[9] Furthermore, the limited 'track record' of international courts in obtaining judgment-obedience from state parties (particularly strong states and rogue states) and the relative obscurity of the judges sitting on these courts undermine their traditional and charismatic authority.[10] Hence, whereas domestic courts derive much of their authority from the widespread acceptance of the rationality of domestic law, the tradition of obeying court decisions and the personal charisma of certain notable judges, international courts have fewer legitimating assets to rely on.

A useful taxonomy, which may further help in elucidating differences between the legitimacy of international courts and that of national courts, is the distinction between source, process and outcome legitimacy. Acceptance of a court's legal authority is influenced by perceptions of the legitimacy of the source of its legal power, the processes it deploys in exercising legal power and the overall outcomes it produces.[11] Thus, if an international court had been established by an competent body – a group of states or an organ of an international organization, such as the Security Council – in a manner that is fair, proper and lawful – the court is invested with an initial source legitimacy capital, which allows it to legitimize its own operations and those of other international actors whose conduct it reviews.[12] Further legitimacy capital accrues to the court by the very designation of the adjudicative institution as an 'international court', with all the symbolism attendant

---

[8] Max Weber, *The Theory of Social and Economic Organization* (New York: The Free Press, 1947), p. 328.

[9] See, e.g., W. G. Werner, 'The politics of expertise: Applying paradoxes of scientific expertise to international law' in M. Ambrus et al. (eds.), *The Role of 'Experts' in International and European Decision-Making Processes: Advisors, Decision Makers or Irrelevant Actors* (Cambridge University Press, 2014), pp. 44, 56.

[10] See, e.g., Daniel Terris, Cesare P. R. Romano, and Leigh Swigart, *The International Judge: An Introduction to the Men and Women Who Decide the World's Cases* (Waltham MA: Brandeis University Press, 2007), xii. See also Joost Pauwelyn's contribution to this volume, Chapter 8.

[11] See, e.g., Wolfrum, above note 1, at 6.

[12] See, e.g., Yuval Shany, *Assessing the Effectiveness of International Courts* (Oxford University Press, 2014), pp. 145–7.

thereto,[13] and by its integration into the structures of international governance (especially in areas where international governance enjoys a 'halo effect', such as human rights and international criminal law).[14] Still, the initial legitimacy capital of some international courts may be depreciated by the low levels of legitimacy held by the international institutions with which international courts are associated. Such institutions are sometimes viewed, especially in the eyes of constituencies deeply skeptical of the project of global governance, as having a dubious pedigree and a low quality of performance[15]. Allegations of politicized or ineffective judicial processes and outcomes might further erode the legitimacy of international courts, when compared to the well-established and relatively efficient judicial processes taking place before national courts in liberal democracies, and to the acceptance by influential domestic constituencies of the fairness and justice of their outcomes and of the system of governance to which they belong.[16] To be sure, additional structural factors may affect the legitimacy capital held by any given international court, such as the professional expertise or independence of its judges, the acceptance of the relevant court's jurisdiction by key states, its actual level of utilization and perceptions about the very necessity of creating it.[17]

Of the three aforementioned legitimacy categories, outcome legitimacy presents a particular challenge for our understanding of judicial legitimacy, as unlike the other two categories of legitimacy aspects, it is not content independent: While source and process legitimacy are evaluated regardless of whether one supports or objects to any judicial decision, outcome legitimacy evaluation involves an assessment of the compatibility

---

[13] It is interesting to note that the drafters of the WTO Dispute Settlement Understanding consciously avoided using the term 'court' for the permanent adjudicative forum they created, opting instead for the less symbolically laden title of 'Appellate Body'. See, e.g., J. H. H. Weiler, 'The Rule of lawyers and the ethos of diplomats: Reflections on the internal and external legitimacy of WTO dispute settlement' in R. B. Porter et al. (eds.), *Efficiency, Equity and Legitimacy* (Washington DC: The Brookings Institution, 2001), 334, 343.

[14] Shany, above note 12, at 146.

[15] See e.g., A. von Bogdandy, P. Dann, and M. Goldman, 'Developing the publicness of public international law: Towards a legal framework for global governance activities' in A. von Bogdandy et al. (eds.), *The Exercise of Public Authority by International Institutions: Advancing International Institutional Law* (Heidelberg: Springer, 2010), pp. 3, 9.

[16] See, e.g., E. Benvenisti and G. Downs, 'Prospects for the increased independence of international courts' in A. von Bogdandy and I. Venzke (eds.), *International Judicial Lawmaking* (Heidelberg: Springer, 2012), pp. 99, 123–4.

[17] Shany, above note 12, at 148, 153–4. See also Anastasia Telesetsky's contribution to this volume, Chapter 7.

STRONGER TOGETHER? 359

of judicial decisions, with applicable legal norms and substantive standards of justice. For example, the ICTY and ICTR case law on the doctrine of Joint Criminal Enterprise[18] has been criticized both for its low degree of compatibility with legal precedent and for standing in tension with basic notions of criminal responsibility,[19] leading to challenges directed against the legitimacy of parts of the jurisprudence of the two ad hoc tribunals. Note, however, that source, process and outcome legitimacy all constitute building blocks of institutional legitimacy, and that, as a result, strength in one legitimacy aspect may compensate for weakness in another aspect. Hence, a 'healthy' international court, properly established and generally deemed to be operating pursuant to a fair procedure can most probably withstand legitimacy challenges directed against a few misguided decisions. But if key decisions issued by the tribunals are viewed as lacking in legal foundation or grossly unjust, the legitimacy of the court may suffer badly, especially if such 'blunders' occur on a chronic basis.[20] Furthermore, the aftermath of the *South West Africa*[21] and *Nicaragua*[22] ICJ cases shows that there may be points in the life of an international court in which outcome legitimacy concerns can seriously affect the acceptance of the court's authority by important constituencies.[23]

---

[18] See, e.g., *Gotovina and Markač v. Prosecutor*, Case No. IT-06–90-A, Judgment of 16 November 2012, para. 89 (AC); *Brđanin v. Prosecutor*, Case No, IT-99-36-A, Judgment of 3 April 2007, at para. 430 (AC); *Karemera v. Prosecutor*, Case No. ICTR-98-44-A, Judgment of 29 September 2014, para. 145 (AC).

[19] See, e.g., A. M. Danner and J. S. Martinez, 'Guilty associations: Joint criminal enterprise, command responsibility, and the development of international criminal law', *California Law Review*, 93 (2005), 75, 134–7; A. Bogdan, 'Individual criminal responsibility in the execution of a "joint criminal enterprise" in the jurisprudence of the ad hoc International Tribunal for the Former Yugoslavia', *International Criminal Law Review*, 6 (2006), p. 63, 119.

[20] Although not an international court, one may allude to the demise of the Human Rights Commission as a cautionary tale about what may happen to an institution chronically lacking in outcome legitimacy – i.e., repeatedly engaged over a number of decades in 'selective justice' and political score-settling. UN Secretary General's Address to the Commission on Human Rights, 7 April 2005, www.un.org/sg/STATEMENTS/index .asp?nid=1388; S. Joseph and J. Kyriakakis, 'The United Nations and human rights' in S. Joseph and A. McBeth (eds.), *Research Handbook on International Humanitarian Law* (Cheltenham, 2010), pp. 1, 9.

[21] *South West Africa* (*Liberia v. SA*; *Ethiopia v. SA*), 1996 ICJ 6.

[22] *Military and Paramilitary Activities in and against Nicaragua* (*Nicaragua v. US*), 1986 ICJ 14.

[23] R. Mullerson, 'Aspects of legitimacy of decisions of international courts and tribunals: comments' in *Legitimacy in International Law*, above note 1, at 190; Eric A. Posner, *The Perils of Global Legalism* (Chicago: University of Chicago Press, 2009), pp. 147–8.

In any event, it is important to note that the legitimacy capital available to an international court fluctuates over time, partly in response to changes in its structure, procedures or performance. Hence, for instance, the adherence by new states to an international court's statute or the denunciation of the statute by existing member states may influence the jurisdictional structure of the court and affect its source legitimacy capital (allowing it to derive authority from fewer or more states); and developments in the law-application procedure, such as exercising case-selection discretion to ensure diversity of prosecutions before international criminal courts may affect the perceived fairness and process legitimacy of the relevant court's proceedings.[24] Finally, legitimacy capital may also vary in light of reactions to judicial performance, sometimes resulting in virtuous cycles in which growing acceptance of the decisions generated by an international court may encourage it to adopt even bolder decisions, which may produce greater outcome legitimacy dividends (e.g., allowing the court to address deep-seated injustices caused by structural social problems);[25] at other times, reactions to performance may result in vicious cycles in which an international court's diminishing credibility leads it to avoid issuing bold decisions.

Arguably, the ECHR's case law on narrowing over time the margin of appreciation afforded to member states demonstrates the Court's willingness to gradually impose more burdensome and more specific human rights obligations[26] – thereby setting the stage for a virtuous cycle of increasing legitimacy. By contrast, the ICC's timid approach toward the prosecution of Kenyan President Uhuru Kenyatta, following the strong AU criticism of the Court's decisions to indict a number of African leaders, may foreshadow a vicious cycle entailing gradual loss of judicial legitimacy by the Court.[27]

---

[24] See, e.g., Mark Osiel, *Making Sense of Mass Atrocity* (New York: Cambridge University Press, 2009), pp. 158–9.

[25] One explanation for the European Court of Human Rights' (ECtHR) increased assertiveness in prescribing remedies is the increased legitimacy capital it has attained as a result of compliance with its 'low cost' judgments. See, e.g., Shany, above note 12, at 127–8.

[26] See, e.g., P. G. Carozza, 'Subsidiarity as a structural principle of international human rights law', *American Journal of International Law*, 97 (2003), 38, 75; D. L. Donoho, 'Autonomy, self-governance, and the margin of appreciation: Developing a jurisprudence of diversity within universal human rights', *Emory International Law Review*, 15 (2001), 391, 465.

[27] See, e.g., S. D. Mueller, 'Kenya and the International Criminal Court (ICC): Politics, the election and the law', *Journal of Eastern African Studies*, 8 (2014), 25, 37; BBC News, African Union urges ICC to defer Uhuru Kenyatta case, 12 October 2013, www.bbc.com/news/world-africa-24506006.

STRONGER TOGETHER? 361

B   Aspects of Judicial Effectiveness

Evaluation of the effectiveness of international courts proceeds from a different point of departure than evaluation of their legitimacy, focusing more on the performance of international courts and less on the attitude of their constituencies. The organizational sociology literature offers three principal approaches to gauge the effectiveness of organizations, including public organizations such as courts: the rational systems approach, the open system approach and the system resource approach.[28] The first approach revolves around the degree in which organizations actually attain the goals set for them by important constituencies, the second approach revolves around the impact of organizations on their social environment and the third approach on the ability of organizations to attract the resources necessary for their survival and growth. Under all three approaches, however, evaluating effectiveness requires examining the record of achievement of international courts: Have they met the goals set for them by their mandate providers (the natural or legal persons that established them and defined their tasks)[29] and other relevant constituencies? Have they influenced the operations of other international actors, norms and institutions, constituting their social environment? And have they attained, over time, a significant amount of resources, which enables them to exercise their functions?

Still, external perceptions are important for the effectiveness of international courts for a number of reasons. First, as discussed in the next part, perceptions of legitimacy by international court constituencies can support (or undermine) international court effectiveness. In the same vein, external perceptions of judicial effectiveness influence perceptions of legitimacy.[30] This is because outside observers may reasonably assume that the success of international courts cannot occur without constituency support, and that such support is unlikely to be provided without a justification. An international court that appears to enjoy widespread support is thus likely to be regarded as enjoying justified

---

[28] See, e.g., J. L. Price, 'The study of organizational effectiveness', *Sociological Quarterly*, 12 (1972), 3, 3–7; Richard W. Scott and Gerald F. Davis, *Organizations and Organizing: Rational, Natural and Open Systems Perspective* (Upper Saddle River, NJ: Pearson, 2007), p. 31; S. E. Seashore and E. Yuchtman, 'A system resource approach in organizational effectiveness', *American Sociological Review*, 32 (1967), 891, 898.

[29] For a discussion of the concept of mandate providers, see Shany, above note 12, at 31–5.

[30] See C. J. Carrubba and M. Gabel, 'Courts, compliance, and the quest for legitimacy in international law', *Theoretical Inquiries in Law*, 14 (2013), 505, 509.

authority – i.e., legitimate. Such external perceptions of sociological legitimacy may generate, in turn, pressure to comply with international court decisions and further strengthen its ability to operate effectively, transforming thereby perceptions of effectiveness into self-fulfilling prophecies. Second, the goals of international courts sometimes include shaping external perceptions. For example, the ICC's mission of ending impunity[31] and the WTO DSB's mission of increasing the predictability of trade rules[32] almost inevitably require these international courts to consider the attitudes and expectations of external actors – political and military leaders, economic operators and the general public. Third, changes in the conduct of external actors, which are critical for enhancing the effectiveness of international courts, are often predicated on the anticipated impact or utility of adjudication. Thus, expectations of short-term sanctions or long-term gains may explain instances of state compliance with specific court decisions,[33] the alignment of state practice with legal standards developed by international courts (even in cases decided with respect to other states),[34] or the provision of material resources to international courts by relevant stakeholders. Such expectations may also explain instances of noncompliance, rejection of a court's jurisprudence and lack of political support for its operation.

Although evaluating the effectiveness of international courts is, in essence, not a normative exercise, because it focuses on what courts actually do, the process of evaluating judicial effectiveness is informed by normative considerations. First, all three approaches to organizational effectiveness appear to stem from normative propositions – i.e., that organizations should strive to attain their goals, that they should strive to meaningfully influence their social environment and that they should strive to survive and grow. Second, purposive efforts by international courts to attain certain goals and to impact certain external actors and processes are almost always based on a normative conception of the desirability of the relevant outcomes– i.e., on what it is that international courts should be trying to do.

---

[31] Statute of the International Criminal Court, 17 July 1998, preamble, 2187 U.N.T.S. 90.

[32] Agreement Establishing the World Trade Organization, Annex 2: Dispute Settlement Understanding, 15 April 1994, art. 3(2), 1869 UNTS 401.

[33] See, e.g., Constanze Shulte, *Compliance with Decisions of the International Court of Justice* (Oxford University Press, 2004), p. 91 *et seq.*

[34] David J. Harris et al., *Law of the European Convention on Human Rights*, 3rd ed., (Oxford University Press, 2014), pp. 34–5.

At the same time, it is worth noting that the evaluation of judicial legitimacy is more comprehensive than the evaluation of judicial effectiveness in the sense that the latter focuses on organizational outcomes, whereas the former assesses the desirability of these outcomes and of their attainment, but it may also attribute as much significance to assessing the source of judicial authority and the process of exercising it. Although the structure of international courts (including their source of authority) and their decision-making processes influence to a large degree their judicial outcomes, effectiveness analysis ultimately revolves around judicial performance and not about the factors controlling it. By contrast, judicial legitimacy is often invoked to explain content-neutral obedience by a target audience – i.e., obedience to judicial decisions whose contents are controversial and enjoy only a limited degree of support from relevant target audiences. As a result, judicial legitimacy analysis is typically divorced from any specific judicial output (although a series of judicial decisions, leading to noteworthy legal and factual outcomes, may affect the legitimacy analysis).[35]

III Interplay between Legitimacy and Effectiveness

A Similarities between Judicial Legitimacy and Judicial Effectiveness

Despite the analytical differences between notions of judicial legitimacy and effectiveness, as applied to the evaluation of international courts, the two notions are in fact very much intertwined. As explained later, a more effective court is likely to be more legitimate than an ineffective court, and a more legitimate court is likely to be more effective. Still, under certain special circumstances, legitimacy and effectiveness factors may pull in opposite directions, resulting in a focus on certain legitimating factors, which are divorced from effectiveness considerations, and which outweigh other legitimating factors, which are aligned with effectiveness considerations.

For starters, a rational system (or goal-based) approach to international court effectiveness may result in some conflation of legitimacy and effectiveness: One important goal of international courts is the conferral of legitimacy on their own operations and on other relevant norms and institutions,[36] and under these conditions enhancing judicial legitimacy and bolstering judicial effectiveness appear to be directly correlated.

---

[35] Shany, above note 12, at 149.   [36] See, e.g., Shany, above note 12, at 44–6.

In fact, one *raison d'être* of introducing adjudication as a form of international dispute settlement or law enforcement is the high level of legitimacy attached to decision making by judges pursuant to a judicial procedure. Arguably, decisions reached by courts are not always more 'correct' than decisions reached by other decision makers, such as politicians, academic experts or experienced bureaucrats. Still, for many disputes, judicial decisions by well-respected professional judges issued pursuant to a legal process are deemed more authoritative – i.e., legitimate – than other, equivalent nonjudicial decisions. This is partly so because observance of judicial independence and impartiality standards and legal procedures founded on the principle of 'equality of arms' appear to contain strong guarantees of fairness, and because the combination of full argumentation of the case by the parties and judicial expertise in legal decision making appear to provide strong quality assurances. These attributes render international courts as particularly well situated to confer legitimacy on their own decisions (internal legitimatization) and on decisions of other international actors, who constitute part of the global governance apparatus and whom international courts monitor and review (external legitimization).

At a more general level, one may posit that the different outcomes generated by international courts are likely to be legitimized by the designation of judicial decisions as authoritative in nature and vice versa. Hence, legitimate judicial decisions may help to generate external constituency support for changes in the actual state of the world brought about by them. For example, generic goals of international courts such as dispute settlement, norm interpretation and norm-application and regime support,[37] or specific goals of international governance such as promoting trade liberalization[38] or greater unity between the peoples of Europe,[39] are likely to command a greater degree of acceptance, over and beyond that appertaining to their inclusion in an international treaty, if they are perceived to also be endorsed by the legitimate authority of an international court. At the same time, such goals might be more easily rejected if they are perceived to originate from or be tainted by illegitimate exercises of decision-making authority. In addition, authoritative international court decisions render changes in the social environment in which international courts operate more legitimate and assist

---

[37] See ibid., at 38–44.   [38] Ibid., at p. 192 (co-authored with Sivan Shlomo-Agon)

[39] European Convention on Human Rights and Fundamental Freedoms, 4 November 1950, preamble, ETS 5.

international courts in portraying their efforts to attain more resources as more acceptable. Put differently, legitimate courts are more likely to generate support for the specific outputs they produce, and relevant constituencies are more likely, in turn, to support the attainment of judicial outcomes – i.e., support an increase in international court effectiveness. At the same time, illegitimate judicial outputs might generate contested outcomes and lead to a perception that it may not be desirable for an international court advancing controversial outcomes to be effective.

Another important connection between legitimacy and effectiveness is that legitimacy – especially, sociological legitimacy – helps international courts in sustaining judicial effectiveness. This is because the authoritative nature of legitimate judicial decisions attracts the support and cooperation by relevant constituencies (including the parties to adjudication and other actors), which may facilitate an even greater degree of subsequent effectiveness on the part of the relevant international courts under the various approaches to judicial effectiveness – i.e., better attainment of judicial goals, greater impact on the environment and securing of more resources. Hence, for example, acceptance of the legitimacy of WTO DSB reports by WTO member states and economic operators, which is accompanied by habitual compliance on their part with legal pronouncements contained in the reports, facilitates the goal of the DSB of providing for increased security and predictability of the trading system.[40] In the same vein, acceptance by WTO members of the legitimacy of the trade liberalization agenda found in many DSB reports[41] is likely to result in stronger commitment to a pro-trade policy agenda, impacting thereby the global economy (i.e., the economic environment). A perception that decisions of the WTO DSB are, by and large, legitimate (sociological legitimacy) may also explain why member states have been willing over time to fund the system and provide it with the resources needed for its continued operation.

It can also be noted that from a sociological legitimacy perspective, outcome legitimacy is tied to source and process legitimacy in the sense that judicial decisions issued by an international court with recognized competence following a professional decision-making procedure that

---

[40] WTO Dispute Settlement Understanding, *supra* note 30, art. 3(2).
[41] S. P. Subedi, 'The WTO dispute settlement mechanism as a new technique for settling disputes in international law' in D. French, M. Saul, and N. D. White (eds.), *International Law and Dispute Settlement: New Problems and Techniques* (Portland OR: Hart Publishing, 2010), p. 173, 187.

appears to be fair are more likely to be regarded as legitimate by external constituencies than decisions issued ultra vires or in violation of due process standards.[42] Judicial decisions deemed as legitimate are, in turn, more likely than decisions deemed as illegitimate to bestow legitimacy on legal developments or changes in the state of the world that are brought about by them (such as new interpretations of legal standards or a peace agreement following the terms of a judicial decision).

Significantly, the link between different aspects of legitimacy that exists for sociological legitimacy also exists for normative legitimacy in the sense that competent international courts taking decisions pursuant to a fair procedure might be better situated to reach just decisions than courts operating outside their scope of authority or applying an unfair judicial procedure.[43] The upshot of this analysis is that source and process legitimacy also serve to render effective outcomes more legitimate, although it cannot be excluded, of course, that a legitimate institution, following a legitimate process, will nonetheless render illegitimate outcomes. Furthermore, to the extent to which the goals of international courts are normatively legitimate, an international court that generates outcomes that advance such goals, like resolving disputes or deterring international crimes, would more likely to be produce legitimate outcomes than a court that fails to obtain such goals.[44]

In short, an international court that has attained its goals, had an impact on its social environment and been successful in obtaining the needed resources for its operations can usually refer back to a track record of support and acceptance of its work by external constituencies that react to its decisions, modify their conduct accordingly and provide it with the said resources. Such support and acceptance is indicative of sociological legitimacy and may generate further social legitimacy by virtue of mimicry and acculturation.[45] To the extent that the goals are

---

[42] See, e.g., T. R. Tyler and J. T. Jost, 'Psychology and the law: Reconciling normative and descriptive accounts of social justice and system legitimacy' in A. W. Kruglanski and E. T. Higgins (eds.), *Social Psychology: Handbook of Basic Principles*, 2nd ed., (New York: Guilford Press, 2007), p. 807, 818.

[43] See, e.g., M. Adler, 'Understanding and analyzing administrative justice' in M. Adler (ed.), *Administrative Justice in Context* (Oxford University Press, 2010), pp. 132–3; J. Rawls, 'Political liberalism: Reply to Habermas' in J. G. Finlayson and F. Freyenhagen (eds.), *Habermas and Rawls: Disputing the Political* (New York: Routledge, 2011), p. 46, 82.

[44] See, e.g., M. Haugaard, 'Power and legitimacy' in M. Mazzotti (ed.), *Knowledge as Social Order: Rethinking the Sociology of Barry Barnes* (Aldershot: Ashgate, 2008), p. 119, 123.

[45] Ryan Goodman and Derek Jinks, *Socializing States: Promoting Human Rights through International Law* (New York: Oxford University Press, 2013), p. 45; G. C. Shaffer, 'The

legitimate, that the impact on the state of the world is desirable and that the authority of court is fundamentally justified, courts that effectively generate such outcomes are also more legitimate from a normative point of view than courts that fail to do so.

The ICTY's record of prosecuting virtually all indicted suspects in the commission of international crimes in the former Yugoslavia illustrates the relationship between effectiveness and legitimacy. To the extent that the goal of prosecuting and punishing those bearing the greatest responsibility for international crimes in the former Yugoslavia was deemed by large segments of the international community as legitimate and can be objectively justified, attaining this goal of increased the legitimacy of the Tribunal.[46] Furthermore, the effective impact of the Tribunal on legal developments in the Balkans[47] and the longevity of the Tribunal (notwithstanding its hefty budget)[48] are indicative of broad acceptance of its authority and strong support for its operations by important constituencies, who regard the Tribunal as legitimate. If such impact is indeed desirable than the operation of the Tribunal, and perhaps its very existence, can be justified.

B   Conflicts between Judicial Legitimacy and Judicial Effectiveness

Note, however, that the interplay between judicial legitimacy and judicial effectiveness is not one directional in nature. At times, protecting the legitimacy of an international court inevitably leads to the issuance of ineffective judicial decisions – e.g., decisions that fail to attain some of the court's goals, fail to have an impact on the social environment or lead to backlash involving withdrawal of resources or even termination of the court's existence. For example, the Weberian notion of the rational-legal authority attributes a legitimacy-enhancing effect to decisions issued pursuant to a legal procedure and grounded in positive law. Still,

---

dimensions and determinations of state change', in G. C. Shaffer (ed.), *Transnational Legal Ordering and State Change* (New York: Cambridge University Press, 2013), p. 23, 35.

[46] United Nations resolution 827 of 25 May 1993, UN Doc. S/RES/827 (1993) ('Determined to put an end to such crimes and to take effective measures to bring to justice the persons who are responsible for them').

[47] See, e.g., Y. Shany, 'How can international criminal courts have a greater impact on national criminal proceedings? Lessons from the first two decades of international criminal justice in operation', *Israel Law Review*, 46 (2013), 431, 437–8.

[48] For example, in 2014, the 20 annual budget of the ICTY – more than 20 years after the establishment of the Tribunal – was almost $90 million. See www.icty.org/sid/325.

a judicial decision reflecting a 'correct' application of legal doctrine may fail to generate the desirable outcome or impact or could lead to counterproductive consequences.

For example, it is plausible that the ECtHR judgment in *Hirst*,[49] the ICJ judgment in *Kosovo*[50] and the SADC Tribunal judgment in *Campbell*[51] all represented plausible applications of the relevant norms of international law. Still, their effectiveness appears to be questionable: The first decision has not been complied with at the time of writing, thus failing to lead to better implementation of the ECHR by the UK;[52] the second decision appears not have had any impact on the state of the world because of the narrowness of its legal holding;[53] and the third decision generated withdrawal of member state support from the Tribunal, leading to its collapse.[54] Arguably, the judicial effectiveness problems of the UK prisoner voting cases (such as *Hirst*) correspond to concerns about the substantive justice of the final outcome; and the judicial effectiveness problems of the *Kosovo* ICJ opinion and SADC's 'activist' human rights judgment in *Campbell* are tied to concerns about the two judicial bodies adopting excessively narrow or broad understandings of their scope of authority. These explanations underscore the overlap between the judicial illegitimacy and judicial ineffectiveness evaluative frameworks; still, they also point to the coexistence of multiple legitimacy-influencing factors pointing at times in different directions. Whereas some legitimacy-influencing factors implicated in international adjudication (such as procedural regularity or correcting injustice) may support judicial effectiveness, other concurrently applicable legitimacy-influencing factors may undermine it. Note that difficulties of predicting the effects of judicial decisions that include both effectiveness-enhancing and effectiveness-detracting factors is further complicated by the influence of intervening actors, such as the Council

---

[49] *Hirst v. United Kingdom*, ECtHR Judgment of 6 October 2005 (Grand Chamber).

[50] *Accordance with international law of the unilateral declaration of independence in respect of Kosovo*, 2010 ICJ 403.

[51] *Campbell v. Zimbabwe*, Case 2/2007, SADC Tribunal judgment of 28 November 2008.

[52] See, e.g., J. Fraser, 'Conclusion: The European Convention on Human Rights as a common European endeavor' in S. don Flogaitis, T. Zwart, and J. Fraser (eds.), *The European Court of Human Rights and Its Discontents: Turning Criticism into Strength* (Cheltenham: Edward Elgar, 2013), pp. 192, 200.

[53] See, e.g., John Cerone, 'The World Court's non-opinion, opinion juris' (25.7.2010), http://opiniojuris.org/2010/07/25/the-world-court%E2%80%99s-non-opinion/.

[54] See, e.g., E. de Wet, 'The rise and fall of the Tribunal of the Southern African Development Community: Implications for dispute settlement in Southern Africa', *ICSID Review*, 28 (2013), 45, 48.

of Europe Committee of Ministers (responsible for enforcing ECtHR judgments), the UN General Assembly (which requested the Advisory Opinion from the UN) and the SADC Summit of Heads of States (which decided to suspend the Tribunal), whose acts and omissions often determine the actual effectiveness of judicial outcomes.

Moreover, effective judicial bodies are not always sociologically or normatively legitimate. As suggested earlier, a goal-based approach to judicial effectiveness would allow for overlaps between legitimacy and effectiveness only if the sought goals themselves are normatively justified or empirically supported and accepted. Similarly, under an open systems approach to judicial effectiveness, the desirability of proven impacts may be questioned, just like under a resource system approach the very justification for the continued existence of a judicial institution may be questioned. For example, it is has been suggested that the legitimacy of the CJEU has suffered notwithstanding its marked contribution to promoting European integration because of the growing unpopularity of the integration project it facilitates,[55] that ICSID has lost support because it has been accused of generating negative impacts – hindering the ability of member states to adopt structural economic reforms in reaction to economic emergencies,[56] and that the very justification for the establishment of ITLOS had been put in question in the past.[57] In these type of inquiries too, it appears as if legitimacy-enhancing or detracting factors may exist simultaneously, pointing in opposite directions and having a disparate influence on judicial effectiveness.

The uncertainty of the interplay between legitimacy and effectiveness is further compounded by the subjective nature of sociological legitimacy: Different constituencies may view the same legitimacy-influencing factors differently – some attributing to them legitimacy-enhancing value, while others regarding them as detracting from judicial legitimacy.

---

[55] See, e.g., M. A. Loth, 'Courts in search of legitimacy: A case of wrongful life' in Mortimer Sellers (ed.), *Autonomy in the Law* (New York: Springer, 2007), 85; E. Voeten, 'Public opinion and the legitimacy of international courts', *Theoretical Inquiries in Law*, 14 (2013), 411, 424.

[56] See, e.g., W. Burke-White, 'The Argentine financial crisis: State liability under BITs and the legitimacy of the ICSID system' in M. Waibel et al. (eds.), *The Backlash against Investment Arbitration: Perceptions and Reality* (Alphen aan den Rijn: Kluwer, 2010), p. 407, 411.

[57] See, e.g., S. Oda, 'Dispute settlement prospects in the law of the sea', *International and Comparative Law Quarterly*, 44 (1995), 863, 864.

Furthermore, judicial effectiveness indicators themselves may point in different directions – e.g., prompt resolution of disputes may conflict with the definitive resolution of disputes.[58] Under those circumstances, the same measure may, at least according to the rational system approach, increase judicial effectiveness in some respects and decrease it in others. The legitimacy-enhancing or detracting implications of such inconclusive effectiveness influencing measures are therefore unclear and would appear to depend on multiple contextual factors.

IV Conclusion

Notions of judicial legitimacy and judicial effectiveness are strongly interrelated: Legitimacy is one of the strategic assets that courts may deploy to increase their effectiveness (attain their goals, impact their environment or attain necessary resources), and effectiveness can be a legitimacy-enhancing factor (whenever the judicial goals or impact themselves are legitimate, and whenever the existence of the court is generally supported and accepted). Hence, one may expect that mutually reinforcing patterns of support would often hold between judicial legitimacy and judicial effectiveness. At the same time, given the complexity and diversity of legitimacy and effectiveness influencing factors and the multiplicity of relevant constituencies that monitor their implementation, there would inevitably be situations in which effective practices would lead to loss of legitimacy, and legitimacy-enhancing measures would nonetheless result in loss of effectiveness.

Ultimately, a chronic gap between judicial outcomes and 'client preferences' – i.e., the outcomes deemed to be desirable by the relevant constituencies – would result in the sociological delegitimization of the relevant international court. This is partly because of the role of politics in legitimacy challenges – parties may be induced to raise legitimacy challenges when they view the outcomes generated by an international court as fundamentally contrary to their values and interests – and partly because perceptions of justice are tied to perceptions of interest.[59] Furthermore, an international court that is viewed as ineffective might not attract the support and resources necessary for its continued operations,

---

[58] See, e.g., Shany, above note 12, at 196.

[59] See, e.g., Melvin J. Lerner and Susan Clayton, *Justice and Self-Interest: Two Fundamental Motives* (New York: Cambridge University Press, 2011), p. 10.

its decision may not be complied with, and it may find itself trapped in a vicious circle of declining fortunes. Finally, lack of effectiveness for fear of loss of legitimacy may constitute a self-fulfilling prophecy: It could encourage international courts not to address controversial issues, possibly limiting thereby their ability to attain their goals and make a lasting impact on their environment (though probably extending their longevity).

INDEX

ABMs. *See* Appellate Body Members
accountability
  for global constitutionalism, 313–14
  of human rights treaty bodies, 286, 300–2
  non-electoral, 313–14
actual legitimacy
  assessment of, 339
  diversity of judges and, 350
  sociological legitimacy compared to, 338–9
  types of, 341
ad hoc arbitral tribunals, 258–60, 273
adherence
  ITLOS and, 198–9
  sociological legitimacy and, 240–1
adjudicators
  for ICSID
    as closed network, 231–2
    demographic of, 221–4
    impartiality of, 230–1
    legitimacy capital of, 228–32
    WTO adjudicators compared to, 221–4, 232–3
  for WTO
    ICSID adjudicators compared to, 221–4, 232–3
    legitimacy capital of, 224–8
African Court of Human and Peoples' Rights, 141–2
Alemanno, Alberto, 159
Alston, Philip, 299
Alter, Karen, 46–7, 102, 104–5
Alvarez, José, 239
amicus curiae briefs, 17, 228, 248–9, 267, 277, 289
Andean Court of Justice, 120–1

annulment, of awards, of ICSID judgments, 264–6, 279–80
appeals, of ICSID judgments, 265–6
Appellate Body Members (ABMs), of WTO, 221–4
arbitral rosters, 258–60
arbitral tribunals. *See ad hoc* arbitral tribunals
arbitrators. *See* adjudicators
Arnull, Anthony, 156
artificial justice, 345
assessment, of normative legitimacy, 7–9
atrocity crimes, 116
  in Colombia, 121–3
  IACtHR and, 121–3
AUC. *See* United Self-Defense Forces of Colombia
audience
  for CJEU, 163–4
  legitimacy influenced by, 18–19
authority
  morality and, 87–8
  Raz on, 57–9
  Solomonic judgments and, 57–9

Balasco, Lauren Marie, 81
Ban Ki-Moon, 284
Bangladesh, 182, 190–1
Barry, Brian, 316
Belarus, 182
Bensouda, Fatou, 72, 135–6
bias
  of CJEU, 150–1, 153–5
  ICJ and, 53–5
  normative legitimacy and, 150–1
  Solomonic judgments and, 53–5

INDEX

373

Bilateral Investment Treaties (BITs)
  ICSID and, 29–30
  Indonesia-Netherlands, 257
  multiplication of, 18–19
  in South Africa, termination of, 242
bindingness
  of human rights treaty bodies, lack of
    legal status for, 286–7, 292–3
  legitimacy of international courts
    and, 27–31
BITs. *See* Bilateral Investment Treaties
Bjorklund, Andrea, 18–19, 21–3,
  25–6
Bobek, Michal, 155
Bolivia, withdrawal from ICSID, 242
Branch, Adam, 74–5
British exit (Brexit), 113
Broches, Aron, 257–8
Brownlie, Ian, 47
Buchanan, Allan, 7, 329–30

Caldeira, Gregory, 164–70
Carter, Linda, 69–70
case load
  for ECtHR
    effectiveness influenced by, 295–6
    legitimacy challenges as result of, 91
  for human rights treaty bodies, 303
CCC. *See* Constitutional Court of
  Colombia
CEDAW. *See* Committee on the
  Elimination of Discrimination
  against Women
CESCR. *See* Committee on Economic,
  Social and Cultural Rights
CETA. *See* Comprehensive Economic
  and Trade Agreement
Churchill, Robin, 290–1
CJEU. *See* Court of Justice of the
  European Union
Clark, Phil, 74–5
coherence
  in ICJ judgments, 55–6
  in ICSID judgments, 272–6
  legitimacy and, 55–6
  in sociological legitimacy, 240–1
  in Solomonic judgments, 55–6
Coke, Edward, 344

Colombia, 58–9
  atrocity crimes in, 121–3
  AUC in, 119
  CCC in, 127, 135–6
  conflict in, 118–20
    history of, 118
    IACtHR and, 120–3
    as low-intensity war, 118–19
  constitutional block and, 127
  FARC in, 118–20
  Framework for Peace Law, 134–6
  ICJ and, 120–1
  Justice and Peace Law, 128, 130–1
  in OAS, 121, 123
  Pact of Bogotá, 58–9
  Rome Statute and, ratification of,
    123–4
Colombian peace process, 115–16
  atrocity crimes and, 121–3
  early history of, 119–20
  IACtHR and, 117–18, 120–3, 140–2
    complementary goals of, 126–9
    convergence with ICC, 126–36
    goal-setting by, 129–34
    international agreements and,
      imbalance in, 136–40
    legitimacy of, 126–36
  ICC and, 117–18, 123–6, 140–2
    complementary goals of, 126–9
    convergence with IACtHR, 126–36
    goal-setting by, 129–34
    international agreements and,
      imbalance in, 136–40
    legitimacy of, 126–36
    retreat from, 139–40
  jurisdiction issues in, 115–16
  under Rome Statute, 137–8
Committee against Torture, procedures
  for, 289–90
Committee on Economic, Social and
  Cultural Rights (CESCR), 290–1
Committee on the Elimination of
  Discrimination against Women
  (CEDAW)
  competency of members, 288–9
  composition of, 287–9
  obligation of states' parties under, 298
  procedures for, 289–90

INDEX

compensable regulatory measures, 273
competency
  of CEDAW members, 288–9
  of Human Rights Committee
    members, 288–9
  of human rights treaty bodies,
    288–9
competitive elections, in democracies,
  320–1
compliance
  for ITLOS, with orders and
    judgments, 184–6
  legitimacy of international courts
    through, 99–102
  through shaming, 103
  sociological legitimacy influenced
    by, 103
Comprehensive Economic and Trade
  Agreement (CETA), 283
consent, of states, 69–70
consistency, of ICSID, 245–6, 272–6
Constitutional Court of Colombia
  (CCC), 127, 135–6
constitutional culture, 104–5
constitutionalism. *See* global
  constitutionalism
constructive interference, in
  international law, 115
correctness, of ICSID, 245–6
cosmopolitanism
  institutional, 313
  normative, 312–13
Court of Justice of the European Union
  (CJEU), 143–4
  audience for, 163–4
  bias of, 150–1, 153–5
    integrationist, 154–5
    national, 154
  crisis of legitimacy and, 162–3
  diffuse support for, 146
  fairness of, 150–1
  framework for analysis, 145–6
  historical legacy of, 172–3
  input legitimacy of, 145
  judicial activism and, 155–8
  judicial outputs and, 161
  legal reasoning in, 155–8
  legal soundness of, 151–2

  normative legitimacy of, 145, 147–62
    criteria for, 149–52
    critiques of, 152–62
    democratic deficit, 147–9
  opacity of, 158–62
  openness of, 152
  output legitimacy of, 145
  political acceptability of, 151–2
  preliminary reference procedures for,
    162–3
  public legitimacy of, 164–70
    contemporary studies on, 168–70
    defined, 164
    diffuse support of, 165–8
    public awareness as factor in,
      165–6
  public trust and support for, 146,
    164, 168–9
    EU and, 170
    after financial crises, 170–2
    in new EU member states, 172
    in UK, 172
  sociological legitimacy of, 145–6,
    162–72
  structure of, 143
  transparency of, 152
crimes against humanity, 116
crisis of legitimacy, 162–3

Danner, Allison Marston, 74
De Búrca, Gráinne, 307, 332–3
decision-making institutions
  under democracy, 315–16, 325–9,
    332–4
  human rights treaty bodies as, 290–3
  ICs as, 328–9
  ITLOS as, 202
democracy, democracies and
  active opposition parties in, 321
  building blocks of, 332–6
  central use of, 335
  competitive elections and, 320–1
  concepts of, 315–18
  in decision-making institutions,
    315–16, 325–9, 332–4
  deficit of, 335
  defined, 318–25, 342–3
  effective power under, 318–19

INDEX

features of, 317
free media and, 321
GBS and, 322–5
  fallacy of accumulation in, 323–4,
    332–4
  fallacy of composition in, 322–3
  normative assessment of, 329–32
global constitutionalism and, 310,
  336–7
historical development of, 342–3
human rights and, 317–18
ICs and, 342–3, 352–3
  principle of democracy for, 326
  reforms of, 309–10
incrementalism and, 331–2
independent judiciary as part of,
  321–2
institutionally-established
    procedures under, 318
instrumental justification of, 320
justifiability of, 336
legitimacy and, of international
    courts and, 13, 307–11, 324
  with normative legitimacy, 7–8
  under rule of law, 308–9
majoritarian, 319
normative standards of, 316–17,
  326–7, 336
  assessment of, 329–32
procedural control and, 318–19, 333
public deliberations under, 320–1
reform of international courts and,
  309–10
rule of law and, 308–9, 317–18
social value of, 318–25, 331
as theory, 315–29
transparency and, 317
democratic deficit, 335
  of CJEU, 147–9
  within EU, 147–9
DePalma, Anthony, 247
dependence thesis, 57
determinacy, in sociological legitimacy,
  240–1
diffuse support
  of CJEU, 165–8
  of ECJ, 167–8
  four hypotheses for, 167–8

Dispute Settlement Body (DSB), of
  WTO, 225
dispute settlements. *See also*
    International Centre for
    Settlement of Investment
    Disputes
  through human rights bodies, 304
  through ICSID, 253–6
  through ITLOS, 197–8
distributive fairness, 104
diversity, of judges, 349–50
  actual legitimacy and, 350
  sociological legitimacy and, 349–50
doctrine of execution immunity.
    See execution immunity
DSB. *See* Dispute Settlement Body
dual nationality rule, 263–4

Easton, David, 146
ECJ. *See* European Court of Justice
Economic Community of West African
    States (ECOWAS), 141–2
ECtHR. *See* European Court of Human
    Rights
Ecuador, withdrawal from ICSID, 242
effectiveness
  defined, 355–63
  of ECtHR, expansion of case load as
    factor for, 295–6
  goal-based approach to, 363–4
  of human rights bodies, 293–300
    in domestic legal systems, 297
    legal fragmentation as influence
      on, 296
  of international courts
    of ICC, 65
    judicial, 86–7
    legitimacy and, 8–9, 13–14, 65
    sociological legitimacy and, 65
  of judges, 361–3
    evaluations of, 362–3
    external perceptions of, 361–2
    judicial legitimacy and, 363–71
    legitimacy and, of international
      courts, 8–9, 13–14, 65, 363–70
Ejercito Libertador National (ELN), 118
elections. *See* competitive elections
ELN. *See* Ejercito Libertador National

INDEX

embeddedness
  of ICs, 326
  of ICSID adjudicators, 229
enforcement
  of ICSID awards, 266–7
  of ITLOS judgments, 210–12
equity
  ex aequo et bono compared to, 47–9
  in ICJ judgments, 47–9
EU. *See* European Union
European Court of Human Rights
    (ECtHR)
  case load for
    effectiveness influenced by, 295–6
    legitimacy challenges as result of,
      91
  design structure of, 17
  human rights treaty bodies
    judgments compared to, 291
  judicial legitimacy and, 360
  legitimacy challenges at, 91–9
    case load as factor for, 91
    expansionist methodologies, 92–5
    in prisoner voting cases, 83–4,
      95–9, 101–12
  living instrument approach to, 93
  pilot judgments of, 298–9
  post-conflict involvement, 141–2
  on prisoner voting, in UK, 83–4,
    95–9
    competing illegitimacy in, 106–12
    declarations of incompatibility
      and, 102
    *Greens and M. T. v. United
      Kingdom*, 97–9
    judicial compliance and, 101,
      103–5
    public debate on, 101–2
  state sovereignty and, 89–90
  transparency of, CJEU compared to,
    159–60
European Court of Justice (ECJ),
    diffuse support of, 167–8
European Union (EU)
  CJEU and, public trust for, 170
  democratic deficit within, 147–9
  NMIs in, 148–9
  TTIP and, negotiations for, 255

ex aequo et bono, 47–9
execution immunity, doctrine of,
    266–7
exit, 27–31
expansionist law making
  definition of, 94–5
  in ECtHR, 92–5
external consent, 257–8
external legitimacy, 5
  of ICSID, 232
  of WTO, 227
external stakeholders, ITLOS and
  dispute settlement and, prioritization
    of, 197–8
  incremental jurisprudence of, 194–6
  jurisdictional issues and, 189–92
  legal objectives of decisions, 192–4
  legitimacy for, creation of, 188–99
  other international court decisions as
    influence on, 198–9

fairness
  of CJEU, 150–1
  distributive, 104
  of ITLOS, 204–5
  legitimacy and, 104
  normative legitimacy and, 150–1
  procedural, 104
fallacy of accumulation, 323–4, 332–4
fallacy of composition, 322–3
FARC. *See* Revolutionary Armed
    Forces of Colombia-People's
    Army
Fichetelberg, Aaron, 71
Findlay, Mark, 77
Fletcher, Laurel, 80
forum shopping, 280. *See also* treaty-
    shopping
Framework for Peace Law (2012),
    Colombia, 134–6
Franck, Thomas, 55, 151, 234–5, 273
  on sociological legitimacy, 240–1
free media, in democracies, 321
Frei, Eduardo, 58–9
Frodl v. Austria, 107–8

GBS. *See* Global Basic Structure
general state consent, 179

INDEX

genocide, 116
Gibson, James L., 164–70
Glasius, Marlieus, 81
Global Basic Structure (GBS), 311
in democratic theory, 322–5
fallacy of accumulation in, 323–4, 332–4
fallacy of composition in, 322–3
normative assessment of, 329–32
in global constitutionalism, 311
global constitutionalism, 311–15
critiques of, 314–15
democracy and, 310, 336–7
through interdependence among institutions, 312
limitations of power under, 313
main functions of, 311
non-electoral accountability, 313–14
normative cosmopolitanism and, 312–13
global justice, ICC and, 17
global norms, ICC and, 77
global-local dilemma
defined, 66–7
for ICC legitimacy, 68–82
input legitimacy, 74–9
legal scope of, 63–6
of origin, 69–72
output legitimacy, 79–81
personal elements of, for judges and prosecutors, 72–4
victim participation and, 78–9
Rome Statute and, 66–7
Greens and M. T. v. United Kingdom, 97–9
Grossman, Nienke, 7, 15, 18–19, 23, 86, 116, 234–5, 307
on building blocks of democracy, 332–3
on normative legitimacy, 10
critiques of, 236–9
on sociological legitimacy, 241–2
Grotius, Hugo, 344, 348
Guinea, 208–9
gunboat diplomacy, 254
deGuzman, Margaret, 16, 19, 32

Habermas, Jürgen, 316
Hansen, Thomas, 75
Helfer, Larry, 102
Hirst, John, 96
Hollobone, Philip, 98
Hoover, Joseph, 75
HRW. *See* Human Rights Watch
human rights. *See also* European Court of Human Rights; human rights treaty bodies; Inter-American Court of Human Rights
courts for, 286
democracy and, 317–18
ICs for, 330–1
Universal Declaration of Human Rights, 351
Human Rights Act (1998), UK, 97
Human Rights Commission, 359
Human Rights Committee
competency of members, 288–9
composition of, 287–9
right to life approach and, 290–1
substantive decisions of, 290–3
Human Rights Council, 297–8
human rights courts, 286
non-human rights courts, 87
World Court of Human Rights, 299
human rights treaty bodies
accountability of, 286, 300–2
case load for, 303
competency of, 288–9
composition of, 287–9
criticism of, 285
dispute settlement functions of, 304
ECtHR judgments compared to, 291
effectiveness of, 293–300
in domestic legal systems, 297
legal fragmentation as influence on, 296
function and purpose of, 284–5
ICJ on, 292–3
legitimacy of, 286
limitations of, 288
margin of appreciation for, 291–2, 302–3
NGOs and, 289
non-binding legal status of, 286–7, 292–3, 303–4

human rights treaty bodies (cont.)
  principle of subsidiarity and, 302–3
  procedures of, 289–90
    for individual complaints, 294
  separation of powers for, 298–9
  substantive decisions of, 290–3
Human Rights Watch (HRW), 139–40
Huneeus, Alexandra, 21

IACtHR. *See* Inter-American Court of
    Human Rights
ICC. *See* International Criminal Court
ICJ. *See* International Court of Justice
ICs. *See* international courts
ICSID. *See* International Centre for
    Settlement of Investment
    Disputes
ICTY. *See* International Criminal
    Tribunal for the Former
    Yugoslavia
impartiality
  of ICSID, 255
    for adjudicators, 230–1
  of ITLOS, 204–5
  of judges, 348
incremental jurisprudence, 194–6
incrementalism, 331–2
independence. *See* judicial
    independence
India, 182
Indonesia-Netherlands BIT, 257
injustice, legitimacy and, 87
input legitimacy, 74–9, 145
institutional cosmopolitanism, 313
interaction models, 21–34
  legitimacy capital in, 31–4
  regime-embedded, 23–7
Inter-American Court of Human
    Rights (IACtHR)
  atrocity crimes and, 121–3
  Colombian conflict and, 120–3
  Colombian peace process and,
    117–18, 120–3, 140–2
  complementary goals of, 126–9
  convergence with ICC, 126–36
  goal-setting by, 129–34
  international agreements and,
    imbalance in, 136–40

  legitimacy of, 126–36
  jurisdiction for, 115–16, 120–1
  Organization of American States
    and, 121
interference. *See* constructive
    interference; negative
    interference
internal legitimacy, 5
  of ICSID, 228–9
  of ITLOS, 199–205
  of WTO, 227
International Centre for Settlement
    of Investment Disputes
    (ICSID), 189
  accessibility of, 277–8
  adaptability of, 283
  appeal of decisions, 265–6
  arbitrators and adjudicators for
    as closed network, 231–2
    demographic of, 221–4
    impartiality of, 230–1
    legitimacy capital of, 228–32
    WTO adjudicators compared to,
      221–4, 232–3
  BITs and, 29–30
  coherence in, 272–6
  consistency of, 245–6, 272–6
  correctness of, 245–6
  as dispute settlement body, 253–6
  dual nationality rule and, 263–4
  embeddedness of, 229
  establishment of, 281
  external legitimacy of, 232
  functions of, 234–5, 256–68
    ad hoc arbitral tribunals, 258–60,
      273
    annulment of arbitral awards,
      264–6, 279–80
    arbitral rosters, 258–60
    enforcement of awards, 266–7
    external consent as, 257–8
    investment definition as, 260–3
    investor identification, 263–4
  goals of, 253–6
  impartiality of, 255
    for adjudicators, 230–1
  institutionalization of, 229
  internal legitimacy of, 228–9

INDEX   379

legal scope of, 234–5
legitimacy capital of, 216–17
legitimacy of, 25–6
   through administrative processes,
     278–80
   through coherence, 272–6
   critiques of, 242–53, 269–80
   definitions of, 235–42
   through state sovereignty, 269–72
   through transparency, 276–8
as multilateral convention, 262–3
nationality planning and, 250,
    278–9
neutrality of, 258
normative legitimacy of, 236–9,
    253–69, 271–2
predictability of, 245–6
process for
   critiques of, 250–3
   legitimacy through, 278–80
as regime-specific court, 26–7
sociological legitimacy of, 232,
    240–2, 271–2, 281–2
sovereignty of states and, 244–5
   legitimacy through, 269–72
transparency of, 247–50, 267–8
   legitimacy through, 276–8
treaty-shopping and, 250, 278–80
withdrawal from, 242
International Court of Justice (ICJ).
    See also Solomonic judgments
authority of, 206–10
bias and, 53–5
coherence in, 55–6
Colombia and, 120–1
delegated authority of, 45–53
design structure of, 17
equity and, in judgments, 47–9
ex aequo et bono and, in judgments,
    47–9
human rights treaty bodies and,
    292–3
ITLOS and, 174, 176–7
legitimacy of, 45–53
   through foundational instruments,
    45–6
   in future legal cases, 206–14
   judicial process and, 46–7

   normative, 44–5
   sociological, 44–5, 59–60
Maritime Dispute (Peru v. Chile), 43,
    51–3
North Sea Continental Shelf Cases,
    47–9
post-conflict involvement of,
    141–2
practices of, revision of, 206–10
sociological legitimacy and, 44–5,
    59–60
Statute of, 349
international courts (ICs). *See also*
    legitimacy; *specific courts*
as decision-making institutions,
    328–9
democracy and, 342–3, 352–3
   principle of, 326
   reforms of ICs through, 309–10
as dispute settlement organization,
    15
effectiveness of
   of ICC, 65
   judicial, 86–7
   legitimacy and, 8–9, 13–14, 65
   sociological legitimacy and, 65
embeddedness of, 326
external stakeholders and, 198–9
global expansion of, 1–2
human rights, 330–1
judges in, 347–9
   diversity of, 349–50
   selection of, 350–2
judicial independence of, 348–9
judicial role in, 347–9
justice through, 344–5
legitimacy capital of, 217–19
   normative, 217–19
   sociological, 217–19
minimal moral acceptability of, 330
reforms of, in democracies, 309–10
rule development through, 15
rule of law and, 347–9
trade law in, 19
undemocratic, 323
VCLT and, 325–6
International Covenant on Civil and
    Political Rights, 351

380 INDEX

International Criminal Court (ICC)
case selection for, 74–6
Colombian peace process and,
117–18, 123–6, 140–2
complementary goals of, 126–9
convergence with IACtHR, 126–36
goal-setting by, 129–34
international agreements and,
imbalance in, 136–40
legitimacy of, 126–36
retreat from, 139–40
effectiveness of, 65
fairness of, 76–7
flaws of, 62–3
global justice vision of, 73
global norms promotion by, 77
global-local dilemma for, 68–82
input legitimacy and, 74–9
legal scope of, 63–6
legitimacy of origin, 69–72
output legitimacy and, 79–81
personal elements and, for judges
and prosecutors, 72–4
Rome Statute and, 66–7
victim participation factors, 78–9
judges in, selection of, 73
judicial legitimacy and, 360
jurisdiction for, 115–16, 120–1
justice goals of, global compared to
local, 17
legal norms and, 64–5
legitimacy of, 65, 126–36
local justice vision of, 73
moral norms and, 64–5
OTP, 117, 123–6, 132
Rome Statute and, 63
global-local dilemma and, 66–7
preamble to, 66
sentencing practices, 79–80
in Uganda, 75–6
victims and
impact on, 80–1
participation by, in cases, 78–9
International Criminal Tribunal for the
Former Yugoslavia (ICTY), 367
international law. See also international
courts; legitimacy
constructive interference in, 115

hierarchy in, absence of, 114–15
judicialization and, 114
negative interference in, 115
International Tribunal for the Law of
the Sea (ITLOS)
adherence strategy of, 198–9
compliance with, for orders and
judgments, 184–6
design and structure of, 176–7
enforcement options for, 210–12
external stakeholders and
dispute settlement and,
prioritization of, 197–8
incremental jurisprudence of,
194–6
jurisdictional issues and, 189–92
legal objectives of decisions,
192–4
legitimacy for, creation of, 188–99
other international court decisions
as influence on, 198–9
fairness of, 204–5
function of, 174–5
ICJ and, 174, 176–7
impartiality of, 204–5
judges, 202, 204
jurisdiction of, 176, 178
conflicts with other courts, 20
external stakeholders and,
189–92
legal standards and terms for,
201–2
legitimacy capital and, 33–4
legitimacy of, 175–86, 214–15
authority and, definitions of, 175
for external stakeholders, 188–99
institutionalization of, 187–205
internal, 199–205
limited state referrals and, 180–4
outcome-based theories for, 176
procedure-based theories for, 176
prompt release cases, 183
provisional measure cases, 183
relevance of, 212–14
rule of law and, 200–1
Russian Federation and, 184–6
scope of work, 204
source-based theories for, 176

sovereignty of states and, 202–4
state consent and, 175–86
  denial of, 179
  general, 179
  specific, 179
UK and, 209
UNCLOS and, 174, 176–7, 181–2
uniformity of decisions for, 202
use of force issues for, 196
investment law, 276
investment treaty arbitration, 235–42, 281. *See also* International Centre for Settlement of Investment Disputes
investments, definitions of, 260–3
investors, identification of, 263–4
investor-state tribunals, 231
ITLOS. *See* International Tribunal for the Law of the Sea

Jackson, John, 226–7
Jaconelli, Joseph, 50
judges. *See also* judicial independence; judicial legitimacy
  effectiveness of, 361–3
    evaluations of, 362–3
    external perceptions of, 361–2
    judicial legitimacy and, 363–71
  in ICC, selection of, 73
  in ICs, 347–9
    diversity of, 349–50
    selection of, 350–2
  impartiality of, 348
  for ITLOS, 202, 204
  legitimacy of, 355–60
  personal legitimacy of, 72–4
judicial activism
  CJEU and, 155–8
  meanings of, 156
judicial independence
  in democracies, 321–2
  history of, 344
  of ICs, 348–9
  rule of law and, 346
judicial legitimacy, 355–60
  ECtHR and, 360
  ICC and, 360
  judicial effectiveness and, 363–71

conflicts between, 367–70
similarities between, 363–7
outcome legitimacy and, 358–9
judicial outputs, 161
judicialization, 114
jurisdiction
  in Colombian peace process, 115–16
  of IACtHR, 115–16, 120–1
  of ICC, 115–16, 120–1
  of ITLOS, 176, 178
    conflicts with other courts, 20
    external stakeholders and, 189–92
jurisprudence. *See* incremental jurisprudence
justice
  artificial, 345
  definitions of, 88–9, 344–5
  global, 17
  ICC goals of, global compared to local, 17
  ICs and, 344–5
  in legal practice, 344
  legitimacy of international courts and, 12, 84–91, 99–112
    complementary, 85–6
    as interdependent, 85–6
    as moral dissonance, 103–6
    as mutually constitutive, 85–6
    with normative legitimacy, 7
    as perceived legitimacy, 99–102
  local, 17
  procedural, 104
  substantive, 86, 88
Justice and Peace Law (2005), Colombia, 128, 130–1
justice effect, 113

Kaufmann-Kohler, Gabrielle, 274
Kelemen, R. Daniel, 168–9
Kenyatta, Uhuru, 360
Keohane, Robert, 7, 329–30
Khaliq, Urfan, 290–1
Kmiec, Keenan, 156
Krisch, Nico, 104

Land, Molly, 16, 29
law, morality and, 87–8
legal fragmentation, 296

legal legitimacy, 5
legal norms, ICC and, 64–5
legal reasoning
  in CJEU, 155–8
  in Solomonic judgments, 55–7
legal soundness, of CJEU, 151–2
legality, legitimacy compared to,
    340–1
legitimacy, of international courts. *See
    also* normative legitimacy;
    public legitimacy; sociological
    legitimacy; *specific courts*
  approaches to, 4–9
  bindingness and, 27–31
  coherence and, 55–6
  through compliance with decisions,
    99–102
  components of, 341
  crisis of, 162–3
  defined, 64, 340–1, 355–63
  democracy and, 13, 307–11, 324
    with normative legitimacy, 7–8
    under rule of law, 308–9
  for ECtHR, 91–9
    case load as factor for, 91
    expansionist methodologies, 92–5
    in prisoner voting cases, 83–4,
      95–9, 101–12
  effectiveness as result of, 8–9, 13–14,
    65, 363–70
  exit and, 27–31
  external, 5
    of ICSID, 232
    of WTO, 227
  fairness and, 104
  global context for, 14–34
    audience as factor in, 18–19
    through design choices, 16–18
    institutional environment as factor
      in, 19–22
    normative goals in, 15–16
    types of elements in, 15–22
  human rights treaty bodies, 286
  of IACtHR, 126–36
  of ICC, 65, 126–36
  of ICJ, 45–53
    through foundational instruments,
      45–6

judicial process and, 46–7
  normative, 44–5
  sociological, 44–5, 59–60
injustice and, 87
input, 74–9
interaction models, 21–34
  legitimacy capital in, 31–4
  regime-embedded, 23–7
  regime-independent, 23–7
  regime-neutral, 24–5
  regime-specific, 26–7
internal, 5
  of ICSID, 228–9
  of ITLOS, 199–205
  of WTO, 227
of ITLOS, 175–86, 214–15
  authority and, definitions of, 175
  for external stakeholders, 188–99
  institutionalization of, 187–205
  internal, 199–205
justice and, 12, 84–91, 99–112
  with normative legitimacy, 7
legal, 5
legality compared to, 340–1
of origin, 69–72
output, 79–81
performance and, 8–9
personal, 72–4
process-oriented factors, 5–6
purpose of, 2–3
questions about, 2–3
Razian critique of, 57–9
result-oriented factors, 5–6
Solomonic judgments and, 44–5,
  59–60
source-based, 179
source-oriented factors, 5–6
stakes and, 27–31
state consent and, 69
substantive outcomes and, 11–14
transparency and, 8
voice and, 27–31
legitimacy capital, 5, 31–4
  defined, 217
  of ICs, 217–19
    normative legitimacy for, 217–19
    sociological legitimacy for, 217–19
  of ICSID, 216–17

INDEX

for adjudicators, 228–32
  appointment patterns, 220–4
  normative legitimacy for, 217–19
  sociological legitimacy for, 217–19
for ICSID adjudicators, 228–32
ITLOS and, 33–4
of WTO, 216–17
  of adjudicators, 224–8
  adjudicators for, 224–8
  appointment patterns, 220–4
  normative legitimacy for, 217–19
  sociological legitimacy for, 217–19
Lenaerts, Koen, 151–2
limited state referrals, 180–4
living instrument approach, to ECtHR,
  93
local justice, ICC and, 17
Luban, David, 70–1, 76–7
Lupu, Yonatan, 146

Madison, James, 344
majoritarian democracy, 319
margin of appreciation, 291–2, 302–3
maritime boundary delimitation cases,
  49–50
Maritime Dispute (Peru v. Chile), 43,
  51–3
Mavroidis, Petros, 226–7
May, Theresa, 113
Mechlem, Kerstin, 290
media. *See* free media
Mera, Gòngoro, 127
minimal moral acceptability, 330
moral authority, 87–8
  of human rights courts, 106
moral norms, ICC and, 64–5
morality
  authority and, 87–8, 106
  law and, 87–8
Moreno Ocampo, Luis, 74–5, 124, 131
Morris, Madeline, 70
Myanmar, 182, 190–1

NAFTA. *See* North American Free
  Trade Agreement
nationality planning, 250, 278–9
negative interference, in international
  law, 115

the Netherlands. *See* Indonesia-
  Netherlands BIT
Neumann, Thore, 159
neutrality, of ICSID, 258
Ngane, Sylvia, 77
NGOs. *See* non-governmental
  organizations
NMIs. *See* non-majoritarian
  institutions
non-governmental organizations
  (NGOs), 289
non-human rights courts, 87
non-majoritarian institutions (NMIs),
  148–9
normal justification thesis, 57
normative cosmopolitanism, 312–13
normative legitimacy, 4–14
  academic literature on, 9–14
  assessment standards for, 7–9
  bias, 150–1
  of CJEU, 145, 147–62
    criteria for, 149–52
    critiques of, 152–62
    democratic deficit, 147–9
    critique of, 236–9
    defined, 85, 179
  democratic theory and, 7–8
  fairness, 150–1
  Grossman on, 10
    critiques of, 236–9
  of ICSID, 236–9, 253–69, 271–2
  judicial legitimacy and, 355–60
  justice and, 7
  legal soundness, 151–2
  openness, 152
  political acceptability, 151–2
  Shany on, 238–9
  sociological legitimacy and, 9–11
  Solomonic judgments and, 44–5
  transparency, 152
normative standards, of democracy,
  316–17, 326–7, 336
  assessment of, 329–32
norms. *See* global norms; legal norms;
  moral norms
North American Free Trade Agreement
  (NAFTA), 247–8
  tribunals for, 268

North Sea Continental Shelf Cases, 47–9
Nowak, Manfred, 299

OAS. *See* Organization of American States
O'Boyle, Michael, 98
Office of High Commissioner for Human Rights (OHCHR), 295
Office of the Prosecutor (ICC) (OTP), 117, 123–6, 132
OHCHR. *See* Office of High Commissioner for Human Rights
On Law and Policy in the European Court of Justice (Rasmussen), 156–7
opacity. *See also* transparency of CJEU, 158–62
openness
of CJEU, 152
normative legitimacy and, 152
opportunistic legitimacy, 341
Organization of American States (OAS), 121, 123
Ossom, Aminta, 72
OTP. *See* Office of the Prosecutor
outcome legitimacy, 358–9
outcome-based theories, for ITLOS, 176
output legitimacy, 79–81, 145
The Oxford Guide to Latin in International Law, 47

Pact of Bogotá, 58–9
Paulsson, J., 273
Pauwelyn, Joost, 17, 19, 23, 29–30
peace, Solomonic judgments for, 50–1
performance, 8–9
personal legitimacy, 72–4, 341
Peru v. Chile case. *See Maritime Dispute (Peru v. Chile)*
Petersmann, Ernst-Ulrich, 226–7
Pettit, Philip, 322–3
pilot judgments, 298–9
political acceptability, of normative legitimacy, 151–2
The Power of Legitimacy (Franck), 55

predictability, of ICSID, 245–6
preliminary reference procedures, 162–3
principle of subsidiarity. *See* subsidiarity
prisoner voting cases, in UK, 83–4, 95–9
competing illegitimacy in, 106–12
declarations of incompatibility and, 102
Greens and M. T. v. United Kingdom, 97–9
judicial compliance and, 101, 103–5
public debate on, 101–2
procedural controls, in democracies, 318–19, 333
procedural fairness, 104
procedure-based theories, for ITLOS, 176
prompt release cases, 183
prosecutors, personal legitimacy of, 72–4
provisional measure cases, 183
public legitimacy, of CJEU, 164–70
contemporary studies on, 168–70
defined, 164
diffuse support of, 165–8
public awareness as factor in, 165–6
public trust and support, for CJEU, 146, 164, 168–9
EU and, 170
after financial crises, 170–2
in new EU member states, 172
in UK, 172

Rasmussen, Hjalte, 156–7
Raz, Joseph, 57–9
reconciliation, Solomonic judgments for, 50–1
reform, of international courts, democratic principles and, 309–10
regime-embedded courts, 23–7
examples of, 24
regime-independent courts, 23–7
regime-neutral courts, 24–5
regimes, defined, 16
regime-specific courts, 26–7

INDEX 385

Representation of the People Act
(1983), UK, 97
Resolution System, of WTO, 120–1
Revolutionary Armed Forces of
Colombia-People's Army
(FARC), 118–20
right to life, 290–1
Romano, Cesare P. R., 46–7
Rome Statute, 63
Colombia and, ratification of,
123–4
Colombian peace process under,
137–8
global-local dilemma and, 66–7
preamble to, 66
rule of law
defined, 345–7
democracy and, 308–9, 317–18
ICs and, 347–9
independent judiciary under, 346
ITLOS and, 200–1
supranational, 173
Russian Federation, 182
ITLOS and, 184–6

Sarkin, Jeremy, 81
Scharpf, Fritz, 145, 148
Scheffer, David, 116
Scheinin, Martin, 296, 299
Scheppele, Kim Lane, 105
Sen, Amartya, 318
sentencing, by ICC, 79–80
separation of powers, 298–9
shadow of the law, 117–18
shaming, compliance through, 103
Shany, Yuval, 9, 20, 30, 46–7, 65,
234–5
on judicial effectiveness, 86–7
on normative legitimacy, 238–9
Sheffield, Kai, 74–5
Simma, Bruno, 159
Singh, Nagendra, 56
sociological legitimacy, 4–14
academic literature on, 9–14
actual legitimacy compared to,
338–9
adherence factors for, 240–1
of CJEU, 145–6, 162–72

coherence factors in, 240–1
compliance as influence on, 103
defined, 85, 116, 179
determinacy factors for, 240–1
effectiveness and, 65
Franck on, 240–1
Grossman on, 241–2
of ICSID, 232, 240–2, 271–2,
281–2
judicial legitimacy and, 355–60
normative legitimacy and, 9–11
Solomonic judgments and, 44–5,
59–60
symbolic validation as factor in,
240–1
Solomonic judgments
coherence of, 55–6
conception of authority and, 57–9
defined, 43–4
equity in, 47–9
ex aequo et bono in, 47–9
legal legacy of, 60–1
legitimacy and, 45
normative, 44–5
sociological, 44–5, 59–60
in maritime boundary delimitation
cases, 49–50
Maritime Dispute (Peru v. Chile), 43,
51–3
for peace, 50–1
Razian critique of, 57–9
for reconciliation, 50–1
sound legal reasoning in, 55–7
UNCLOS and, 49–50
source-based legitimacy, 179
source-based theories, for ITLOS, 176
South Africa, BITs and, termination
of, 242
sovereignty, of states
ECtHR judgments and, 89–90
ICSID and, 244–5
legitimacy of, 269–72
ITLOS and, 202–4
under UNCLOS, 194–5
specific state consent, 179
SRFC. *See* Sub-regional Fisheries
Commission
stakes, 27–31

386 INDEX

state consent. *See also* external consent
  ITLOS and, 175–86
    denial of, 179
    general, 179
    specific, 179
Statute of the International Court of
    Justice, 349
Stefan, Oana, 159
Struett, Michael, 71
Sub-regional Fisheries Commission
    (SRFC), in West Africa, 209
subsidiarity, principle of, 302–3
substantive justice, 86, 88
supranational rule of law, 173
symbolic validation
  in investment law, 276
  in sociological legitimacy, 240–1
systemic legitimacy, 341

Telesetsky, Anastasia, 23, 33–4
Tomka, Peter, 52
TPP. *See* Trans-Pacific Partnership
trade insiders, 226–7
trade law, in ICs, 19
Transatlantic Trade and Investment
    Partnership (TTIP), 243, 255,
    275, 282
Trans-Pacific Partnership (TPP), 282
transparency
  of CJEU, 152
    ECtHR compared to, 159–60
  democracy and, 317
  of ECtHR, CJEU compared to, 159–60
  of ICSID, 247–50, 267–8
    legitimacy of, 276–8
  legitimacy of international courts
    and, 8
  normative legitimacy and, 152
  of UNCITRAL, 248
treaty-shopping, 250, 278–80
trust. *See* public trust
TTIP. *See* Transatlantic Trade and
    Investment Partnership
Tyler, Tom, 104

Uganda, ICC in, 75–6
UK. *See* United Kingdom
Ukraine, 182

UNCITRAL. *See* United Nations
UNCLOS. *See* United Nations
undemocratic ICs, 323
United Kingdom (UK)
  Brexit and, 113
  CJEU and, public trust in, 172
  Human Rights Act, 97
  ITLOS and, 209
  prisoner voting in, ECtHR
    judgments on, 83–4, 95–9
    competing illegitimacy in,
      106–12
    declarations of incompatibility
      and, 102
    *Greens and M. T. v. United
      Kingdom*, 97–9
    judicial compliance with, 101,
      103–5
    public debate on, 101–2
  Representation of the People Act, 97
United Nations (UN). *See also* human
    rights treaty bodies
  UNCITRAL, 220, 231–2
    arbitrations under rules of, 273
    transparency of, 248
  UNCLOS, 49–50
    dispute settlements and,
      prioritization of, 197–8
    enforcement options for, 210–12
    ITLOS and, 174, 176–7, 181–2
    state sovereignty of, 194–5
United Nations Charter, 351
United Self-Defense Forces of
    Colombia (AUC), 119
United States (U.S.)
  NAFTA and, 247–8
    tribunals for, 268
  TPP and, 282
  TTIP and, negotiations for, 255
Universal Declaration of Human
    Rights, 351
Universal Periodic Review (UPR),
    297–8
Unterhalter, David, 226–7
UPR. *See* Universal Periodic Review
Uribe, Alvaro, 119–20
U.S. *See* United States
use of force, ITLOS cases and, 196

INDEX

validation. *See* symbolic validation
Vattel, Emer de, 344, 351
VCLT. *See* Vienna Convention on the
    Law of Treaties
Venezuela, withdrawal from ICSID,
    242
victims, ICC cases and
    long-term impact on, 80–1
    participation in, 78–9
Vienna Convention on the Law of
    Treaties (VCLT), 325–6
Voeten, Erik, 169–70
voice, 27–31

Wallerstein, Shlomit, 70
war crimes, 116
Weiler, Joseph, 151–2, 162–3,
    226–7
Wheaton, Henry, 344, 351

withdrawal, from ICSID, 242
Wolfrum, Rudiger, 179
World Court of Human Rights, 299
World Trade Organization (WTO)
    ABMs for, 221–4
    adjudicators for
        ICSID adjudicators compared
            to, 221–4, 232–3
        legitimacy capital of, 224–8
    design structure of, 17
    development history of, 26–7
    DSB of, 225
    external legitimacy and, 227
    internal legitimacy and, 227
    legal scope of, 225
    legitimacy capital of, 216–17
        of adjudicators, 224–8
    Resolution System of, 120–1
    trade insiders, 226–7

For EU product safety concerns, contact us at Calle de José Abascal, 56–1º, 28003 Madrid, Spain or eugpsr@cambridge.org.